Not Playing Around

Not Playing Around

Intersectional Identities, Media Representation, and the Power of Sport

Edited by
Andrew M. Colombo-Dougovito,
Tracy Everbach, and Karen Weiller-Abels

LEXINGTON BOOKS
Lanham • Boulder • New York • London

Published by Lexington Books
An imprint of The Rowman & Littlefield Publishing Group, Inc.
4501 Forbes Boulevard, Suite 200, Lanham, Maryland 20706
www.rowman.com

86-90 Paul Street, London EC2A 4NE, United Kingdom

British Library Cataloguing in Publication Information Available

Library of Congress Cataloging-in-Publication Data

Names: Colombo-Dougovito, Andrew M., 1986– editor. | Everbach, Tracy, 1962– editor. | Weiller-Abels, Karen, editor.
Title: Not playing around : intersectional identities, media representation, and the power of sport / edited by Andrew M. Colombo-Dougovito, Tracy Everbach, and Karen Weiller-Abels.
Description: Lanham, Maryland : Lexington Books, [2022] | Includes bibliographical references. | Summary: "This book reveals how sports provide spaces for marginalized communities and create unique platforms that shift how society defines identity. Each chapter delves into how those identities—such as race, gender, disability, and sexuality—have developed and influenced social change"—Provided by publisher.
Identifiers: LCCN 2022028239 (print) | LCCN 2022028240 (ebook) | ISBN 9781793654670 (cloth) | ISBN 9781793654694 (paperback) | ISBN 9781793654687 (epub)
Subjects: LCSH: Sports—Social asepcts. | Social change. | Marginality, Social. | Group identity.
Classification: LCC GV706.5 .N678 2022 (print) | LCC GV706.5 (ebook) | DDC 306.4/83—dc23/eng/20220708
LC record available at https://lccn.loc.gov/2022028239
LC ebook record available at https://lccn.loc.gov/2022028240

To all the athletes who have been and continue to be marginalized.

Contents

Contents

Acknowledgments

When we embarked on putting together the call for contributions for this collection, the world was several months into the pandemic that had begun the previous March. Never in our wildest imaginations did we believe at the book's completion would we still be contending with the same contagion. We are beyond thankful for the diligence and hard work of all the authors that shared their work with us. Their product represents the best of this collection.

We would also like to thank our partners, spouses, and family. Without their support through these difficult times, this book would not be possible. Through personal challenges, workplace stresses, and the general dumpster fire that the last year has been, our families have supported us indelibly. We love you all.

Introduction

At the Confluence of Sport and Identity

Andrew M. Colombo-Dougovito,
Tracy Everbach, and Karen Weiller-Abels

Writing a book about the influence of sport on culture during the ongoing, seismic global shift in the recognition of marginalized identities has not been an easy endeavor. Just this week, as we worked to finalize this book, the Texas Legislature passed yet another bill (H.R. 25, 2021) effectively banning trans athletes from participating on sports teams that do not match their assigned sex at birth, going so far as not accepting birth certificates that have been legally amended. As a response to H.R. 25 and other recent discriminatory legislation, in an open letter to the players associations of all the major professional sports leagues, the National Association for the Advancement of Colored People (NAACP) called on athletes to refuse to sign with Texas sports teams unless these laws are overturned (Franklin, 2021). Though Texas is seemingly an epicenter of discriminatory legislation in recent months, this oppressive response to the ever-increasing social acceptance of diversity is not an issue solely relegated to this state alone, as 33 states have introduced bills banning transgender athletes (Krishnakumar, 2021). Moreover, the injustices that we are presented with today are not novel but a product of the capitalist system that has been developed by those who have versus those who don't have. This capitalist system, though allowing for opportunity, often affords that opportunity for only for a small few while restricting many opportunities for a minoritized many.

Though markedly improved from racially segregated sports leagues or the lack of opportunities for women prior to Title IX, inequality still reigns supreme among the sporting world and broader culture: immense gender pay gaps continue to exist among professional-level athletes (Murray, 2021); Paralympians are perceived and presented as unable to match their Olympic peers (Weiller et al., 2021); and trans athletes are often unable to participate at the outset (Krishnaumar, 2021). Yet, no matter where injustice is being confronted, sports—more specifically, athletes—often play a central role in either starting such civil rights movements or amplifying their cause: players in the Women's National Basketball Association (WNBA) don Black Lives Matter (BLM) jerseys and warm-up in shirts with bullet holes (Blackwelder, 2020); former San Francisco 49ers quarterback Colin Kaepernick kneels in solidarity with BLM to protest police brutality, and remains a free agent (White, 2020); disabled athletes compete on a global stage but are treated like second-class citizens at home (Johnston et al., 2015): openly gay athletes get engaged while audiences support and applaud them, yet, though legal, still often have to justify their ability to marry to those around them (Graham, 2021); and trans athletes continue to fight ardently for the right to compete at all levels of sport with respect to their gender identities (Buzuvis, 2016). All the while, athletes—particularly those from marginalized communities—are told to keep their personal politics out of sport competition, play the sport and keep quiet. Yet, as Dr. Muqtedar Khan, Professor in the Department of Political Science and International Relations at the University of Delaware, stated, in a webinar held by the United States (US) Department of State's Sports Diplomacy Division, "Politics is as much a part of sports as it is a part of life" (Tandon, 2021, para. 16).

POLITICS AND SPORT: THE VENN DIAGRAM IS A CIRCLE

Some believe sports, and more broadly sports competitions, should not include the personal views or political rhetoric of athletes, particularly if that view differs from their own. In other words, many wish that athletes should just "shut up and dribble" (Sullivan, 2018). To do so, however, would ignore the myriad examples of the intertwined nature of politics and sport. Sport, through the media's lens, has often offered a platform to (re)examine these identities and their acceptance within society (Collins, 2019; Collins & Bilge, 2020; bell hooks, 1981; DePauw, 1997). More specifically, sport athletes have leveraged their platform to express views on social justice and social movements to force society to examine the preconceived notions of ability, worth, and identity (Steidinger, 2020; Zirin, 2008). Though imperfect messengers on their own, athletes such as Jackie Robinson and Billie Jean King served as examples of the power of sport to create a larger wave of societal change. Yet, as Kane and Barber (2019) have suggested, our examples of the disruption of past hegemonic practices in sport have privileged a few rather than many. Thus, larger social change would only be effective with "strategic initiatives" (Kane & Barber, 2019, p. 223) to address the changes that are needed and lead to an emancipatory movement.

The "Battle of the Sexes" match between King and Bobby Riggs—a match that King won—addressed a needed shift in societal and cultural beliefs about women's place in sport; playing a major role in increasing public support for Title IX of the Education Amendments Act of 1972 (2018). As a *New York Times* editorial phrased it, "In a single tennis match, Billie Jean King was able to do more for the cause of women than most feminists can achieve in a lifetime" (as cited in Ware, 2011, p. 2). A through line can be traced from King's victory to the 1999 US women's soccer win and their present legal battle for equal pay (Murray, 2021).

Preceding Billie Jean King and other activists' pursuit of gender equality, the story of Jackie Robinson and his integration into Major League Baseball served as one of the most visible, and potentially most important, moments in American civil rights history (Shropshire, 1997). Though certainly not the first Black athlete to confront racial injustice, Jackie Robinson's presence in a professional sport competition, during a period before any major civil rights legislation, serves as an example for small changes reverberating through time and how broader media coverage can encourage societal shifts toward justice. Without the success of Jackie Robinson, the civil rights movement may have been set back decades (Lester, 2002). Robinson's experience, however, continues to be reflected in the present struggles facing today's athletes and their pursuit of equality more than the predominately white spectators would like to admit. Robinson, as a condition of his contract, pledged to "turn the other cheek in the face of white physical and verbal abuse" (p. 11) facing racial taunts, rough treatment during game play, and death threats (Lester, 2002). In his autobiography, Robinson explained,

> I learned that as long as I appeared to ignore insult and injury, I was a martyred hero to a lot of people who seemed to have sympathy for the underdog. But the minute I began to answer, to argue, to protest—the minute I began to sound off—I became a swell-head, a wise guy, and "uppity" [n-word]. (Robinson & Duckett, 1972, p. 80)

It does not take much imagination or creative thought to see the parallels of Jackie Robinson's experience—or those of Muhammad Ali, Jessie Owens, Tommie Smith and John Carlos, Althea Gibson, or Wilma Rudolph—with today's athletes. Colin Kaepernick, former quarterback of the San Francisco 49ers, perhaps most clearly reflects Robinson's experience in the wake of his eventual protest of his poor treatment. Prior to the national and international attention on the BLM movement following the death of George Floyd at the hands of the police in March 2020, Kaepernick began his protest of police brutality by sitting, later kneeling, during the US national anthem nearly four years prior, stating:

I am not going to stand up to show pride in a flag for a country that oppresses black people and people of color. . . To me, this is bigger than football and it would be selfish on my part to look the other way. There are bodies in the street and people getting paid leave and getting away with murder. (Wyche, 2016, para. 3)

Though not the first athlete to address the issue of racial injustice in the modern era—several high-profile professional men's and women's basketball players were already drawing attention to the issue of police brutality at the time—like Robinson, Kaepernick represents the most prominent representation of the continued injustices of sport and hypocrisy of society. No team would—as of publishing this collection—sign Kaepernick after his protests, despite the evidence that he still retains the skill and talent to play.

THROUGH THE LOOKING GLASS: MEDIA AS A MIRROR OF SOCIETY

Whether it be print, television, or social media, media have served for many years as a conduit, for better or worse, in shaping the views of society. Outside of sport arenas, media coverage of global events has long been used to mold the cultural views of events, past and present. For instance, upward of four-fifths of news coverage between 1942 and 1946 in the United States was devoted to war themes such as supporting family members in combat, importance of being a "good citizen," and encouraging women to work as laborers (Maynard, 1997). Ebbing with the views of society, media have adapted and changed to model that of the broader culture, encouraging growth or acceptance as well as reinforcing stereotypes and stigma.

Media's amplification of those movements have helped bend the arc of the moral universe toward justice, slightly. Ultimately, media gatekeepers' decisions on what is stressed in coverage and how it is presented affect public perception (Weiller-Abels et al., 2021). Indeed, prior examinations have found that coverage of women athletes is likely to be represented in passive and sexual poses intended for the male gaze (Bishop, 2003; Daniels, 2009; Davis, 1997; Hardin et al., 2005; Salwen & Wood, 1994), and the framing within media coverage emphasizes their femininity and conformity to traditional gender roles (Kane & Greendorfer, 1994). Among disabled athletes, media coverage focuses on medicalized descriptions focused on impairments and "overcoming" their disability (Ellis, 2009) in pursuit of an "able-bodied ideal" (Berger, 2008), indeed, serving to further otherize disabled individuals and perpetuate stigma of disability (Pullen et al., 2019). This stigmatization not only roots stigma in those without disabilities but has been shown to be internalized by those with disabilities as well (Hardin, 2003), thus, continuing a hierarchy among athletes with disabilities (Howe, 2011). Howe described this phenomenon as media focusing on the stereotype of the "supercrip"—that is, inspirational stories that depict athletes with disabilities as having special powers to "overcome" adversity and perform athletically. By defining athletic accomplishment in such a way, media continue to give permission to those who cheer for marginalized athletes in competition to excuse their own discriminatory actions in other aspects of society.

Sport can "mobilize the sentiments of people in all countries in an unrivalled manner" (Carlin, 2003; as cited in Smart, 2007, p. 114). Yet, ongoing media coverage and the existing infrastructure of sport continue to support the oppressive systems that marginalize a great number of communities to satisfy a broader, whiter audience. Indeed, opportunities for ethnic and racial minorities, women, and those with disabilities have improved in the 80 years since Jackie Robinson first stepped onto the field as a Brooklyn Dodger; however, as the civil protests of 2020 have shown, society still has a tremendously long way to go before we can claim equality.

A NEED TO EXPLORE OUR INTERCONNECTEDNESS

In the opening of her poem, "All Oppression Is Connected," poet and activist Stacyann Chin states:

Being queer has no bearing on race
my white publicist said . . .
true love is never affected by color
I curb the flashes of me crashing across the table
to knock his blond skin from Manhattan to Montego Bay
to bear witness to the bloody beatings of brown boys
accused of the homosexual crime of buggery
amidst the new fangled fads and fallacies

In this poem, Chin emphasizes how the individual oppressions that each marginalized group suffers are rooted in the same hatred, the same bigotry. She calls us—white "progressives"—out for celebrating the victories of some oppressed groups that often come at the expense of other, even more vulnerable people. As we examine the oppressions that have and continue to be addressed by society, we—all participants, stakeholders, and powerholders—must examine our interconnectedness within sports and how sports may continue to whitewash ongoing oppressions by celebrating the small improvements made for "accepted" groups of minoritized persons. The hypocrisy of progressive ideals in addressing prejudice is most apparent in the United States, though it is present across the globe. The United States, a self-proclaimed beacon of individual freedoms and "champion" of human rights, has long touted love of multiculturalism abroad, yet has continually failed to address these concerns at home. Sport offers an avenue to examine this duality. In the years since the integration of Black athletes into the Major League Baseball association in the 1950s, inarguable progress has been made for racial and ethnic minorities, women, and disabled persons. Yet, within each of those gains, multiple marginalization and oppression remains.

Using an intersectional framework (Collins, 2019; Crenshaw, 1989), we—the editors—and each of the chapters' authors will examine how sport offers a platform for the development of individual identity and provides a mechanism for influencing societal perceptions. We will present aspects of how individual identities and individual acts of activism can create opportunity to build a more inclusive society, as well as examine media's role in such depiction. Each included chapter presents an aspect of the confluence of identity, sport, and the media that represents it, through both academic and community scholarship; thus, rooting the focus of the book in both theoretical understanding of identity, sport, and representation as well as its lived experience. In examining this product in its entirety, we present an intersectional argument for the use of sport to encourage collective identity while respecting and supporting our individual affinities.

Within this collection, we have aimed to provide an accessible space for interdisciplinary scholarship and narrative surrounding the intersectionality of sports, media, politics, social justice, and social movements. Rooted in the theoretical framework of intersectionality (Crenshaw, 1989; Collins, 2019), this collection examines how identities coalesce in sports and how sport itself can offer a mechanism for driving social change. We argue that sports are political and that they provide spaces for marginalized communities to participate. The forum of sport offers a unique platform for shifting how society sees identity and, in turn, how society views the identities of those outside of sport. Athletes' identities and actions, and the mass media's representation thereof, can influence the perceptions of society as a whole and, also, how an individual views themself. Each included chapter intends to examine how those identities—such as race, gender, disability, and sexuality—have developed and influenced social change. Indeed, we have come a long way; yet we have so far left to go.

A strong focus in this book is the representation of lived experiences from both a scholarly perspective and a lived perspective. Included are athletes from marginalized groups as they form their experiences concerning each chapter's foci. The discourse consists of how these lived experiences are a collection of multiple marginalization and how they align with the theory presented. Sports can highlight societal injustice; yet, it can also offer opportunities for unity in pursuit of a fair, equitable, and just society. Within this interdisciplinary collection, we have sought to emphasize scholars and writers who examine sport, media, and society and how they shape popular thought on political and social issues. We have also included a stakeholder narrative as a part of each chapter to provide firsthand accounts of athletes or other sports stakeholders' lived experiences.

Through the investigation of identity and sport, this collection is intentional in probing the intersectionality of these identities and sport as a transformational force within broader society. Furthermore, the presented collection includes a diverse group of academic scholars from the United States as well as from South America and Europe. Each chapter includes a contribution from a community member that relates the chapter's topic to their own lived experience through short narratives or personal reflection. We intentionally wanted to represent community voices to add depth and personal meaning to the chapters. This collection is meant for the academic community but also, we hope, applies to a broader audience. We believe athletes, journalists, educators at several levels, and sports fans in general will not only gain knowledge from it but also consider the perspectives of those marginalized groups described in these chapters.

OUR PRAXIS

As the editors of this collection, we recognize the influence of our own identities, views, and biases in the gathering and editing of the narratives held within. We have been conscious of our limitations in examining identity and have intentionally sought to include diverse discussions of identity and sport, particularly from those outside traditional academic discourse. To root the positionality of this book and the conversations more transparently within, we have each detailed our own beliefs and identities.

I, Dr. Andrew M. Colombo-Dougovito, am a 35-year-old white, cisgender, hetero male raised in the Midwest. I identify as disabled and athletic. My scholarship is rooted in my experience as a public educator and seeks to improve the physical activity access of disabled people across their lifespan. My scholarship is guided by my own paradigm as a radical pragmatic researcher. Informing my decisions to guide my research toward practical solutions, I root my scholarship heavily within participatory and emancipatory frameworks of research so that solutions are closely aligned with community need. With my pragmatism, however, I draw from critical examinations of injustice within our existent systems, thus borrowing from radical ideology that the most practical solution is the most radical of changes.

I, Dr. Tracy Everbach, identify as white, female, and cisgender. My research focuses on the ways media represent race, gender, sexuality, disability, and other marginalized groups. As a former journalist, I can look back on my work at a newspaper and see that I wrote through the lens of my own experiences and only sometimes was able to present the views of those who often are voiceless in media. Joining the academic world and reading scholarship on media effects and media framing, I have learned a great deal, including being able to acknowledge my own white privilege. I hope that my research and teaching help students, other academics, journalists, and others in the larger community to understand how the hierarchy of our society works and how it affects the way media content is presented to audiences, whether it is news, entertainment, or social media. Stereotypes persist, although society has changed little by little. The work never ends.

I, Karen Weiller Abels, identify as a white female, lesbian, and cisgender. I have been in a relationship with my spouse for over 40 years and married for 11 years. We have two children, 28 and 22. Many years ago when our son was young, we wondered how he and we would be accepted in preschool and in society in general. It has been a journey of learning for all, though through proactive measures, we have been always well received with both of our children. My work has centered on gender issues in the media, with recent work in disability. Examining and presenting the lived experiences of those who played in the All-American Girls Professional Baseball League afforded me a glimpse into the gendered world of sport in the 1940s and 1950s. I have seen improvement in how media presents women in sporting roles, though the hegemonic perspective appears to be ever present. It's this work and the hope that we can continue to envision a more open world that fosters my continued interest in this work.

WHAT THIS COLLECTION IS (AND ISN'T)

As described above, this collection of academic and community-based writing aims at identifying the ways that identity and sport are infused in every aspect of our global culture and how media mediation of those elements of socialization can shift cultural acceptance of historically marginalized identities. This collection is not meant to be an exhaustive history of each identity or sport but a snapshot of the ways in which these elements are intertwined. Each element of this book highlights aspects of this phenomenon but is not all-inclusive. As the editors, we recognize that there are elements of identities that are not well represented nor well considered. We still believe that this collection could be of great benefit to novices and experts alike, as it is rooted in. . . historical and contemporary examples of the ever-evolving exploration of one's identity and the influence of sport and media. We also hope that this collection can serve as an example to academics seeking to make greater connection to the communities in which they work, as well as spark a conversation among those with power and privilege to recognize the vast amount of work that is needed in pursuit of a just and equitable society.

Beginning with Our Cover

As the first and most visual element of this collection, the cover features a soccer ball and a baseball that have been thrown at and shattered a television (TV) screen. We have intended through this depiction to show the dynamic relationship between media and sports, as well as how athletes must at times work in confrontational ways to push media toward equity.

The choice to use a TV screen was intentional; though media have shifted toward a more digital, mobile Internet base that will likely be the sole means of consumption in the decades to come, the TV still plays a central role in many households, particularly those in Western, Euro-centric cultures. Its destruction lays bare the imperfections among media coverage and under-scores the need to repair, or build a new, the foundations of a just and equitable media environment.

Lastly, the choice of a baseball and soccer ball was also intentional. The baseball hearkens back to the most visible representation of sport's influence on society and the beginning of our long-running civil rights movement: that of Jackie Robinson, who represents one of our most visible examples. The soccer ball represents the ongoing fight for gender equality headed by the US Women's National Soccer Team (USWNT). This highlights the growth and positive change that has emerged in the last half century, yet also represents the continued inequality. Both the soccer ball and baseball are torn and tat-tered to show how although sports are used for change, they continue to be points of contention by such advocacy and, like the media that covers it, are not perfect in the pursuit of justice.

The Construction of This Collection

In recruiting authors to share in this collection, we intentionally sought narra-tives that explored the breadth of intersecting identities, media representation, and the influence of sport. Ultimately, the chapters were organized so similar ideas and constructs shared equal space. We begin the book with discussions of how space can define our identities and how our identities can define that space. Next, we acknowledge the power of Black activism and dedication to ensuring that not only are people afforded their equal rights but also share that freedom with other oppressed peoples. Lastly, we finish with the influence of media and its inherent power to shift societal consciousness.

Section I: *Spaces that Define*

The first section of the book, *Spaces that Define*, explores the interconnected nature of the policies and organization of sport with identity. In other words, the section details the many ways in which our construction of sport has influenced our cultural construction of identity, for good and bad. Across this section, how sport and recreation spaces govern themselves, as well as their impact on our cultural beliefs, begin our journey.

In the first chapter, "'Keep It in the Locker Room': How College Athletic Departments Stifle Controversy and Dissent," Frank LoMonte and Dionne Koller argue that we have entered a transformative period regarding college athlete free speech. They review legal actions that have defied the suppression of college athletes' speech and contend that these athletes have the constitutional right to speak out. Using First Amendment law as a basis, LoMonte and Koller maintain that athletes are legally, albeit slowly, gaining the right to speak to the media and participate in democracy without being muzzled by their universities.

Joshua Rubin's chapter, "On Balls, Players, Tackle Boxes, and Other Footballing Objects: The Politics of Being in the NFL Rulebook," examines the 2018 edition of the NFL official playing rules. The analysis is applied as a document of social and political history, examining the changes in the NFL rulebook over time. This investigation includes a discussion of how the social and political aspects intersect into the conditions in which the game has and is being played. The rulebook takes on an identity of its own as Rubin presents both the meanings of football on society and on the bodies of the athletes who play the game.

William P. Cassidy in "Shattering the Glass Ceiling Twice: Sports Journalism Framing of Katie Sowers" has provided us with an analysis of Katie Sowers, who made sports history by coaching in a male-dominated sport, professional football, the NFL. This chapter presents readers with a discussion of sport journalism's approach to Sowers's history-making accomplishments. With a focus on both the gender and sexual orientation component, Cassidy contends journalists in the process of doing their job can and should take a stand in addressing social and cultural issues. Using a framing lens, Cassidy examines the space, time, and prominence of the media presentation of Sowers's entrance onto the major sport NFL stage.

In our fourth chapter, "Queer Recreation: LGBTQ Sporting Spaces, Community, and Impact," Austin R. Anderson and Eric Knee focus on how recreation and leisure spaces outside of the mainstream have provided opportunities for the LGBTQ+ community to find belonging. They offer insight into how traditional sporting spaces can reinforce heteronormativity despite lipstick marketing such as Pride events or use of the rainbow flag. In analyzing the intersection of queer identity with other forms of identity, Anderson and Knee highlight the difficulties that many from the LGBTQ+ community can face and why queer spaces are vital.

In "A 'Permissible Prejudice': An Exploration of the Systemic Ableist Barriers to Sport and Leisure Activities for Disabled People," Andrew M. Colombo-Dougovito and Suzanna Rocco Dillon examine the ingrained cultural beliefs that limit, even prevent, many disabled individuals from engaging in physical activity or sport, as well as how these beliefs can be transferred and exacerbated by the disabled people. Using a thematic metasynthesis, Colombo-Dougovito and Dillon have aggregated first-person narratives and experiences to explore the ways in which society has defined ability. Stemming from critical disability discourse, they assess societal barriers through the lens of ableism and scrutinize the duplicity of media in pursuit of inclusion.

Section II: *Black Athletes as Activists*

The second section, *Black Athletes as Activists*, looks at the many ways Black athletes have and continue to serve as advocates for justice within sports. The chapters emphasize how, using their platform, Black athletes push for equity not only for themselves but for all. Rooted in relevant, ongoing conversations, this section gives light to that which is obscured by bad actors in the fight for racial justice.

Tracy Everbach, Gwendelyn S. Nisbett, and Karen Weiller-Abels examine the activism of WNBA players in "#SayHerName: The WNBA and Black Women's Athletes' Social Activism." This chapter ties the WNBA's social justice campaigns and actions to a long history of Black feminist activism and an intersectional approach to fighting racism and sexism. The authors demonstrate how WNBA players and coaches organized a collective to speak out about social justice, which their male counterparts followed and emulated. In this way, they embraced a long history of Black American women, including athletes, who have fought for human rights, social justice, and equality.

Teveraishe Mushayamunda and Mildred F. Perreault, in "How Social Media Gives Black NBA Athletes a Platform to Rally Around Racial Injustice During the #BlackLivesMatter Movement," explore the strategies Black male athletes have employed to demonstrate their endorsements and support of the #BlackLivesMatter movement. The authors investigate Black male NBA athletes' social media engagement through political advocacy statements on YouTube and Twitter using the lens of critical race theory and the theory of social media engagement. They find that the athletes also seek to engage their fan communities around their concerns for racial injustice using both traditional media and personal social media engagement.

In "Athletes as Activists: Exploring Audience Evaluations of Black Celebrity Athlete Activism," Gwendelyn S. Nisbett, Newly Paul, and Stephanie Schartel Dunn also examine Black athlete activism through the lens of celebrity endorsements. Using social identity theory and white racial frames, they explore audience responses to athletes' support of the #BlackLivesMatter movement, finding three themes: identification with the athletes, different responses depending on the tone of the athlete's message, and ambivalent responses to the use of their platform for activism.

Section III: *After the Lights Go Out*

In the final section, *After the Lights Go Out*, the authors investigate the role of media narrative in the acceptance of marginalized identities. Via a running theme through the preceding chapters, this section explores how storylines can linger beyond what occurs on the playing field. In this section, you will be confronted with how media can exacerbate stigma or be the agent of its change.

In "Fairness, Without the Inclusion: A Critical Discourse Analysis of Trans-Exclusionary Sports Bans," Vincent Peña presents a study of sports from a view that focuses on the construction and portrayal of transgender athletes. How are they portrayed by the media? What is the discourse presented by journalists? Peña also provides a critical discourse analysis through feminist theory in his presentation and discussion of two recent cases (from Connecticut and Idaho) surrounding the question: Why do media often disregard and exclude trans athletes from their presentation? His discussion includes commentary not only on this lack of inclusiveness by journalists but also on how sports journalists might more effectively portray trans athletes.

Allison R. Tsuchida and Nathan M. Murata provide a chapter focused on the creation of a program that prepared students with disabilities and their peers to participate together in interscholastic competition, "In High Demand: Friday Night Prime Time and High-School Athletes with Disabilities." The intent of the program called *Friday Night Prime* was to utilize sport as the focal point in developing well-being for students with and without disabilities. This program focused on physical, emotional, and psychological well-being, helping students to develop a sense of purpose. Three constructs formed the basis for this project: sense of belonging, self-esteem and self-efficacy, and social justice. The *Friday Night Prime Program* was rooted in equity, motivation, a sense of purpose and relationship building for all students. Students who participated in this program, based in Hawaii, were truly part of an authentic experience that allowed students with and without disabilities to participate in sport together, build bonds, and form lasting friendships.

Paolo Lucattini, in "Migrant Children with Disabilities in Italian Schools: Educational and Sport-Related Experiences," explores the experiences of those that face "double belonging" because of their disability and migratory status. In this chapter, Italy serves as a case study for discussion regarding how existing policies can benefit and hinder individuals' ability to find connection with their new community. As global migration has increased due to civil unrest, famine, and climate-related disasters, Lucattini provides an overview of how cultures can better prepare themselves through sport.

In our final chapter, "Criticism of Stereotypes in Paralympism and Expectations of Media Portrayals of Latin American Athletes" Sandra Meléndez-Labrador probes the influence of media coverage on the broader culture of Latin American athletes and provides guidance on how journalists can better cover disability without further stigmatization. This chapter gives insight into how athletes in the global south are confronted with stigma regarding their disability and how they are using their new platform to push for equitable coverage. Examining the interviews of athletes from South American countries, she presents firsthand accounts of how media can more appropriately cover disability, particularly among ideologies that are so rooted in the overarching culture.

LET US BEGIN

As we start this exploration, we hope this book will ignite a conversation among all those who would consider themselves stakeholders or stewards of sports. It has become evident that the status quo no longer works—if it ever did—and there is a desperate need for critical reflection on the historically oppressive practices that have and continue to exist. We hope you enter this book with an open mind to exploring the experiences of those whose are, potentially, vastly different from your own. We also expect that many will find similarity and camaraderie in the narratives within.

Enjoy.

REFERENCES

Berger, R. J. (2008). Disability and the dedicated wheelchair athlete: Beyond the "supercrip" critique. *Journal of Contemporary Ethnography, 37*(6), 647–678.

Bishop, R. (2003). Missing in action: Feature coverage of women's sports in Sports Illustrated. *Journal of Sport and Social Issues, 27*(2), 184.

Blackwelder, C. (2020, August 27). WNBA players wear shirts with 'bullet holes' to protest Jacob Blake shooting, racial injustice. *American Broadcast Channel (ABC)*

News. https://abcnews.go.com/GMA/Culture/wnba-players-wear-shirts-bullet -holes-protest-jacob/story?id=72650367.

Buzuvis, E. E. (2016). "As who they really are": Expanding opportunities for transgender athletes to participate in youth and scholastic sports. *Law & Inequality, 34*, 341–384.

Chin, S. (2014, July 25). *All oppression is connected*. http://whyaminotsurprised .blogspot.com/2014/07/staceyann-chin-all-oppression-is.html.

Collins, P. H. (2019). *Intersectionality as critical social theory*. Durham and London: Duke University Press.

Collins, P. H., & Bilge, S. (2020). *Intersectionality*. 2nd ed. Medford, MA: Polity Press.

Crenshaw, K. (1989). Demarginalizing the intersection of race and sex: A Black feminist critique of antidscrimination doctrine, feminist theory, and antiracist politics. *University of Chicago Legal Forum, 1989*(1, 8). https://chicagounbound.uchicago .edu/cgi/viewcontent.cgi?article=1052&context=uclf.

Daniels, E. A. (2009). Sex objects, athletes, and sexy athletes: How media representations of women athletes can impact adolescent girls and college women. *Journal of Adolescent Research, 24*(4), 399–422.

Davis, L. R. (1997). *The swimsuit issue and sport: Hegemonic masculinity in Sports Illustrated*. State University of New York Press.

DePauw, K. P. (1997). The (in)visibility of disability: Cultural contexts and "sporting bodies." *Quest, 49*(4), 416–430.

Education Amendments Act of 1972, 20 U.S.C. §§1681 – 1688 (2018).

Ellis, K. (2009). Beyond the aww factor: Human interest profiles of Paralympians and the media navigation of physical difference and social stigma. *Asia Pacific Media Educator, 19*, 23–35.

Franklin, J. (2021, October 28). NAACP urges pro athletes not to sign with Texas teams over voting and abortion laws. *National Public Radio [NPR]*. https://www .npr.org/2021/10/28/1050175142/naacp-pro-athletes-not-sign-texas-teams-voting -abortion-laws?utm_medium=social&utm_source=twitter.com&utm_campaign =npr&utm_term=nprnews.

Graham, R. (2021, October 26). Texas effectively banned abortion. Now it's targeting same-sex marriage [opinion]. *The Boston Globe*. https://www.bostonglobe.com /2021/10/26/opinion/texas-effectively-banned-abortion-now-its-targeting-same -sex-marriage/.

Hardin, M., Lynn, S., & Walsdorf, K. (2005). Challenge and conformity on "Contested terrain": Images of women in four women's sport/fitness magazines. *Sex Roles, 53*(1), 105–111.

hooks, b. (1981). *Ain't I a woman: Black women and feminism*. Boston: South End Press.

Howe, P. D. (2011). Cyborg and supercrip: The Paralympics technology and the (dis)empowerment of disabled athletes. *Sociology, 45*(5), 868–882.

Johnston, K. R., Goodwin, D. L., & Leo, J. (2015). Understanding dignity: Experiences of impairment in an exercise facility. *Adapted Physical Activity Quarterly, 32*(2), 106–124.

Kane, V., & Barber, H. (2019). Creating a new sport culture. In. V. Krane, *Sex, Gender and Sexuality in Sport: Queer Inquiries* (pp. 223–235). Routledge Books.

Krishnakumar, P. (2021, April 15). This record-breaking year for anti-transgender legislation would affect minors the most. *Cable News Network (CNN)*. https://www.cnn.com/2021/04/15/politics/anti-transgender-legislation-2021/index.html.

Lester, C. T. (2002). Mirror of the times: The racial politics of sport from Jackie Robinson to Muhammad Ali. *Perspectives in History is a journal publication, 17*, 9–23.

Maynard, K. (1997). Rosie the Riveter Pittsburgh style: The representation and experiences of Pittsburgh working women during the Second World War. *The Sloping Halls Review-1997*, 13–23.

Murray, C. (2021, July 23). USWNT to fight U.S. Soccer in equal pay row: Appeal says judge's decision 'defies reality'. Entertainment and Sports Programming Network [ESPN]. https://www.espn.com/soccer/united-states-usaw/story/4437227/uswnt-to-fight-us-soccer-in-equal-pay-row-appeal-judges-decision-as-it-defies-reality.

Pullen, E., Jackson, D., Silk, M., & Scullion, R. (2019). Re-presenting the Paralympics: (Contested) philosophies, production practices and the hypervisibility of disability. *Media, Culture, and Society, 41*(4), 465–481.

Relating to requiring public school students to compete in interscholastic athletic competitions based on biological sex, H. R. 25, 87th Leg., 2021.

Robinson, J., & Duckett, A. (1972). *I never had it made, an autobiography of Jackie Robinson*. New York: Ecco Press.

Salwen, M. B., & Wood, N. (1994). Depictions of female athletes on Sports Illustrated covers, 1957–1989. *Journal of Sport Behavior, 17*(2), 98.

Shropshire, K. L. (1997). Where have you gone, Jackie Robinson: Integration in America in the 21st century. *S. Tex. L. Rev., 38*, 1043.

Smart, B. (2007). Not playing around: Global capitalism, modern sport and consumer culture. *Global Networks, 7*(2), 113–134.

Steidinger, J. (2020). *Stand up and shout out: Women's fight for equal pay, equal rights, and equal opportunities in sport*. Rowman & Littlefield.

Sullivan, E. (2018, February 19). Laura Ingraham told LeBron James to shut up and dribble; He went to the hoop. *National Public Radio [NPR]*. https://www.npr.org/sections/thetwo-way/2018/02/19/587097707/laura-ingraham-told-lebron-james-to-shutup-and-dribble-he-went-to-the-hoop.

Tandon, T. (2021, May 2021). Why sport is always political. *Sportanddev.org*. https://www.sportanddev.org/en/article/news/why-sport-always-political.

Ware, S. (2011). *Game, set, match: Billie Jean King and the revolution in women's sports*. UNC Press Books.

Weiller-Abels, K., Everbach, T., & Colombo-Dougovito, A. M. (2021). She's a lady; he's an athlete; they have overcome: Portrayals of gender and disability in the 2018 Paralympic winter games. *Journal of Sports Media, 16*(1), 123–148.

White, M. (2020, September 7). Kap's NFL absence still notable despite Goodell's claims. *National Broadcast Channel (NBC) Sports*. https://www.nbcsports.com/bayarea/49ers/colin-kaepernicks-nfl-absence-notable-despite-roger-goodells-claims.

Wyche, S. (2016, August 27). Colin Kaepernick explains why he sat during national anthem. *National Football League [NFL] News*. https://www.nfl.com/news/colin-kaepernick-explains-why-he-sat-during-national-anthem-0ap3000000691077.

Zirin, D. (2008). *A people's history of sports in the United States: 250 years of politics, protest, people and play*. New York and London: The New Press.

Section I

SPACES THAT DEFINE

Chapter 1

"Keep It in the Locker Room"

How College Athletic Departments Stifle Controversy and Dissent

Frank LoMonte and Dionne Koller

Disgusted by the meager fitness equipment provided for competitors in the women's NCAA basketball tournament, Oregon Ducks player Sedona Prince did what any young person in the twenty-first century does to stir discussion: She filmed a TikTok video (Mickanen, 2021). When the video went viral, drawing some 5.2 million views, Prince became a sought-after interviewee, featured on CNN and NBC Nightly News. Her publicity campaign succeeded. The NCAA was shamed into adding a greatly expanded weight room, and Prince was acclaimed as an empowering voice for women in sports (Hahn, 2021; Wisniewski, 2021). Yet nearly every time college athletes like Prince go public to express dissatisfaction, they risk their educational and professional futures because college rulebooks typically forbid speaking publicly, about anything, without the athletic department's approval. In this chapter, we look at why such rigid restraints—which would not be tolerated if applied to other college students or even to salaried state employees—are regarded as "standard operating procedure" in the world of college sports and whether anything can or should be done to reform them.

This is a period of transformative change for college sports and free speech. Following the lead of California in 2019, numerous states enacted legislation providing that college athletes may earn income from third-party use of the athletes' name, image, and likeness (commonly referred to by the initials "NIL" rights) (McInerney, 2021). The legislation overrode NCAA rules that strip athletes of their NIL rights and prohibit college players from earning compensation beyond the "cost of attendance" scholarship benefits offered by their schools (Myerberg, 2021; Berkowitz, 2019). Finally, in June 2021, under the combined weight of pressure from state lawmakers and

Congress, and adverse court rulings, the NCAA changed its long-standing rules and agreed to allow athletes to profit from endorsements and licensing deals (McInerney, 2021), a watershed moment for athletes reclaiming their power. Antitrust challenges to the NCAA model also have forced change. More than 43,000 former college players received checks as part of a $208.7 million settlement with the NCAA and 11 athletic conferences in a lawsuit alleging that the NCAA unlawfully restrained its member schools from fully compensating athletes for the costs of attending college (Berkowitz & Epstein, 2019). A parallel case, alleging that the NCAA's limits on outside earnings also violated federal antitrust law, resulted in a US Supreme Court ruling largely in the players' favor in June 2021 (*NCAA v. Alston*, 2021). In the courts and in legislative corridors, athletes and their advocates are organizing as never before, seeking to challenge the NCAA's definition of "amateurism" and recalibrate a regime of overbearing institutional control that critics have derided as a "plantation" system (Branch, 2011, para. 16).

But as athletes are taking ownership of their economic power, their political and social capital still largely remains constrained by century-old conventions that—like the "vow of poverty" accompanying NCAA definitions of "amateurism"—are overdue for reconsideration. While athletes appear to be winning the freedom to reclaim their NIL rights, they remain under tight institutional restraints when they seek to engage with the press and public on contemporary issues, within or beyond their athletic programs (LoMonte & Hamrick, 2020). The same college athlete who will be legally permitted to endorse a product or develop a YouTube channel could also be subject to disciplinary sanctions for giving an interview to a journalist about the endorsement. Beyond the ubiquitous campus rulebooks that forbid athletes from speaking publicly without permission, the unofficial "rules" may be more powerful still. The culture of silence that envelops college sports strongly discourages outspokenness, especially where the athlete's remarks might reflect unfavorably on the reputation of the athletic program, provoke political controversy, or alienate powerful boosters (Hansen, 2020).

Both the law and the culture surrounding college athletes' freedom of speech demand reconsideration. It is becoming increasingly evident that while competitive sports can provide important life lessons and generate long-term socioeconomic benefits for athletes (NCAA/Gallup, 2020), there is another side that is often overlooked. Issues such as concussions and their long-term effects (Murphy, 2019), allegations of abusive workouts (Murphy, 2019), uncompensated medical expenses, and predatory and abusive coaches and trainers, who opportunistically capitalize on the culture of silence to re-offend without accountability, among other issues, deserve to be part of the discourse around college sports (Brake & Nelson, 2012). The contemporary "rights revolution" overtaking college sports will be incomplete unless it also includes unleashing the full power of athletes' voices, even when doing so means that potentially uncomfortable, inconvenient, and unwelcome conversations result.

THE VALUE OF ATHLETE VOICES

Athletes have long been in the forefront of reform movements, including the movements for racial and gender equality, and they are again in the forefront today. Sports are an obvious vehicle for social change: They command intense public interest, athletes and coaches are admired role models, and sports bring individuals of different races and socioeconomic backgrounds together. When a Black college basketball player, Jerry Harkness, extended a handshake to a white opposing player during a 1963 NCAA tournament game between Loyola and Mississippi State, the gesture reverberated across the nation and the game—which became known as "The Game of Change"—was credited with helping speed the demise of segregation in higher education (O'Neil, 2012).

Today, college athletes are taking the baton from Loyola's Jerry Harkness and continuing to advocate for the rights of the underrepresented, within college sports and beyond. Starting with the NFL's Colin Kaepernick, but trickling down to colleges and high schools, athletes have used their role-model status and followings to express their outrage over police brutality and of the underlying systemic inequities that produce violent police confrontations in Black communities (Anderson, 2020; Svrluga, 2017; Walker, 2016). For instance, after a 43-year-old Black man, Eric Garner, died in the grips of a New York City police officer's chokehold while being arrested for a petty infraction, Georgetown University men's basketball players donned matching T-shirts bearing Garner's indelible dying words—"I can't breathe"—during a practice session (Curry, 2018).

Coming into their power as campus opinion leaders, and recognizing their value as economic assets to their athletic programs, players have begun speaking up more forcefully about closer-to-home concerns on their own campuses. At the University of Missouri, when college football players organized in opposition to the university's failings in responding to an uncomfortable climate for Black students, the power of their collective gesture was widely credited with accelerating the ouster and replacement of the university's ineffective chancellor (Bump, 2015). Boycotting Utah State University football players forced the school to cancel its 2020 season-ending game, after they took offense to remarks made by the university's president that they perceived as pejorative toward their coach's faith and ethnicity (Martin, 2020). Star football players have helped bring pressure on colleges to reconsider their association with antiquated symbols evoking racism, including Confederate iconography long displayed at the University of Mississippi (Nietzel, 2020). The sense of urgency about engaging on issues of university governance was amplified by the COVID-19 pandemic of 2020, as many campuses brought athletes back to the playing field as "test subjects," even while other students were taking classes online for fear of contracting the deadly virus (Peter & Schad, 2020). It is remarkable, then, that athletes largely remain constrained by their school's policies from using what is perhaps the most effective channel of communication to reach a mass audience: Speaking to the news media.

LEAVE YOUR CONSTITUTIONAL RIGHTS IN THE LOCKER ROOM?

Along with their playbooks, college athletes are handed a raft of regulations that govern their on- and off-duty behavior, often including regulations that restrict speech. As colleges have built their own media platforms enabling them to reach a large audience without the intermediation of professional news organizations, journalists say their access to athletes and coaches has dwindled. In a column for the Poynter Institute, longtime sports reporter Ed Sherman documented how heavy-handed gatekeeping by athletic departments has diminished the ability to tell athletes' stories; one South Carolina sportswriter told Sherman he had been afforded only a single one-on-one conversation with a college athlete in five years (Sherman, 2015). It is increasingly becoming common for coaches in high-profile sports to declare first-year players ineligible to speak to the media for any reason, which—in the era of "one-and-done" college basketball careers—effectively means that soon-to-be NBA superstars may never be interviewed by the news media until turning pro (Michaux, 2017). These restrictions, when combined with aggressive information crackdowns on coverage of practice sessions and player injuries, are corrosive to candid news coverage; one sports columnist has bemoaned that coaches' assertive control over access to information is "more likely to generate more disinformation as reporters have to piece together what's happening exclusively from second-hand sources" (Michaux, 2017, p. B1).

During 2019, the Brechner Center for Freedom of Information at the University of Florida surveyed sports editors at news organizations across the country and found that journalists regularly have difficulty getting access to interviews with college athletes because of university policies that require any communication to be filtered through a public relations apparatus, typically referred to as a "sports information" office (LoMonte & Hamrick, 2020). Out of 32 editors whose publications regularly cover college sports, two-thirds said that they are "never" able to speak to an athlete without getting permission from the athletic department. Just three of the thirty-two editors said that they are "always" able to secure the interviews they need by obtaining approval through sports information gatekeepers.

Equipped with these findings, the researchers then asked public universities across Division I, the largest and most competitive programs, for copies of any rules governing communications between athletes and the news media. Fifty-six athletic programs produced responsive documents, and fifty of them contained restrictions that expressly forbid speaking to journalists without athletic department approval (LoMonte & Hamrick, 2020). The requirement of prior approval sends an intimidating message: The university is watching who you speak with and what you say and reserves the right to control speech that might be unflattering.

Erasing any doubt, some policies explicitly prohibit whistleblowing, indicating that athletes can face punishment for taking complaints about the athletic program to the press and public. At Iowa State University, a handbook issued to football players stated: "Do not take your complaints to the newspaper. The coaches' office is the only place for these. Keep it in the family." Kent State University's athlete handbook similarly provided: "Don't take your complaints to the media. The coaches' office is the only place for these." Texas Tech University produced a policy document that instructs football players: "Anything that happens with this team—anything within the program or locker room—stays with the football program and in the locker room." East Carolina University's football program cautions players emphatically: "If you do not have anything good to say, do not say anything at all. DO NOT COMPLAIN ABOUT THE COACHES, TEAMMATES OR THE UNIVERSITY" (LoMonte & Hamrick, 2020).

Augmenting these constraints on interviewing, many athletic departments exert comparably rigid control over players' use of social media (Berman, 2020). Some coaches require athletes to allow a private monitoring service to scan their online posts for references to drugs or other red-flag keywords, and others ban the use of certain social media platforms entirely, either during the team's playing season or year-round (Berman, 2020). The combined effect of these restrictions is to cut off the only two channels by which a 19-year-old without the means to purchase advertising can reach a mass audience—channels that would be available to any other college student.

"PRIOR RESTRAINTS" AND THE FIRST AMENDMENT

Public educational institutions, like all government agencies, are subject to the constraints of the Constitution, including the First Amendment. As a general principle, the First Amendment strongly disfavors any restriction that can be interpreted as a "prior restraint" against speaking (*CBS, Inc. v. Young*, 1975). While government agencies can sometimes justify imposing after-the-fact consequences on harm-causing speech, they almost never can justify preventing a speaker from being heard by a willing audience. Moreover, First Amendment freedoms do not stop with the speaker. The Supreme Court has recognized a constitutional right to receive information as well as to share it (*Stanley v. Georgia*, 1969), so the interests of the listening audience are of legal relevance whenever speakers are silenced.

When a government agency, like a public university, sets itself up as a gatekeeper deciding who is allowed to speak, the Constitution requires rigorous safeguards to keep the agency from impermissibly picking and choosing which speakers can be heard based on favored or disfavored viewpoints (Hatch, 2003). Any regulation that purports to reserve unbridled discretion to decide who can and cannot speak will, invariably, be struck down as unconstitutional if challenged.

DEGREES OF CENSORSHIP: THE FIRST AMENDMENT ON CAMPUS

First Amendment protections diminish when the speaker is in a special relationship with the government regulator, such as employee/employer or student/teacher. In those instances, the courts afford greater deference to the government, on the theory that managers need leeway to use their expertise to make time-sensitive judgment calls when acting in a supervisory role (Chemerinsky, 2013). Still, the Supreme Court has generally been protective of college students' free speech rights and has never said that the First Amendment applies with diminished force on a college campus. To the contrary, the Court has emphasized that a college campus is "the marketplace of ideas," where speakers need extra latitude to test out new-and-different theories without fear (*Healy v. James*, 1972, p. 180). Thus, when a University of Missouri college student, presaging the modern-day "Black Lives Matter" movement, distributed an offensive self-produced magazine replete with strong profanity denouncing the police, the justices unanimously overturned her expulsion and ordered her reinstated (*Papish v. Bd. of Curators of Univ. of Mo.*, 1973). But the Court has never set a comprehensive standard by which all college-speech cases are to be determined, leaving uncertainty whether college students enjoy the robust "real-world" First Amendment protections that apply in typical citizen/government interactions or some stepped-down version more akin to the K–12 school environment.

In K–12 public schools, the guidestar is the Supreme Court's landmark Vietnam-era *Tinker* case, in which the justices recognized a halfway measure of First Amendment protection when the speaker is a student and the disciplinarian is a school (*Tinker v. Des Moines Indep. Cmty. Sch. Dist.*, 1969). There, the Court determined that speech becomes punishable only if the school can concretely foresee that it will "materially" disrupt classwork or create "substantial" disorder (*Tinker v. Des Moines Indep. Cmty. Sch. Dist.*, 1969, p. 509). A generation after *Tinker*, a more conservative Court carved out a broad exception to *Tinker* that gives schools much greater authority when students are using a school-provided "forum," such as a newspaper or a commencement address, to deliver their speech (*Hazelwood Sch. Dist. v. Kuhlmeier*, 1988). In neither *Tinker* nor *Hazelwood* did the justices purport to be speaking about higher education, but lower courts have regularly fallen back on the Court's K–12 school standards when adjudicating college-speech cases, even though the equities seem decisively different: The listeners are all adults, and no one is compelled by law to attend (LoMonte, 2013). Thus, in a recent case brought by a University of Connecticut soccer player who lost her scholarship for flipping a celebratory middle finger to the ESPN sideline camera after a game-clinching goal, a US district court looked to K–12 school case law in ruling that the college had reasonable grounds to regard her gesture as constitutionally unprotected (*Radwan v. Univ. of Conn.*, 2020).

In sum, while the quantum of constitutional protection has never been conclusively settled, the First Amendment applies with some degree of force when a state college or university enforces a regulation that prohibits or punishes speech. The question is not whether the First Amendment applies but what level of justification that college must produce to overcome the student's presumptive right to speak. There is no history of athletes challenging their colleges' prohibition on giving interviews, so it is uncertain how a court would analyze a First Amendment claim in that context. There is instructive guidance, however, in the somewhat analogous setting of the government workplace—and in that setting, the employee speaker invariably wins.

"Gag Rules" Don't Work in the Workplace

First Amendment rights notwithstanding, the Supreme Court has given government agencies latitude to manage employees' workplace speech, particularly when the speech is made "on duty" and might undermine the agency's effectiveness or call the employee's fitness into question. A government employer's authority to punish speech is greatest when the speech is part of an official work assignment, such as writing a memo (*Garcetti v. Ceballos*, 2006). But the employer's authority diminishes if the employee is speaking as a private citizen addressing a matter of public concern (*Pickering v. Bd. of*

Educ., 1968). Importantly, speech does not lose First Amendment protection merely because it is about the workplace or draws on expertise gained in the workplace, because the Court recognizes that government employees have valuable inside knowledge about the workings of government that the public needs to hear (*Lane v. Franks*, 2014). These principles apply whenever a public employee is punished for a particular instance of speech and brings a First Amendment challenge.

A different analysis applies, however, when an agency tries to enforce a blanket prohibition against speaking—a "prior restraint"—that applies across the workforce. Because of the First Amendment's aversion to prior restraints, the Supreme Court has erected a far more demanding burden for the employer to surmount. In a 1995 case brought on behalf of US Treasury Department employees (referred to colloquially as the *NTEU* case), the Court struck down a statute prohibiting federal workers from accepting payment for speeches or articles (*United States v. Nat'l Treasury Employees Union*, 1995). The Court did not apply the same deference to the employer that might apply to an individualized disciplinary decision. Instead, because the decision was a broad-based restraint silencing all employees, the Court assigned a heavy burden of justification, which the government failed to meet. When a restriction inhibits an entire class of workers from speaking, the Court decided, the government must concretely identify harms that the speech will cause and show that the restriction "will in fact alleviate these harms in a direct and material way" (*United States v. Nat'l Treasury Employees Union*, 1995, p. 475).

In the years since the *NTEU* decision was handed down, no government employer has ever successfully defended a prohibition on speaking to the news media. Court after court has concluded that a rule forbidding employees from discussing work-related matters with the media, or requiring a supervisor's permission before speaking, offends the First Amendment as a prior restraint (LoMonte, 2019). In an oft-cited case applying *NTEU*, a federal appeals court found that New York City child welfare agency overreached in prohibiting employees from communicating with the media about agency policies or activities without prior supervisory approval (*Harman v. City of New York*, 1998). The policy declared unconstitutional—which is comparable to the policies on the books in college athletic programs across the country—stated that employees must refer all media contacts "regarding any policies or activities of the Agency" to a public relations officer rather than offering any information themselves (*Harman v. City of New York*, 1998). Time and again, judges have struck down agency policies that prevent government employees from discussing their work with the press and public, including a Rhode Island fire department's policy forbidding anyone but the chief from speaking to the media (*Providence Firefighters*

Local 799 v. City of Providence, 1998), and a New Jersey police agency's regulation forbidding disclosure of any information acquired in the course of duty, which inhibited Black officers from speaking to the media about their concerns over racism within the agency (*Davis v. N.J. Dept. of Law & Pub. Safety*, 1999).

In the college sports context, a federal appeals court cited the *NTEU* case and invalidated a University of Illinois regulation forbidding anyone "associated with" the university from communicating with a prospective athletic recruit without the athletic director's authorization. (*Crue v. Aiken*, 2004). The rule was found to be unconstitutionally broad, because it even forbade discussing issues of public concern, such as an ongoing controversy over the university's racially divisive Native American mascot.

In addition to the First Amendment considerations, workplace interview prohibitions also flunk constitutional scrutiny when they reserve unbridled discretion to approve or deny an interview, without recourse for the employee who has been silenced to challenge the decision (*Swartzwelder v. McNeilly*, 2002). For example, a federal district judge threw out a Massachusetts fire department's policy requiring prior written approval before firefighters could make comments on any department matter, because the policy failed to provide "narrow, objective and definite" criteria to assure that the department would not withhold approval for impermissible viewpoint-punitive reasons (*Spain v. City of Mansfield*, 1996, p. 923).

To be clear, there is no basis to believe that a public university has the same level of control over athletes as it has over salaried employees. Indeed, universities have fought for decades to avoid categorizing athletes as employees, to avoid owing them workers' compensation, death benefits, and other employee rights (Branch, 2011). For instance, when Texas State University basketball player Basil Brown II filed suit alleging that his scholarship was revoked in retaliation for filing complaints over mistreatment by the coaching staff and inadequate medical care, the university successfully secured dismissal of the lawsuit by convincing a judge that Brown was not entitled to the same whistleblower protection as college employees (*Brown v. Texas Univ. Sys. Bd. of Regents*, 2013). In the relatively few instances in which the "employee" status of athletes has been put to the test, the courts have agreed: Athletes may wear a school-issued uniform, but they are not "agents" of their institutions in the same way that paid employees are. Given that gag rules are universally recognized as unconstitutional when applied even to employees, and that universities almost certainly have less authority over athletes than over employees, there is no basis for believing that the commonplace rules forbidding athletes from having unapproved contact with the news media are constitutional.

From Basketball Court to District Court

For understandable reasons, athletes rarely sue their institutions. Suing is adversarial, it costs money, and it is unlikely to yield results, such as restoration to a team, while the relief is still meaningful on a college student's limited timetable (Hauer, 2012). As one commentator memorably put it, "if forced to choose between their sport and free speech rights, the speech rights lose" (Hauer, 2012, p. 420). The dearth of litigation means that courts have furnished little guidance about the athlete/school dynamic. What precedent exists is largely in the context of high-school athletes challenging removal from their teams—a situation in which the relationship is already broken, so the plaintiff has little to lose.

High-school athletes typically have won their constitutional cases when disqualification from the team seems nakedly retaliatory for whistleblowing speech, particularly speech addressing discrimination or abuse. For instance, when eight players were suspended from the basketball team at an Oregon high school because they signed a petition asking for their abusive coach— who had threatened to "make [their] lives a living hell"—a federal court found their petition to be constitutionally protected speech (although their subsequent refusal to attend a road game was not) (*Pinard v. Clatskanie Sch. Dist. 6J*, 2006).

But courts are less protective of athlete speech if it comes across as a personal grievance rather than a complaint of wrongdoing, particularly if the speech is accompanied by defiant conduct or inflammatory words calculated to incite others. The most prominent of these cases, and perhaps the most deferential, is the Sixth Circuit's ruling in *Lowery v. Euverard* (2007), a case involving a high-school football team's revolt against a coach many players found intolerable to play for. The appeals court decided that the school did not violate the First Amendment in kicking four players off the team for circulating a petition seeking the coach's firing, even though the players presented evidence that the coach was abusive, degrading, and violated rules against excessive practices. Analogizing high-school sports to a workplace, the judges concluded that athletes voluntarily agree to be bound by the coach's rules and obey the coach's orders in service of the greater good of the team.

In a rare college-level case, a federal appeals court ruled against college basketball players whose scholarships were revoked after they complained to their athletic director, and to the press, about their head coach (*Marcum v. Dahl*, 1981). Because the complaints were purely about internal team dynamics—the complainants preferred to play for an assistant coach they regarded as more competent—the court found that the complaints did not address any matter of public concern. Accordingly, because the complaints created "disharmony" among the players disruptive to the basketball program, the university could punish the speakers without running afoul of the First Amendment.

Courts are prone to treat the success of carrying out the coach's plan as the "point" of sports rather than the educational development of young people. For instance, a court upheld the discipline of a high-school athlete who wrote a letter to her teammates criticizing her coach, noting that the coach was entitled to enforce "team unity" and "cohesiveness" and that coaches deserve "respect" from athletes (*Wildman*, 2001). One prominent legal scholar who played intercollegiate sports as an undergraduate has defended colleges' rigid control over athletes' use of social media thusly:

> The primary goal of college athletics, actually all athletic pursuits, is successful athletic performance. No one shows up to a game or tournament hoping or preparing to lose. No athlete suits up hoping to perform in mediocre fashion. Athletics, by its very nature, separates teams and individual athletes into winners and losers. (Penrose, 2014)

Courts have further exacerbated the power imbalance between athlete and institution by declining to recognize that the Due Process Clause—which prohibits government agencies from taking away government benefits arbitrarily—gives an athlete a constitutional claim for deprivation of the opportunity to play sports (*Colorado Seminary v. NCAA*, 1978; Johnson, 2010; *Justice v. NCAA*, 1983). Because it is relatively difficult for athletes to win legal challenges against their institutions, it is doubly important for them to have a clearly protected right to speak out against abusive or discriminatory conditions within their programs or college sports generally, as Oregon's Sedona Prince did.

How Colleges Rationalize Restraints

The NCAA and its member institutions often claim that they deserve substantial deference from courts and policymakers because intercollegiate sports are a unique and important feature of the broader educational experience and process of higher education (*NCAA v. Alston*, Pet. Brief, 2021). In cases ranging from antitrust challenges to the "amateurism" model to the application of disability rights statutes, the NCAA and its member schools argue for latitude, asserting that freedom to operate sports programs as coaches and administrators see fit is necessary if college athletics is to happen at all (*NCAA v. Alston*, Pet. Brief, 2021, p. 20). These arguments frequently invoke the preferences of sports consumers (*NCAA v. Alston*, Pet. Brief, 2021, p. 17). Indeed, colleges and universities often rationalize limitations on athlete speech because the speech will be disfavored by the program's fans. In this way, athletes are treated less like human beings with a voice, or students engaging in the learning process, and more like products. For instance, in *NCAA v. Alston*, a key part of the NCAA's argument was that "consumers" do not want to watch athletes who are paid (*NCAA v. Alston*, Pet. Brief, 2021, p. 44). Colleges and universities extend this thinking to athlete speech, seeking to curtail athlete speech on sensitive political issues at least partially for fear of how fans, politicians, and donors might overreact.

In one especially dramatic example, players for the Texas Longhorns football team said that, during their 2020 season, they were ordered to remain on the field during the traditional singalong of "The Eyes of Texas," even though many found the anthem's racial overtones troubling and wanted to walk off in silent protest (McGee, 2021). Players told the *Texas Tribune* that athletics officials discouraged the protest because the university was receiving irate emails from donors defensive of the song, who were threatening to withdraw their support for the program and interfere with UT graduates' job prospects if the protest went forward (McGee, 2021). At Georgia's Kennesaw State University, the university's recently hired president was forced to resign after mishandling a controversy over cheerleaders emulating the Kaepernick kneeling protest on the sideline of football games; text messages obtained by the *Atlanta Journal-Constitution* showed that Republican elected officials influenced the president's decision to exclude cheerleaders from future pre-game activities, out of fear that they would continue their protests and cost the university political support (Lutz, 2017).

Some college attorneys maintain that athletes may legitimately be required to waive any claim that social media monitoring violates their privacy or free-expression rights, as part of the Financial Aid Agreement that sets forth the terms of athletic scholarships. But neither contract law nor constitutional law would recognize a blanket surrender of First Amendment rights as legitimate.

While the initial choice of a college is a freely bargained transaction, renewing the contractual relationship in subsequent years is not. College athletes are under infirmities that significantly limit their mobility and thus their ability to walk away from an onerous bargain. Athletes who are unpleasantly surprised by an unexpected regulation in the handbook cannot seamlessly change colleges without interrupting their educational and playing careers. For an athlete in the second, third or fourth years of college, renewing the Financial Aid Agreement is a take-it-or-leave-it proposition. The only "option" may be walking away and quitting college—which is, practically speaking, no option at all. Moreover, there is no indication that the ability to speak freely to the media is a "benefit" that *any* college athletic department offers, so an athlete interested in pursuing that benefit would be unlikely to find a better offer by transferring schools.

The argument that athletes "contract away" their free-speech rights in exchange for free tuition, housing, and meals ignores the reality that, according to NCAA statistics, nearly half of all college athletes (46%) "walk on" to their college teams (Leccesi, 2017). Walk-on players receive no compensation beyond the intangible benefits of athletic participation. It is highly unlikely that a coach would accede to two differing levels of control over players, one for those receiving financial benefits and another for walk-ons. Since a coach will assert the same level of control over non-scholarship as well as scholarship athletes, an athletic department's authority over players' speech cannot be based on the scholarship contract.

It is often observed that playing intercollegiate sports is a "privilege" to which no one has a guaranteed right, suggesting that the organizers are free to impose conditions on participating. (*Equity in Athletics, Inc. v. Dept. of Education*, 2009; *Brennan v. Board of Trustees for Univ. of Louisiana Sys.*, 1997; *NCAA v. Gillard*, 1977). But that notion is irreconcilable with a half-century's worth of First Amendment jurisprudence. While it was once believed that a discretionary government benefit could be withheld or conditioned on a surrender of constitutional rights, the Supreme Court swept away the so-called rights/privileges distinction during a series of rulings reacting to McCarthy-era persecution of suspected Communists. In the most prominent of these decisions, the *Keyishian* case (1967), the justices decided that, even though no one has an "entitlement" to receive a government job, a state university could not condition employment on disclosing any past affiliation with the Communist Party and forswearing any future involvement. It has been clearly established for decades that a public agency, including a state university, cannot condition a "privilege" on forfeiting First Amendment rights.

Furthermore, requiring a student to sign away constitutional rights in exchange for the opportunity to play sports risks running afoul of the "unconstitutional conditions" doctrine. A requirement to waive constitutional rights as a condition of receiving a government benefit will be held unconstitutional if the right "has little or no relationship" to the withheld benefit (*Dolan v. City of Tigard*, 1994). Interposing the artifice of a contract so as to make the government coercion appear voluntary does not legitimize the exaction because "the state cannot accomplish indirectly that which it has been constitutionally prohibited from doing directly" (*Lebron v. Secretary, Fla. Dept. of Children and Families*, 2013, p. 1217).

In a 2013 ruling, the Supreme Court decided that it was unlawfully coercive for a federal agency to require an applicant to sign a broad waiver of First Amendment freedoms in exchange for a government grant, even an entirely discretionary one that the applicant had no legal entitlement to receive (*Agency for Int'l Development v. Alliance for Open Society Int'l, Inc.*, 2013). While a grantee can be required to agree to conditions within the scope of the grant program, the justices said any surrender of free-speech rights must be limited to what is necessary for the government program to operate success- fully. Under that standard, it would be quite difficult for a university athletic department to justify a wholesale prohibition on speaking to the media about any subject, even during the offseason when the program is not actively operating.

The Price of Silence

Limiting athlete speech causes a wide range of harm to athletes, to fans, to policymakers and others who are denied information that could lead to sport reforms, and, perhaps most importantly, to the games themselves. Indeed, while it may appear in our sports-obsessed culture that there is more sports information than ever before, there is relatively little coming from athletes themselves. We have a one-dimensional sport narrative, curated by coaches and administrators, and lacking the insight of those who play and bear the highest costs and burdens of the games. It is time to recalibrate.

In June 2020, the University of Iowa bought out the contract of its long- time football strength coach, Chris Doyle, after multiple former Hawkeye players accused him of singling out Black athletes for differential mis- treatment (Sallee, 2020). The floodgates opened after one former player, James Daniels, posted his criticism on Twitter: "There are too many racial disparities in the Iowa football program. Black players have been treated unfairly for far too long." (Daniels, 2020). The university commissioned an external review from a law firm specializing in athletic compliance issues, Husch Blackwell, which released a report in July 2020 identifying concerns within the football program's culture (Husch Blackwell, 2020). The report documented a phenomenon within the program widely known as "The Iowa Way," which current and former players described as signifying: "Do not speak up about things" and "Be quiet and do what you're told" (Husch Blackwell, 2020, at p. 7). The report found that top coaches on the Iowa staff were widely unaware of the perception that Black players were subjected to disfavored treatment:

> None of the individuals interviewed said they raised concerns about differential treatment due to a fear of facing repercussions. One current player explained that players were scared to come out with this because they were afraid of the treatment they would receive. (Husch Blackwell, 2020, p. 16)

Unsurprisingly, it took *former* players—safely removed from retaliation— to speak out about a problem within the program that had been festering for years.

The Iowa findings echo what players reported at the University of Maryland, where a culture of silent obedience within the football program produced especially tragic results. In May 2018, Jordan McNair, a highly sought-after athlete recruited to play offensive line for the Maryland Terrapins, collapsed on the practice field, suffering symptoms of heat stroke. He died 15 days later, at the age of 19 (Dougherty, 2018). McNair's death brought to light deeper cultural issues pervading the football program. An exhaustive, 192-page report by a commission of outside experts determined that Maryland's coaches and athletic department fostered "a culture where problems festered because too many players feared speaking out," even when members of the coaching staff subjected them to serious physical and verbal abuse (Maese & Alexander, 2018).

As these cases exemplify, silence is the accomplice of mistreatment. But they are hardly isolated occurrences.

In recent years, scandals involving the abuse of athletes have become public knowledge with disturbing regularity: At Ohio State University, where a wrestling team physician molested young men for decades; at Michigan State University, where generations of young gymnasts were criminally sexually abused by team physician Larry Nassar, while university authorities looked the other way; and at the University of Michigan, where a physician was allowed to keep treating Wolverine athletes for 37 years despite multiple complaints that he sexually molested patients or made sexually inappropriate remarks during examinations (Jesse, 2021; Levenson, 2018; Kwiatkowski, 2016). Abusive coaching tactics have surfaced at Rutgers University (verbal and physical abuse by the head basketball coach) (Eder & Zernike, 2013), at the University of Utah (swimming coach removed after years of complaints from athletes about violent temper outbursts and cruel mistreatment went unaddressed) (Whitehurst & Faulk, 2013), at Purdue University-Fort Wayne (women's basketball coach accused of "toxic abuse" that drove players to panic attacks and self-harm) (Benbow, 2021), and at many other institutions, as former team members—no longer vulnerable to retaliation—come forward and speak about the abuse they suffered.

The Benefits of Uncensored Whistleblowing

It cannot be overlooked that college sports programs are overwhelmingly run by white administrators and disproportionately populated by students of color (Harper, 2018). In other words, policies that empower athletic departments to silence the voices of athletes disproportionately result in white administrators serving as the gatekeepers over what Black and brown people are allowed to say. Similarly, while women constitute 44% of all athletes and women's teams represent 54% of all intercollegiate sports teams (Schwarb, 2018), women are underrepresented in intercollegiate athletics administration and coaching (Bower & Hums, 2013). Gender alone certainly cannot guarantee better or different policies for women's sports. However, the lack of women's voices in leadership coupled with limitations on speech predominately crafted by male coaches and administrators makes it even more important that athletes be permitted greater speech rights so that the full range of experiences and voices may be heard. This is especially true given that statistics show the full promise of Title IX and gender equity in sports has yet to be realized (Heckman, 2003). Thus, the current model of restrained athlete speech serves to privilege a very limited group of voices in intercollegiate sports—those of predominantly white male coaches and administrators—with the cost being a richer discourse around intercollegiate sports.

The price of limiting athlete speech goes beyond harm to athletes and also includes harm to the public interest. Restraining athlete speech serves to sustain the traditional deference from regulation the NCAA and its member institutions have long enjoyed. Amateur athletes have few rights: they have no right to participate and no right to form unions. They are not members of the NCAA and have little ability to shape the policies that directly affect their athletic and educational experiences (Mitten & Davis, 2008). When athletes cannot communicate fully about their experiences and the sports structures that shape them, the narrative of intercollegiate sport is limited to what the public sees at game time and the carefully curated statements about the team and its play. But the social construct that is intercollegiate sport goes well beyond the games themselves. Sports are embedded in educational institutions, many of them public, and both public and private institutions receive federal funding and enjoy other public support. Intercollegiate sports programs are matters of public importance. Without the perspective of athlete speech, policymakers at all levels are left with an incomplete picture of intercollegiate sports. That blurry conception of college athletics is generally focused only at times of scandal or crisis, such as the death of Jordan McNair, the discovery of Larry Nassar's crimes, the athlete concussion crisis, and the University of North Carolina's systemic academic fraud. Indeed, the full scope of issues such as these are appreciated only through the discourse of litigation or investigations—one of the few places where athletes are able to speak freely, but only after considerable harm has occurred. Without a wider, more consistent discourse around intercollegiate sports that includes athletes' voices, policymakers are left to inquire into specific incidents after the fact, if at all, rather than proactively consider or adopt reforms that take account of the true reality of intercollegiate sports and its impact on the public good. Athletes and the games themselves are worse for it.

Loosening the limits on athlete speech is similarly important because it can allow for a type of collective action that is generally lacking in intercollegiate sports. This is speech that communicates from athlete to athlete, such as through the use of social media. Without the benefit of a union, athletes are not protected in their ability to seek collective redress for the variety of harms they may suffer in their athletic careers. The ability to speak to other athletes and generate consensus or momentum for issues of importance therefore cannot be discounted, and athlete speech may also create new forms of collective action, by engaging fans. While colleges and universities typically restrain athlete speech to satisfy team fans and donors, athletes have an opportunity to engage a wider audience, beyond those that follow their particular school or have differing beliefs. Instead, athletes can use their speech to activate the interest of those who are supportive of athletes' rights and concerns and who might join the cause of seeking reform. In this way, consumers of sports information are not simply those who follow game scores and traditional team rivalries. They are also potential allies.

To appreciate what is at stake, consider the story of Syracuse University's softball team. After a dozen players transferred schools or quit the sport entirely over the three-and-a-half-year tenure of head coach Shannon Doepking, the *Daily Orange* student newspaper sought to find out why. Relying almost entirely on accounts from former players, the newspaper assembled a picture of a highly controlling coach unsympathetic to players' struggles with mental health, who browbeat and insulted players to the point that at least one contemplated suicide (Alandt & Smith, 2021). The reporters pieced together their story by speaking with seven former players and one current player, most of whom insisted on anonymity—even after having left the program—for fear of retaliation. In response, Syracuse hand-picked two players that the athletic department authorized to speak to *Daily Orange* reporters, both of whom "said everyone on the team gets along and enjoys being a part of Doepking's softball program" (Alandt & Smith, 2021). The reporters noted that a Syracuse official "sat in on the interviews." This is the price of institutionalizing reputation management as a virtue in college sports. If not for the enterprise of reporters who refused to settle for the stage-managed version of reality, people concerned about the welfare of Syracuse athletes would have been left with an officially sanitized account.

A PATH FORWARD: UNCHAINING ATHLETE VOICES

In August 2015, California labor lawyer David A. Rosenfeld filed a wide-ranging complaint with federal regulators on behalf of football players at Northwestern University, a private institution where workplace standards are governed by the National Labor Relations Act (NLRA) (Edelman, 2017). In his complaint to the National Labor Relations Board (NLRB), Rosenfeld alleged that Northwestern engaged in unfair labor practices by, among other things, unduly restricting players' ability to speak to the media about working conditions. The NLRA has long been understood to protect employees' freedom to discuss work-related issues with the press, because enlisting public support can be an essential step in improving working conditions. The Northwestern complaint sent shockwaves through the college sports world, because it asked the NLRB to recognize football players as "employees" for purposes of federal workplace rights, a decision with seismic consequences for the NCAA's entrenched business model.

While the NLRB would ultimately punt on the "employee" question, leaving the Northwestern complaint unaddressed (*Northwestern Univ.*, 2015), the complaint itself produced a significant change in the university's relationship with its athletes. An NLRB staff attorney investigating Rosenfeld's complaint concluded that many of the restrictions in Northwestern's athlete handbook would constitute unlawful labor practices under the NLRA (Kearney, 2016). Practices identified as unlawful included prohibiting interviews with the press without approval from a public relations officer and directing students and employees to say only "positive" things to the media and avoid "negative" remarks (Kearney, 2016, p. 5). However, during the investigation, Northwestern rewrote the handbook to bring it into compliance with prevailing NLRA standards—for instance, making consultation with a sports-information officer an optional convenience and not mandatory. For that reason, the Board found no violations to act on and closed the case (LoMonte & Hamrick, 2020).

The revised Northwestern manual can serve as a roadmap for what colleges everywhere can legitimately do to offer assistance to athletes who want help navigating conversations with the news media, without crossing the line into coercively discouraging them from speaking. It affirmatively informs athletes that they are free to speak to the press with or without the athletic department's assistance, as long as they refrain from sharing confidential medical information about their teammates, which is the type of "narrowly tailored" restriction that the First Amendment finds tolerable at a state institution.

The moment is opportune to rethink the relationship between athletes and their institutions, because the "name, image and likeness" movement is forcing a recalibration of the power dynamic. Long-held assumptions about amateurism are being upended as a result of court rulings and state legislation. Protecting athletes' ability to endorse products or sign autographs for money is an incomplete remedy without also protecting their ability to speak publicly about the issues they care about, whether internal to the athletic program or external to the wider world. We are living at a moment of civic reckoning in which it is increasingly understood that educational institutions have failed to prepare young people to engage critically with issues of governance. It disserves higher education's civic mission to maintain a constitutional underclass of students who never during their waking hours enjoy the freedom to participate in the democracy they are soon to inherit.

Response

Restricting Athletes' Speech Puts Athletic Programs at Risk

Paula Lavigne, ESPN Investigative Reporter

During the 2020 football season, there was much debate over how college athletic departments were managing the threat of COVID-19. Reporters were hearing that some parents and athletes were concerned about returning to play and feeling pressured to rejoin the team before they felt it was safe to do so. I reached out over social media to one male college athlete who might have been at higher risk for complications due to COVID-19. "Would you mind talking to me for this story?" I asked. He quickly responded, "Hi. I'd be more than happy to but you'd have to contact (the school) first."

I knew that was coming. And I had a pretty good idea of what would happen next. I contacted the sports information director for the athletic department, and no one ever set up that interview. I messaged the athlete on social media a few more times, and each message went unanswered. I admit I don't know exactly what transpired after my first message, but I can guess based on what I've heard from former athletes and coaches at other schools who talked about the culture of silence within college athletics.

I once spoke to a (since retired) chancellor of a major football university who complained about the inability to get information from athletics, referring to the department as the "North Korea" of campus for its siloed and isolated nature. And these were employees that technically reported to him. I've even had parents tell me that if they talk to a reporter without permission their son or daughter will be in trouble. It's not just the major powerhouse programs. A sports information director at a Division III school sent me a scolding email one time for directly reaching out to a female athlete and not going through the "proper channels."

The proper channel is to go to the athlete directly. If that doesn't work, maybe there's a parent or someone the athlete has chosen to represent him or her outside of the school. Athletes have a right to speak out on their own behalf. An athlete has a right to hear the question or the topic and decide if she or he wants to speak without the filter or the implied or direct intimidation from a coach or other team official. This is always important, but especially so when the topic is how an athlete is being treated or how there might be a problem within the team, with a coach or with any aspect of the athletic department.

Policies that punish athletes for posting on social media or speaking to journalists, and sports information directors who cherry-pick athletes to give comments on controversial topics, are how serious problems get buried. That is how people get hurt.

We have seen how this culture of silence—this "keep it in the family" mentality—also prevents or discourages athletes from going directly and speaking candidly to law enforcement, to school Title IX investigators, and to other regulatory entities or investigators, even if laws or rules require that they do so. In some cases, these bans have even contradicted class assignments from professors.

If coaches and administrators are so threatened by what their athletes might say, then maybe instead of gagging them, they should start to listen to them.

REFERENCES

Agency for Int'l Development v. Alliance for Open Society Int'l, Inc., 570 U.S. 205 (2013).

Alandt, A. & Smith, C. (2021, March 9). Former SU softball players allege abuses by head coach Shannon Doepking. *The Daily Orange.* http://dailyorange.com/2021/05/former-syracuse-softball-players-allege-abuses-by-shannon-doepking/

Anderson, G. (2020, July 2). On the offensive and in the lead. *Inside Higher Ed.* https://www.insidehighered.com/news/2020/07/02/athletes-push-and-achieve-social-justice-goals

Benbow, D.H. (2021, January 20). Toxic abuse alleged inside Purdue-Fort Wayne women's basketball: 'It was brutal.' *Indianapolis Star.* https://www.indystar.com/story/sports/college/purdue/2021/01/20/purdue-fort-wayne-womens-basketball-program-accused-toxic-abuse/3592918001/

Berkowitz, S. (2019, September 30). California governor signs bill that makes it easier for college athletes to profit from name, likeness. *USA Today.* https://www.usatoday.com/story/sports/college/2019/09/30/college-sports-california-governor-signs-image-and-likeness-bill/2367426001/

Berkowitz, S. & Epstein, J. (2019, October 4). NCAA's $208.7 million in legal settlement money finally reaching athletes' mailboxes. *USA Today.* https://www.usatoday.com/story/sports/2019/10/04/ncaas-208-7-million-legal-settlement-reaching-athletes-mailboxes/3859697002/

Berman, J. (2020). Dribbling around the first amendment: Analyzing the constitutionality of university-imposed restrictions on student-athletes' use of social media. *U. Denv. Sports & Ent. L.J. 23*, 79–117. https://heinonline.org/HOL/LandingPage?handle=hein.journals/denversel23&div=8&id=&page=

Bower, G.G. & Hums, Mary A. (2013). Career paths of women working in leadership positions within intercollegiate athletic administration. *Advancing Women in Leadership, 33*, 1–14. https://awl-ojs-tamu.tdl.org/awl/index.php/awl/article/view/93

Branch, T. (2011, October). The shame of college sports. *The Atlantic.* https://www.theatlantic.com/magazine/archive/2011/10/the-shame-of-college-sports/308643/

Brennan v. Board of Trustees for Univ. of Louisiana Sys., 691 So.2d 324 (La. Ct. App.1997).

Brown v. Texas Univ. Sys. Bd. of Regents, No. A-13-CA-483, 2013 WL 652025 (W.D. Tex. Dec. 12, 2013).

Bump, P. (2015, November 9). How the Missouri football team took down its university's president. *Washington Post*. https://www.washingtonpost.com/news/the-fix/wp/2015/11/09/missouri-football-players-and-the-untapped-political-power-of-the-college-student-athlete/

CBS, Inc. v. Young, 522 F.2d 234 (6th Cir. 1975).

Chemerinsky, E. (2013). The Hazelwooding of the first amendment: The deference to authority. *First Amend. L. Rev. 11*, 291–304. https://scholarship.law.uci.edu/faculty_scholarship/10/

Colorado Seminary v. NCAA, 570 F.2d 320 (10th Cir. 1978).

Crue v. Aiken, 370 F.3d 668 (7th Cir. 2004).

Curry, M. (2018). "Get that son-of-a-***** off the field:" Regulating student-athlete protest speech in public university sports facilities. *Howard L.J. 61*, 669–696. https://heinonline.org/HOL/LandingPage?handle=hein.journals/howlj61&div=32&id=&page=

Dator, J. (2021, February 26). A comprehensive timeline of the Larry Nassar case. *SB Nation*. https://www.sbnation.com/2018/1/19/16900674/larry-nassar-abuse-timeline-usa-gymnastics-michigan-state

Davis v. N.J. Dept. of Law & Pub. Safety, 327 N.J. Super. 59 (N.J. Super. 1999).

Doe v. Alvey, No. 1:20-CV-410, 2021 WL 1099593 (S.D. Ohio Mar. 23, 2021).

Dolan v. City of Tigard, 512 U.S. 374 (1994).

Dougherty, J. (2018. August 13). Experts say Maryland may not have acted quickly enough to save football player. *Washington Post*. https://www.washingtonpost.com/sports/colleges/experts-say-maryland-may-have-not-acted-quickly-enough-to-save-football-player/2018/08/13/261b6122-9f25-11e8-8e87-c869fe70a721_story.html

Edelman, M. (2017). The future of college athlete players unions: Lessons learned from northwestern university and potential next steps in the college athletes' rights movement. *Cardozo L. Rev. 38*(**5**), 1627–1662. http://cardozolawreview.com/the-future-of-college-athlete-players-unions-lessons-learned-from-northwestern-university-and-potential-next-steps-in-the-college/

Eder, S. & Zernike, K. (2013, April 3). Rutgers leaders are faulted on abusive coach. *New York Times*. https://www.nytimes.com/2013/04/04/sports/ncaabasketball/rutgers-fires-basketball-coach-after-video-surfaces.html

Equity in Athletics, Inc. v. Dept. of Education, 675 F.Supp.2d 660 (W.D. Va. 2009).

Garcetti v. Ceballos, 547 U.S. 410 (2006).

Hahn, J.D. (2021, March 29). What to know about university of Oregon basketball player Sedona prince. *People.com*. https://people.com/sports/what-to-know-about-oregon-basketball-player-sedona-prince/

Hansen, J. (2020, June 12). Cultures of secrecy and silence gag college athletes when speaking on racism. *Missoulian*. https://missoulian.com/sports/college/jordan-hansen-cultures-of-secrecy-and-silence-gag-college-athletes-when-speaking-on-racism/article_3355949b-8ad0-573e-8f54-083d2cdbd016.html

Harman v. City of New York, 140 F. 3d 111 (2d Cir. 1998).

Harper, S.R. (2018, March 14). White NCAA coaches profit off black players. *Hartford Courant*. https://www.courant.com/opinion/hc-op-harper-white-coaches -profit-off-black-players-20180313-story.html

Hartocollis, A. (2021, February 5). Students punished for 'vulgar' social media posts are fighting back. *New York Times*. https://www.nytimes.com/2021/02/05/us/col-leges-social-media-discipline.html

Hatch, T. (2003). Keep on Rockin' in the free world: A first amendment analysis of entertainment permit schemes. *Colum. J. of Law & Arts, 26*, 313–334. https://hei-nonline-org.lp.hscl.ufl.edu/HOL/Page?handle=hein.journals/cjla26&id=321&col-lection=journals

Hauer, M. (2012). The constitutionality of public university bans of student-athlete speech through social media. *Vt. L. Rev. 37*, 413.

Healy v. James, 408 U.S. 169 (1972).

Heckman, D. (2003). The glass sneaker: Thirty years of victory and defeats involving title IX and sex discrimination in athletics. *Fordham Intell. Prop. Media & Ent. L.J. 13*, 551–616. https://ir.lawnet.fordham.edu/cgi/viewcontent.cgi?article=1261 &context=iplj

Hunt v. Board of Regents of Univ. of New Mexico, 792 Fed. Appx. 595 (10th Cir. 2019).

Husch Blackwell, Report of External Review, Football Program Culture, University of Iowa (July 2020).

James Daniels [@jamsdans]. (2020, June 5). Twitter. https://twitter.com/jamsdans/ status/1269058668663844864.

Jesse, D. (2021, May 11). Report: U-M could have stopped Anderson sexual assaults on athletes. *Detroit Free Press*. https://www.freep.com/story/news/education/2021 /05/11/robert-anderson-sexual-assaults-university-michigan/5038960001/

Johnson, N. (2010). Tinker takes the field: Do student athletes shed their constitutions rights at the locker room gate? *Marq. Sports L. Rev. 21*(**1**), 293–314.

Justice v. NCAA, 577 F. Supp. 356 (D. Ariz. 1983).

Kearney, B.J. (2016, September 22). Advice memorandum to Peter Sung Ohr, Reg'l Dir. of Region 13. *National Labor Relations Board*.

Kessler v. City of Providence, 167 F.Supp.2d 482 (D.R.I. 2001).

Kwiatkowski, M., Alesia, M., & Evans, T. (2016, August 4). A blind eye to sex abuse: How USA Gymnastics failed to report cases. *Indianapolis Star*. https://www.indys-tar.com/story/news/investigations/2016/08/04/usa-gymnastics-sex-abuse-protected -coaches/85829732/

Lane v. Franks, 573 U.S. 228 (2014).

Lauretano v. Spada, 339 F.Supp.2d 391 (D.Conn. 2004).

Lebron v. Secretary, Fla. Dept. of Children and Families, 710 F.3d 1202 (11th Cir. 2013).

Leccesi, J. (2017, April 13). The 5 most commonly asked questions about being a col-lege walk-on. *USA Today High School Sports*. https://usatodayhss.com/2017/the-5 -most-commonly-asked-questions-about-being-a-college-walk-on

Levenson, E. (2018, February 5). Larry Nassar apologizes, gets 40 to 125 years for decades of sexual abuse. *CNN.com*. https://www.cnn.com/2018/02/05/us/larry-nas-sar-sentence-eaton/index.html

Lindsay, M. (2012). Tinker goes to college: Why high school free-speech standards should not apply to post-secondary students. *Wm. Mitchell L. Rev. 38*(**4**), 1470–1514.

LoMonte, F.D. (2013). "The key word is student:" Hazelwood censorship crashes the ivy-covered gates. *First Amend. L. Rev. 11*, 305–363.

LoMonte, F.D. & Hamrick, V. (2020). Running the full-court press: How college athletics departments unlawfully restrict athletes' rights to speak to the news media. *Neb. L. Rev. 99*(**1**), 86–140.

Lowery v. Euverard, 497 F.3d 584 (6th Cir. 2007).

Lutz, M. (2017, December 14). Cobb sheriff, lawmaker pushed to keep KSU cheerleaders off field. *Atlanta Journal-Constitution.* https://www.ajc.com/news/local-govt--politics/ksu-cheerleader-protest-sheriff-lawmaker-say-olens-caved/y4VLs2DlTY82rOskdXvfcJ/

Maese, R. & Alexander, K.L. (2018, October 25). Report on Maryland football culture cites problems but stops short of 'toxic' label. *Washington Post.* https://www.washingtonpost.com/sports/2018/10/25/report-maryland-football-culture-cites-problems-stops-short-toxic-label/

Marcum v. Dahl, 658 F. 2d 731 (10th Cir. 1981).

Martin, J. (2020, December 12). Utah State football game canceled after players reportedly vote not to play because of comments from university president. *CNN.com.* https://www.cnn.com/2020/12/11/us/utah-state-football-game-canceled-spt-trnd/index.html

McGee, K. (2021, March 3). UT-Austin football players say they were forced to stay on field for "The Eyes of Texas" to appease angry donors and fans. *Texas Tribune.* https://www.texastribune.org/2021/03/03/ut-austin-eyes-of-texas-donors/

McInerney, K. (2021, July 2). What is NIL? NCAA rules are changing regarding athlete pay. Here's what it means. *Boston Globe.* https://www.bostonglobe.com/2021/06/30/sports/ncaa-nil-rules-change/

Michaux, S. (2017, August 3). Media restrictions are a disservice to college programs. *Augusta Chronicle.* https://www.augustachronicle.com/columnists/sports/2017-08-03/michaux-media-restrictions-are-disservice-college-programs

Mickanen, D. (2021, March 19). Sedona Prince's viral TikTok shows the NCAA had enough space for an equal weight room. *NBCSports.com.* https://www.nbcsports.com/northwest/oregon-ducks/sedona-princes-viral-tiktok-shows-ncaa-had-enough-space-equal-weight-room

Mitten, M.J. & Davis, T. (2008). Athlete eligibility requirements and legal protection of sports participation opportunities. *Va. Sports & Ent. L.J. 8*(**1**), 71–146.

Myerberg, P. (2021, May 26). Confused about NIL? 10 questions explore how name, image and likeness laws will change college sports. *USA Today.* https://www.usatoday.com/in-depth/sports/college/2021/05/26/how-name-image-likeness-laws-change-college-game/5184304001/

National Collegiate Athletic Association. (2021). Staying in bounds: An NCAA model policy to prevent inappropriate relationships between student-athletes and athletics department personnel. https://www.ncaapublications.com/p-4308-staying-in-bounds.aspx

NCAA v. Alston, Case No. 20-512, Brief for Petitioner (U.S. Feb. 1, 2021).

NCAA v. Alston, 141 S.Ct. 2141 (2021).

NCAA v. Gillard, 352 So.2d 1072 (Miss. 1977).

NCAA / Gallup. (2020). A study of NCAA student-athletes: Undergraduate experiences and post-college outcomes. https://ncaaorg.s3.amazonaws.com/research/other/2020/2020RES_GallupNCAAOutcomes.pdf

Nietzel, M.T. (2020, June 28). Black athletes are leading the new college protest movement. *Forbes.* https://www.forbes.com/sites/michaeltnietzel/2020/06/28/black-athletes-lead-the-new-college-protest-movement/?sh=1a91fdc162fa

Northwestern Univ., 362 N.L.R.B. 1350 (2015).

Office of Senator Christopher Murphy. (2019, December 16). *Madness, Inc.: How college sports can leave athletes broken and abandoned.* https://www.murphy.senate.gov/imo/media/doc/Madness%203.pdf

O'Neil, D. (2021, December 13). A game that should not be forgotten. *ESPN.com.* https://www.espn.com/blog/collegebasketballnation/post/_/id/69914/oneil-a-game-that-should-not-be-forgotten

Papish v. Bd. of Curators of Univ. of Mo., 410 U.S. 667 (1973).

Penrose, M. (2014). Tinkering with success: College athletes, social media and the first amendment. *Pace L. Rev. 35*(**1**), 30–72.

Peter, J. & Schad, T. (2020, August 6). From #WeAreUnited to COVID-19 whistleblowing, college athletes are raising their voices like rarely before. *USA Today.* https://www.usatoday.com/story/sports/ncaaf/2020/08/06/weareunited-covid-19-whistleblowing-college-athletes-speak-out/3299442001/

Pickering v. Bd. of Educ., 391 U.S. 563 (1968).

Pinard v. Clatskanie Sch. Dist. 6J, 467 F. 3d 755 (9th Cir. 2006).

Providence Firefighters Local 799 v. City of Providence, 26 F.Supp.2d 350 (D.R.I. 1998).

Raab, S. (2021, February 23). The wrestler. *Esquire.* https://www.esquire.com/sports/a35120040/richard-strauss-ohio-state-wrestling-sexual-abuse/

Radwan v. Univ. of Conn., 465 F. Supp. 3d 75 (D. Conn. 2020).

Sallee, B. (2020, June 15). Iowa splits with strength coach Chris Doyle after allegations of racial disparity. *CBSSports.com.* https://www.cbssports.com/college-football/news/iowa-splits-with-strength-coach-chris-doyle-after-allegations-of-racial-disparity/

Schwarb, A.W. (2018, October 10). Number of NCAA college athletes reaches all-time high. NCAA.org. https://www.ncaa.org/about/resources/media-center/news/number-ncaa-college-athletes-reaches-all-time-high

Sherman, E. (2015, December 3). The problem with the dwindling media access to college athletes. *Poynter.org.* https://www.poynter.org/reporting-editing/2015/the-problem-with-the-dwindling-media-access-to-college-athletes/

Spain v. City of Mansfield, 915 F.Supp. 919 (D. Mass. 1996).

Stanley v. Georgia, 394 U.S. 557 (1969).

Svrluga, S. (2017, October 16). Some college students keep taking the knee, too. *Washington Post.* https://www.washingtonpost.com/news/grade-point/wp/2017/10/16/some-college-students-keep-taking-the-knee-too/

Swartzwelder v. McNeilly, 297 F.3d 228 (3d Cir. 2002).

United States v. Nat'l Treasury Employees Union, 513 U.S. 454 (1995).

Walker, R. (2016, September 15). High school football players following Kaepernick's lead. *The Undefeated.* https://theundefeated.com/features/high-school-football-players-following-kaepernicks-lead/

Whitehurst, L. & Faulk, A. (2013, July 2). Report: Former U. swim coach should have been fired for alcohol abuse. *Salt Lake Tribune.* https://archive.sltrib.com/article.php?id=56542931&itype=CMSID

Wildman v. Marshalltown School District, 249 F.3d 768 (8th Cir. 2001).

Wisniewski, L. (2021, March 21). Sedona Prince inspired to lead the change in empowering women in sports. *NBC Sports.* https://www.nbcsports.com/northwest/ducks/sedona-prince-inspired-lead-change-empowering-women-sports

Chapter 2

On Balls, Players, Tackle Boxes, and Other Footballing Objects

The Politics of Being in the NFL Rulebook

Joshua D. Rubin

This chapter examines the 2018 edition of the *Official Playing Rules of the National Football League* (henceforth: "the NFL rulebook" or "the rulebook").[1] The rulebook could be analyzed in a host of ways. One could, for example, study it as a document with a social and political history of its own, and chart across time how the changes in rules map (or fail to map) onto changes to technology (cf. Gelberg, 1995), to in-game strategies, to the economic and social conditions in which football is played, and to medical and scientific understandings of football and its impacts on players and their bodies. One could also study the rulebook as a text that must be learned and navigated by coaches and players in actual sporting practice. Though these approaches certainly have merit, this chapter takes a different approach. Rather than focusing on the rulebook's regulations and policies directly, it considers the rulebook as a theoretical text.[2] This approach teases out the underlying formulations—sometimes explicitly articulated and sometimes left implicit—of what footballing things *are*, in the context of the game, such that the regulations applied to them make sense. Seen in this way, the rulebook is a document that hinges on a situated theory of being—a sporting ontology. It is to this ontology, I argue below, that a significant strain of football's politics (and political possibilities) can be traced.

While one might suppose that, in keeping with the hypermasculine ideal that predominates in American footballing rhetoric, the rulebook would center the human player and elevate them to a place of special importance, the present analysis suggests otherwise. As far as the rulebook is concerned, the player is neither special nor singularly meaningful. He is a being without a fully realized identity, and what identity he possesses is acquired situationally. That identity is established not by the player's own behavior (or their lived experience) but rather by the contexts that surround him. What is more, because those contexts—featuring the space, time, and objects of the field most centrally—are not just important to the play of football but actually dictate what the player can become, the ontology of the rulebook is fundamentally flat. The player, the ball, and the helmet are, instead, *all* objects in Graham Harman's sense of the term—"anything that cannot be entirely reduced either to the components of which it is made or to the effects that it has on other things" (2018, p. 43). As this reference to Harman's work suggests, the NFL rulebook's flat ontology mirrors a strain of recent philosophical work, which theorizes speculatively about ontologies that, rather than privileging the human, locate humanity within a wider universe that is not wholly of its own design. Like such work, the rulebook attempts to cultivate a space beyond history, politics, culture, and identity where a novel (and desubjectivized) theory of being can emerge. By doing so, the rulebook—again like theorists of object-oriented speculative realisms—attempts to recognize the agentive capacities of non-human things.

This project might appear to be a purely academic exercise, but recent events point to a broader significance. Following Colin Kaepernick's solemn protests of police brutality, and former president Trump's response to such protests, the connections between football and politics in contemporary American life are commonly acknowledged if not appreciated. This chapter elaborates on Kaepernick's protests and many other protests like them, insofar as it takes the question "What kinds of political expression are permissible in American football today?" more literally than most of its askers might intend. Drawing inspiration from Nguyen's observation that objects, and structured framings of objects, are integral to locking conceptions of personhood into place (2015), the present reading of the NFL rulebook as a theory of ontology suggests that forms of political expression in football must be thought together with the sorts of beings that the footballing rulebook permits. If players are objects among objects, for example, what consequences does this carry for player speech? For embodied expression? And what roles do conceptions of space and time play in these expressions? If non-human objects are given a place of importance alongside human actors, what new agentive qualities do those objects possess?

Building on the work of Nguyen as well as Ruha Benjamin (2019), Fred Moten (2003), Karen Barad (2007), and other critical theorists of race and gender, this chapter demonstrates that the rulebook's attempt to clear away human political considerations is itself a political project. The NFL rulebook is not so much a disinterested text as a text that adopts a disinterested "orientation" (Ahmed, 2006, 2007, p. 155) with respect to its objects by bringing some things close and pushing others away. The rulebook theorizes players as (mostly) silent objects, but it does so by first positing itself as uninterested in the ways that human actors have been, and continue to be, objectified and silenced in domains beyond its own theoretical concerns. While it can strip away the lived subjectivities of its players in pursuit of a flat ontology, then, it cannot extract that project from a broader political context in which lived subjectivities are unevenly recognized. Furthermore, because the NFL rulebook seems to mirror so precisely other work in object-oriented speculative realism, this chapter suggests that the political position adopted by the rulebook can be extended to those more explicitly theoretical works on object-oriented ontologies as well.

TAUTOLOGICAL DEFINITIONS AND CONTEXTUAL BEING IN THE RULES OF THE NFL

The NFL rulebook, first and foremost, is a document that is intended to outline the terms of a situated reality.[3] It is therefore fitting that its opening sections are devoted not to the practical or moral conditions of the play of football but instead to defining the sport's ontological status—what the field is, what things inhabit the field, what actions those things do, how those things impact other things, and when actions are thought to begin and end. Rule 3, Section 21, Article 1, for example, defines a Player or Official Out of Bounds "when he touches a boundary line, or when he touches anything that is on or outside a boundary line, except a player, an official, or a pylon" (p. 8).

Because the rules are positing football's ontology, we should not be surprised that many of the claims made about the entities participating in football seem exceedingly odd. The defining quality of those claims is that they are tautological—The field is the field because it is the field, and it has certain dimensions. The length of the game is the length of the game, and it is measured in seconds and minutes. In short, the conditions of play are what they are because there is really no good reason for them to be that way. Indeed, the things of play are ordinarily *not* that way, off the field and outside of the game. The "player," for example, is named as a person and assigned he/him pronouns,[4] but that person is left entirely undefined and his gender identity is allocated no specific content. As far as the rulebook is concerned, the player matters exclusively as a *player*, defined according to their presence in a playing space and time. The rulebook is quite clear on this point. "A player," Rule 3, Section 24 states, "is a participant of either team who is in the game" (p. 9). Fittingly and tautologically, a "team" is defined, and only in passing, as comprised of 11 players (Rule V, § 1, Art. 1, p. 17). These founding tautologies are easily framed as the premise of the autotelic character of play—given that the purposelessness of play is commonly explained in terms of the arbitrariness of its goals—but thinking of it ontologically shifts the rules onto a different, arguably more meaningful, terrain. Seen as a text about a situated sporting *reality*, with attendant practices that emerge from and produce relations between things, the NFL rulebook becomes a document about how things do actually exist and behave. Football players do act in a real world, even if they act in pursuit of arbitrary goals, and these real aspects of football's world are foreclosed when play is thought necessarily to be purposeless and therefore distinct from the purpose-driven world of everyday life.[5]

In contrast to the player, who goes almost undefined, the football *does* get a definition as a thing beyond the conditions of play that make it so. The ball, the rules tell us, must be "an inflated (12½ to 13½ pounds) urethane bladder enclosed in a pebble grained, leather case (natural tan color) without corrugations of any kind" (Rule 2, § 1, p. 3). This contrast—between the tautologically defined player and the extremely well-defined ball—seems stark, but I will suggest that it can be explained. One of the core features of the rulebook is its dedication, maybe even obsession, with defining the qualities of non-human things. More to the present point, though, the rulebook says nothing at all about *why* the ball needs to be this shape and size. Its significance is grounded in no "origin story" of purpose or design. It needs to be this size, shape, and quality because that is what the rules need it to be.

Once the rulebook has defined the qualities of the ball, the text moves quickly to what the football *does*—How it links up with other things in space and time. Within the ontology of football's rules, the ball as a footballing thing—rather than as a thing in a home or in a factory or lying on the grass of someone's backyard—oscillates explicitly between two dominant conditions: alive and dead. While one might expect that the ball will come alive when the play begins and die when it ends, this isn't true in any straightforward sense. The beginning of the play does seem to bring life to the ball ("it becomes a live ball when it is legally snapped or legally kicked" [Rule VII, § 1, Art. 1, p. 26]), but in both instances the player action (the throwing of the ball in the snap or the impact of foot to ball in the kick) happens precisely when the ball comes alive. Play, then, brings the ball to life, but the ball brings play to life, too. The ball can also die in numerous ways, some brought about by players and others by the ball itself. If, for example, a living ball touches the boundaries of the field, it immediately dies. The ball is the author of the play's conclusion. Importantly, for reasons considered in detail below, the ball needs to be *declared* dead, to be seen to be dead by an observer, for it to die. ("A Down is a period of action that starts when the ball is put in play [3-2-3] and ends when the ball is declared dead [7-2-1]" [Rule III, § 9, p. 5].) At other times, the ball dies when a player is handling the ball. If a player is carrying the ball, the player's contact with the boundary travels through their body like an electrical shock, killing the ball as well.

The fact that the ball not only lives but can actually dictate the terms of play as it lives and dies should alert us to the possibility that the entities privileged by the rules may not be the entities we expect. We might assume, from experiences we have of observing the live play of football and from our familiarity with its many popular discourses, that players control the game, but the ontology of the rulebook represents the situation differently. Players throw and kick the ball, but their actions are not awarded special importance in the sanctioning of the reality of play. The ball sanctions that reality as well.

This sanctioning extends beyond players and ball to the space of the field and the temporality of play. In the case of the field, the definition of "Possession" explains that a player must have "control" over the ball with his "hands or arms" in order to possess it, but he must also have his feet and/or other body parts on the ground as well (Rule III, § 2, Art. 7, p. 4). A body that simply holds the ball, then, cannot claim to possess it (never mind control it). The body must collaborate with its setting in order for those actions to count as valid. The temporality of play extends from this. While one might expect that time would serve as the backdrop against which football happens, the rulebook is clear that game-time stops and starts with football too. The relationship is reciprocal, as is demonstrated in the case of the forward pass. If the ball goes forward, from a passer to a receiver, and the pass is not completed (or successfully possessed by the receiver, we could say) the 60-minute game clock stops (Rule IV, § 4, p. 13). As this implied connection with possession and movement directionally across space suggests, game time reacts to its environment. If plays are "in time," then time is "in plays" too.[6]

Because space and time are not the backdrop against which play happens (as is often understood to be the case) but are in fact active participants in the world posited by the rulebook, everything about that world is necessarily contextual. This contextuality manifests in two ways. The first manifestation emerges in the connections drawn between physical locations in space, across time. This sort of contextuality is most apparent in "penalties," when actions in one space or time reverberate to other "enforcement spots," elsewhere on the field (Rule 8, § 6, Art. 1, p. 34). (Some penalties can even result in a 10-second loss of time.) Second is a thoroughgoing commitment to the live present of play. In the case of the field, this present appears as a focus on spaces and the points of material contact between those spaces and the bodies (human and non-human) that touch it. To the NFL rulebook, spaces and actions only register as mattering to the extent that they happen together. Time, for its part, matters in relation to the occurrence of a play—when it comes alive and when it dies. It would not be inappropriate, in this sense, to imagine that the snap of the ball to begin a play marks the definitive creation of a new temporal-spatial moment, the simultaneous eruption of time, space, and action.

As these two forms of contextuality demonstrate, little is inevitable or stable in football's world; everything appears to sanction everything else. The "Pocket Area" and the "Tackle Box," for example, are delineated spaces on the field. Even though they are not demarcated on the field in paint, they are not fictions. They are rule-bound creations (they are even visible to the naked eye) and are therefore no more and no less real than any other rulebook-bound creation in football's ontology. In both cases, these spaces lose their reality the instant play leaves them. "After the ball leaves the pocket area," the rulebook states, "this area no longer exists" (Rule III, § 26, p. 9). "After the ball leaves the tackle box, this area no longer exists" (Rule III, § 26, p. 10). Rules like these suggest a fundamental *flatness* of being in the rulebook, which privileges neither player agency nor the agency of the object nor even the spatio-temporal environment in which player and object interact but which rather requires the interconnection and co-dependence of space, time, object, and player in the play of the game.

THE FLATNESS OF THE RULEBOOK'S ONTOLOGY

Flatness is perhaps the central orienting principle of the NFL rulebook's ontology. Levi Bryant (2011) has characterized the project of thinking onto-logical flatness as one of refusing "correlationism"—the notion that reality can only be theorized by humans through human experience. Quentin Meil-lassoux, for his part, has elegantly summarized "correlationism" as "there can be no X without a givenness of X, and no theory about X without a positing of X. If you speak about something, the correlationist will say, you speak about something that is given to you, and posited by you" (2014, p. 10). In response to this position, Bryant, Meillassoux, Harman, and other speculative realists (Gratton, 2014, p. 52) hold that non-human entities are not "screens upon which humans project their intentions, meanings, signs, and discourses," they are "genuine actors in their own right" (Bryant, 2011, p. 247; cf. De Landa, 2002, p. 47). The resulting perspective, writes Bryant, "diminish[es] the obsessive focus on the human, subjective and the cultural within social, political, cultural theory and philosophy" (2011, pp. 246–247). This diminishing does not "exclude" human actors (p. 247), but rather places interactions between objects "on the same footing" as interactions between humans and objects (Harman, 2011, p. 6).

The NFL rulebook models this perspective precisely. The subjectivities of football's players are not simply reduced in the flat ontology of the rulebook. They are, instead, constituted differently around things in the game in con-textually specific ways. If the ball moves back and forth between alive and dead, player identities shift around the ball with great frequency and those identities are accompanied by special qualities. Passers, Runners, Blockers, Kickers, and more have unique limitations, rights, and responsibilities and no person permanently occupies one of these positions. Passers become Runners and Runners Passers, Passers become Blockers, Kickers become Passers, and more. Consistent with a theory that locates human actors within broader networks of influential non-human ones, these shifting roles show that players on the field are identified not on the basis of what they *are*, which would presume some absolute knowledge about them as beings, but on the basis of what they *do* and what they do things *with*.

While this might seem to be an unnecessarily literal interpretation of the language of the rulebook, the consequences for human agency are apparent in any actually occurring game. All displays of human athletic prowess must emerge from this framework, with its shifting roles, established boundaries, active situation, and living ball. All other actions register as peripheral, forbidden, or unrecognizable. If there is an ideological commitment at the heart of this formulation, then, it emerges not in the commonsensical conception of the unfettered player pursuing their autonomous aspirations on the field, but rather in that position's almost exact opposite; in the rulebook's rigorous dedication to a *fettered* player, whose identity is fundamentally shaped by the processes in which they find themselves. Pass Plays demonstrate the phenomenon of the fettered player with special clarity. The rulebook defines a Pass Play as a play that "begins with the snap and ends when a forward pass is thrown from behind the line of scrimmage is caught by a player of either team or is incomplete. After the pass is caught, a Running Play begins" (Rule 3, § 22, Art. 3, p. 8). On the surface, this might seem to follow the standard human actor-driven narrative of sporting performance. A player receives the ball from a snap and throws it to another player. A closer reading, though, shows a more complicated set of relationships and actions. The ball comes to life in the snap. At that moment, any number of actions are possible. The play proclaims itself to be a "Pass Play" when the ball is set in forward motion in the air.[7] This Pass Play transforms the player holding the ball into an entirely different being (a "Passer" [Rule 3, § 22, Art. 2, p. 8]) and, when the live ball is caught, when the ball comes to be held by another player after traveling through the air, the situation changes again—into a Running Play. As this brief example demonstrates, the rules give ball, situation, and player(s) equal determining weight. Ball and player dictate the start of play, thrower initiates the passing situation, player and ball create a Passer, the ball initiates running situation, and the ball finally dies (sometimes with the player and sometimes without) to end the sequence of action.[8]

This complex relationship is worked out most explicitly in instances when the stakes are highest—when the ball is close to the goal line. In such instances, the rulebook introduces a special term—"impetus" (Rule 3, § 14,

p. 7)—to characterize the relationship between things in the game. Though impetus is ultimately used by the rulebook to tease out player intention through a network of relationships, that intention cannot be decoupled from context.[9] In this sense, "impetus" is an extremely appropriate term. Impetus may describe the force of a thing, but it also carries the connotation of that thing moving not by its own continuous volition but instead by a process of propulsion. When "impetus" is applied to, for example, "the initial velocity of a projectile" in combat (OED, March 2021), the shell's trajectory is attributed not to its own actions but to the thing that sets it into motion. This definition matches perfectly how the rulebook understands player momentum—as components of a flat ontology, players can never set themselves fully into motion or dictate entirely their own trajectory. Rather, they initiate motions in concert with the environment that surrounds them, get carried into motion by other players and things, and sustain their motion by means of their surrounding environment.

It is this flat ontology, too, that helps explain the rulebook's commitment to taking its readers through, in intimate and loving detail, the sensuous qualities of the other objects that inhabit the player's world. If those objects are going to be recognized as truly capable of acting together with the players in the game, then the qualities of those objects must receive their due attention. A player does not transition from a Receiver to a Runner by touching any old thing. They do so by touching the grass of the field, within its designated boundaries, at a point somewhere near yard markers measuring four inches wide by two feet high (p. iv), while grasping "an inflated (12½ to 13½ pounds) urethane bladder enclosed in a pebble grained, leather case (natural tan color) without corrugations of any kind" (Rule 2, § 1, p. 3). What is more commonly read as a set of exclusive practices (since you can't play true National Football League football if you do things wrong) or petty officiousness can be understood instead as an attempt on the part of the rulebook to reckon with the sheer potency of non-human agents. The shape of the football, the length of the game, and the size of the field impact the play of the game significantly, and the special qualities of each of these agents must be acknowledged.

TOUCH, ONTOGRAPHY, AND DISINTERESTED
DISCERNMENT IN FLAT ONTOLOGIES

As words like "grasping" and "touching" are meant to suggest, the interconnection and co-dependence that define football's flat ontology happen through literal contact. Player identities shift on the basis of what they do, the ball moves from alive to dead, pockets of space come into being and disappear, because of touch. This conception is consistent with an ontological approach that is sensitive to the autonomy of objects because, as Graham Harman notes, anything with its own autonomous reality can qualify as an "object" (2011, p. 116) whether it is material or not. The "Pocket Area" is an object, even though it vanishes as soon as it is no longer touched, because when it exists and when it is touched, it changes the behavior of things around and inside of it.

For Harman, objects enter into "genuine" relations with each other when they "give rise to a thing that exceeds them" rather than "merely stroking one another's sensual facades" (2011, p. 117).[10] In the NFL rulebook's ontology, this excess emerges through contact. Rule 7, Section 2, Article 1 captures this understanding well: "An official shall declare the ball dead and the down ended," it reads, "when a runner declares himself down" by touching the ground and "making no immediate effort to advance" (p. 26). The official's declaration, and its significance, will be addressed below. Right now, it suffices to point out that the player's declaration is clearly a physical one, which emerges from the unity of player, ball, moment of action, and ground. While these elements might simply scrape against each other in passing, and the field is indeed full of similar elements scraping together, the unity of *these* elements creates a contextually meaningful novelty: a declaration, which generates a new location of the ball and a new situation.

From what perspective, though, can this distinction between "stroke" and "thing" be drawn? In practice, the rulebook equivocates on this point—it occasionally frames declared actions in terms of player intention (Rule 3, § 3, p. 5) and, at other times, in terms of *demonstrated* (Rule 8, § 4, Art. 7, p. 33) or *signaled* (Rule 3, § 10, p. 6) intention. The explicit mention of signals and demonstrations, though, reveals ultimately the importance of a discerning arbiter—any of the seven officials, but particularly the Referee, who has "general oversight and control of the game" (Rule 15, § 1, Art. 3, p. 62)—who receives these messages and recognizes them as declarations. The players, ball, field, and time are in their arbitrary and shifting relations, and the officials are charged with tracking their mattering. In the case of work in speculative realism, though, the source of the mattering is less clear. In *The Quadruple Object*, Harman introduces the field of "ontography," which "maps the basic landmarks and fault lines in the universe of objects" (Harman, 2011, p. 125). While the ontographer might therefore be tasked with marking the distinction between "stroking sensual facades" and "giving rise to a thing," it is not evident what can and cannot be an ontographer. Can things, in relations, be ontographers? If so, how and for whom are they marking distinctions? While Gratton has posed similar questions of speculative realism (2014, p. 106), Peterson (2018, p. 73) and Pasek (2015) consider more explicitly the possibility that the *theorist* might in practice be the ontographer who assumes responsibility for adjudicating a superficial touch from a deep one. If this is the case, speculative realists would seem to be smuggling in—much more subtly than the NFL rulebook—a discerning, apparently disinterested, arbiter. Pasek writes that, for theorists like Ian Bogost, who adopts a similar approach in his *Alien Phenomenologies* (2012),

> all objects and experiences may be said to exist equally in so far as they enjoy material grounding, though human access to them is not equally secured (nor secured equally to all humans) and at the end of the day it is humans who write philosophy.

In the particular case of Bogost, she adds, his "own situated epistemology as a human becomes occluded" (Pasek, 2015).

In Pasek's view, what matters is not just the flatness of things in their relations but *also* the angle from which that flatness comes into view and what can be seen, or not, from the angle in question. This approach is consistent with that of Karen Barad, who draws from Niels Bohr's work on quantum mechanics, and the theory of the "intra-action" of scientist, equipment, and world-under-observation she finds there, to argue that the scientist is no detached reader of an objective world. Neither is the scientist simply positioned by, and participating in the production of, a broader regime of truth. In Barad's view, the scientist affects an "agential cut" into reality, which draws a boundary between the world-under-observation and the scientist themselves. As she writes, "Only part of the world can be made intelligible to itself at a time, because the other part of the world has to be the part that it makes a difference to" (2007, p. 351). Though this agential cut severs the scientist from the world, constituting them as a subject to the world's object, the cut means also that the scientist is constructing reality as they observe it. In this formulation, ontology may be manufactured but it is no less real for its manufacture.

Because the nature of reality is manufactured, and because it is manufactured specifically through the scientist and their apparatuses (which they use, ostensibly, to "detect" the preexisting nature of reality), reality itself is explicitly and unavoidably political. Put simply, the reality that scientists manufacture—the reality that they purport to find—is marked by identity because scientists and their tools are gendered (and raced and classed too). Barad therefore describes the result of scientific research into quantum mechanics as "gender-and-science-in-the-making" (Barad, 2007, p. 167) to indicate both the gendering of the research and, as noted above, the processual dimension of the "agential cut" that parts the scientist/subject from the world.

Reading the rulebook through Barad and Pasek, then, places the official-and-ontographer at the boundary of the reality they chart. Seen from this vantage point, it would make sense that the official is exempt from football's relations. If Barad is correct that "only part of the world can be made intelligible to itself at a time, because the other part of the world has to be the part that it makes a difference to" (2007, p. 351), then the official cannot both adjudicate the arbitrary intra-actions of things discussed in the rulebook and also be a component of those intra-actions. The official's identity cannot shift, based on the position of the field or whether they are holding the ball, because the rulebook would have to register those shifts as mattering to someone or something *else*, and the official would cease to be an official. This position also explains Pasek's concerns about Bogost's un-interrogated epistemology, which, like other object-oriented ontological work in her estimation, "evinces politically suspect motivations" (Pasek, 2015). The philosophical distinction between "things giving rise to a thing that exceeds them" and "merely stroking one another's sensual facades" is adjudicated not from within those relations, as a component of them, but from a detached position—that of the philosopher of objects. There is nothing to suppose that this philosopher of objects could not be attached to, and constituted with, other things at other times, but their philosophical standpoint is dependent on that detachment. It too, is "correlationist," but the theorist, like the footballing official, cannot be touched.[11]

Since objects have the capacity to act only to the extent that the theorist recognizes them as doing so, they are not permitted to adjudicate their own relations and, thereby, to speak back to how they are framed. Consequently, the position of the philosopher—or the position of the official—becomes the only recognizable vantage point. In the case of the NFL rulebook, the official is quite clearly the rulebook embodied in the game. In the case of object-centered work in speculative realism, this outcome manifests in the fact that such work issues from the theorist's own cultivated position of detachment. Without a philosophical vocabulary to document the emergent points of contact between things from the perspective of those things themselves, this work is blocked from taking seriously things in their objecthood. The "democracy of objects" (Bryant, 2011) offered by both the rulebook and object-centered work in speculative realism is a democracy so dependent upon the parameters of recognition imposed from without that it is effectively a structured system of interactions that allows little room for objects—including persons—to define themselves (cf. Peterson, 2018, p. 74).[12]

Though this consequence might seem utterly paradoxical in the case of football, it can be traced to the explicit arbitrariness of the rulebook and, indeed, of work in speculative realism. For Quentin Meillassoux, for example, non-correlationist thinking requires a refusal on the philosopher's part to take anything that is derived from human experience as an absolute. The human experience of time cannot be absolute, for example, because the universe existed prior to human experience. Similarly, objects extend beyond our knowledge of them, so neither can our experience of objects be taken as absolute. Without time and objects, there can be no universal causality. The result, writes Gratton, is "hyper-chaos," in which all relations are arbitrary and absolutely everything must be posited (2014, p. 61). Unmoored from contexts beyond the rulebook, footballing objects work similarly. Players are players not because they are intrinsically or objectively players in any respect. They have to be posited as players, and they are posited as such because they are on the field. The field, in turn, must be posited too. It is not objectively a field, it is a field because of the play that occurs on it. The ball is the ball because it is used in football, and so on. Given that everything in the rulebook must be posited, everything in the rulebook is arbitrary and could always be otherwise. As such, all the different ways that things can and should interact during play are necessarily shadowed by infinitely more possible interactions (and non-interactions) that are expressly forbidden or that occur but are not sanctioned as legitimate by the rulebook.

THE TERMS AND CONDITIONS OF OBJECT AGENCY, IN THE RULEBOOK AND BEYOND

As Fred Moten has argued, however, "the history of blackness is a testament to the fact that objects can and do resist" (2003, p. 1). While speculative realists would undoubtedly agree with this statement on its face, given their avowed interest in detaching objects from worlds of human significance, Moten is also reminding us to be suspicious of theories that pursue the elevation of the agency of things, and the reduction of the agency of the human, without thinking that project in conjunction with broader histories of objectification and alterity. Without, that is to say, recognizing that the current valuation of things is *not* arbitrary and carries real determining weight. This is true not only in the world of human relations but also in the realm of theory. It has been observed, for example, that theories that celebrate the objecthood of all things—whether human or non-human—often fail to remark upon the fact that humans *have* been perceived as objects, in colonialism and in slavery, and that this kind of ontological flatness has always been a monstrous and unforgivable crime (cf. Chen, 2012, p. 33; Chen, 2018, p. 442; Fanon, 1967; Mbembe, 2003, pp. 20–21). Elaborating on this point, Schuller argues that theorists in the nineteenth century were more than willing to think ontologically and to mobilize conceptions of agentive matter to justify their racism (2018, p. 26). A related critique has been raised by Ruha Benjamin, who argues that moves toward post-humanism are often premised on the notion that thinking about humanity has been exhausted. This is a view she contests. *"Post humanist visions assume that we have all had a chance to be human,"* she writes (2019, p. 32, emphasis in original), sounding the alarm that moves to post-humanism could close off, rather than open up, politics at the level of human experience.

This exhaustion, and the complicated politics of non-human and post-human orientations toward persons and objects that can accompany exhaustion, is perhaps depicted nowhere with more clarity than in Nick Srnicek's comments in an interview with Paul Ennis. "Do we really need," Srnicek wonders,

> another analysis of how a cultural representation does symbolic violence to a marginal group? This is not to say that this work has been useless, *just that it's become repetitive*. In light of all that, speculative realism provides the best means for creative work to be done, and it provides genuine excitement to think that there are new argumentative realms to explore. (Ennis, 2009, as cited in Bogost, 2012, p. 132, emphasis added)

Rather than considering the value of an analysis of symbolic violence to a member of that marginal group, or theorizing the political and cultural context that demands repeated analyses of symbolic violence against marginal groups, or even plotting political courses of action that could correct and redress such symbolic harms, Srnicek prefers instead to shift the theoretical conversation elsewhere, to a new and (in his view) more fertile argumentative terrain. In their unwillingness to reckon with these symbolic harms, Srnicek's remarks would appear to realize Benjamin's worst fears—The flatness of speculative realist thought comes explicitly at the expense of marginalized groups, whose experiences of harm cease to matter before they are adequately addressed. Worse still, the conversion of members of those groups into objects among objects—whose communication is audible only to the object theorist—affords them little space to speak back in their own voices.

The NFL rulebook is so dedicated to its flat ontology that it attends even to this silencing. The distinction between the verbal declarations of the official and the embodied declarations of the player is again relevant. While the rulebook devotes pages and pages to the ways that players' bodies are permitted to communicate in accordance with the rules, player verbal communication receives only cursory attention. For the most part, players are communicated *to*, in a manner consistent with flatness—via mediating objects, spaces, and times. "The Coach-to-Player system," the rulebook states,

> allows a member of the coaching staff in the bench area or the coaches' booth to communicate to a designated offensive or defensive player with a speaker in his helmet. The communication begins once a game official has signaled a down to be over, and is cut off when the play clock reaches 15 seconds or the ball is snapped, whichever occurs first. (Rule V, § 3, Art. 3, p. 19)

When players do get positive instructions about their own verbal communication, those instructions are also limited to particular spaces and moments. "If [a player] approaches the huddle and communicates with a teammate, he is required to participate in at least one play before being withdrawn," the rulebook says (Rule V, § 2, Art. 5, p. 17). Additionally, players may speak back to their coach "provided the coach is in his prescribed area during dead-ball periods" (Rule XIII, § 1, Art. 1, p. 54) and make "the call of 'heads' or 'tails'" at the coin toss (Rule IV, § 2, Art. 2, p. 12).

Put into the context of Ruha Benjamin's concerns about post-human theorizing, the political implications of these regulations become clear. Player speech is only recognized when it manifests in the appropriate relationships. Should the player speak out of turn and out of context, that speech is almost entirely illegible to the rulebook. When it *is* legible, notably, it reads as a transgression—as "unsportsmanlike conduct." Logically, this reading makes sense. Permissible and recognized speech must be consistent with the game's flat ontology. Unrecognized speech, by definition, does not appear in the rulebook at all. It escapes the gaze of the rulebook entirely. All that remains to be addressed, then, are recognized but impermissible forms of speech—statements that emerge from within the context of the game but ignore the rules of the game's theory of being—particularly expressions of outrage, described as abusive, threatening, or insulting language or gestures that are directed at opponents, teammates, officials, or representatives of the league (Rule XII, § 3, Art. 1, p. 52). Given that these uses of language and gesture break from the permissible flat associations between things, they are attributed solely to the player performing them. Any player can, in the right circumstances, become a Kicker or a Passer. Only "personal" fouls belong to the player. The player's speech becomes correlationist and inadmissible, and the sanctity of the referee is preserved. Just as there is no space in the rulebook for players to speak for themselves, so too is there no place for them to "come to voice" on the field.

In 2005, the Fox television network introduced a new mascot for its NFL programming—a CGI-rendered, football-playing android, later named "Cleatus." This chapter suggests that Fox could hardly have chosen a more appropriate mascot. Though Cleatus seems to be alive and certainly plays football, he occupies no position in particular. Sometimes he is a Kicker and sometimes a Passer. His identity would therefore seem to be consistent with that of the amorphous "player" whose role can shift based on his position on the field and his relationship with the ball. And though Cleatus can move and act, he cannot speak (so far as I have been able to determine). Everything he communicates he does by means of the impetus of his body. Cleatus, in short, is an object, comprised of objects but not reducible to them, and he interacts with other objects in ways that create new objects. If we consider the NFL rulebook as a theoretical document that posits a flat ontology, the football playing "person" that emerges from that project would seem to look, act, and interact almost exactly like Cleatus.

CONCLUSION: POLITICAL DECLARATIONS IN FOOTBALL'S FLAT ONTOLOGY

While Meillassoux understands "correlationism" as "there can be no theory of x without a positing of x" (2014, p. 10) and therefore that escaping correlationism means thinking speculatively about the pockets of the universe where humanity cannot reach, the work of Moten and Benjamin seems to suggest an alternative conception. For the latter theorists, there can be no theory of objects that is not already located in a prior landscape of objectification. This conception decenters the work of the theorist and places them into a broader moral and political context. Even if the theorist manages to avoid positing x, their avoidance is always already political because they are not reckoning adequately with what x has meant, still does mean, and will mean in the human contexts that surround their theorizing. Because marginalized persons have already been, and continue to be, thought of as objects, object-oriented speculative realism does not manifest socially as a "promising new argumentative realm to explore" (Ennis, 2009). It manifests instead as a recapitulation of prior processes of objectification, rendered in a new philosophical vocabulary. What is more, because object-oriented speculative realism explicitly rejects correlationism, the theorist becomes justified in detaching their work from those prior objectifications (which others nevertheless find meaningful), thereby representing themselves, and their work, disinterested.

I have argued above that the NFL rulebook enacts a similar procedure and encounters similar political consequences. It defines the human (arbitrarily) as a "person" who is also a "player," and it envelops that player in a network of relationships with things, spaces, and times. Those relationships constitute a flat ontology that decenters the agency of the player and calls up the unique qualities of the things with which they interact. In order to keep these arbitrary relations meaningfully organized, though, the rulebook must also posit an official who is detached from those relations—one who, in the language of Barad, implements the "agential cut" between the arbitrary world of the game and the already meaningful—but correlationist—world of everyday life. The result is a world that is political in its arbitrariness not because of its positing, but because of the political context from which that positing emerges. The referee, like the speculative realist, is detached, capable of adjudicating relations, and able to speak. The player is embedded, interested, and capable of communicating almost exclusively with their body alone—a thing among things. Cleatus.

How, then, can a player—occupying the position of Cleatus—speak back to the rulebook and to the referee? How do they make themselves legible in politically meaningful ways? Breaking into speech would appear to be one option, but because the rulebook represents players as objects among objects, they come to voice through predetermined relationships. There is little opportunity for emergent and unstructured speech, and the unstructured speech that does emerge is either illegible to the rulebook or a read as a failure of comportment on the part of the individual player. Because this emergent language is attributable only to the player, as a solitary being, furthermore, the rulebook renders it impossible to think backward, from the profane talk to the relationships that exceed the predetermined limits of associations set by the rules—Things that occur off the field, for example, but that nevertheless inform what happens on it. These occurrences amount to the wider political landscape in which the rulebook theorizes its ontology, and they are written out of the rulebook as surely as they are written out of object-oriented speculative realist thought.

When NFL players like Colin Kaepernick knelt or linked arms in silent protest of police violence, their actions pointed us toward an alternative response. These protests were certainly meaningful for many reasons—they occurred on national television during the stillness and solemnity of the National Anthem, they were explained and justified off the field, and so on—but the present chapter suggests that the form of these protests is also notable because it is consistent with the footballing ontology posited by the NFL rulebook. The rulebook, in this sense, already allows players (as objects among objects) to "declare" positions with their bodies in ways that are not tolerated in speech. The rulebook may have considered them to be undifferentiated players, converting to Runners or Passers or Kickers in conjunction with the times, spaces, and objects of play, but these embodied protests allowed athletes to show that they were more than arbitrary and interchangeable objects.

Furthermore, the rulebook's language of "impetus" provides an avenue for athletes to set themselves into embodied motion in a way that is not permitted with speech. If "impetus" ordinarily places human actors within football's arbitrary causality, athletes can still use it to stake out positions on, and drag wider political concerns into, the space of the field. This being the case, these actions declare in body what Moten, Benjamin, and others declare in text—that attempts to imagine a "flat" ontology *without* situating that ontology within a wider historical and political landscape do not so much open up promising new realms of exploration as reproduce prior acts of silencing and alienation. By mobilizing their bodies, then, Kaepernick and others were able to show themselves to be black (footballing) objects that resist (Moten, 2003, p. 1), insofar as they insisted that spectators think together the objectification required by the ontology of football with other forms of legal and illegal, judicial and extrajudicial, objectification that black people have experienced since the earliest days of European colonialism.

Response

Football

Louis Jenkins

I take the snap from the center, fake to the right, fade back . . .
I've got protection. I've got a receiver open downfield . . .
What the hell is this? This isn't a football, it's a shoe, a man's
brown leather oxford. A cousin to a football maybe, the same
skin, but not the same, a thing made for the earth, not the air.
I realize that this is a world where anything is possible and I
understand, also, that one often has to make do with what one
has. I have eaten pancakes, for instance, with that clear corn
syrup on them because there was no maple syrup and they
weren't very good. Well, anyway, this is different. (My man
downfield is waving his arms.) One has certain responsibilities,
one has to make choices. This isn't right and I'm not going
to throw it.

NOTES

1. Every quotation in this chapter is sourced from the NFL rulebook unless otherwise indicated.

2. The NFL rulebook includes many distinct actors, both human and non-human, each with its own definitions and unique qualities. The rulebook is also extremely concerned with locating those actors in space and time and shifting their definitions accordingly. Because those definitions need to be marked as they shift if actors are going to be regulated, the rulebook tends to be extremely self-referential. It continually doubles back on, refines, and disambiguates itself from itself on the basis of minute differences in context. The rulebook, for example, cannot assert where on the field the play should resume after a penalty (Rule 9, § 5, Art. 1, pp. 38–9) without five exceptions that reference four rules located elsewhere in the rulebook. Given this complexity, I merely intend to trace here the outlines of the rulebook's underlying principles and to examine those principles alongside more explicitly theoretical texts in object-oriented speculative realism.

3. Though the NFL has produced policies and documents that explicitly stipulate how players can and should act, this chapter is premised on the notion that the NFL rulebook is more structurally fundamental to football than those policies, not just because of the centrality of footballing performance to football as a phenomenon, but

also because the rulebook is tasked with offering up a theory of football as a situated reality in a way that other policies are not. That having been said, a consideration of the relationship between NFL policies and the NFL rulebook would certainly be a fascinating and worthwhile analytical project.

4. So, for example, "A player is Offside when any part of his body or his person is in the Neutral Zone, or is beyond his free kick line, or fair catch kick line when the ball is put in play, unless he is a holder of a placekick for a free kick (6-1-3-b-1) or fair catch kick (11-4-3), or a kicker (6-1-3-b-2). The snapper is offside if any part of his body is beyond the neutral zone" (Rule III, § 20, p. 8).

5. This ontological approach can be read as taking Johan Huizinga's theory of "the magic circle" of play more seriously than Huizinga takes it himself. For Huizinga, play unfolds within a "consecrated spot," "within which special rules obtain." Whether the magic circle surrounds a card-table, a temple, a stage, or a tennis court, the results are similar—"*All are temporary worlds within the ordinary world*, dedicated to the performance of an act apart" (Huizinga, 1980, p. 10, emphasis added). If Huizinga has been critiqued for failing to reckon adequately with the ways that actions that occur within play's "magic circle" carry real significance for the worlds that surround that circle (cf. Consalvo, 2009; Vossen, 2018), this present chapter considers the extent to which the NFL rulebook might provide that "temporary world" with its own situated theory of being.

6. Interestingly, the rulebook is adamant that "during any timeout, including an intermission, all playing rules continue in effect" even if the game clock is stopped and the ball is dead (Rule 3, § 37, Art. 1, p. 10). Timeouts and other pauses in action, therefore, enforce specific transformations in the relationships between players, objects, space, and time, but they absolutely do not nullify those relationships.

7. Fumbles on passes show how complicated, and counterintuitive, this conception can be. When a player begins a forward movement of their hand, holding the ball, it is a forward pass and a Pass Play begins. It continues to be a pass play even if "contact by an opponent materially affects the passer, causing the ball to go backward" (Rule 8, § 1, Article 1, p. 30). Even though the ball ultimately goes backward, the rulebook still deems the thrower to be a "Passer" and the movement of the ball to be "forward."

8. Rule 12, Section 2, Article 7 "Players in a Defenseless Posture" lends credence to this interpretation. Among the categories of being that are situationally unavailable for contact is a "receiver attempting to catch a pass who has not had time to *clearly become* a runner" (p. 49). In this formulation, the player is evidently transformed into a runner by the catch. If that transformation isn't complete, the player cannot be recognized according to their new identity.

9. Nor does the rulebook presume that *all* players are necessarily agents in such interactions. Note 1 of Rule 3, Section 14 addresses exactly this: "*If a passive player is pushed or blocked into any kicked or fumbled ball or into a backward pass after it has struck the ground, causing the Loose Ball to touch a goal line or anything on or behind a goal line, the impetus is attributed to the pusher or blocker, provided that the pushed (blocked) player was not making an attempt to block an opponent*" (p. 7, emphasis in original). In such instances, impetus is tracked backward from the goal line through the ball and the "passive player" to the player who pushed him.

10. Importantly, for Harman, neither genuine relations nor sensuous touching amount to a full erasure of an object's autonomy. Some "real" part of the object must always recede from any contact lest the object collapse entirely into that which it touches (Gratton, 2014, p. 91; Harman, 2011, p. 98). The NFL rulebook shows this ongoing autonomy clearly—Even as a player, a ball, and a field might enter into a genuine relation with each other, creating a new object with its own internal integrity, they are nevertheless considered by the rulebook to retain something of what they previously were.

11. This is not to suggest that critiques of "correlationism" are invalid. As Cramer (2019, p. 42) shows, accusations of "correlationism" can be useful in challenging the objectivity of artificial intelligence and other allegedly disinterested domains of research and theory. Rather, a close reading of the NFL rulebook as a work of object-oriented theory does open the possibility that speculative realism succumbs to "correlationism" as well.

12. Harry Walker (2013) has come to a similar conclusion, albeit from a different direction. In his ethnographic study of soccer in Amazonian Peru, Walker suggests soccer is a "political ontology" insofar as it demands that the players abstract themselves from their context and place themselves into a new collectivity, constituted of contextually specific roles. Drawing on George Herbert Mead (1934), Walker argues that, "underneath their roles, [players] are essentially 'the same'" (Walker, 2013, p. 388). If Walker is correct about the "political ontology" of soccer, and if that ontology is traceable to the formulation of the sport in its rulebook, then his work serves as an important reminder that the "flat ontology" posited by the NFL rulebook (and, perhaps, by sporting rulebooks in general) is less a speculative, and potentially universal, theory of being than a cultural and political project derived from a Western ontology. As such, it would appear to silence not just those who carry the burden of past objectifications but also those indigenous persons who inhabit other ontologies and may already, in their own ways, decenter the human (de la Cadena, 2010; Viveiros de Castro, 2015).

REFERENCES

Ahmed, S. (2006). *Queer phenomenology: Orientations, objects, others*. Durham: Duke University Press.

Ahmed, S. (2007). A phenomenology of whiteness. *Feminist Theory, 8*(2), 149–168.

Barad, K. (2007). *Meeting the universe halfway: Quantum physics and the entanglement of matter and meaning*. Durham: Duke University Press.

Benjamin, R. (Ed.). (2019). *Captivating technology: Race, carceral technoscience, and liberatory imagination in everyday life*. Durham: Duke University Press.

Bogost, I. (2012). *Alien phenomenology, or what it's like to be a thing*. Minneapolis: University of Minnesota Press.

Bryant, L. R. (2011). *The democracy of objects*. Ann Arbor: Open Humanities Press.

Chen, M. Y. (2012). *Animacies: Biopolitics, racial mattering, and queer affect*. Durham: Duke University Press.

Cheng, A. A. (2018). Ornamentalism: A feminist theory for the yellow woman. *Critical Inquiry, 44*(3), 415–446.

Consalvo, M. (2009). There is no magic circle. *Games and Culture, 4*(4), 408–417.

Cramer, F. (2019). Crapularity hermeneutics: Interpretation as the blind spot of analytics, artificial intelligence, and other algorithmic producers of the postapocalyptic present. In C. Apprich, W. H. K. Chun, F. Cramer, & H. Steyerl (Eds.), *Pattern discrimination* (pp. 23–58). Minneapolis: University of Minnesota Press.

de la Cadena, M. (2010). Indigenous cosmopolitics in the Andes: Conceptual reflections beyond "politics". *Cultural Anthropology, 25*(2), 334–370.

De Landa, M. (2002). *Intensive science and virtual philosophy*. London: Continuum.

Ennis, P. (2009). Interview with Nick Srnicek. Retrieved from http://anotherheid eggerblog.blogspot.com/2009/08/interview-with-nick-srnicek.html

Fanon, F. (1967). *Black skin, White masks* (C. L. Markmann, Trans.). New York: Grove Press.

Gelberg, J. N. (1995). The Lethal weapon: How the plastic football helmet transformed the game of football, 1939–1994. *Bulletin of Science, Technology, and Society, 15*(5–6), 302–309.

Gratton, P. (2014). *Speculative realism: Problems and prospects*. New York: Bloomsbury Publishing Plc.

Harman, G. (2011). *The quadruple object*. Washington: Zero Books.

Harman, G. (2018). *Object-oriented ontology: A new theory of everything*. London: Penguin.

Huizinga, J. (1980). *Homo Ludens*. New York: Routledge.

Mbembe, A. (2003). Necropolitics. *Public Culture, 15*(1), 11–40.

Mead, G. H. (1934). *Mind, self, and society from the standpoint of a social behaviorist*. Chicago: University of Chicago Press.

Meillassoux, Q. (2014). *Time without becoming*. Sesto San Giovanni: Mimesis International.

Moten, F. (2003). *In the break: The aesthetics of the black radical tradition*. Minneapolis: University of Minnesota Press.

Nguyen, M. T. (2015). The Hoodie as sign, screen, expectation, and force. *Signs: Journal of Women in Culture and Society, 40*(4), 791–816.

OED, O. (2021, March). impetus, n. Retrieved from https://www.oed.com/view/Entry /92389?redirectedFrom=impetus

Official Playing Rules of the National Football League. (2018). National Football League. Accessed June 30, 2022. https://operations.nfl.com/media/3277/2018-nfl-rulebook_final-version.pdf.

Pasek, Anne. 2015. "The Problem of Nonhuman Phenomenology: or, What is it Like to Be a Kinect?" *InVisible Culture* (22: Opacity). http://ivc.lib.rochester.edu/ the-problem-of-nonhuman-phenomenology-or-what-is-it-like-to-be-a-kinect/.

Peterson, C. (2018). *Monkey trouble: The scandal of posthumanism*. New York: Fordham University Press.

Schuller, K. (2018). *The biopolitics of feeling: Race, sex, and science in the nineteenth century*. Durham: Duke University Press.

Viveiros de Castro, E. (2015). Who is afraid of the ontological wolf: Some comments on an ongoing anthropological debate. *The Cambridge Journal of Anthropology, 33*(1), 2–17.

Vossen, E. (2018). The magic circle and consent in gaming practices. In K. L. Gray, G. Voorhees, & E. Vossen (Eds.), *Feminism in play* (pp. 205–220). Cham, Switzerland: Palgrave Macmillan.

Walker, H. (2013). State of play: The political ontology of sport in Amazonian Peru. *American Ethnologist, 40*(2), 382–398.

Chapter 3

Shattering the Glass Ceiling Twice

Sports Journalism Framing of Katie Sowers

William P. Cassidy

Katie Sowers, an assistant coach for the San Francisco 49ers of the National Football League (NFL), burst onto the national scene in 2020 when she became the first woman and openly LGBTQ+ person to coach in the Super Bowl, the NFL's marquee event. Her inspiring story was featured in a Microsoft commercial broadcast during the game. She called the experience "surreal," but Sowers seemed to realize the significance of her status as someone who had shattered the proverbial glass ceiling—twice. Speaking directly to the camera in the Microsoft ad, she stated, "All it takes is one, and then it opens the door for so many" (Graham, 2020, para. 2). In addition, she told reporters, "I am willing and happy to be a trailblazer because I know that other women, other young girls are watching this and maybe their path seems a little clearer now" (Wagoner, 2020, para. 24).

This chapter examines how sports journalists in the United States framed Katie Sowers in the weeks leading up to and immediately after the 2020 Super Bowl. Her history-making accomplishments are analyzed via the theoretical framework of media sociology, which examines the "creation of news content . . . within a larger institutional and ideological context" (Reese, 2019, p. 1). Many media sociology studies look at journalism as a social practice, created in part by the routines of the profession because journalists "mediate reality through the mere process of doing their work" (Shoemaker & Reese, 2014, p. 29). Such an analysis is especially appropriate considering that historically sports journalism has been labeled "the toy department" by critics who contend it often lacks a critical perspective and fails to reflect the connection between sport and cultural/societal issues (Boyle, 2013; Rowe, 2007).

Examining sports reporting about Sowers is a worthy subject of study given that she represents two historic firsts in a male-dominated sport. An extensive stream of literature documents the miniscule amount of media coverage women athletes receive compared to men (e.g. Adams & Tuggle, 2004; Billings & Young, 2015; Bruce, 2013). Furthermore, media response to the presence of lesbians in sport has largely been one of silence or at best an occasional mention of lesbianism as an obstacle for women athletes in their quest to be relevant (Hardin & Whiteside, 2010; Kane & Lenskyj, 1998). With that in mind, a central question of this chapter is which of those "firsts"—Sowers's gender or sexuality—received greater emphasis in coverage?

KATIE SOWERS'S STORY

When Sowers was a little girl living in the small town of Hesston, Kansas, all she wanted to do was play football, writing in her diary, "When I grow up, I want to be on a real football team" (Walsh, 2020, para. 3). However, as she got a bit older she noticed there didn't seem to be a place for her in the sport. "I started to realize how much bigger the boys I grew up playing football with in the backyard became compared to me," she said. "I was forced into the societal norms that told me girls don't play football" (Buzinski, 2017, para. 21). From there Sowers set her sights on coaching, even though along the way she played pro football in the Women's Football Alliance and helped guide the US team to a world title and gold medal in 2013 (Buzinski, 2017). The total lack of female representation in the NFL had her thinking she might end up coaching basketball. After all, she was a scholarship player and a team captain for Goshen College in Indiana (Benbow, 2020). But football remained her first love and Sowers began to believe there might be a place for her in the NFL when former women's basketball star Becky Hammon in 2014 became an assistant coach with the NBA's San Antonio Spurs. "That was when it really clicked that 'Oh my God, I could coach football,'" Sowers said. She revealed her intentions by posting "NFL, I'm coming for you" on her Instagram account (MacKenzie, 2019, para. 4).

Three years later, in 2017, Sowers became the NFL's second full-time female assistant coach, securing a position with the San Francisco 49ers, working primarily with the team's wide receivers. Her appointment was also noteworthy because of her status as the league's first openly LGBTQ+ coach (Buzinski, 2017). Sowers publicly disclosed her sexual orientation because

> there are many people who identify as LGBT in the NFL. . . . The more we can create an environment that welcomes all types of people, no matter their race, gender, sexual orientation, religion, the more we can help ease the pain and burden that many carry every day. (Buzinski, 2017, paras. 2 & 3)

COVERAGE OF WOMEN'S SPORTS
AND OF LESBIAN ATHLETES

The numerous studies devoted to examining the vast disparities in media attention given to women athletes in comparison to men are important because their results identify "ideologies and practices that . . . point to a critical marking of sport as male territory" (Bruce, 2013, p. 128). A recent study found that only 5.1% of stories on local TV network affiliate sports-casts and 5.7% on ESPN's *Sportscenter* were devoted to women (Cooky et al., 2021). Incredibly, those results were an improvement over a similar study conducted several years earlier which reported that 3.2% of stories on local TV network affiliates and 2% on *Sportscenter* were about women (Cooky et al., 2015).

Much of the research on media coverage of women athletes examines the issue through the lens of hegemonic masculinity (Cassidy, 2019), which is seen as "the culturally idealized form of masculine character" (Connell, 1990, p. 83). Hegemonic masculinity defines sports as a masculine pursuit and male athletes symbolize "what it means to be a man" (Anderson, 2002, p. 860). Women athletes are often viewed as deviant and/or lesbian, especially those who are strong and powerful and participate in sports are perceived to be more masculine in nature (Dann & Everbach, 2016; Duncan, 1990; Kane & Lenskyj, 1998). Numerous researchers argue that sports media reinforces hegemonic masculinity (Hardin et al., 2009; Trujillo, 1991) with the end result being that women athletes are essentially ignored (Bruce, 2013). Further compounding this issue is the overwhelmingly white and male sports journalism workforce. The 2018 *AP Sports Editors Racial and Gender Report Card* reported that more than 80% of sports editors, reporters, and columnists were white males (Fischer & Baker, 2020). Male sports journalists surveyed by Schmidt (2018) tended to say that the minuscule level of coverage given to women's sports was appropriate, while another study reported that newspaper sports editors perceived their audience had only limited interest in women's sports (Laucella et al., 2017).

The trivialization of women athletes by sports journalists remains front and center in analyses of coverage. For example, a study examining the front pages of newspaper sports sections at 10-year intervals between 1932 and 2012 found that the percentage of stories about women athletes in major city newspapers never rose above 4% (Kaiser, 2018). Even with the advent of social media, where arguably time and space constraints do not apply, the attention devoted to women's sports remains small. Only 10.2% of posts on Twitter by leading national sports outlets were about women (Cooky et al., 2021) and Hull (2017) discovered that just 4.3% of tweets by local television sports journalists were about women's sports.

Other research has found that sports media requires women athletes to "overcompensate for their masculine behavior on the field by acting in traditionally feminine ways off the field" (Knight & Giuliano, 2003, p. 273) in order to combat their perceived image problem (Kane & Lenskyj, 1998). As a result, much of the coverage emphasizes the femininity of women athletes instead of their athletic prowess (e.g., Hardin et al., 2009; Lenskyj, 2013), although one study noted a trend toward acknowledging the talents of women, albeit it in a "lackluster, matter-of-fact manner" (Musto et al., 2017, p. 590). While Bullingham and Postlethwaite (2019) caution that the literature examining women athletes cannot be assumed to represent the experiences of lesbian athletes in the media, the two subjects are intertwined. Certainly, sexuality intersects with gender and other societal forces (King, 2009). This is particularly true in the case of Sowers, especially when one considers her achievements in American football, the most "macho" sport of all (Butterworth, 2014). Historically, many women athletes have been presumed to be lesbians (Dann & Everbach, 2016; Hardin et al., 2009) and when lesbianism has been mentioned in coverage it has often been presented as a problem (Hardin & Whiteside, 2010). Stories have historically tended to highlight the risk of being out and the presence of lesbianism has been treated as a hindrance to the success of women's sports (Kane & Lenskyj, 1998; Krane & Barber, 2003). Significant amounts of media coverage about the outings of tennis champions Billie Jean King and Martina Navratilova in the 1980s emphasized the damage to their pocketbooks (Cassidy, 2019, 2020). King reported she lost all of her endorsements within 24 hours after acknowledging her affair with a former assistant (Shuster, 2013), while Navratilova said she lost approximately $10 million in endorsements after being outed (Zeigler, 2011). Both also worried about the impact their sexuality would have on their sport, a sentiment echoed by Basketball Hall of Fame member Sheryl Swoopes when she came out more than 20 years later (Cassidy, 2019; Swoopes & Granderson, 2005). Similarly, Brittney Griner, who led her teams to NCAA and WNBA championships, said her coaches at Baylor University told her not to discuss her sexuality (Fagan, 2013).

However, a recent study looking at media reports about the coming-out stories of soccer players Megan Rapinoe and Casey Stone, found evidence that journalists were covering lesbian athletes with greater nuance, and focused on the specific contributions of each athlete to their sport (Bullingham & Postlethwaite, 2019). In that same vein, another analysis discovered that in the years since King's outing in 1981, reporting had evolved to include greater emphasis on societal issues and subjects related to the challenges faced by lesbian athletes (Cassidy, 2019).

Hardin and Whiteside's (2010) research examining coverage of a lawsuit filed against Penn State women's basketball coach Rene Portland is of particular interest to this study in part because it looked at the intersection of sexuality and race in reporting. Jennifer Harris, a former player alleged that Portland, who had a history of reported homophobic behavior, dismissed her from the team because the coach suspected that Harris was a lesbian. Although Harris said Portland was more likely to target African American players suspected of being gay, the lawsuit focused on Portland's homophobia. However, despite this, articles about the lawsuit tended to emphasize racial discrimination, even after an investigation by Penn State officials dismissed those charges. Lesbianism and homophobia were treated as insignificant issues. This preoccupation with race, Hardin and Whiteside (2010) said is "evidence of the discomfort, resistance, and perhaps even fear of journalists in dealing with stories about homophobia" (p. 31).

JOURNALISM ROUTINES

The reluctance of journalists to tackle the issue of homophobia in the case of Rene Portland can be traced in part to the routines of journalism, the "patterned, repeated practices, forms and rules that media workers use to do their jobs" (Shoemaker & Reese, 2014, p. 165). Similarly, routines have been referred to as "the crucial factor which determines how newsworkers construe the world of activities they confront" (Fishman, 1980, p. 14). Much of the content created by journalists, including sports journalists, is influenced by the routines of the profession (Lowes, 1999; Shoemaker & Reese, 2014).

An enduring routine of sports journalism has been that coverage rarely extends "beyond the game." The sociological, political, and economic issues connected to sports are often neglected (Salwen & Garrison, 1998). Thus reporting about sports lacks a critical perspective and fails to uphold the traditional watchdog role of the press (Hardin et al., 2009; Oates & Pauly, 2007). According to Rowe (2007), sports journalists "are likely to leave sustained, intensive, critical inquiry into sports and its relationship with other major areas of society to others" (p. 399). Another observer put it more harshly stating that most "are fans with an audience . . . who aren't looking to uncover truths, they're interested in talking with their sports heroes and sharing their love of the sports world" (Zeigler, 2016, p. 158). Similarly, other research has said that sports journalists are often too dependent and too close to the athletes and team officials they cover, with the result being largely uncritical reporting because they do not want to risk losing access to information (Lowes, 1999; Sugden & Tomlinson, 2007). The perception that sports journalism functions under more lenient standards and ethics than other areas of the profession also contributes to its designation as the "toy department" (Fink, 2001).

Yet, there is some developing evidence that sports journalism is moving away from that moniker. A study examining coverage of the coming-out announcements of NBA veteran Jason Collins and football All-American Michael Sam found that a sizable portion of the coverage addressed the potential issues a gay athlete faces in professional sports (Cassidy, 2017).

Broussard (2020) said that many of the sports journalists he interviewed enjoyed covering political and social issues related to sports and are working to change perceptions of the field by "moving toward an issue-based approach to covering beats" (p. 1641). In addition, he noted that athletes are now more likely to be activists and sports reporters regularly cover those activities as part of their work, signaling a change in the routines of sports journalism.

FRAMING AS A ROUTINE OF JOURNALISM

Many media sociology studies employ framing (e.g., Benson, 2004; Carragee & Roefs, 2004; Revers & Brienza, 2018) and it is helpful in research such as this because of its connection to journalistic practice and the routines of the profession (Chyi & McCombs, 2004; Schildkraut & Muschert, 2014). Shoemaker and Reese (2014) regard framing as a routine because journalists utilize it "ritualistically in a predictably structured way . . . and that it adds meaning to a seemingly disconnected list of facts" (p. 176).

Entman (1993), in perhaps the most renowned articulation of framing, said to frame is "to select some aspects of a perceived reality and make them more salient in a communicating text in such a way as to promote a particular problem definition, causal interpretation, moral evaluation, and/or treatment for the item described" (p. 52). McCombs and Ghanem (2001) call framing "the construction of an agenda with a restricted number of thematically related attributes to create a coherent picture of a particular subject" (p. 70). Tankard (2001), in another oft-cited definition, wrote that a media frame is a "central organizing idea for news content that supplies a context and suggests what the issue is through the use of selection, emphasis, exclusion and elaboration" (pp. 100–101).

Although framing is an extremely popular area of research among a wide variety of communication and journalism scholars (Weaver, 2007), there is no common agreement on a specific set of frames used by journalists. Many framing studies can only be applied to one particular event or issue (Ghanem, 1997; Shoemaker & Reese, 2014). In an effort to address such concerns, Chyi and McCombs (2004) developed a two-dimensional framing measurement scheme, which has been utilized in numerous studies (e.g., Holody & Daniel, 2017; Kwon & Moon, 2009; Muschert & Carr, 2006; Park et al., 2012;

Schildkraut & Muschert, 2014). Their framework organizes the measurement of frames around the dimensions of space and time because both are "central organizing ideas in journalistic practice" (Chyi & McCombs, 2004, p. 25).

There are five levels of the space dimension, viewed as a continuum: (1) Individual: the news event is framed within a scope limited to the individuals involved in an event, (2) Community: the news event is framed as relevant to a particular community, (3) Regional: the news event is framed as relevant to a more general population such as residents of a metropolitan area or state, (4) Societal: the news event is framed in terms of social or national significance, and (5) International: the news event is framed from an international perspective. The time dimension consists of three levels: (1) Past, (2) Present, and (3) Future. The two dimensions are combined and sorted by space and time.

Chyi and McCombs (2004) tested their framework in a content analysis of *New York Times* coverage of the 1999 Columbine High School shootings in Littleton, Colorado. They found that more than half (54%) of the stories utilized the societal level as the primary space frame, and 70% employed the present time frame. Several other studies have utilized the same methodology in examinations of mass shootings, enabling scholars to compare shifts in coverage of these events. For example, a study of the 2015 shootings at Emanuel African Methodist Episcopal Church in Charleston, South Carolina, discovered that journalists used a wider variety of frames in their stories compared to other studies, suggesting that routines utilized in reporting about the topic are evolving and not as cut-and-dried as some critics have contended (Cassidy et al., 2018).

Some researchers have utilized Chyi and McCombs's (2004) measurement scheme to aid in analyzing the quality of media coverage. A study examining newspaper reports about methamphetamine usage contended that the common use of the individual space frame signaled that reporters did not view it as a serious problem for the general population (Schwartz & Andsager, 2008). Other studies have utilized the framework as a foundation and made adjustments. In a comparison of US and South Korean newspaper coverage of the 2005 mass shootings at Virginia Tech, Kwon and Moon (2009) incorporated a collectivist storytelling frame into their analysis. Cassidy (2017, 2019) added identity-based components into the space frame levels because there was little geographic relevance (in terms of community and region) in studying sports journalism framing of gay and lesbian athletes.

RESEARCH QUESTIONS AND ANALYSIS

The study I conducted for this chapter sought to answer five specific questions. The first two relate directly to Chyi and McCombs's (2004) framing measurement scheme and serve to provide a general overview of the results. Those questions are:

1. What space dimension frames are most prominent in stories about Katie Sowers?
2. What time dimension frames are most prominent in stories about Katie Sowers?

As mentioned earlier, I was also interested in knowing which of Sowers's historic firsts was emphasized most in coverage. So, the third question addressed in the study is:

3. What is the level of prominence given to gender and sexuality in stories about Katie Sowers?

The remaining two questions address the presence of space frames at the community, regional, and societal levels in the articles analyzed. They are the following:

4. How prevalent are space dimension frames (other than the individual level) in stories about Katie Sowers?
5. Are any relationships apparent between discussions of gender and sexuality and the use of space level frames (other than the individual level) in stories about Katie Sowers?

I used content analysis to analyze sports journalism coverage of Katie Sowers. To locate articles for the study, I utilized the NexisUni database, Google News, and Google along with the websites for the major sports publications, *SI.com, ESPN.com, Yahoo! Sports, Deadspin.com, Bleacher Report*, and *SB Nation* (Cassidy, 2019; Dann & Everbach, 2016). I conducted keyword searches for "Katie Sowers" and "Super Bowl" for a 30-day time period starting on January 20, 2020, the day after the San Francisco 49ers defeated the Green Bay Packers to advance to the Super Bowl (which was played on February 2) and concluding on February 19, 2020. I only examined articles where Sowers was the main focus or played a prominent role, along with stories written as a consequence of her becoming the first woman and openly LGBTQ+ individual to coach in the Super Bowl (Holody & Daniel, 2017). I did not include letters to the editor and used stories appearing in multiple outlets only once. A trained graduate student from my university and I coded each article on five variables: date published, most prominent space frame, most prominent time frame, the presence of other space frames, and if the story discussed Sowers's gender and sexuality.

I applied the space frame levels utilized by Chyi and McCombs (2004) as a starting point, but I made some adjustments. First, the community and regional levels were altered because there appeared to be little geographic relevance at those levels to Sowers's historic firsts (Cassidy, 2017, 2019). In addition, given this study's interest in the comparative emphasis of Sowers's gender and sexuality in the sample, categories related to both gender and sexuality at the regional and societal levels were added. I replaced Community with NFL/Football Community and regional with Women Athletes/Coaches and LGBTQ+ Athletes/Coaches and divided the Societal level into Women in Society and LGBTQ+ Individuals in Society. The International category was not used because no stories employed this frame. Therefore, the six levels of space frames were:

1. *Individual*—Focus on individuals (e.g., Sowers, her fellow coaches, NFL players, family members, or others); the interaction among them; or description of their acts, reactions, or background information. Editorial pieces telling personal stories are also part of this category.
2. *NFL/Football Community*—Focus on the community of the NFL and football. This category includes women and LGBTQ+ gay/Lesbian coaches in the NFL and other football leagues.
3. *Women Athletes/Coaches*—Focus on the issues and challenges concerning women athletes and/or coaches both in general and beyond the NFL and football.
4. *LGBTQ+ Athletes/Coaches*—Focus on the issues and challenges concerning LGBTQ+ athletes and/or coaches both in general and beyond the NFL and football.
5. *Women in Society*—Focus on concerns, events, or discussions with nationwide interests such as social problems and/or the problems, issues, and concerns of women in society—in other words, the impact of Sowers's milestone at the first woman coach in a Super Bowl on the nation as a whole.
6. *LGBTQ+ Individuals in Society*—Focus on concerns, events, or discussions with nationwide interests such as social problems and/or the problems, issues, and concerns of LGBTQ+ individuals in society—in other words, the impact of Sowers's milestone as the first openly LGBTQ+ coach in the Super Bowl on the nation as a whole.

The time frames consisted of three levels based on Chyi and McCombs's (2004) definitions:

1. *Past*—If the story focuses on previous events with no direct linkage to the key event (Sowers being the first woman and openly LGBTQ+ coach

in the Super Bowl), analysis with a historical perspective, or editorial pieces based on past experiences (e.g., LGBTQ+ coaches and athletes in the past; Sowers's life history)

2. *Present*—Focus on events/developments surrounding the key event— Sowers's status as the first woman and openly LGBTQ+ coach in the Super Bowl—in time, immediate consequences of the event or current social phenomena.

3. *Future*—Focus on the long-term effects of Sowers being the first woman and/or openly LGBTQ+ coach in the Super Bowl, suggestions to solve problems, or actions to be taken.

After coders decided on the most prominent space and time frames in each story, they were also asked to code for whether any or all of the aforementioned Community, Regional, and Societal space frames were present in each story. This additional procedure provides insight into the depth and quality of information provided in the stories, enabling the study to further assess if reporters went beyond the basics of Sowers's achievements. The Individual space frame was cut from this part, because by definition the entire sample consisted of stories that included Sowers.

For reliability purposes, 20 articles (15% of the sample) were coded by both coders. Using Scott's Pi, a summary statistic that corrects for the possibility of chance agreements, the level of agreement was .95 for the most prominent space frame and 1.0 for the most prominent time frame. The level of agreement for the presence of specific frames at the Community, Regional and Societal levels was .88 and 1.0 for if the story mentioned Sowers's gender and/or sexuality.

TIME AND SPACE FRAME FINDINGS

Of the 130 stories ($N = 130$) analyzed in this study, the most prominent space frame in the vast majority was Individual ($n = 117$, 90%). Women Athletes/ Coaches was the second leading category with 5 stories (3.8%). The results were similar for the most prominent time frame, with most ($n = 125$, 96.2%) framed as Present. No story had Future as the most prominent time frame, while the remaining 5 stories (3.8%) were framed as Past (table 3.1).

This result is not surprising given that by design this study focused on stories published in the immediate aftermath of Sowers's history-making accomplishments. Therefore, it stands to reason that coverage would also focus on Sowers's personal story because of its uniqueness and that she was making history at that very moment in time. Although stories can be framed in a variety of ways, Chyi and McCombs (2004) say that some are more relevant to

Table 3.1   Dimensions of Framing in Coverage of Katie Sowers (N = 130)

Dimension	Number	Percentage
Space		
Individual	117	90
NFL/Football Community	4	3.1
Women Athletes/Coaches	5	3.8
LGBTQ+ Athletes/Coaches	0	0
Women in Society	3	2.3
LGBTQ+ Individuals in Society	1	0.8
Time		
Past	5	3.8
Present	125	96.2
Future	0	0

the nature of an event than others. For example, a study examining coverage of the coming-out stories of NBA veteran Jason Collins and football All-American Michael Sam found that 80.6% and 90% of stories respectively, were framed at the Present time level (Cassidy, 2017), no doubt at least in part to the newsworthiness of their announcements (Billings et al., 2015).

However, it is important to note that stories about Sowers were much more likely to emphasize the Individual space level than in other studies of lesbian athletes. Only 29.7% of stories about the coming out of Basketball Hall of Fame member Sheryl Swoopes were framed at that level, while 59.1% of stories about WNBA and NCAA champion Brittney Griner were focused on the Individual level (Cassidy, 2019). Research utilizing Chyi and McCombs's (2004) framing measurement scheme has argued that the use of space frames beyond the Individual level can provide indications of the quality of coverage because the utilization of other frames in coverage serve as evidence that journalists were looking at the bigger picture by examining connections between sport and cultural/societal problems (Cassidy, 2017, 2019; Schwartz & Andsager, 2008). In other words, the more often other space frames are emphasized, the more it can be said that sports journalists are engaging in critical, issue-oriented coverage.

Thus, at first glance, the level of Individual dominance in coverage of Sowers's could be seen as alarming, although as noted earlier, the time frame of this study likely influenced the usage of dominant space dimension frames. In addition, some have criticized Chyi and McCombs's measurement scheme for lacking detail (Park et al., 2012). Therefore, it was deemed important in this study to also examine the 130 stories for the presence of other frames—particularly those addressing issues related to the NFL, gender and sexuality—in order to provide a more nuanced analysis of the coverage. The level of attention given to the aforementioned community, regional, and societal space frames in stories about Sowers offers insight into how well sports journalists addressed issues related to, but also beyond the basic elements of, her story, a quality researchers say is often lacking in coverage (Hardin et al., 2009; Oates & Pauly, 2007; Rowe, 2007).

As discussed throughout this chapter, Sowers was responsible for two historic firsts. She was both the first woman to coach in the Super Bowl and the first openly LGBTQ+ individual to coach in the NFL's marquee event, which attracted an audience of more than 100 million viewers in 2020, more than double that of any other sporting event in the United States that year (Statista.com., n.d.). In particular I was interested in which of those "firsts" received more attention in coverage, especially considering that numerous studies have lamented the lack of coverage given to both women and lesbian athletes (e.g., Cooky et al., 2021; Hardin & Whiteside, 2010; Hull, 2017; Kane & Lenskyj, 1998).

As shown in table 3.2, 122 stories (93.8%) discussed that Sowers was the first woman coach in Super Bowl history while 97 (74.6%) noted her status as the first openly LGBTQ+ individual to coach in the game. Thus, Sowers's gender was mentioned significantly more than her sexuality X^2 (1, N=130) = 6.20, p = .013. Sowers's gender and sexuality are both essential elements of her story in the context of this study and their varying levels of prominence are relevant to discussions concerning the quality of coverage. Rowe (2007) argued that sports journalists must get at the inherent questions of any issue they are covering. In the case of Sowers's those would be questions emanating from her gender, and sexuality, coupled with her position as a coach in the NFL, which has been referred to as the most masculine sport (Butterworth, 2014; Rader, 2008) "where sexuality is the most ferociously policed" (Glazek, 2014). By looking at those questions and going beyond the mere mention of her being the first woman and openly LGBTQ+ individual, journalists would be providing more thorough reporting that addresses the political and/or social implications of the story.

When looking at frames beyond the Individual space level utilized in coverage, the NFL/Football Community frame was present in 103 (79.2%)

Table 3.2   Presence of Gender, Sexuality, and NFL Frames in Coverage of Sowers (N = 130)

Frame	Number	Percentage
First Woman Coach	122	93.8
First LGBTQ+ Coach	97	74.6
NFL/Football Community	103	79.2
Women Athletes/Coaches	96	73.8
LGBTQ+ Athletes/Coaches	44	33.8
Women in Society	52	40.0
LGBTQ+ Individuals in Society	39	30.0

Table 3.3   Pearson Correlation Coefficients for Gender, Sexuality, and NFL Frames in Coverage of Katie Sowers

Frames	2.	3.	4.	5.	6.	7.
1. First Woman	.22[a]	.19[a]	.14	.05	.08	.03
2. First LGBTQ+ Individual	—	.18[a]	.10	.31[c]	.03	.27[b]
3. NFL/Football Community		—	.47[c]	.05	-.01	.01
4. Women Athletes/Coaches			—	.13	.16	-.03
5. LGBTQ+ Athletes/Coaches				—	-.05	.70[c]
6. Women in Society					—	.19[a]
7. LGBTQ+ Individuals in Society						—

Note: [a]$p < .05$, [b]$p < .01$, [c]$p < .001$

stories and the Women Athletes/Coaches frame appeared in 96 (73.8%) of the stories. The frames related to LGBTQ+ issues were addressed less frequently. The LGBTQ+ Athletes/Coaches frame appeared in 44 (33.8%) of stories, while the LGBTQ+ Individuals in Society frame was present in 39 (30%) of the stories (table 3.2). The mean number of frames used in each story (including gender and sexuality) was 4.25 (M = 4.25, SD = 1.56).

Some interesting patterns in the coverage were also reserved in that the foundational elements of Sowers's story were significantly correlated. Table 3.3 shows significant correlations between discussion of Sowers's status as the first woman to coach in the Super Bowl and discussion of her sexuality, ($r = .22$, $p = .013$) as well as the NFL/Football Community frame ($r = .19$, $p = .036$). Significant correlations were also found between discussion of Sowers's status as the first openly LGBTQ+ individual to coach in the game and the NFL/Community frame ($r = .18$, $p = .040$), the LGBTQ+ Athletes/ Coaches frame ($r = .31$, $p < .001$) and LGBTQ+ Individuals in Society frame ($r = .27$, $p = .002$). Stories containing the NFL/Football Community frame were highly correlated with the Women Athletes/Coaches frame ($r = .47$, $p = < .001$), while the LGBTQ+ Athletes/Coaches frame was strongly correlated with the LGBT+ Individuals in Society frame ($r = .70$, $p < .001$). There was also a significant correlation between the Women in Society frame and the LGBTQ+ Individuals in Society frame ($r = .19$, $p = .035$).

CONCLUSION: PROGRESS BUT NOT PARITY

This chapter examined how sports journalists covered Katie Sowers in the 30-day time period after it became official she would be the first woman and first openly LGBTQ+ person to coach in the Super Bowl. The results add to the body of literature about women and lesbian sports figures, in part by heeding the call of other researchers (e.g., King, 2008; Lenskyj, 2013) for intersectional analyses of sexual identity that also pay attention to other variables such as gender. The fact that 130 stories were published about Sowers's historic firsts and that most of them addressed her sexuality can be seen as confirmation of an advancing societal environment that is more tolerant of gay and lesbian sports figures (Anderson, 2015; Dann & Everbach, 2016; Lenskyj, 2013). Such changes have increased the likelihood that journalists will write about issues of sexuality (Billings et al., 2015; Cassidy, 2019; Kian & Anderson, 2009; Zeigler, 2016).

Yet, despite these positive developments, the results cannot and should not be taken as proof that relative parity has been achieved in media coverage of women and lesbian athletes. Homophobia, not to mention "long standing forces of orthodox masculinity and compulsory heterosexuality" (Moscowitz et al., 2019, p. 263) are still present in society. Undoubtedly, a contributing factor to the media attention given to Sowers is that her accomplishments came in the NFL, which according to sports columnist Dave Zirin (2014) "is the closest thing we have in [the United States] to a national obsession" (para. 3) and a league considered emblematic of traditional norms of masculinity (Glazek, 2014). Thus, the novelty of her status in the most popular *and most masculine* spectator sport in the United States elevated her level of newsworthiness, which is indicated in the results of this study. Issues related to the NFL/Football Community were present in more stories about Sowers than mentions of her being the first openly LGBTQ+ coach in the Super Bowl. This finding is somewhat similar to those of Hardin and Whiteside (2010) in that media coverage of the lawsuit against former Penn State women's basketball coach Rene Portland alleging homophobic behavior in dismissing a player from the team, focused on issues of race, rather than homophobia and sexuality, which they said "reinforced lesbianism as an insignificant issue" (p. 31).

However, that is not to say that Sowers's sexuality was rendered insignificant in the findings here. When compared to other studies, the results indicate progress in media coverage and increased openness to discussing issues related to LGBTQ+ individuals in sports. Yet, they also show that such issues were present less frequently in stories about Sowers and that more attention was given to gender and subjects related to the NFL. This suggests there is still some reluctance on the part of journalists to discuss such topics. LGBTQ+ sports reporters interviewed for a volume examining sports journalism coverage of coming-out stories said many in the field felt athletes were reluctant to discuss such a personal topic. Furthermore, access to athletes is limited in the COVID-19 media environment, which makes it less likely that an athlete will confide in a reporter about issues of sexuality because they rarely get one-on-one time with them. As one noted, "When you're around a lot of reporters, you can't just say 'Hey Sue, you mentioned that you're gay!'"

(Cassidy, 2019, p. 104). Issues related to LGBTQ+ Athletes/Coaches were mentioned in just 33.8% (*n* = 44), while issues concerning LBGTQ+ Individuals in Society were present in 30% of the stories (*n* = 39). Interestingly, articles discussing Sowers's sexuality tended to also explore issues related to LGBTQ+ Athletes/Coaches, as well as LGBTQ+ Individuals in Society. So, when sports journalists addressed these issues of sexuality, they tended to go beyond the basics and explore other inherent, ingrained issues related to Sowers's role as the first openly LGBTQ+ coach in Super Bowl history.

Taken as a whole, the results here show that Sowers's history-making feats were indeed covered extensively by sports journalists. Although part of the reason for her acclaim can be attributed to her success as a woman in a male-dominated sport, that fact arguably made her accomplishments all the more newsworthy, and thus worthy of high levels of coverage. Additionally, significant attention was given to her sexuality—although not at the levels paid to gender and NFL issues. Nevertheless, the amount of discussion related to issues of sexuality in the stories represents a substantial improvement from other studies whose findings report little attention given to lesbians in sports (e.g., Hardin & Whiteside, 2010; Kane & Lenskyj, 1998). Finally, the results also demonstrate an increased inclination of sports journalists to explore issues related to and beyond the subject or event being covered, an indication that the "toy department" designation may not be as accurate as it once was.

Still, while sports journalists have certainly moved beyond Zeigler's (2016) unflattering proclamation that they are little more than fans interested only in rubbing shoulders with their athletic heroes, the advances reported here cannot be taken as an indication that the profession is doing all it can to provide substantive coverage of LGBTQ+ athletes or (especially) women athletes. Research mentioned in this chapter has documented improvements in portrayals of LGBTQ+ athletes (e.g., Billings et al., 2015, Cassidy, 2017, 2019), yet the fact remains that LGBTQ+ women athletes and women athletes in general tend to be ignored by the sports media. One need look no further than the discrepancy in coverage devoted to the coming-out stories of basketball players Jason Collins and Brittney Griner, who both announced they were gay in 2013. Collins, an NBA journeyman, received significantly more attention than Griner, who was fresh off being selected as the No. 1 pick in the WNBA draft and already acknowledged as one of the greatest women's college basketball players of all time (Cassidy, 2019; Dann & Everbach, 2016). One could argue that this finding signals that being a woman contributes more to a lack of newsworthiness than being LGBTQ+. Furthermore, the numerous studies documenting the sparse amount of media attention given to women athletes indicates that sports journalism has many miles to go before it can be said the industry provides quality coverage of women athletes.

Response

Women Succeed in Coaching and Family Life

Lisa Carlsen

Early on in my career, a friend of mine said "I don't think you can be a great Mom and a great Coach at the same time, something's gotta give."

I remember feeling challenged by her statement and all I could think of was, JUST WATCH ME! When I first got my first college women's basketball head coaching job, I had three small boys, ages five, two, and a newborn. Life was crazy to say the least. I was trying to find my way as a young head coach, I was trying to be a great Mom to my boys, and I was loving every minute of it!

I don't know if I knew it then, but I definitely know it now, 20 years later, certain things have to be in place for this all to work. Women in coaching are faced with this challenge in a much different way than men. The stereotypes are alive and well!

Moms are the caregivers, the keepers of the house, and the planners of the schedule. The only way to have great success in work and life is to have a tremendous support system, (family, spouse, friends) and leadership who understand your demands and to work to blend it all together. It's not about work life balance, it's about work life blending.

We've seen tremendous growth in many areas of diversity in women coaches, but the challenges of having a family and a successful coaching career still remain and our need to continue to fight for equality is ongoing. Efforts made to normalize raising a family in this business have only just begun.

I've been extremely fortunate to be able to work for people who value family in our business. Knowing how much of a role model you can be to young professionals and for them to see how to make it all work is critical. Athletics is so much more than wins and losses. It's about life lessons, handling adversity, building relationships, and mentoring young people as they grow.

I've now been in this business for over 25 years and I understand the demands and the toll it takes. I have loved the chance to raise my kids around the game, in a gym, on a field, on the road, in the stands, all of it! They have been informally adopted by hundreds of big sisters that they have looked up to. I wouldn't trade it for the world.

Every great coach wants what every great Mom wants, to help their kids be happy and successful. To teach them to always work hard, strive for excellence, and surround yourself with people who make you better and people who love you. Build confidence for them to see they can be anything they want to be.

Sometimes it takes tough love and hard lessons, but you always do it because you care. Be a strong hand, a shoulder to cry on, a voice of reason and sound advisor. Coach and Mom: sounds like a perfect combination for success! Those that have done it well and paved the way owe it to the next generation to create an environment where there is no question that women can be great at both.

REFERENCES

Adams, T., & Tuggle, C. A. (2004). ESPN's *SportsCenter* and coverage of women's athletics: "It's a boys' club." *Mass Communication and Society, 7*(2), 237–248.

Anderson, E. (2002). Openly gay athletes: Contesting hegemonic masculinity in a homophobic environment. *Gender and Society, 16*(6), 860–877.

Anderson, E. (2015). Assessing the sociology of sport: On changing masculinities and homophobia. *International Review for the Sociology of Sport, 50*(4–5), 363–367.

Benbow, D. H. (2020, January 28). 49ers' Katie Sowers lost college coaching job because she's gay, moved on to Super Bowl. *Indianapolis Star.* Retrieved from https://www.indystar.com/story/sports/nfl/colts/2020/01/28/katie-sowers-49-ers -coach-rejected-coaching-role-indiana-college/4597571002/

Benson, R. (2004). Bringing the sociology of media back in. *Political Communication, 21*(3), 275–292.

Billings, A. C., Moscowitz, L. M., Rae, C., & Brown-Devlin, N. (2015). The art of coming out: Traditional and social media frames surrounding the NBA's Jason Collins. *Journalism & Mass Communication Quarterly, 92*(1), 142–160.

Billings, A. C., & Young, B. D. (2015). Comparing flagship news programs: Women's sports coverage in ESPN's *SportsCenter* and FOX Sports 1's *Sports Live. Electronic News, 9*(1), 3–16.

Boyle, R. (2013). Reflections on communication and sport: On journalism and digital culture. *Communication & Sport, 1*(1–2), 88–99.

Broussard, R. (2020). 'Stick to sports' is gone: A field theory analysis of sports journalists' coverage of socio-political issues. *Journalism Studies, 21*(12), 1627–1643.

Bruce, T. (2013). Reflections on communication and sport: On women and femininities. *Communication & Sport, 1*(1–2), 125–137.

Bullingham, R., & Postlethwaite, V. (2019). Lesbian athletes in the sports media: Ambivalence, scrutiny and invisibility. In R. Magrath (Ed.), *LGBT athletes in the sports media* (pp. 51–74). London: Palgrave Macmillan.

Butterworth, M. L. (2014). The athlete as citizen: Judgement and rhetorical invention in sport. *Sport in Society, 17*(7), 867–883.

Buzinski, J. (2017, August 22). San Francisco assistant Katie Sowers is first out LGBT coach in NFL. *Outsports.* Retrieved from https://www.outsports.com/2017 /8/22/16175286/katie-sowers-san-francisco-49ers-coach-gay-coming-out

Carragee, K. M., & Roefs, W. (2004). The neglect of power in recent framing research. *Journal of Communication, 54*(2), 214–233.

Cassidy, W. P. (2017). *Sports journalism and coming out stories: Jason Collins and Michael Sam.* New York: Palgrave Macmillan.

Cassidy, W. P. (2019). *Sports journalism and women athletes: Coverage of coming out stories.* New York: Palgrave Macmillan.

Cassidy, W. P. (2020). Martina Navratilova: Out in the (relative) open. In J. Carvalho (Ed.), *Sports media history: Culture, technology, identity* (pp. 150–162). New York: Routledge.

Cassidy, W. P., La France, B. H., & Babin, S. (2018). Routine adjustments: How journalists framed the Charleston shootings. *International Journal of Communication, 12,* 4668–4688.

Chyi, H. I., & McCombs, M. (2004). Media salience and the process of framing: Coverage of the Columbine school shootings. *Journalism & Mass Communication Quarterly, 81*(1), 22–35.

Connell, R. W. (1990). An iron man: The body and some contradictions of hegemonic masculinity. In M. A. Messner & D. F. Sabo (Eds.), *Sport, men and gender order: Critical feminist perspectives* (pp. 83–95). Champaign, IL: Human Kinetics.

Cooky, C., Council, L. D., Mears, M. A., & Messner, M. A. (2021). One and done: The long eclipse of women's televised sports, 1981–2019. *Communication & Sport, 9*(3), 347–371.

Cooky, C., Messner, M. A., & Musto, M. (2015). "It's dude time!": A quarter century of excluding women's sports in televised news and highlight shows. *Communication & Sport, 3*(3), 261–287.

Dann, L., & Everbach, T. (2016). Opening the sports closet: Media coverage of the self-outings of Jason Collins and Brittney Griner. *Journal of Sports Media, 11*(1), 169–192.

Duncan, M. (1990). Sports photographs and sexual difference: Images of women and men in the 1984 and 1988 Olympic Games. *Sociology of Sport Journal, 7*(1), 22–43.

Entman, R. M. (1993). Framing: Toward clarification of a fractured paradigm. *Journal of Communication, 43*(4), 51–58.

Fagan, K. (2013, May 29). Owning the middle. *ESPN: The Magazine.* Retrieved from http://www.espn.com/espn/feature/story/_/id/9316697/owning-middle.

Fink, C. (2001). *Sportswriting: The lively game.* Ames: Iowa State University Press.

Fischer, S., & Baker, K. (2020, July 7). Sports media's race reckoning. *Axios.com.* https://www.axios.com/sports-media-race-reckoning-985b6ca2-acf3-4df6-8eeb-8b092ed8bcf8.html

Fishman, M. (1980). *Manufacturing the news.* Austin, TX: University of Texas Press.

Ghanem, S. I. (1997). Filling in the tapestry: The second level of agenda setting. In M. E McCombs, D. L. Shaw, & D. H. Weaver (Eds.), *Communication and democracy* (pp. 3–14). Mahwah, NJ: Lawrence Erlbaum.

Glazek, C. (2014, July 9). Michael Sam and the draw that changed American sports forever. *Out.* Retrieved from http://www.out.com/entertainment/sports/2014/07/09/michael-sam-and-draw-changed-american-sports-forever

Graham, M. (2020, January 28). Microsoft's super bowl ad thanks Katie Sowers, the first woman to coach in the big game. *CNBC.com.* Retrieved from https://www

.cnbc.com/2020/01/28/microsoft-super-bowl-thanks-katie-sowers-first-woman-to
-coach-in-super-bowl.html

Hardin, M., Kuehn, K. M., Jones, H., Genovese, J., & Balaji, M. (2009). Have you got game? Hegemonic masculinity and neo-homophobia in U.S. newspaper sports columns. *Communication, Culture & Critique, 2*(2), 182–200.

Hardin, M., & Whiteside, E. (2010). The Rene Portland case. In H. L. Hundley & A. C. Billings (Eds.), *Examining identity in sports media* (pp. 17–36). Los Angeles: Sage.

Holody, K. J., & Daniel, E. S. (2017). Attributes and frames of the Aurora shootings: National and local news coverage differences. *Journalism Practice, 11*(1), 80–100.

Hull, K. (2017). An examination of women's sports coverage on the Twitter accounts of local television sports broadcasters. *Communication & Sport, 5*(4), 471–491.

Kaiser, K. (2018). Women's and men's prominence in sports coverage and changes in large, medium and small-city newspapers, Pre-and post-Title IX: A local play for equality? *Communication & Sport, 6*(6), 762–787.

Kane, M. J., & Lenskyj, H. J. (1998). Media treatment of female athletes: Issues of gender and sexualities. In L. Wenner (Ed.), *MediaSport* (pp. 186–201). New York: Routledge.

Kian, E. M., & Anderson, E. (2009). John Amaechi: Changing the way sport reporters examine gay athletes. *Journal of Homosexuality, 56*(7), 799–818.

King, S. (2008). What's queer about (queer) sport sociology now? A review essay. *Sociology of Sport Journal, 25*(4), 419–442.

King, S. (2009). Homonormativity and the politics of race: Reading Sheryl Swoopes. *Journal of Lesbian Studies, 13*(3), 272–290.

Knight, J. L., & Giuliano, T. A. (2003). Blood, sweat and jeers: The impact of the media's heterosexist portrayals on perceptions of male and female athletes. *Journal of Sport Behavior, 26*(3), 272–284.

Krane, V., & Barber, H. (2003). Lesbian experiences in sport: A social identity perspective. *Quest, 55*(4), 328–346.

Kwon, K. H., & Moon, S.-I. (2009). The bad guy is one of us: Framing comparison between the US and Korean newspapers and blogs about the Virginia Tech shooting. *Asian Journal of Communication, 19*(3), 270–288.

Laucella, P. C., Hardin, M., Bien-Aime, S., & Antunovic, D. (2017). Diversifying the sports department and covering women's sports. A survey of sports editors. *Journalism & Mass Communication Quarterly, 94*(3), 772–792.

Lenskyj, H. J. (2013). Reflections on communication and sport: On heteronormativity and gender identities. *Communication & Sport, 1*(1–2), 138–150.

Lowes, M. D. (1999). *Inside the sports pages: Work routines, professional ideologies and the manufacture of sports news.* Toronto: University of Toronto Press.

MacKenzie, M. (2019, July 16). Katie Sowers: The ceiling shattering coach. *Glamour.* Retrieved from https://www.glamour.com/story/football-has-a-woman-problem-coach-katie-sowers-wants-to-solve-it

McCombs, M. E., & Ghanem, S. I. (2001). The convergence of agenda setting and framing. In S. D. Reese, O. H. Gandy, & A. E. Grant (Eds.), *Framing public life:*

Perspectives on media and our understanding of the social world (pp. 67–81). Mahwah, NJ: Lawrence Erlbaum.

Moscowitz, L. M., Billings, A. C., Ejaz, J., & O'Boyle, J. (2019). Outside the sports closet: News discourses of professional gay male athletes in the mainstream. *Journal of Communication Inquiry, 43*(3), 249–271.

Muschert, G. W., & Carr, D. (2006). Media salience and frame changing across events: Coverage of nine school shootings, 1997–2001. *Journalism & Mass Communication Quarterly, 83*(4), 747–766.

Musto, M., Cooky, C., & Messner, M. A. (2017). "From fizzle to sizzle!": Televised sports news and the production of gender-bland sexism. *Gender & Society, 31*, 573–596.

Oates, T. P., & Pauly, J. (2007). Sports journalism as moral and ethical discourse. *Journal of Mass Media Ethics, 22*(4), 332–347.

Park, S.-Y., Holody, J. J., & Zhang, X. (2012). Race in media coverage of school shootings: A parallel application of framing theory and attribute agenda setting. *Journalism & Mass Communication Quarterly, 89*(3), 475–494.

Rader, B. G. (2008). *American sports: From the age of folk games to the age of televised sports* (6th ed.). Upper Saddle River, NJ: Prentice Hall.

Reese, S. D. (2019). Hierarchy of influences. In T. P. Vos & F. Hanusch (Eds.), *International encyclopedia of journalism studies*. Hoboken, NJ: Wiley-Blackwell. Retrieved from https://doi.org/10.1002/9781118841570.iejs0023

Revers, M., & Brienza, C. (2018). How not to establish a subfield: Media sociology in the United States. *American Sociologist, 49*(3), 352–368.

Rowe, D. (2007). Sports journalism: Still the toy department of the news media? *Journalism: Theory Practice & Criticism, 8*(4), 385–405.

Salwen, M. B., & Garrison, B. (1998). Finding their place in journalism: Newspaper sports journalists' professional "problems". *Journal of Sport & Social Issues, 22*(1), 88–102.

Schildkraut, J., & Muschert, G. W. (2014). Media salience and the framing of mass murder in schools: A comparison of the Columbine and Sandy Hook massacres. *Homicide Studies, 18*(1), 23–43.

Schmidt, H. C. (2018). Forgotten athletes and token reporters: Analyzing the gender bias in sports journalism. *Atlantic Journal of Communication, 26*(1), 59–74.

Schwartz, J., & Andsager, J. L. (2008). Sexual health and stigma in urban newspapers' coverage of methamphetamine. *American Journal of Men's Health, 2*(1), 56–67.

Shoemaker, P. J., & Reese, S. D. (2014). *Mediating the message in the 21st century: A media sociology perspective*. New York: Routledge.

Shuster, R. (2013, May 22). Billie Jean King: Tennis star least of her important roles. *USA Today*. Retrieved from https://www.usatoday.com/story/sports/2013/05/22/billie-jean-king-icons-innovators-world-team-tennis-womensrights/2159071/

Statista.com no date Number of TV viewers of most watched sporting events in the United States in 2020. https://www.statista.com/statistics/619023/number

-tv-viewers-sporting-events-usa/#:~:text=According%20to%20the%20source%2C %20the,viewers%20in%20the%20United%20States

Sugden, J., & Tomlinson, A. (2007). Stories from planet football and sportsworld: Source relations and collusion in sport journalism. *Journalism Practice, 1*(1), 44–61.

Swoopes, S., & Granderson, L. Z. (2005, October 26). Outside the arc. *ESPN.com*. Retrieved from http://www.espn.com/wnba/news/story?id=2204322

Tankard, J. W. (2001). The empirical approach to the study of media framing. In S. D. Reese, O. H. Grandy, & A. E. Grant (Eds.), *Framing public life: Perspectives on media and our understanding of the social world* (pp. 95–106). Mahwah, NJ: Lawrence Erlbaum.

Trujillo, N. (1991). Hegemonic masculinity on the mound: Media representations of Nolan Ryan and American sports culture. *Critical Studies in Mass Communication, 8*(3), 290–308.

Wagoner, N. (2020, January 28). 49ers' Katie Sowers calls becoming first woman to coach at Super Bowl 'surreal.' *ESPN.com*. Retrieved from https://www.espn.com /nfl/story/_/id/28580558/49ers-katie-sowers-calls-becoming-first-woman-coach -super-bowl-surreal

Walsh, S. M. (2020, February 4). Katie Sowers: 5 fast facts you need to know. *Heavy*. Retrieved from https://heavy.com/sports/2020/02/katie-sowers/

Weaver, D. H. (2007). Thoughts on agenda setting, framing and priming. *Journal of Communication, 57*(1), 142–147.

Zeigler, C. (2011, October 3). Moment #2: Martina Navratilova comes out. *Out-sports*. Retrieved from https://www.outsports.com/2011/10/3/4051944/moment-2 -martina-navratilova-comes-out

Zeigler, C. (2016). *Fair play: how LGBT athletes are claiming their rightful place in sports*. New York: Akashic Books.

Zirin, D. (2014, February 24). What Michael Sam can't do. *Socialistworker.org*. Retrieved from https://socialistworker.org/2014/02/25/what-michaelsamcant-do ?quicktabs_sw-recent-articles=11-8.

Chapter 4

Queer Recreation

LGBTQ+ Sporting Spaces, Community, and Impact

Austin R. Anderson and Eric Knee

The LGBTQ+ community has long employed sport, recreation, and leisure as sites of identity and community development, socialization, activism, and celebration. However, these spaces can also act as sites of exclusion, oppression, and harm toward this population. Indeed, much discussion has taken place about the relationship between sport and the LGBTQ+ community, whether in the form of how a high-profile coming-out story is framed in popular media (Carl Nassib, Jason Collins, etc.), media questioning why there is a "limited" number of out gay men in professional sport (Hernandez, 2021), coverage of homophobic actions by sporting fans (Borg, 2021), or popular media campaigns for LGBTQ+ inclusion within sport (such as the Rainbow Laces campaign, an initiative from the Stonewall organization that celebrates LGBTQ+ inclusion in sport). As such, sport at the professional and collegiate levels receive widespread academic and media attention with regards to their relationship to the LGBTQ+ community (Anderson et al., 2021b; Anderson et al., 2019; Billings & Moscowitz, 2018).

However, while discussed less frequently, recreation and leisure spaces have an opportunity to have a large impact on the LGBTQ+ community, particularly in localized contexts (Knee, 2019; Theriault, 2014). By their very nature, more persons participate in recreation and leisure than elite sport; as such, opportunities typically have fewer barriers for participation, and recreation/leisure are embedded within the fabric of local communities through governmental and nonprofit agencies. So, while there have been some high-profile cases of queer athletes in professional and collegiate sports and organizational initiatives to promote LGBTQ+ inclusion, recreation and leisure spaces have provided an outlet for queer populations to be included and, when done well, have the potential to shift/disrupt heteronormative narratives (Elling et al., 2003; Gillig et al., 2019; Krane et al., 2002; Litwiller, 2018, 2021; Theriault, 2014). Common examples include public parks and recreation spaces acting as sites of Pride events, LGBTQ+-exclusive recreation clubs sharing spaces and equipment with public and nonprofit recreation agencies, and queer community formation and activism growing out of social gatherings in leisure spaces.

Leisure and recreation, conversely and often more perniciously, can uphold heteronormativity. In so doing, this creates spaces of exclusion and oppression. As such, recreation and leisure scholars and practitioners have outlined the importance of cultural competence in promoting LGBTQ+ inclusion within "mainstream" recreation and leisure organizations, often citing this as the promotion of social change on a larger scale (Anderson et al., 2021; Dattilo et al., 2019). However, at times these attempts, while well-meaning, lack a critical gaze which can inadvertently uphold heteronormativity and lead to assimilation and cultural practices that are antagonistic to queerness and LGBTQ+ lives.

In response, specialized recreation and leisure spaces built by the queer community and for the queer community have been found to promote safe spaces for queer expression, community-building, and counter-hegemony. These spaces range from local community organizations, such as a queer volleyball league, to large international endeavors, such as the quadrennial international Gay Games. At any level, such spaces have not only provided a safe space for queer individuals to participate in recreational sporting activities, but they also have leveraged recreation to provide community services and promote social change. For example, queer sport organizations were instrumental in advocacy during the early stages of the HIV pandemic, have pushed back against gender binaries, promoted queer community formation, and engaged in social activism (Knee & Anderson, 2021; Markwell, 1998; Pronger, 2000). Indeed, the role of queer recreational sport has been well-documented in both mainstream media, largely through optimistic coverage of the Gay Games (Lee et al., 2014), and through queer-media outlets/authors, which can emphasize this connection between queer recreational sport and social change (see Stahl, 2019). Indeed, queer recreational sport organizations themselves have implemented multiple communications tools internally to promote community-formation and implement counter-hegemonic discourse, often challenging mainstream media's homophobic narratives. Today, this includes the leveraging of social media as a tool for connection. Pre-Internet, such communications included the publication of newsletters. Queer media and communications, including examples, will be discussed further later in this chapter.

Similar to representations of mainstream or LGBTQ+-specific spaces, spaces for recreation and leisure can reflect more than simple physical spaces of activity. These sites can also serve as places of discourse, politics, and action where questions of insider and outsider status are constantly negotiated and re-created along intersectional identity lines (Watson & Ratna, 2011). Such negotiation can occur through traditional media representations of these spaces (Jarvis, 2018), debates within queer communication outlets (Knee & Anderson, 2021), or internal community boundary-maintenance (Knee, 2019). Thus, increased attention to the state of LGBTQ+ engagement within recreation is important to recognize these discourses. To do so, both mainstream recreation spaces and LGBTQ-specific recreational sport spaces will be discussed in this chapter. In the case of the former, specific managerial and administrative processes will be noted to understand how these organizations attempt to promote a discourse of inclusion for LGBTQ+ persons. For the latter, motivations for participation and outcomes will be discussed with specific attention to the assimilative or transformative potential of these LGBTQ+-specific recreation spaces. In both cases, intersectional identities, such as race, religion, and athletic identity, are discussed. First, we begin this chapter with a brief discussion on why discussing LGBTQ+ recreation and leisure matters.

LGBTQ+ RECREATION AND LEISURE

While both popular narratives and research points to a liberalizing of social norms regarding gender and sexuality within dominant recreation and sporting structures—for instance, the relaxing of compulsive masculinity (see Anderson, 2014)—recreation and sport opportunities for LGBTQ+ individuals through mainstream systems remain largely constrained by heteronormativity and the homophobia/transphobia inherent therein (Anderson & Mowatt, 2013; Hargie & Mitchell, 2017; Trussell, 2017). This has influenced the leisure identity, constraints, and negotiation of LGBTQ+ individuals in such spaces. For example, Fletcher (2014) has argued that LGBTQ+ persons "just want to be like everyone else" (p. 460) and that recreation can either enable inclusion based on a shared love of activity and the acceptance of difference or constrain inclusion by reinforcing dominant hierarchies—with the latter often inhibiting LGBTQ+ persons' participation in recreation and leisure activities.

Similarly, Kivel's (1994) and Kivel and Kleiber's (2000) pioneering work showed that LGBTQ+ individuals do not conceptualize their leisure enjoyment differently from heterosexual peers (their research focused on sexual minorities); rather differences in leisure behaviors based in sexual identity are determined by heterosexism and homophobia. Johnson (2013), for example, reflected upon his discomfort having painted his toenails within a park as a challenge to feelings of acceptance within a heteronormative, mainstream recreation space. Such challenges can be particularly salient for trans and gender nonconforming individuals, who often face higher levels of oppression and violence than their cisgender LGBTQ+ peers. Lewis and Johnson's (2011) narrative inquiry on negotiating transgender identity within leisure spaces demonstrated the complex relationship between a leisure space's dominant discourse and personal identity-presentation. They found that gender identity-negotiation may vary based on the (perceived) social structure of recreation and leisure spaces, particularly the perceived politics of openness and queerness of the space. The case of one transwoman's experience in leisure spaces specifically demonstrated identity openness within "friendly" spaces based in a queer politic (for example a queer-friendly coffee shop) and a closed-identity in hegemonic leisure spaces (for example at youth sporting events). In other words, this particular transwoman negotiated and tailored their authentic presentation based on how "safe" they believed their location to be. Johnson (1999) has further referred to this as a game of "hide and seek" in which leisure comfort is predicated by the negotiation of comfort within leisure, experiences of homophobia/transphobia, and the desire for group enclosure.

This negotiation toward comfort in (hetero)normative leisure spaces particularly matters as the ability to successfully engage in recreation and leisure opportunities has been found to have multiple positive effects for the LGBTQ+ population. On the surface, physical activity has been shown to moderate negative physical and psychosocial outcomes associated with anti-LGBTQ+ discrimination (Woodford et al., 2015). LGBTQ-specific leisure spaces have proven particularly salient in creating spaces apart from heteronormativity and homonegativity where identity-development, community development, sense-of-belonging, and anti-heteronormative transgression can flourish (Elling et al., 2003; Gillig et al., 2019; Krane et al., 2002; Litwiller, 2018, 2021; Theriault, 2014). Media representations of leisure and recreational spaces often focus on normative and highly exclusionary environments (i.e., intercollegiate athletics and professional sport). This focus can undermine the importance of general sport-based leisure and recreational spaces and its impact on marginalized populations.

Intersectionality of Identity: Social Categorization and Managerial Impacts

When considering diversity issues related to self-identity and how those may impact the experiences of individuals in social and/or cultural settings, it is important to consider the multitude of identities that individuals may express at any one time, and how the intersection of these identities can impact experience. This concept, known as intersectionality, was first introduced by Crenshaw (1989) and has grown "to engage a range of issues, social identities, power dynamics, legal and political systems, and discursive structures in the United States and beyond" (Carbado et al., 2013, p. 304). Related to and pre-dating the introduction of "intersectionality" as a term, the social categorization framework (Tajfel & Turner, 1979; Turner et al., 1987) examines the ways in which social groups are constructed, their reliance on the individual categorization of identities, and the prioritization of normative identities over non-normative identities in social spaces.

Over the past decade, intersectionality and social categorization theory have been applied to the queer experience within contemporary society, both inside and outside of sport and recreational settings (Anderson et al., 2019, 2021b; Duong, 2012; Fotopoulou, 2012; Knee, 2019). Integrating queer identity with other aspects of identity (e.g., race, religion, athletic identity, etc.) is vital to a comprehensive understanding of queer recreation spaces, participation, and experience. The political pressures that are present within sport and recreation spaces that are inextricably linked to participant identity and representation, and media representations of inclusion within these spaces often fail to fully recognize the layering of identity, instead focusing simply on the aspect of identity that is most salient. A better understanding of the ways in which queer identity can intersect with racial, religious, and athletic identity allows those with vested interest in sport and recreation settings to form a more accurate representation of inclusion (or exclusion) of queer participants in these participatory environments.

Queer Identity and Racial, Religious, and Athletic Identity

The impact of racial identity within sport for participants and athletes has been relatively well-examined throughout the late twentieth and early twenty-first centuries (Bimper & Harrison, 2011; Harrison et al., 2002). Racial impact on participation has been tied to decisions to engage in recreational activities (Coakley, 2021; Sage et al., 2018), program and sport choices (Durant & Sparrow, 1997; Harrison et al., 1999) and the ability to sustain participation in chosen activities.

In conjunction with the impact of racial identity on recreation participation, the intersection of queer identity and race can carry significant impacts on participatory experiences within a variety of sport settings. Generally, researchers have found that LGBTQ+ status and white identity are closely associated (Whitley et al., 2011) and that "racial minorities in the LGBT[Q+] community are likely to experience more negativity and prejudice than are their white peers" (Cunningham, 2019, p. 282). Culturally, identifying as both a racial minority and a sexual minority is also often extremely difficult to navigate, particularly within highly structured and normative organized sport and recreation settings like those most often represented in popular media (intercollegiate athletics, professional, and elite sport).

Individual religious identity is often in direct conflict with minority sexual and gender identities, due to framing of such identities as "sinful" or unvalued in many major religions. In sport and recreation environments that are populated by participants with salient religious identities, this can be problematic for LGBTQ+ participants. Within recreational sport settings, this has been seen in campus recreational sports (Anderson, 2017) as well as in higher levels of elite sport in university settings (Anderson et al., 2019, 2021b). Generally, as the religious identity of participants becomes more salient—for instance, within religiously oriented or church-run recreational leagues—the more likely it is for LGBTQ+ participants to feel unwelcome or to choose not to participate. As discussed below, it is important that professional competencies reinforce the openness of recreation spaces to LGBTQ+ participants, especially in instances of potential conflict as outlined.

Athletic identity and queer identity have also intersected within sport and recreation participants in important ways, both historically and contemporarily. Hegemonic masculinity, which emphasizes and values traits that are traditionally and normatively "male" over those who are traditionally and normatively "female" (Connell, 1987), permeates the culture of sport and physical recreation settings, and this has a tremendous impact on the experiences of participants. For example, female recreation and high-level sporting participants often feel they must over-accentuate their femininity and heterosexuality throughout their sporting participation because the participation itself is often viewed as a "masculine" domain (Anderson et al., 2021b). Female sport and recreation participants are generally forced to defend their sexual identity, under the assumption that they are lesbians, in ways that male sporting participants are not (Blinde & Taube, 1992; Krane, 2012). Media representations of women and girls in high-level sport have also more largely focused on sexuality and sexualized presentation of athletic participants when compared to media representations of high-level male athletes, serving to reinforce hegemonic masculinity in these settings (Clavio & Eagleman, 2011; Daniels & Wartena, 2011). The prevalence of these assumptions has permeated throughout the highest levels of elite sport into the settings of adult and youth recreational sport. There is some evidence that while LGBTQ+ youth may express just as much interest in sport and recreational activity as non-LGBTQ+ youth, that interest significantly deteriorates as youth matriculate through middle school to high school, and is unlikely to be recaptured (Zipp, 2011). Because of this, it is even more important that recreational opportunities outside of elite-level sport actively engage the LGBTQ+ participant population and exhibit programs and policies aimed at curbing the impact of hegemonic masculinity, homophobia, and sexism within recreational sport settings.

COMPETENCIES FOR RECREATION MANAGERS: SERVING QUEER POPULATIONS IN MAINSTREAM RECREATION

Due to the serious impacts that leisure and recreational activities can have on the physical, emotional, social, and mental health of participants, it is necessary for recreation managers (and those otherwise engaged with marginalized populations) to develop managerial competencies to best serve queer populations within sport and recreation spaces. Specifically, recreational sport administrators often employ managerial strategies that focus on inclusion as a general practice, as opposed to targeted activities to increase inclusion for specific marginalized groups (Anderson et al., 2020). While the notion of overarching inclusion within these spaces is laudable, untargeted inclusive recreation aims and programming often lead to reactive (rather than proactive) management and can also result in the creation of spaces that continue to perpetuate built-in inequities, rather than exhibit qualities of inclusion for marginalized participant groups.

Mainstream Recreation Spaces and LGBTQ+ Cultural Competence

Mainstream recreation spaces, while numerous, are sometimes found to be implicitly or explicitly out of reach for LGBTQ+ populations, particularly at-risk youth populations who are far more likely to be homeless and transient than their non-LGBTQ+ counterparts (Durso & Gates, 2012). Additionally, in the neighborhoods and urban areas that are generally more accepting of LGBTQ+ residents, gentrification has caused of myriad issues that has served to effectively make recreation spaces off-limits to many in the LGBTQ+ community—particularly those without the means to engage in gentrified recreation and leisure opportunities. Because of these shortcomings, LGBTQ+ population groups may not be able to take advantage of normative recreational spaces, and as such will look for other outlets for participation, including LGBTQ+-specific recreational sport clubs and spaces, discussed in further detail later in this chapter.

As LGBTQ+-specific recreational sport clubs and spaces are largely, though not exclusively, located in metropolitan areas with larger LGBTQ+

populations, it is important that mainstream recreation opportunities are managed and represented in a way that serves to encourage queer participation. While the politicization of public recreation is not new, it seems to have taken on increased vigor as we have entered the 2020s. The way these spaces are politicized, represented in the media, and managed by staff are all of importance when creating queer-inclusive opportunities. For example, while Title IX of the Education Amendments Act of 1972 has been used effectively to vastly increase the opportunities for young girls and women to participate in sport and recreation at all levels, it is now being relied upon to ensure similar opportunities for transgender participants, with high-profile impacts. As of early 2021, 24 US states had introduced legislation attempting to ban transgender girls and women from participating in high-school sport and other educational and recreational opportunities, with more expected to follow (ACLU, 2021). Given the increased politicization and media attention around the right to participate for queer persons in sport, increased cultural competency for recreational sport managers, inclusionary programs, and the presence of queer-specific sport clubs and spaces are important.

Cultural competence is often cited as a foundational concept for recreation managers wishing to implement inclusive recreation programming (Allison & Hibbler, 2004). Cultural competency can be generally understood as a set of skills that allows administrators, managers, and providers to act in culturally appropriate ways when serving individuals of different cultures than their own. Cultural competence may prove difficult to develop for those that do not have personal experience nor identify as members of the LGBTQ+ community (Theriault, 2017). However, targeted trainings related to the LGBTQ+ community within sport and recreation settings, particularly around vocabulary, attitudes, and programming, have shown efficacy in helping sport and recreation managers to be more confident in their engagement with the queer community (Anderson et al., 2020, 2021a).

Managerial Impact: Administration of Inclusive LGBTQ+ Recreation Programming

As has been explored above, the work of implementing inclusive sport and recreation programming is ongoing, dynamic, and difficult. Many managers within sport and recreation settings have embraced an "open" approach to their programming that equates the elimination of exclusionary criteria to inclusive programming. That is, managers often design programs as openly as possible, relying on that openness to create an atmosphere of inclusion. However, often recreation programming designed in such a way simply reinforces the implicit exclusionary aspects that have historically been a part of sport, including hegemonic masculinity and normative sexual and gender identities. For example, youth recreation programming is very often explicitly delineated along binary "gender" lines (boys/girls) to be "inclusive" of *everyone*. However, what this also serves to do is reinforce the normative gender binary and may serve to discourage transgender or nonbinary youth from participating.

To combat this, research has supported the idea of creating LGBTQ+-specific programs, outreach, advertising, and training for recreational sport managers to create greater knowledge, skills, and competencies related to queer recreational sport (Anderson et al., 2021a). Additionally, where possible, it is often advisable to provide non-gendered participatory opportunities within recreation and sports settings. Some recreational sport managers have expressed reluctance to offer programming aimed at any one demographic group of participants, instead relying on an aim of including everyone, while not making any structural changes to their programs to ensure such inclusion (Anderson et al., 2020). While this reluctance may be understandable, contemporary recreational sport managers must recognize the historical inequities that are present within these participatory settings, including those perpetuated by popular media representations of sport, and how they impact LGBTQ+ participants. Without this recognition, these inequities will continue to perpetuate themselves and continue to create environments where participants with normative sexual and gender identities feel welcomed and secure, while those who are marginalized remain marginalized.

Even when steps are taken to proactively increase the cultural competency of recreation managers and implement programming specifically aimed at inclusion for the LGBTQ+ community, mainstream recreation spaces may not be able to meet all the needs of all queer participants. In those cases, queer (and queer-friendly) sport and recreation participants may turn to recreational spaces that have been specially designed for LGBTQ+ inclusion and participation. These spaces have an important historical and contemporary purpose in the creation of safe and open sport and recreational participation for queer populations.

LGBTQ+-SPECIFIC RECREATIONAL SPORTS

There is little doubt that LGBTQ+ individuals are more visible in today's sporting structures, including popular media representations of sport (Magrath, 2019), and their needs are being examined more closely in terms of cultural competencies within mainstream recreational sporting spaces. Even so, LGBTQ+-specific recreational sport spaces continue to act as important sites of leisure outside of dominant cultural, sporting, and recreational norms. Numerous recreational sport clubs, community organizations, and governing bodies are organized specifically for LGBTQ+ participants and their allies. Such organizations range from community-based sporting organizations centered on a specific sport to nonprofit camps to national and international sport governing bodies. These organizations and opportunities also cover a range of activities including traditional sports (i.e., volleyball, swimming), outdoor experiences (i.e., hiking, summer camp), artistic, cross-disciplinary activities (i.e., dance, cheerleading, choirs), and so on. See table 4.1 for examples of such organizations.

LGBTQ+-specific recreational sport organizations developed with the goals of providing safe spaces for recreational skill-development, competition, and socialization outside the confines of mainstream society and heteronormativity. For example, The Gay Games were founded in 1982 to challenge dominant cultural ideologies of queer persons (namely gay men) as unskilled in sport, while also creating more opportunities for athletic participation for individuals regardless of sexuality, gender, age, or ability. Held every four years, The Gay Games reflect an international event that mixes sporting competition and cultural events. While this sporting event is, quite obviously, structured after the Olympic Games, media coverage and representation of the event has remained niche, even if participation has steadily increased with over 10,000 participants from over 90 countries at the 2018 games in Paris (Federation of Gay Games, 2018). Where popular media representation of the event is present, it is largely superficial and supportive in nature, representing the games as more festival than sport (Lenskyj, 2002), and focused on the local hosting city (Lee et al., 2014). Additionally, local LGBTQ+-specific recreational sport clubs exist to provide comparable benefits to this population at a more localized level, however such clubs receive far less attention from mainstream media outlets.

Motivations for participation in LGBTQ+-specific recreational sports clubs vary from those related to more traditional sporting outcomes (i.e., competition and skill-mastery) to those more specific to queer populations (i.e., community development and counter-hegemony). Pronger (2000) found that these recreational sport clubs provide sites beyond bars where LGBTQ+ persons could socialize and engage in authentic self-expression outside the restrictions of heteronormativity. As such, motivations for participation in such spaces include community and network-building, security, support, and health promotion. Social and popular media has also contributed to the proliferation of these recreational sport clubs. The queer community has a long history of relying on forms of media to create virtual community space and connection (Blackwell et al., 2014), and this reliance has transferred into the creation of physical spaces as well. Those interested in participating in

Table 4.1 Examples of LGBTQ+-Specific Recreational Sport Organizations

Organization Name	Organization Type	Mission Statement	Website
Gotham Volleyball	Community volleyball not-for-profit organization in New York City	"The mission of Gotham Volleyball is to improve the quality of life for GLBTQ individuals by building community through the sport of volleyball."	https://www.gothamvolleyball.org/
North American Gay Volleyball Association (NAGVA)	International not-for-profit volleyball organization—Canada, Mexico, Puerto Rico, United States	"The mission of NAGVA is to provide a safe environment for the LGBTQ+ (and allied) community through the sport of volleyball. We value inclusivity, equality and fair play."	https://nagva.org/
Federation of Gay Games	International governing body for Gay Games	"The mission of the Federation of Gay Games is to promote equality, diversity and inclusion through sport and culture."	https://gaygames.org/
Chicago Metropolitan Sports Association (CMSA)	Community not-for-profit multi-sport organization in Chicago	"The Chicago Metropolitan Sports Association (CMSA) provides inclusive and competitive sports leagues focused on the LGBTQ+ community."	https://chicagomsa.org/
Camp Aranu'tiq	Summer camp for transgender, non-binary, and gender-nonconforming youth	"Camp Aranu'tiq's mission is to build confidence, resilience, and community for transgender & non-binary youth and their families through camp experiences."	https://www.camparanutiq.org/
Team New York Aquatics	Community aquatics not-for-profit organization in New York City	"We are an inclusive community of aquatics athletes that welcomes adults (18 years of age and older) of every ability, sexual orientation, gender identity and expression, race, ethnicity, nationality, and creed."	https://www.tnya.org/
The International Association of Gay/Lesbian Country Western Dance Clubs	International not-for-profit country dance organization with affiliate members across North America and Europe	"To promote country western dancing, activities, and music to all persons without regard to age, sex, gender or gender identity, religion, national or cultural origin, sexual orientation, disability or HIV status."	https://www.iaglcwdc.org/main.php

LGBTQ+-specific recreational sport clubs often initially locate those opportunities via popular social media platforms and connect to other participants via those as well.

Returning to motivations for participation, Place and Beggs (2011) surveyed participants in an LGBTQ+ sports association using the Leisure Motivation Scale and found social factors (i.e., the desire for a social outlet), intellectual factors (i.e., to learn about themselves/expand knowledge), competency mastery (i.e., to demonstrate physical abilities), and stimulus avoidance (i.e., stress relief) as motivational factors. Recently, Mock and colleagues (2022) found that factors of ego involvement, such as identity affirmation and social bonding, predict participation in LGBTQ+-recreational sport organizations. Specifically, as participant identity affirmation needs were increasingly being met by their participation, the more actively participants engaged within these clubs. Importantly, however, limited research delineating motivations within the LGBTQ+ community exists. Place and Beggs (2011) did note that there were no differences in motivations between cisgender men and women, while Krane and Romont (1997) found that women participating in The Gay Games were motivated by the importance of an inclusive sporting environment, self-empowerment, and the social/political nature of the event. One important limitation of this research is the specific motivations of trans and gender-nonconforming participants remain unknown, perhaps suggesting gaps in participation benefits for these populations in favor of sexual minorities.

As these motivations suggest, LGBTQ+-specific recreational sport clubs can be powerful tools in promoting positive psychosocial outcomes by creating safe spaces of socialization that both exist outside of and challenge heteronormative conventions of hegemonic recreation and sporting culture. Such clubs can promote counter-hegemonic norms by questioning conventions in more mainstream sporting spaces and raising broader awareness of issues affecting LGBTQ+ individuals. For example, Jarvis (2018) argued that the presence of The Gay Games can provide sociocultural and discursive benefits to their host location by representing a "disruptive and playful platform to challenge and question dominant heteronormative ideologies, change attitudes towards LGBTQ+ people, and raise awareness about wider gay-related legal battles," while also helping to "contest and undermine prevailing heteronormative and masculine values" (p. 992). At the individual level, participation in LGBTQ+ sport clubs has been found to increase both self-esteem and collective identity, while also leading to an increased likelihood of participants to work toward social change in their communities through increased political activity, being visibly "out," and community engagement (Krane et al., 2002). Research in both LGBTQ+ sport clubs (Jones &

McCarthy, 2010) and LGBTQ+ camp sites (Gillig et al., 2019) found that participants experience a sense-of-belonging to a community for the first time. Specifically, Gillig and colleagues (2019) found that such psychosocial benefits can increase resilience and reduce depressive symptoms in LGBTQ+ youth participants.

Benefits have also been found for heterosexual-identified cisgender men who participate in LGBTQ+-specific sport clubs or leagues. Indeed, while these clubs aim to promote participation outside of hegemonic norms, this does not preclude participation by heterosexual and cisgender individuals. While research has not explored these outcomes for cisgender and heterosexual women, Jarvis (2015) found that heterosexual men who participated on an LGBTQ+ sport team have more inclusive notions of masculinity and diminished cultural homophobia.

While academic scholarship pays increased attention to the motivations for and outcomes from participation in these LGBTQ+-specific recreational sport organizations, their importance is also shared discursively through participant narratives in traditional and new media outlets. While one study (Lee et al., 2014) looked at the ways in which The Gay Games were discussed in media, often reflecting optimistic images of the event, LGBTQ+ sport-organizations and their members utilize multiple media sources to share both their experiences in and the role of such organizations. As one example, Gotham Volleyball, an LGBTQ+ volleyball not-for-profit organization in New York City, actively highlights their members' "coming out stories" on YouTube as an attempt to show solidarity among members and those who remain in the closet in some aspects of their lives. This same organization has detailed its historical development during the early HIV/AIDS epidemic in New York City through the publication of "Love, Death, and Volleyball: The Four-Decade Run of a Trailblazing Gay Sports League" (Stahl, 2019). This article highlights the role the organization plays in breaking heteronormative stigmas, challenging the stigma of being HIV-positive (largely promulgated through popular media at the time), and promoting a collective identity and safe space; particularly during the era of increased homonegativity that defined 1980s America (Anderson, 2014). Examples of this include holding drag volleyball events, fundraising for local LGBTQ+ organizations, raising awareness among topics within the community through forums, and the use of personal and collective narratives to memorialize and recognize queer lives (such as publishing the names and memories of club members who died from AIDS in the 1980s and 1990s to those who died from COVID-19 in 2020). In addition to these macro-level discursive outcomes, a Gotham member also published a cartoon depiction of their personal growth from participating in this organization—emphasizing the unlearning of hegemonic norms, self-discovery, and community development (Varner, 2017). The case of Gotham Volleyball's use of mainstream and alternative discourse outlets demonstrates the ways in which this organization, along with other LGBTQ+-organizations, shows their continued role in community-formulation and counter-hegemonic transgression. An acute awareness of these organizations as more than a recreational sporting-space is clearly articulated through these efforts. Indeed, a discourse of political transgression is actively articulated.

However, while counter-hegemonic outcomes and positive psychosocial development have been found in scholarship and shared discursively by these organizations themselves, some scholars have questioned how transgressive LGBTQ+-specific recreational sport spaces truly are. Pronger (2000) argued that there is a binary between being transformative and assimilationist within LGBTQ+-specific recreational sport clubs. A transformative approach to LGBTQ+ recreational sport clubs represents the counter-hegemonic approach that centers a desire for societal changes, whereas an assimilation approach represents tolerance for (largely cisgender) lesbians and gay men within existing sporting structures. In other words, an assimilationist approach does not desire to subvert mainstream approaches to sport but rather (re)create them within an LGBTQ+ sporting structure. This assimilation approach can be problematic if it subverts the potential transformative nature of alternative discourses that can arise from the political nature of LGBTQ+ recreational sporting practices. Thus, instead of centering a challenge to oppressive systems, such initiatives can favor the improving of individual lives of certain assimilative segments of the LGBTQ+ population (namely cisgender, upper-class, white gay men) within the confines of these systems. Examples of the assimilationist approach include upholding hegemonic masculinity as the standard of sporting practice, essentializing gender difference, promoting competition and winning over community development, and using sport as a means to promote sameness between gender and sexual minorities and their cisgender and heterosexual counterparts.

For example, Gay Games participants, while acknowledging the importance of community-building from participation, did not necessarily view the event as radical. Instead, it represented an opportunity to challenge stereotypes of effeminacy and poor athleticism within gay men (Rowe et al., 2006). While the challenging of stereotyping itself can be a transgressive act, these narratives can also reinforce the devaluing of effeminacy and the dominance of masculinity within both sport and society—maintaining the discourses of sport as a masculine arena. Intersectionally, LGBTQ+-specific recreation spaces have been critiqued as spaces that enforce upper-class, white values to distance themselves from discursively being labeled as outsiders/abnormal. For example, Davidson's (2014) critique of The Gay Games pointedly demonstrated how these events leveraged racism, consumption, and neoliberal ideology to gain acceptance in the mainstream. Indeed, Duggan (2002) critiqued LGBTQ+ spaces, and the gay-rights movement specifically, for their complicacy in individualism, consumption, and privatization. Defining this process as the new homonormativity, Duggan argued these outcomes reinforce and recreate the racism, sexism, and intersectional forms of oppression that are formed in mainstream heteronormative society, while further de-politicizing queerness. Similar arguments were made in opposition to the construction of the world's first LGBTQ+ recreational sport facility, which was viewed largely as a tool to uphold the desires of an assimilationist gay community, while gentrifying more transgressive queerness out of the community (Knee & Anderson, 2021).

Other examples show the ways in which LGBTQ+-specific recreational sport clubs can reify essentialist, biological notions of gender through policy. Policy changes can attempt to promote trans inclusion while also refusing to challenge binary notions of gender—thus rendering individuals who identify outside of the gender binary invisible. Such policies can be written so that they allow for self-identification of gender, thus allowing transwomen to compete with cisgender women and transmen to compete with cisgender men. However, so doing still promotes a gender-segregated approach to sport. In other words, inclusion in these clubs is possible for trans individuals who identify as a binary gender (i.e., transman or transwoman), but not necessarily for those who identify outside of the gender binary (Travers, 2006). In these cases, the heterogendering of sport remains unchallenged. Furthermore, even in these cases of limited trans inclusion, biological notions of gender can prevail in the club's discourse. For example, Caldwell (2007) found that a lesbian soccer team produced transphobic notions of individuals assigned male at birth as having athletic advantages over cisgender women. Such discourses and exclusionary practices led Carter and Baliko (2017) to question the notion of community found in these clubs and suggest a more nuanced conceptualization that recognizes its complexity.

> Participants' narratives reveal that queer sports teams are still experienced as places of refuge from heteronormativity, places to meet people, and places to have fun, but they also highlight the tensions and constraints around bodies, gender expression and sexuality. By viewing a sense of commonality or shared identity as the basis of community, and then, to postulate that this can create a safe place for the community as a whole denies the struggle and exclusionary practices that maintain inequalities, and thus only serves to reinforce membership boundaries that support and protect some at the discomfort, expense and exclusion of others. (p. 705)

CONCLUSION

Spaces for leisure are not only physical sites, but sites of discourse. Recreational sport spaces have long provided an outlet for queer populations to be included and, when managed well, shift/disrupt the heteronormative narratives in sport that are often supported by popular media. Recreation and leisure spaces provide holistic health and well-being benefits that include, but extend beyond, the physical. Recreational sport spaces provide environments for socio-emotional development, identity-building, sense-of-belonging, and work within the political arena to further equity and counter-hegemony. Queer populations, as in all demographic groups, balance a multitude of identities that carry over into sport and recreation participatory settings. Sport and recreation administrators, managers, and participants should be cognizant of the ways in which these identities interact, and the ramifications of such intersectionality to provide services for this population adequately. Administrators can also utilize new media, including social media outlets, to work toward undermining the heteronormative nature of sporting spaces. LGBTQ+ participants often discover recreational space and programs in which to participate through these media-based outlets.

At the same time, the tension between assimilationist and transformative notions of LGBTQ+-specific recreational sport clubs raises important questions about the future of such spaces. As cultural competencies and acceptance of LGBTQ+ persons in mainstream sport and recreation spaces continues to grow, are these "segregated" spaces still necessary? If yes, in what capacity? Optimistically, the potential remains for such organizations and spaces to challenge oppressive structures and sporting norms, particularly when mainstream spaces seem continually resistant to such shifts. Certainly, even given the question over assimilationist desires in scholarship, the case of Gotham Volleyball's self-articulation of their transgressive practices, particularly as demonstrated through their publications in media outlets, demonstrates a contemporary desire for counter-hegemonic outcomes.

The need for more transgressive approaches to recreation and sport remains paramount. While popular discourse suggests the liberalizing of attitudes toward the LGBTQ+ population in the United States, the reality can be much different. This is particularly true for trans and gender nonconforming individuals. More US states have introduced and passed anti-trans laws limiting trans participation in organized sport, recreation, and educational opportunities in 2021 than any other year on record (ACLU, 2021). These laws represent an organized attack on trans youth, particularly trans girls, based on transphobic notions of the athletic advantage and gender-based fearmongering. As such, there is an immediate need for a "queering" of recreation and sport in both programming and media representation. While LGBTQ+-specific recreational sport clubs are not immune from furthering transphobia and transphobic discourse, as seen in the discussion above, the queering of recreation and sporting norms will likely need to start from within. Removing the role of hegemonic masculinity in structuring sport, de-essentializing gender differences, challenging homonormativity, recognizing intersectionality, and questioning the role of segregating sport participation by the gender binary are important first steps. Krane and Barber (2019) argue:

> Queering is more than simply acknowledging the presence of LGBTIQ+ people in sport; to queer sport is to destabilize and transgress heteronormative conventions. It involves seeking alternative social practices, norms, and structures that value all sex, sexual, and gender identities and truly embraces sex, sexual, and gender diversity. . . . To queer sport is to challenge hegemonic power configurations and create new ways to be in sport. (p. 225)

Whether this queering is put into practice on a larger scale within recreation, leisure, and their representation in media as we move through the twenty-first century remains to be seen.

Response

Voices from the Field

Warren Perry

I finally came out as gay over the winter of 2009, at the age of 27. Having grown up in a conservative Christian family in rural North Carolina, I always felt a divide in my life, between my sexuality and my spirituality. It was a place of shame, fear, and isolation, and when I arrived at the University of North Carolina–Chapel Hill to join the swim team, I was even more conscious of keeping that part of me hidden. The only examples of being gay I knew in the late 1990s were from the television series *Will & Grace*, which this jock had a hard time relating to.

But finally, thanks to the support of colleagues in a graduate program, I waved the white flag of trying to kill a part of myself and instead turned to embrace my sexuality. It took some time to reconcile it with my spirituality, but that wholeness eventually came. Helping that was a relocation to New York City.

I moved to New York in the spring of 2011, a time when LGBTQ+ rights were on the move. During my first month in the city, I ran into an old college teammate at a gay bar. He and some of his friends told me about a "gay swim club" and invited me to join them sometime. I never imagined being able to live as a Christian gay man, let alone a gay athlete. In the coming weeks, I attended many of the swim practices with Team New York Aquatics and met a welcoming, affirming group of athletes I still count as friends today.

There are many benefits to participating in a sport or recreational program with queer people. The social, emotional, not to mention physical, aspects abound. Being new to the city, I was looking for ways to fit in, meet people, and do the things I had grown to love. Swimming was something I loved and was good at—it had been an integral part of my identity growing up. But so had being gay, even if I was closeted. Being gay had consumed me behind closed doors, and now living as an out gay man in New York City, I was ready to live those two identities out together—as a gay swimmer.

Team New York Aquatics were good swimmers, too. The old adage that you cannot be gay and athletic didn't exist. Neither was there any shame nor hiding on the pool deck or in the locker room. Everyone there, even the straight allies, supported each other in word and deed. I was starting to live my queer identity more fully because of the safe space the club provided alongside other LGBTQ+ individuals. An ember left alone will eventually go out, but stirred together they become a fire, bringing light into the world.

A lot has changed in the decade since then, though there is always work to be done. But my involvement with a gay swim club supported the personal growth I needed to become the truest version of myself; a whole person who confidently lives out of a united identity. I eventually joined the Board of Directors for Team New York Aquatics, elected as president during the global pandemic. It was a rich time of giving back to the program that so aptly served me in a time of identity development.

REFERENCES

ACLU. (2021, February 26). *The coordinated attack on trans student athletes.* https://www.aclu.org/news/lgbtq-rights/the-coordinated-attack-on-trans-student-athletes/

Allison, M. T. & Hibbler, D. K. (2004). Organizational barriers to inclusion: Perspectives from the recreation professional. *Leisure Sciences, 26*(3), 261–280. https://doi.org/10.1080/01490400490461396

Anderson, A. R. (2017). Recreational sport participant attitudes toward lesbians and gay men: Impact of participation, religion, socio-economic status and sexual identity. *Recreational Sports Journal, 41*(1), 27–41. https://doi.org/10.1123/rsj.2016-0002

Anderson, A. R., Knee, E., & Ramos, W. D. (2020). "I'm not an expert, but . . .": Perspectives on aquatic management for LGBTQ participants. *Recreational Sports Journal, 44*(1), 24–37. https://doi.org/10.1177/1558866120909449

Anderson, A. R., Knee, E., & Ramos, W. D. (2021a). Impact of an LGBTQ campus recreation student employee training initiative on professional competencies. *Recreational Sports Journal. 45*(2), 139–148. https://doi.org/10.1177/15588661211010185

Anderson, A. R., Smith, C. M. L., & Stokowski, S. E. (2019). The impact of religion and ally identity on individual sexual and gender prejudice at an NCAA division II institution. *Journal of Issues in Intercollegiate Athletics, 12*, 154–177.

Anderson, A. R., Stokowski, S., & Turk, M. R. (2021b). Sexual minorities in intercollegiate athletics: Religion, team culture and acceptance. *Sport in Society.* https://doi.org/10.1080/17430437.2021.1933452

Anderson, E. (2014). *21st century jocks: Sporting men and contemporary heterosexuality.* London: Palgrave Macmillan.

Billings, A. & Moscowitz, L. (2018). *Media and the coming out of gay male athletes in American team sports.* New York: Peter Lang.

Bimper, A. Y. & Harrison, L. (2011). Meet me at the crossroads: African American athletic and racial identity. *Quest, 63*(3), 275–288. https://doi.org/10.1080/00336297.2011.10483681

Blackwell, C., Birnholtz, J., & Abbott, C. (2014). Seeing and being seen: Co-situation and impression formation using Grindr, a location-aware gay dating app. *New Media & Society, 17*(7), 1117–1136. https://doi.org/10.1177%2F1461444814521595

Blinde, E. M. & Taub, D. E. (1992). Women athletes as falsely accused deviants: Managing the lesbian stigma. *The Sociological Quarterly, 33*(4), 521–533. https://doi.org/10.1111/j.1533-8525.1992.tb00141.x

Borg, S. (2021, July 14). Explaining the homophobic chant that has Mexico's soccer federation in hot water with FIFA. *Sporting News*. https://www.sportingnews.com/us/soccer/news/homophobic-chant-mexico-soccer-federation-fifa/1vfctcoupayz41bbv8mdwxl108

Carbado, D. W., Crenshaw, K. W., Mays, V. M. & Tomlinson, B. (2013). Intersectionality: Mapping the movements of a theory. *Du Bois Review: Social Science Research on Race, 10*(2), 303–312. https://doi.org/10.1017/S1742058X13000349

Carter, C. & Baliko, K. (2017). 'These are not my people': Queer sport spaces and the complexities of community. *Leisure Studies, 36*(5), 696–706. https://doi.org/10.10.1080/02614367.2017.1315164

Caudwell, J. (2007). Queering the field? The complexities of sexuality within a lesbian-identified football team in England. *Gender, Place and Culture, 14*(2), 183–196. https://doi.org/10.1080/09663690701213750

Clavio, G. & Eagleman, A. N. (2011). Gender and sexually suggestive images in sport blogs. *Journal of Sport Management, 25*(4), 295–304. https://doi.org/10.1123/jsm.25.4.295

Coakley, J. (2021). *Sports in society: Issues and controversies*. McGraw-Hill.

Connell, R. W. (1987). *Gender and power: Society, the person and sexual politics*. Oxford: Blackwell Publishers.

Crenshaw, K. (1989). Demarginalizing the intersection of race and sex: A black feminist critique of antidiscrimination doctrine. *University of Chicago Legal Forum, 1989*(1), Article 8, 139–168.

Cunningham, G. B. (2019). *Diversity and inclusion in sport organizations: A multilevel perspective*. Routledge.

Daniels, E. & Wartena, H. (2011). Athlete or sex symbol: What boys think of media representations of female athletes. *Sex Roles, 65*(7–8), 566–579. https://psycnet.apa.org/doi/10.1007/s11199-011-9959-7

Dattilo, J., Siperstein, G. N., McDowell, E. D., Schleien, S. J., Whitaker, E. B., Block, M. E., Spolidoro, M., Bari, J., & Hall, A. (2019). Perceptions of programming needs for inclusive leisure services. *Journal of Park and Recreation Administration, 37*(4), 70–91. https://doi.org/10.18666/JPRA-2019-9514

Davidson, J. (2014). Racism against the abnormal? The twentieth century Gay Games, biopower and the emergence of homonational sport. *Leisure Studies, 33*(4), 357–378. https://doi.org/10.1080/02614367.2012.723731

Duggan, L. (2002). The new homonormativity: The sexual politics of neoliberalism. In R. Castronovo & D. D. Nelson (Eds.), *Materializing democracy: Towards a revitalized cultural politics* (pp. 175–194). Durham, NC: Duke University Press.

Duong, K. (2012). What does queer theory teach us about intersectionality? *Politics & Gender, 8*(3), 370–386. https://doi.org/10.1017/S1743923X12000360

Durant, T. J. & Sparrow, K. H. (1997). Race and class consciousness among lower- and middle-class Blacks. *Journal of Black Studies, 27*(3), 334–351. https://doi.org/10.1177/002193479702700303

Durso, L. E. & Gates, G. J. (2012). *Serving our youth: Findings from a national survey of service providers working with lesbian, gay, bisexual, and transgender youth who are homeless or at risk of becoming homeless.* Los Angeles: The Williams Institute with True Colors Fund and The Palette Fund.

Elling, A., Knop, P., & Knoppers, A. (2003). Gay/lesbian sports clubs and events: Places of homo-social bonding and cultural resistance? *International Review for the Psychology of Sport, 38*(4), 441–455. https://doi.org/10.1177/1012690203384005

Federation of Gay Games. (2018). *Gay Games X – Paris 2018.* https://gaygames.org/Gay-Games-X

Fletcher, G. (2014). 'You just wanna be like everyone else': Exploring the experiences of gay, lesbian, bisexual and queer sportspeople through a languaging lens. *Annals of Leisure Research, 17*(4), 460–475. https://doi.org/10.1080/11745398.2014.956130

Fotopoulou, A. (2012). Intersectionality queer studies and hybridity: Methodological frameworks for social research. *Journal of International Women's Studies, 13*(2), 19–32.

Gillig, T. K., Miller, L. C., & Cox, C. M. (2019). "She finally smiles . . . for real": Reducing depressive symptoms and bolstering resilience through a camp intervention for LGBTQ Youth. *Journal of Homosexuality, 66*(3), 368–388. https://doi.org/10.1080/00918369.2017.1411693

Hargie, O. D., Mitchell, D. H., & Somerville, I. J. (2017). 'People have a knack of making you feel excluded if they catch on to your difference': Transgender experiences of exclusion in sport. *International Review for the Sociology of Sport, 52*(2), 223–239. https://doi.org/10.1177%2F1012690215583283

Harrison, L., Harrison, C. K., & Moore, L. N. (2002). African American racial identity and sport. *Sport, Education and Society, 7*(2), 121–133. https://doi.org/10.1080/1357332022000018823

Harrison, L., Lee, A., & Belcher, D. (1999). Race and gender differences in sport participation as a function of self-schema. *Journal of Sport and Social Issues, 23*(3), 287–307. https://doi.org/10.1177/0193723599233004

Hernandez, J. (2021, July 21). Why there are few openly gay athletes in men's professional sports. *NPR.* https://www.npr.org/2021/07/21/1018404859/openly-gay-athletes-in-mens-pro-sports-few

Jarvis, N. (2015). The inclusive masculinities of heterosexual men within UK gay sport clubs. *International Review for the Sociology of Sport, 50*(3), 283–300. https://doi.org/10.1177/1012690213482481

Jarvis, N. (2018). The transgressive potential of the 2014 Cleveland/Akron Gay Games legacies. *Event Management, 22*(6), 981–995. https://doi.org/10.3727/152599518X15346132863210

Johnson, C. W. (1999). Living the game of hide and seek: Leisure in the lives of gay and lesbian young adults. *Leisure/Loisir, 24*(3–4), 255–278. https://doi.org/10.1080/14927713.1999.9651268

Johnson, C. W. (2013). Feminist masculinities: Inquiries into the leisure, gender, and sexual identity. In V. Freysinger, S. Shaw, K. Henderson, & D. Bialeschki (Eds.), *Leisure, women, and gender* (pp. 245–258). State College, PA: Venture Publishing.

Jones, L. & McCarthy, M. (2010). Mapping the landscape of gay men's football. *Leisure Studies, 29*(2), 161–173. https://doi.org/10.1080/02614360903261487

Kivel, B. D. (1994). Lesbian and gay youth and leisure: Implications for practitioners and researchers. *Journal of Park and Recreation Administration, 12*(4), 15–28.

Kivel, B. D. & Kleiber, D. A. (2000). Leisure in the identity formation of lesbian/gay youth: Personal, but not social. *Leisure Sciences, 22*(4), 215–232. https://doi.org10.1080/01490409950202276

Knee, E. (2019). Gay, but not inclusive: Boundary maintenance in an LGBTQ space. *Leisure Sciences, 41*(6), 499–515. https://doi.org/10.1080/01490400.2018.1441767

Knee, E. & Anderson, A. R. (2021). Gentrification of the (leisure) mind: Organizational justifications and community concerns of a proposed LGBTQ2S sport and recreation center. *Journal of Homosexuality*, Advanced Online Publication. https://doi.org/10.1080/00918369.2021.1984752

Krane, V. (2012). We can be athletic and feminine, but do we want to? Challenging hegemonic femininity in women's sport. *Quest, 53*(1), 115–133. https://doi.org/10.1080/00336297.2001.10491733

Krane, V. & Barber, H. (2019). Creating a new sport culture: Reflections on queering sport. In V. Krane (Ed.), *Sex, gender, and sexuality in sport: Queer inquiries* (pp. 224–237). London and New York: Routledge.

Krane, V., Barber, H., & McClung, L. R. (2002). Social psychological benefits of Gay Games participation: A social identity theory explanation. *Journal of Applied Sport Psychology, 14*(1), 27–42. https://doi.org/10.1080/10413200209339009

Krane, V. & Romont, L. (1997). Female athletes' motives and experiences during the Gay Games. *International Journal of Sexuality and Gender Studies, 2*(2), 123–138. https://doi.org/10.1023/A:1026368527807

Lee, S., Kim, S., & Love, A. (2014). Coverage of the Gay Games from 1980–2012 in US newspapers: An analysis of newspaper article framing. *Journal of Sport Management, 28*(2), 176–188. https://doi.org/10.1123/jsm.2012-0243

Lenskyj, H. J. (2002). Gay Games or gay Olympics? Implications for lesbian inclusion. *Canadian Women Studies/Les Cahiers de la Femme, 21*(3), 24–28.

Lewis, S. T. & Johnson, C. W. (2011). "But it's not that easy": Negotiating (trans) gender expressions in leisure spaces. *Leisure/Loisir, 35*(2), 115–132. https://doi.org/10.1080/14927713.2011.567062

Litwiller, F. (2018). 'You can see their minds grow': Identity development of LGBTQ youth at a residential wilderness camp. *Leisure/Loisir, 42*(3), 347–361. https://doi.org/10.1080/14927713.2018.1535276

Litwiller, F. (2021). Youth perspectives on genderplay recreation programming: Insights and critiques on identity development theories. *Leisure Sciences*, Advanced Online Publication. https://doi.org/10.1080/01490400.2021.1921638

Magrath, R. (2019). *LGBT athletes in the sports media*. Palgrave Macmillan.

Markwell, K. (1998). Playing queer: Leisure in the lives of gay men. In D. Rowe & G. Lawerence (Eds.), *Tourism, leisure, sport: Critical perspectives* (pp. 112–123). Rydalmere, NSW: Hodder Education.

Mock, S. E., Misener, K., & Havitz, M. E. (2022). A league of their own? A longitudinal study of ego involvement and participation behaviors in LGBT-focused community sport. *Leisure Sciences, 44*(6), 750–767. https://doi.org/10.1080/01490400.2019.1665599

Place, G. & Beggs, B. (2011). Motivation factors for participation in GLBT sports league. *Journal of Homosexuality, 58*(10), 1409–1420. https://doi.org/10.1080/00918369.2011.614909

Pronger, B. (2000). Homosexuality and sport – Who's winning? In J. McKay, M. A. Messner, & S. Sabo (Eds.), *Masculinities, gender relations, and sport* (pp. 222–224). London: Sage.

Rowe, D., Markwell, K., & Stevenson, D. (2006). Exploring participants' experiences of the Gay Games: Intersections of sport, gender and sexuality. *International Journal of Media & Cultural Politics, 2*(2), 149–165. https://doi.org/10.1386/macp.2.2.149/1

Sage, G. H., Eitzen, D. S., & Beal, B. (2018). *Sociology of North American sport.* Oxford University Press.

Stahl, D. (2019, April 18). Love, death and volleyball: The four-decade run of a trailblazing gay sports league. *Narratively.* https://narratively.com/volleyball-gay-sports-league/

Tajfel, H. & Turner, J. C. (1979). An integrative theory of intergroup conflict. In S. Worshel & W. G. Austin (Eds.), *The social psychology of intergroup relations* (pp. 33–47). Monterey, CA: Brooks-Cole.

Theriault, D. (2014). Organized leisure experiences of LBGTQ youth: Resistance and oppression. *Journal of Leisure Research, 46*(4), 448–461. https://doi.org/10.1080/00222216.2014.11950336

Theriault, D. (2017). Implementation of promising practices for LGBTQ inclusion: A multilevel process. *Journal of Park and Recreation Administration, 35*(3), 122–134. https://doi.org/10.18666/JPRA-2017-V35-I3-7702

Travers, A. (2006). Queering sport: Lesbian softball leagues and the transgender challenge. *International Review for the Sociology of Sport, 41*(3), 431–446. https://doi.org/10.1177/1012690207078070

Trussell, D. E. (2017). Parents' leisure, LGB young people and "when we were coming out". *Leisure Sciences, 39*(1), 42–58. https://doi.org/10.1080/01490400.2016.1151844

Turner, J. C., Hogg, M. A., Oakes, P. J., Reichter, S. D., & Wetherell, M. S. (1987). *Rediscovering the social group: A self-categorization theory.* Cambridge, MA: Basil Blackwell.

Varner, W. (2017, October 11). What I learned playing in a gay volleyball league. *BuzzFeed News.* https://www.buzzfeednews.com/article/willvarner/things-i-learned-playing-in-a-gay-volleyball-league

Watson, B. & Ratna, A. (2011). Bollywood in the park: Thinking intersectionally about public leisure space. *Leisure/Loisir, 35*(1), 71–86. https://doi.org/10.1080/14927713.2011.549198

Whitley, B. E., Childs, C. E., & Collins, J. B. (2011). Differences in Black and White American college students' attitudes toward lesbians and gay men. *Sex Roles, 64*(5–6), 299–310. https://doi.org/10.1007/s11199-010-9892-1

Woodford, M. R., Kulick, A., & Atteberry, B. (2015). Protective factors, campus climate, and health outcomes among sexual minority college students. *Journal of Diversity in Higher Education, 8*(2), 73–87. https://doi.org/10.1037/a0038552

Zipp, J. F. (2011). Sport and sexuality: Athletic participation by sexual minority and sexual majority adolescents in the U.S. *Sex Roles, 64*, 19–31. https://doi.org/10.1007/s11199-010-9865-4

Chapter 5

A "Permissible Prejudice"

An Exploration of the Systemic Ableist Barriers to Sport and Leisure Activities for Disabled People

Andrew M. Colombo-Dougovito
and Suzanna Rocco Dillon

In 1999, Nancy J. Chodorow—in critiquing the laisse faire cultural response to homophobia—was first to define *permissible prejudices* and identify them as "natural" in society; meaning that society excuses any reason for the dislike, or discrimination, or hatred of another as a rational, and expected, (re)action. Hatred and discrimination are excused or rationalized, in a way, to continue to prioritize the unoppressed. These permissible prejudices are confined not only to sexuality but can also be witnessed across every other form of discrimination—from sexism to racism to ageism—that exists within society. Another form of "-ism" that is broadly accepted within society, even by those advocating for social change, is that of ableism. In an ever-evolving definition, Talila A. Lewis (2021), an abolitionist community lawyer working to prevent and correct wrongful convictions of disabled persons, suggests that ableism is:

> A system that places value on people's bodies and minds based on societally constructed ideas of normality, intelligence, excellence, desirability, and productivity. These constructed ideas are deeply rooted in anti-Blackness, eugenics, misogyny, colonialism, imperialism and capitalism.

Perhaps, most importantly, Lewis implies that "you do not have to be disabled to experience ableism."

As society grapples with purposefully ingrained systemic oppressions that engulf constructed categories of gender and race, discrimination of disabled persons (or those society deems as lacking ability) tends to go unchecked; or as Mia Mingus, a leader in transformative and disability justice, said, "Ableism is connected to all our struggles because it undergirds notions of whose bodies are considered valuable, desirable and disposable" (2011, para. 18). Indeed, as we in the United States celebrate the 30th anniversary of the passing of the Americans with Disabilities Act of 1990 (ADA) (Pub. L. No. 101-336, 104 Stat. 328), it has become evident that little noticeable progress has been made in terms of the accessibility of US society (Abrams, 2020). Though access is much improved from the decades prior to 1990, most disabled people are left to fight for access for even the most basic of civil rights. As American disability rights activist Judy Heumann argued, "In the past, disability has been a cause for shame. This forced acceptance of second-class citizenship has stripped us, as disabled people, of pride and dignity" (1988, p. 74). Given that, within the United States, nearly one in four individuals are classified as having a disability (Centers for Disease Control, 2018), it is shameful that society continues to perpetuate such prejudice. Individually, the stigma related to disability is in some part rooted in the confrontation of human fragility and fears of potential loss (Hahn, 1988; Rauscher & McClintock, 1997); it is connected to a desire to conform to an ideal normal that is perpetuated by cultural expectations (Baglieri & Lalvani, 2019). We do not need to be told "disability is bad"—this permissible prejudice persists unseen and, somewhat, unintentionally.

DEFINING "ABILITY": DISABLISM WITHIN SPORT

In his examination of "normalcy," Lennard Davis (1999), an American scholar in disability studies, described the United States as "the United States of Ability" to depict the centering of ideal forms of movement and function that are inescapable, particularly among euro-centric Western cultures. This hyper focus on "ability," as well as its relationship with individuality and autonomy, has come to be known as "the Empire of the Normal" (Couser, 2000). Within the "Empire," those traits that society idolizes, such as whiteness, maleness, heteronormativity, are centered and prioritized within cultural representations. We see these representations repeated in media such as newspapers and magazines, as well as on television and social media, and media that perpetuates these images has a significant role in shaping those views (Rees et al., 2019). Without intentional thought, we are shown who is important and who is not.

Sport, particularly for those with disabilities, has been suggested as a potential vehicle for navigating the "Empire" and transcending its hierarchy (Berger, 2005). Moreover, disability, as a construct, challenges the perception of a "normal" body by "provid[ing] insight into the fact that all bodies are socially constructed—those societal attitudes and institutions determine far greater than biological fact that representation of the body's reality" (Siebers, 2001, p. 737). As the construct of ability is tied closely to the physical self, sport can provide opportunities for disabled persons to demonstrate their affinities, thus challenging societal constructs of ability and, ultimately, worth.

While sport for disabled persons has allowed for demonstrations of athleticism, the media representation of such achievement has done little on its own to shift societal views of disability. Often, this discourse results in those with impairments being defined as "super" (Howe, 2011)—or more commonly "supercrip"—that "implies a stereotyping process that requires an individual to 'fight against [their] impairment' [to] overcome it and achieve unlikely success" (Silva & Howe, 2012, p. 175). In short, instead of society recognizing the ability of disabled athletes, accomplishments are explained away by defining the achievement despite their disability—thus invalidating the achievement all together. Even among disabled athletes, "supercrip" narratives are internalized and athletes continue to seek an able-bodied ideal (Berger, 2008; Hardin & Hardin, 2004) by internalizing a presumed "hierarchy of disability" (Schell & Duncan, 1999).

Given the ability of sport to reflect society as both a place for the reproduction of dominant societal values and a place for a resistance of those views (Donnelly, 1996), the impacts of sport on disabled bodies or the broader disability rights movement remains elusive and, likely, far more nuanced than typically acknowledged (Berger, 2008). In the last decade, there has been an increase in the media commodification of the Paralympics (Silva & Howe, 2012) and a hypervisibility of disability among the coverage of sport for those with disabilities (Pullen et al., 2019), drawing attention to both greater recognition to the needs of disabled persons and an increased presence of "inspiration porn" (Martin, 2019), which is portraying individuals with disabilities as inspirational wholly or in part based on the basis of their disability for the commodification of non-disabled audiences. Amid this increased visibility, ableist notions of ability are rampant and inseparable from the broader hegemonic views about gender, race and ethnicity, sexual orientation, class, and age.

Appallingly, the interweaving of Paralympic sport into broader nationalistic views of identity by media outlets have led to further entrenchment of ableism and have spawned more broad depictions of the "able-disabled" (Pullen et al., 2020a, p. 727). Among portrayals of "triumph over" and "overcoming" disability, through media representation, society attempts to reconcile such depictions of "ability" with deep-rooted stereotypes of disability, often dismissing an individual's disabled identity and categorizing them among the "able-disabled": still not as worthy as able-bodied peers, but less disabled than "non-athletic" disabled people. More broadly, this ongoing evolution of recognizing the achievements of disabled persons while simultaneously excusing or ignoring their impairment demonstrates the ever-changing societal construction of "ability"—further demonstrating the complexity of narratives about disability and showing that definitions are not static but active reflections of societal values (Schalk, 2016).

A CRITICAL DISABILITY LENS

In 1992, British disability rights activist Mike Oliver argued that research has failed disabled people in at least three ways; namely, research has failed to:

> accurately capture and reflect the experience of disability from the perspective of disabled people themselves;
> provide information that has been useful to the policy making process and has contributed little to improving the material conditions under which disabled people live;
> and
> acknowledge the struggles of disabled people themselves and to recognize that disability is not simply a medical or welfare issue, but a political one.

In the 30 years since Oliver's call for change, little has been done to improve the poor progress regarding outcomes for disabled people. Among those researchers who focus on movement (i.e., kinesiologists), narratives about disability and its analysis are guided primarily by those that would disrelish identifying as "disabled." The cultural values, therefore, of disabled persons are often absent in the exploration of the construction of sport and the influence it has on the daily lives of its participants. This, however, does not mean to infer those presumptions of the meaning of sport for disabled persons wasn't subsumed by non-disabled scholars. When these inferences have occurred, they traditionally have been studied through the lens of "inclusion"—though, "integration" has been suggested as a more honest identifier (Haegele, 2019). As a result of the limited influence of disabled persons, inclusion research, as it relates to sport or physical activity, has examined the ways disabled persons can most readily fit within existing structures of sport or activity without fundamentally changing the construction of that sport or activity. Indeed, under the predominant neoliberal-ableism (Goodley, 2017) in Western cultures where disabled individuals and their allies have their rights eroded under neoliberal governments, inclusion policies "illustrate a utopian vision whereby anyone can be included, but in practice due to the emphasis on market-based values who can become included is often very narrow" (Hammond et al., 2019, p. 312).

Such policies are reliant on impairment-centered practices (Townsend et al., 2018) and perpetuate a medicalized representation of disability (Weiller-Abels et al., 2021). In 1997, adapted physical activity scholar Karen DePauw urged the field to move

> beyond accommodations [e.g., "allowing" disabled individuals to participate in sport but not changing the sport, itself—in other words, *inclusion*][1] to transformation, which requires that sport, as a social institution, undergo fundamental change. (p. 426)

Indeed, for sport to reach a point that transcends our present state of "inclusion," it will take a broader societal shift in the construction of *ability*. Ultimately, this will not occur without the centering of disabled expertise in narratives about ability within sport. Moreover, this transformation will need to consider the intersectionality of such expertise and how those experiences cannot be viewed separately from the neoliberal-ableism pervasive in society that reinforces the stigma of disability.

Therefore, to better understand the imposed barriers that ableism enacts upon disabled persons attempting to engage in sport or leisure activities, and the role of sport in navigating such inclusive barriers, we chose to conduct a qualitative meta-synthesis to thematically examine the overarching similarities among the firsthand accounts of disabled persons. In doing so, we expected to gather recollections of how sport assists disabled persons in their self-identification as well as how ableism influences their participation, thus providing a guide for future inquiries.

A THEMATIC META-SYNTHESIS

Following the prescribed measures to ensure the trustworthiness of the findings by Walsh and Downe (2005), this thematic meta-synthesis of the literature focused on the perspectives and experiences of disabled persons attempting to participate in physical activity, whether it be organized sport, leisurely recreation, or anything in between. Prior to conducting the literature search, we agreed to the search terms used to identify qualitative literature for inclusion in the meta synthesis. The specific search terms, along with the inclusion criteria, guided the gathering of articles and synthesis of their findings. We also defined our paradigms as researchers and situated our own identities within the analysis.

Article Search Procedure

Potential journal articles, published between 1990 and 2021, were initially located via online indexing system searches. We conducted an initial search of the literature using the indexing systems/research platforms of PsychINFO, Proquest, PubMed, SocINDEX, SPORTDiscus, Scopus, Science Direct, and SAGE Global Journals Online. The search results were generated using the following search strategy:

> disability or disabled or impairment or impaired or handicap or special need;
> physical activity or exercise or sport or recreation or sports for persons with disabilities;
> and
> perceptions or experience or barrier or access.

Criteria for Inclusion

The following inclusion criteria were selected by us and were reviewed by an external panel of experts. The outlined procedure required that articles:

> be published between January 1990 and May 2021;
> be published in English language journals;
> be located in peer-reviewed periodical publications; and
> utilize a qualitative research design (i.e., qualitative or mixed methods design).

Reviews of literature and quantitative studies were excluded from the review. Only articles that met these criteria were eligible for evaluation.

Title and Abstract Review

Research studies identified through the initial search procedure were then evaluated using a multi-step process. First, we conducted an identity-hidden title and abstract review on the potential studies identified in the initial search. This identity-hidden review process was conducted using Rayyan software (Ouzzani et al., 2016), which removed 44 duplicate entries and aided in the review process. In the initial review of 701 potential articles, we agreed on 39 articles; were undecided on 42 articles (i.e., either Andrew or Suzanna thought the article should be included/excluded but the other wasn't sure either way); and conflicted on 30 articles (i.e., Andrew or Suzanna thought the article should be included and the other thought it should be excluded). In the second step, we conducted an open review of the 42 articles marked as undecided and 30 articles marked as conflicted. This second review resulted in the inclusion of 27 additional studies for consideration for full article review. In 62 cases, we agreed on the inclusion of the article. In four cases, both of us were unsure if the article should or should not be included—so, we included these in the full-text analysis. At the end of the second review, no articles remained in conflict.

Inter-Rater Agreement

In the third step, we independently conducted a full article review on the 66 identified articles to confirm whether the studies met the criteria for inclusion using a dichotomous scale (yes or no). The resulting 34 articles were confirmed as meeting the inclusion criteria and were, thus, included in the thematic meta-synthesis. In instances of disagreement, articles were re-assessed until an inter-rater agreement of 100% was reached. There were no instances of disagreement during the review; hence, there was 100% inter-rater consensus.

Data Extraction and Analysis

After the full text review, we further reviewed each of the 34 articles to extract primary source data from each recorded instance of participant-provided data within each individual study. During data extraction, it became apparent to us that three of our included studies (Gaskin et al., 2010; Rimmer et al., 2004; Taub & Greer, 1998) did not have the necessary data needed for this analysis; therefore, they were excluded. This resulted in 31 articles to extract data that led to gathering 678 individual quotations. The included quotes ranged from a few words to multiples of sentences. In certain cases, smaller quotes from the same person were aggregated into one quotation.

We then independently heuristically examined each data entry for meaning considering its context. This resulted in a codebook of 45 different individual codes which were discussed and defined—after the initial round of coding, entries were reread for any additional instances not captured during the first round of coding or for instance of quotes that needed to be recoded. Following guidance from Jensen and Allen (1996), we explored each of the included studies for credibility, auditability, fittingness, and confirmability. Specifically, fittingness and confirmability were used to examine how studies related or were dissonant from each other and ensure our processes were coherent for outside observers, respectively. These relationships among the coded entries were discussed until we found aggreement. Resultingly, three broad themes were developed.

(1) *Ableism within and about sport and physical activity is rampant and pervasive—or—"Sometimes you figure you got to become a second-class citizen."*

(2) *Sport can serve as a mediator to psycho-environmental barriers yet is missing justice-oriented approaches—or—"Tak[ing] a break from pretending to be normal."*

(3) *Intersectional examinations of disability are absent and study samples are homogenous, prioritizing certain disabilities thus reinforcing an existing disability hierarchy—or—"They simply cannot help being prejudiced."*

These themes will be described in the following paragraphs—the framing of the findings will be rooted in a broader exploration of disability, sport, and media representation.

FINDINGS: "HOUSTON, WE HAVE A PROBLEM"

D. L. Stewart, a scholar known for their research on minoritized groups in postsecondary education, underscored that "sport serves an arena wherein a multitude of forces are played against and upon individual athletes in the service of competition and winning" (2018, p. 42). More globally, "sport is a part of society and, in some ways, reflects the society (and culture) in which it is embedded" (DePauw, 1997, p. 418). Thus, when we look upon sport with an understanding that the broader cultural issues of ableism are interwoven into the fabric of sport, the injustice of our present construction of sport becomes evident. Zhang and Haller (2013), in examining the role of media in shaping a person's view of their own disability, showed how positive coverage of disability can lead disabled persons to affirmations of their disabled identity; conversely, negative coverage reinforced denials of a disabled identity. Given media's mirrored reflection of society, however, there exists a paucity of positive media representations (Kolotouchkina et al., 2021; Rees et al., 2019). As we reviewed the gathered data from the assembled articles, conflicting patterns of inequity and encouragement were evident across the coded data. It also became apparent how broader systemic issues relating to the inadequacies of knowledge generation continue to impede the ability to generate benefit for those on the margins of an already marginalized population.

Descriptive Findings of Analyzed Studies

Among the thirty-one included articles, all but four (87%) were from researchers situated in global North countries; of those originating in or about the global South, data were shared from Brazil (Haegele et al., 2018),

Australia (Ballas et al., 2022; Mahy et al., 2010), and South Africa (Conchar et al., 2016). Of those from the global North, seven (22%) were from Canada (Bonnell et al., 2021; Jachyra et al., 2021; Jackson et al., 2019; James et al., 2018; Johnston et al., 2015; Raymond, 2019; Rolfe et al., 2009), seven (22%) were from the United Kingdom (i.e., England & Scotland) (Collar & Ellis-Hill, 2019; Canton et al., 2012; Cox & Bartle, 2020; Fitzgerald, 2005; Hackett, 2003; Moffet & Paul, 2019; Richardson et al., 2017), two (6%) were from the Netherlands (Bloemen et al., 2015; van Schijndel-Speet et al., 2014), two (6%) were from Sweden (Barns et al., 2015; Lassenius et al., 2013), eight (25%) were from the United States (Autry & Hanson, 2001; Bendini, 2000; Bendini & Anderson, 2005; Blinde & McClung, 1997; McLoughlin et al., 2017; Pack et al., 2017; Taliaferro & Hammond, 2016; Wilhite et al., 1999), and one study (3%) concurrently recruited participants from the United States, the United Kingdom, and Canada (Javorina et al., 2020). In looking at these studies in aggregate, the oldest were from the United States (Blinde & McClung, 1997; Wilhite et al., 1999) while many of the most recent articles were from Canada or the United Kingdom. This highlights two important factors in understanding the pervasiveness of ableism: (1) much of our understanding of ableism is rooted in euro-centric, Western thought generated either in the United States or the United Kingdom; and (2) an increase in the studies from a broader array of countries around the world is a positive trend, yet further demonstrates the lagging acceptance of US-based researchers toward recognizing the expertise of lived experience.

Nine (29%) of the included articles were published prior to 2010, though only two were published prior to 2000 and none were published prior to 1997 despite searching for articles published as early as 1990. The increase in publications after 2015 (19/31, 61%), following the Paralympic Games in Sochi and London, shows the increasing acknowledgment of the need to capture the lived experiences of disabled athletes, particularly in exploring the factors that greatest influence their movement opportunities. However, only a few authors of the included studies acknowledge their research paradigm, and many provided too little information for their paradigm to be determined by us. Of the nine articles (29%) that included enough information, two (6%) centered findings within the social model of disability (Cox & Bartle, 2020; Rolfe et al., 2009); four (13%) examined data using stigma theory (Bedini, 2000; Bedini & Anderson, 2005; Collard & Ellis-Hill, 2019; Raymond, 2019); two (6%) rooted findings in the Social Ecological model (Taliaferro & Hammond, 2016; Wilhite et al., 1999); and one (3%) grounded their work in a post-structural feminist framework that incorporated Foucault's Concepts of Surveillance (Autry & Hanson,

2001). The remaining articles (22/31; 71%) did not mention a theoretical or conceptual framework for the analysis, though several did acknowledge their general worldview such as interpretivist (Pack et al., 2017; Javorina et al., 2020; Richardson et al., 2017) or constructivist (Bloemen et al., 2015; Bonnell et al., 2021).

Across the included studies, participants ranged in age from 8 to 80 years and were predominantly male. Only two studies (Bedini & Anderson, 2005; Rolfe et al., 2009) focused primarily on female participants; no studies identified participants outside of the gender binary. This homogeneity among sample populations not only within studies but also across studies demonstrates that the gathered findings, though covering the lifespan, may miss the potential "double oppression" (Deegan & Brooks, 1985; Fine & Asch, 1988; Hargreaves, 2000; Wendell, 1989) that impacts disabled women or disabled individuals who do not identify within the gender binary or are transgender. Remaining consistently homogenous, unsurprisingly, study samples were overwhelmingly white; though, several articles did not include enough information about the racial or ethnic breakdown of their sample to determine the makeup of the included participants. These findings, though subtle, suggest that the included data may miss the multiple oppressions faced by racially or ethnically marginalized groups—demonstrating the possible, often unintentional impacts of racism embedded within the data collection and analysis of most academic scholarship (Zuberi & Bonilla-Silva, 2008).

Among the disabilities represented in the studies, participants in the included studies were primarily those with a physical disability, such as cerebral palsy, para- or quadriplegia, spina bifida, polio, and arthritis, which included a mix of perspectives from individuals whose disability was acquired and those that were congenital. Outside of physical impairments, one study (Collard et al., 2019) focused on those with epilepsy, one (Haegele et al., 2018) included those with visual impairments, three (Mahy et al., 2010; Taliaferro & Hammond, 2016; van Schijndel-Speet et al., 2014) focused on those with intellectual disabilities, and one (Jachyra et al., 2021) included perspectives from autistic participants. Overwhelmingly, data were generated through semi-structured interviews or focus groups. Only two studies (James et al., 2018; Johnston et al., 2015) included observations along with interviews; and one study (Moffet & Paul, 2019) used a mixed methods approach. The types of physical activity or sport explored were quite broad with most studies focusing a broadly defined "physical activity" or "recreation" and were primarily in amateur settings; only three studies exclusively included a sample of "elite" athletes (i.e., those that competed in organized competition or at the professional level such as Paralympic athletes) (Ballas et al., 2022; McLoughlin et al., 2017; Pack et al., 2017).

Theme 1: *Ableism within and about Sport and Physical Activity Is Rampant and Pervasive—or—"Sometimes You Figure You Got to Become a Second-Class Citizen"*

Examining sport using a lens centered in the abject understanding that oppressions are a design feature of the broader system and not an unfortunate flaw takes the traditional inquiry regarding sport for those with disabilities a step beyond the usual explorations of this phenomena. As we explored the gathered data, barriers rooted in the ableist notions of worth and value were abundant. Participants across the included studies experienced external barriers such as a cost burden, lack of opportunity, and limited physical access as well as internalized barriers such as loss of dignity and shame. Additionally, the influence of social stigma was apparent as nearly each study included examples of policing disabled people, ignorance of disabled bodies, and bullying—all perpetuated from the broader beliefs held by society and the representation of disability.

Given that the primary disability included were physical disabilities, cost as an identified barrier is not surprising. As one participant put it:

> At the beginning every sport you begin to play, you need adapted equipment and that all requires money to get it to fit to your body, and chairs run about 4 or 5 grand each so you have to find that money to do that. . . . Once you get really into it you realize it (is) an expensive hobby. (McLoughlin et al., 2017)

Though it is not uncommon for individuals to have to purchase specialized equipment to participate in many different sports, disabled persons are at a greater disadvantage due to limited societal supports that allow for the ability to have discretionary income. As this participant stated, "If you have a disability, you're less likely to have a job, less likely to have a house, less likely to have a partner, less likely to have a family. That's real discrimination, they're big things" (Cox & Bartle, 2020, p. 8). This added cost burden highlights the broader societal issues related to the acceptance and accommodation for those with disabilities. Unemployment among disabled persons is much higher than that of non-disabled persons (US Department of Labor, 2021), which directly impacts what types of activity an individual can engage in or access (particularly if transportation is needed).

More broadly, if individuals can afford the added cost burden of many physical activities, there continues to be limited opportunities available for disabled individuals to participate in sport or activity. As participant Katie (Wilhite et al., 1999) summarized, "There are so many spaces [. . .] that are inaccessible, that talk about disability. [. . .] I was constantly showing up to events that they hadn't made accessible." Demonstrating the broader constraints that ableism places on society, a lack of representation or inclusion of disabled people in the development of movement opportunities is mired in an ignorance of disabled people and their needs. Participant Nancy (Rolfe et al., 2009) recollected one example of this ignorance:

> A sighted guide is essential [for me when I use the gym]. A sighted guide is where you get the blind person [to] hold your elbow. And [the sighted guide] just guides them around. Guide dog etiquette is essential too. . . . A lot of the time I found some of the [gym] monitors . . . unfortunately, were saying, "Well [guide dog's name], come [do] this and do that." . . . What they're supposed to [do] is tell me [how] to guide [my dog].

As media representation continues to perpetuate and reinforce the otherizing of disability (Goethals et al., 2022), it is foreseeable that those in the environment with the power to influence a disabled person's success are often poorly equipped to complete the task effectively. This can lead to individuals "policing" the disabled person and their place in physical activity settings. Participant Cindy (Bedini & Anderson, 2005) noted, "Well, I deserve to have the rights to do that [recreate]. Um . . . maybe I can't do all of them by maybe I can if I want to." Participant Marsha (Bedini & Anderson, 2005) stated, "Some people think, you know, that just being handicapped means you can't do anything at all." Ultimately, this increase in policing can cause potential safety issues, particularly for those that are able to "hide" their disability. As a participant with epilepsy, reflecting on their swimming experiences, described, "My experience with that [disclosure to a lifeguard] is that I'd be, not embarrassed, that's the wrong word. But if I tell them, I'd feel like they'd be staring at me the whole time I'm in there" (Collard & Hill, 2019). Another participant (Richardson et al., 2017)—describing the overwhelming fat-phobia embedded into physical activity settings—said:

> I went in as a guide to find out what the prices were and have a look round to see who was there. I can actually remember . . . the look on the face of the receptionist like "Christ!" and one of the membership guys came round. . . . I didn't go to the gym that day, I went back the next say at the crack of dawn 6 o'clock . . . you can kind of, in the gym you can feel the eyes on the back of your head; "what's fatty doing in the gym?"

Given the abundance of evidence to the prevalence of increased weight among those with disabilities, it is possible that many individuals face oppression that is related to their disability as well as their weight. As connection of weight and health is rooted in the ableist notion of an "able-bodied ideal," it is worth considering that, though common among those with disabilities, discrimination based on weight may operate separately, yet parallel to, the discrimination based on disability. In whatever ways these factors may be constructed in society more broadly or influence access for people who are visibly divergent from the assumed norm, social stigma associated to disability heavily influence disabled persons ability to engage with physical activity and sport. Knowing that through participation, particularly through media outlets, the representation of disabled people can assist in dismantling the prejudice of ableism (Ellis & Goggin, 2015). Without authentic representation, however, people are left with stereotyped versions of their future self. As one participant reflected on their transition after acquiring their disability: "I didn't go out for months because I could not stand the stares and being continually ignored. . . . You just feel completely worthless and abandoned" (Richardson et al., 2017).

Rooted heavily in the idea of *dignity*, participants across the studies reflected on how their experiences left them consistently feeling less than and espoused broader internalized ableist beliefs. One participant, describing their acquired disability and a loss of dignity, said:

> Sometimes I wish it would have happened all at once, because I think that might have been easier to cope with than having to face it as I go along. . . . Most of the loss of dignity comes from having to get help for things that either you've done for yourself in the past then all of a sudden you can't do them. You have no choice, you have to give in . . . and admit I need help. (Johnston et al., 2015)

Guided by our prevailing media depictions, much of our identity, particularly in Western cultures, is rooted in ability, individualism, and autonomy thus acquiring a disability or attempting to navigate spaces as a disabled person means that you must confront a system that was not designed for you and needing assistance in some way is a requirement. As we, particularly within sport, associate needing help with "weakness" and worth, those attempting to be physically active while disabled are forced to reconcile with conflicting, often discursive, information. For instance, many participants among the included studies recognized their right to participate yet failed to also recognize their right to appropriate accommodations. Disabled individuals, when engaging in sport and physical activity, are constantly reminded that they are not welcome in such spaces; that they should be grateful if they are allowed; or, as one participant believed, that "sometimes their [requested] help inhibits us more than anything [. . .] but we must always appreciate it, always." This extends to the ways in which disabled people who are attempting to participate in sport are allowed or not allowed the dignity of risk (i.e., being able to make choices that could result in negative consequences and to experience said consequences) (Mental Health and Developmental Disabilities National Training Center, 2020) (Wolpert, 1980). As one participant mentioned:

Nobody really wanted to take me [on any school teams] anymore. So that kind of finished. . . . Um, they were constantly worried I was going to have a seizure cause. . . . I kind of, I like quite challenging sports, I'm not particularly into yoga and things like that, as you can tell. Um, so, none of them wanted to take me on sports I wanted to do. So . . . so, yeah, I didn't really do anything, which was a bit of a shame. (Collard & Hill, 2019)

This can extend to the ways in which ableism is ingrained in society and even be reflected in the attitudes or beliefs among disabled peers. Participant Cindy shared that "I wanted to get on the team but, see, they won't let people with motorized chairs play. That's just the way it is. I don't know why" (Bedini & Anderson, 2005). As a participant in Bedini (2000) stated: "People cannot, they simply cannot help being prejudiced against . . . a person whose mind isn't all there. . . It's just one of those things that is . . . human nature." This innate prejudice reinforces prior stigmas and continues to extend the other-izing of disability. As Bill, a 20-year-old, who had recently acquired a spinal cord injury said: "I just see that people there are in worse situations than I am, and I can do more than what they can do and they can do a little bit more than what I can do" (Autry & Hanson, 2001). These examples (Bedini, 2000; Bedini & Anderson, 2005; Autry & Hanson, 2001) describe the existing hierarchy of disability (Schell & Duncan, 1999) that is generated through the prevalent "supercrip" narrative (Howe, 2001; Schaulk, 2016; Silva & Howe, 2012). Ultimately, the prioritization of physical disabilities within the inquiries of sport, hierarchizes a select group of disabled persons over others, and emboldens *otherizing* (Pullen et al., 2019). For instance, Kelly (Autry & Hanson, 2001) said that she "sometimes feels guilty about not being as disabled as some of the others." Another participant described how

they couldn't really classify me because I'm not like—I am disabled, but I'm not in a wheelchair or blind. And the only judo they had was blind judo, and that is not fair because I have sight and they don't. I'm not blind, but I'm not physically normal. I'm like right in between, and they didn't have competitions for that. (Conchar et al., 2016)

Even among those with disabilities, sport is often described as means to overcome their disability: "[Sport] has shown me that I haven't let my disability get the better of me. . . I haven't let my disability define me, I have defined my disability (Ballas et al., 2022)"; or show the worth of disabled persons to non-disabled people. For example, Tiger, a 16-year-old African American male with cerebral palsy in the study from Wilhite et al. (1999), said: "If we can just get an opportunity to be included, I think we can show them [people without disabilities] that we can do it." The construction of "disability does not equal worthy" was omnipresent:

The problem . . . a problem is that—I don't want to say this. A problem is that I don't feel, I don't always feel like a whole person. I would say like, on a whole I usually feel like not a whole person more than I do like a whole person. (Autry & Hanson, 2001)

These types of reflections are evidence of the extensive ongoing and active segregation of disabled people from society within sport and physical activity. Given media's tendency to focus on impairments and "super" qualities, the opportunities to use positive images of disabled athletes to "help peers 'engage in sport' is lost" (Rees et al., 2019, p. 379). Moreover, the overarching "overcoming" narrative present in many depictions of disability further preserve the presumed incompatibility of disabled bodies in sport (Pullen et al., 2020b).

Experiences of bullying and exclusion, for instance, were rife among the included studies, which reflect our broader understanding of disabled peoples' experiences during physical activity (e.g., Healy et al., 2013; Hutzler et al., 2021; Lindsay et al., 2012). One participant reflected (Jachyra et al., 2021), "One of the guys came up to me and said that I'm a retard, and a waste of space and am good for nothing. All because I did not score" while another participant shared, "Disability, that's like homeless people. Don't want to look at them; don't want to make eye contact. I'm sure a lot of people would like to speak to people in chairs; the thing is a lot of people don't" (Johnston et al., 2015). The pervasive ableist notion of worth of disabled people, within the sport and physical activity contexts, is reflected exponentially as the constructions of ability conflict with societal constructions of sport (DePauw, 1997). Without a prevailing shift in the discussion of disability in the public sphere and a removal of pervasive stereotypes and stigma (Kolotouchkina et al., 2021), the athletic achievements of disabled persons will continue to be ignored (Pullen et al., 2020a, 2020b). This continued dissonance is reflected in the active exclusion of disabled persons and the persistent ignoring their needs. As another participant of Johnston et al. (2015) mentioned:

Sometimes you figure you got to become a second-class citizen. Suck it up get it done. Figure out how to get by. It's frustrating, it's to the point where . . . do I stay in my room where I know everything works or do I go out in public and suffer the slings and arrows?

It is important to highlight that of those views that were included, participants were predominantly able to communicate verbally, and did not rely on augmentative and alternative communication devices as may be the case for participants with autism spectrum disorder or speech disorders. Therefore, it must be considered that if those who have tools to self-advocate experience exclusion and bullying, than those without those tools may experience a greater level of discrimination.

Theme 2: *Sport Can Serve as a Mediator to*
Psycho-Environmental Barriers Yet Is Missing
Justice-Oriented Approaches—or—"Tak[ing]
a Break from Pretending to Be Normal"

Sport and physical activity, though reflective of broad societal inequality, was not a passive conduit onto disabled persons. Within each of the included studies, elements of the positive influence of physical activity were permeative, though sparse. Overarchingly, participants described sport and physical activity as a means to find community and cut through the isolation of being considered "second-class." Individuals were able to use sport as a guide to support their transition from abled to disabled—it gave people perspective and hope. Moreover, sport and physical activity offered individuals a way to seek dignity and gain a sense of self. It should be noted that, though potentially powerful, these determinations were made with groups of individuals that were, often, already socialized into sport before acquiring a disability and likely had a prior affinity with movement. Further still, data were gathered from homogenous sources not dissimilar from the dominant views normalized within sport broadly (e.g., masculine, heteronormative).

Overwhelmingly, as suggested by Ellis and Goggin (2015), sport was perceived as a mediator by many of the participants that allowed them to act against the systemic structures and beliefs that typically limit physical activity for disabled persons. As a participant said:

> I had nothing until I found swimming. I felt like a complete misfit. When I found swimming that all changed. Swimming gives me a focus that I've never had, it is fun and it feels so good having the water on my skin. I feel tired after swimming, but that feeling also is what gets me coming back to the pool. I don't know what I would do without it now. (Jachyra et al., 2021)

Sport and physical activity became outlets for participants to "take a break from pretending to be normal" (Jachyra et al., 2021). As participant Pat shared, by participating in sport, participants showed themselves that they had worth and that their own preconceived stigmas of disability were untrue:

> "It showed me, showed me that I am somebody . . . and that I am a winner." When asked how the camp experience had achieved this he replied, "through people . . . you know, looking me in the eye . . . looking me in the eye, smiling. And saying things, like, 'you can do it.'" (Autry & Hanson, 2001)

Among those with acquired disabilities, participation in sport alongside accepting non-disabled peers helped to build confidence for many individuals:

I grew up playing with my friends who are able-bodied and I played right along-side them. I was really included in everything. . . . (I was) definitely the slowest down the court and things like that, but I still loved it! (McLoughlin et al., 2017)

Sport and other physical activities also helped many "find acceptance" with their disability, whether it be acceptance of an acquired disability and processing the grief of "loss" or acceptance of self and self-worth from finally uprooting assumed ableist notions of one's own disability that are so prevalent among the societal representations of disability. Participant Vince said: "It (swimming) gave me the confidence to recognize that I've got a disability, embrace it rather than saying I don't want to do that because I'm disabled. Now I understand it" (Pack et al., 2017). Another participant, Anne, from Pack et al. (2017), reflected:

I'd always worn a prosthetic unless I swam or slept, so going to swimming at first was a bit of a challenge because people were just so open about their disability, and like obviously when you swim you can't hide it, so that was a bit of an eye opener for me. I kind of learnt to like my disability and that people didn't care, especially when you're in a disability environment.

Similarly, participant William recalled that

when I play hockey in my neighborhood, everybody is welcomed. Even if you do not know how to play, you are welcomed. It is easy to access, thus is allows to see that okay, the barrier is broken, and everybody can play. (Wilhite et al., 1999)

Though sport reflects the broader stigmas embedded in society, it also provides opportunity to resist those stigmas (Donnelly, 1999). As Berger (2005) noted, disabled persons can leverage sport to navigate the covert and overt stigma they endure. One participant reflected:

And, I never thought about wheelchair sports, and . . . so, I was like really, really depressed for a long time, because they said, "no more sports." And that's all I'd done all my life. And, uh, so . . . I was provided this opportunity [to go skiing and] to get involved in something and I loved it, and I didn't do a lot of wheelchair, I mean there wasn't a lot of wheelchair activities. Like we went skiing, snowmobiling . . . and so I realized if I can ski, maybe there's something else I can do. (Autry & Hanson, 2001)

Bill, another participant of Autry and Hanson (2001), explained further:

"I can do more than what I thought I could do." but, he explained, "Ah, before I went there I ain't wanta do nothing, I ain't wanta go nowhere, but now [my friends] call me and I can go places and do things that I thought I never could do."

Likewise, a participant of Ballas et al. (2020) recounted:

> For me, the Paralympics helped normalise and made me realise that I wasn't alone, that I wasn't the only amputee in the world. So, you start talking to other amputees—how do you do this? You learn from them, which is so powerful.

Similarly, Wilhite et al. (1999) included a participant, Pierre, who shared,

> They [friends that live with a physical disability][2] showed me how to do it with my disability, how to get into the kayak and how to get out because it is much different than before!

Yet, sport is not wholly able to transcend all elements of ableism as Ellis and Goggin (2015) or Berger (2005) suggest—in some instances, it may only serve to reinforce it. As a participant from McLoughlin et al. (2017) presumed: "That's one of the big things for people with (physical) disabilities. If they're not introduced to sports at a young age, they don't have the opportunity to do things."

Despite sports' mercurial yet imperceptible influence in broader society, it comes as no surprise that the influence of sport for disabled people exists in among a field of gray. Like few things in society, however, sport offers connection to a greater whole (Smart, 2007) and a way to navigate entrenched stigma of disability (Berger, 2005). When the appropriate supports exist, in other words, "It is a good place if you want to understand that you are not being judged, that we are all the same, that we all have a disability" (Wilhite et al., 1999). Perhaps, more significantly, sport can offer a safe space for those who've benefited from prior success or developed supports. Metaphorically, if all the pieces align, sport can be place of escape or reprieve from society. As one participant stated: "Well, you take a shower and then you go into the swimming pool and . . . it is like entering another world. It feels really good (Lassenius et al., 2013)." Perhaps, our media coverage should do better to acknowledge sport in this role instead of focusing on "excellence."

Theme 3: *Intersectional Examinations of Disability Are Absent and Study Samples Are Homogenous, Prioritizing Certain Disabilities Thus Reinforcing an Existing Disability Hierarchy—or—"They Simply Cannot Help Being Prejudiced"*

Lastly . . . yet, perhaps most importantly . . . there exists in this synthesis a great absence in representation, which attributes to the limitations of the present findings. Though, ableism is apparent throughout the included studies and sport is witnessed as a mediator for such ableism (reinforcing broader evi-denced assumptions), these data are generated from very homogenous sam-ples regarding gender, race or ethnicity, class, and so on. Moreover, evidence has been primarily generated by those with physical impairments, which leaves considerable gaps. This is not to suggest that the those researching sport and activity for disabled persons overlook the barriers faced by other disabled populations—that evidence does exist (for instance, see Nichols et al. (2019) and Buchanan et al. (2017) to see barriers for autistic indi-viduals)—however, this evidence is overwhelmingly generated from those approximate to the disabled person such as their caregiver, teacher, therapist, or sibling. Frank (2006) said that people, "need to hear their own voices and, by knowing others' stories, become empowered to tell their own" (p. 422). Without these stories told, our understanding of the intersecting oppressions faced by disabled athletes will continue to be incomplete.

Perhaps, this theme is encompassing a broader critique of disability and sport scholarship, and the societal influence on our views. As its scholars, we are tasked with the investigation and critique of its practices. Yet, we rarely reflect that lens upon ourselves and examine the influences of our bias. If we are to accept that ableism influences sport in the same ways witnessed in broader society, then we also must accept that we are similarly enamored. As Beacom et al. (2016) highlighted, however, to outwardly condemn the way scholars or journalists cover disability in sport, "would be too simplistic and inevitably involve glossing-over what is indeed a complex area characterized by contested meaning(s)" (p. 56). As we seek to examine sport and its influence on disabled bodies, as well as how those views are espoused in broader society, we must ensure that our lens acknowledges the privileges from which we've benefited. Indeed, intentional effort must be made to encourage the adoption of participa-tory methods within our practice, so that we may understand the full breadth of the influence of society on sport and sports ability to resist such influence.

CONCLUSION: WE ALL HAVE RESPONSIBILITY

In a 1964 speech with Malcolm X that summarized her fight for racial equal-ity, civil rights leader Fannie Lou Hamer said:

> All my life I been sick and tired. Now I'm sick and tired of being sick and tired . . . there's so much hypocrisy in this society and if we want America to be a free society, we have to stop telling lies, that's all. (Brooks & Houck, 2011, p. 62)

As we consider the impacts of identity, representation, and sport across soci-ety and between cultures, we must come to recognize that we have told our-selves fallacies regarding disability; that our centering of able-bodied idols as definitions of sport only serves to perpetuate a dishonest definition of "ability"; and those notions have become pervasive among our media coverage (Rees et al., 2019). Through a critical disability lens, this synthesis reignites a 30-year-old call to action; as DePauw (1997) wrote, "The lens of disability allows us to make problematic the socially constructed nature of sport and once we have done so, opens us to alternative constructions, actions, and solutions" (p. 428). In doing so, we must assume a transformational practice: one that recognizes the ongoing (re)construction of disability and sport in broader society, as well as the role that media plays in how those constructs are designed. We must engage in the transformation of sport culture "to 'see' sport and athlete with a disability without seeing any contradiction, without assuming a physical liability, stigma, or deformity, and without assuming an impaired athletic performance" (DePauw, 1997, p. 428). Only then might we dismantle the persistent authoritarianism of the "Empire of the Normal" (Couser, 2000; Davis, 2013) and throw off the remaining colonizing normativity of our present media culture.

It is vital to acknowledge that this change among representations of disabled athletes is occurring, albeit slowly (Devotta et al., 2013). Persistently, though, this representation continues to be based in heavily medicalized views of disability and propagates stigma related to disability (Goethals et al., 2022; Rees et al., 2019; Weiller et al., 2021). Within sport and physical activity contexts, we see that focusing on "inclusion," even among media, is "more about governing people with disability in sport to achieve integrative standards of normalcy rather than creating more inclusive (in Barton's terms) spaces of a more diverse range of people who do not traditionally participate in sport" (Hammond et al., 2019, p. 318). If we are honestly intent to serve the needs of disabled people through sport and physical activity, immense introspection on the power of our words (Burns, 2010) is required. To fight for justice for disabled persons in sport, we must listen to disabled individuals and recognize their expertise (Stewart & Spurgeon, 2019)—we must push for a shift in our construction of sport and its relationship to historically oppressive constructions of *ability*.

Response

Just Because You Use a Ball Chair Doesn't Mean You're Blameless

John Loeppky

There is a duality in being a national team-level athlete one second and being banned from bringing your wheelchair to school the next. My physical education teachers in high school gave me three options: work in the weight room, get pelted with whatever sports prop was in use that day—puck, basketball, football, and so on—or stay away. No one in administration spoke up when a classmate told me to "sit on the sideline where your crippled ass belongs." I just removed myself from the situation and flew across the country to train the following week. If you're wondering, I'm an ambulatory wheelchair user whose wheelchair was briefly banned because my friends kept using it when I was sitting in class. They expected me to police my chair. All they were doing was policing my body.

It's a standard narrative in parasport to equate competing with saving one's life. I was isolated, I was frustrated, I was angry—I once got thrown out of an anger management session for being too angry. I got to go and play basketball with and against tons of Paralympians across North America and yet when I returned home, I was just another cripple in the corner.

There is a bright side. One of my former opponents was a groomsman at my wedding, I could fly into most major centers in Canada and have a couch to sleep on if so desired, and my inclusion in parasport means that I feel capable and comfortable in my career as a journalist. This community has given me so much, and yet has so much to answer for.

Ableist barriers exist in community, too. A room full of people singing "fa-ker, fa-ker, fa-ker" when I stood up in a hotel lobby the day of a wheelchair rugby tournament, for example. I was on a national team bench when I was denied food—a required need for my body and not a nice-to-have ask from a needy basketball-playing teen.

Look, I'm very privileged on the grand scale of things. I'm white, in the middle of the Canadian prairie, I'm an immigrant but was born with citizenship, my parents were able to get me the adapted equipment and medical model support that I needed. I was lucky, but I won't deny that parasport often hides behind this inspiration narrative, as this undeniable force for social good, this unquestioned space for equality. As I've written about for the Globe and Mail, much of this is a façade. If the parasport movement wants to grow, then it needs to acknowledge that funding makes the world go around, that there is plenty of ableism within the elite parasport environment (coincidentally I wrote about that too, this time for Rooted in Rights), that there is cheating, and—perhaps most importantly—that there is a massive gulf in opportunity between those we see in elite competition and those from marginalized backgrounds.

But, and it's a big but, that unpacking begins with how we treat disability and the political right of disabled people to live in their body, to be active, and to compete. Parasport is problematic, but that's largely a function of our wider ableist notions of what a disabled body can and should be able to do.

NOTES

1. Text between [] was added by us to define accommodations for the reader as Dr. DePauw has in the included quote, which adds necessary context to the quote.
2. Text inside [] is direct quote from original source, Wilhite et al., 1999.

REFERENCES

denotes article included in synthesis.

Abrams, A. (2020). 30 years after a landmark disability law, the fight for access and equality continues. *TIME*. https://time.com/5870468/americans-with-disabilities-act-coronavirus/

Americans with Disabilities Act of 1990. Pub. L. 101-336. § 1. 26 July 1990. 104 Stat. 328.

*Autry, C. E., & Hanson, C. S. (2001). Meaning of sport to adults with physical disabilities: A disability sport camp experience. *Sociology of Sport Journal, 18*, 95–114.

Baglieri, S., & Lalvani, P. (2019). *Undoing ableism: Teaching about disability in K-12 classrooms*. Routledge.

*Ballas, J., Buultjens, M., Murphy, G., & Jackson, M. (2020). Elite-level athletes with physical impairments: Barriers and facilitators to sport participation. *Disability & Society,37*(6), 1018–1037.

*Barns, A., Svanholm, F., Kjellberg, A., Thyberg, I., & Falkmer, T. (2015). Living in the present: Women's everyday experiences of living with rheumatoid arthritis. *Sage Open, 5*(4), 2158244015616163.

Beacom, A., French, L., & Kendall, S. (2016). Reframing impairment? Continuity and change in media representations of disability through the Paralympic Games. *International Journal of Sport Communication, 9*(1), 42–62.

*Bedini, L. A. (2000). "Just sit down so we can talk:" Perceived stigma and community recreation pursuits of people with disabilities. *Therapeutic Recreation Journal, 34*(1), 55–68.

*Bedini, L. A., & Anderson, D. M. (2005). I'm nice, I'm smart, I like karate: Girls with physical disabilities perceptions of physical recreation. *Therapeutic Recreation Journal, 39*(2), 114.

Berger, R. J. (2005). Hoop dreams on wheels. In *Storytelling sociology: Narrative as social inquiry,* edited by R. Berger and R. Quinney, 153–166. Boulder, CO: Lynne Rienner.

Berger, R. J. (2008). Disability and the dedicated wheelchair athlete: Beyond the "supercrip" critique. *Journal of Contemporary Ethnography, 37*(6), 647–678.

*Blinde, E. M., & McClung, L. R. (1997). Enhancing the physical and social self through recreational activity: Accounts of individuals with physical disabilities. *Adapted Physical Activity Quarterly, 14*(4), 327–344.

*Bloemen, M. A., Verschuren, O., van Mechelen, C., Borst, H. E., de Leeuw, A. J., van der Hoef, M., & de Groot, J. F. (2015). Personal and environmental factors to consider when aiming to improve participation in physical activity in children with Spina Bifida: A qualitative study. *BMC Neurology, 15*(1), 1–11.

*Bonnell, K., Michalovic, E., Koch, J., Pagé, V., Ramsay, J., Gainforth, H. L., . . . & Sweet, S. N. (2021). Physical activity for individuals living with a physical disability in Quebec: Issues and opportunities of access. *Disability and Health Journal,* Advanced Online Publication.

Brooks, M. P., & Houck, D. W. (Eds.). (2011). *The speeches of Fannie Lou Hamer: To tell it like it is.* University Press of Mississippi.

Buchanan, A. M., Miedema, B., & Frey, G. C. (2017). Parents' perspectives of physical activity in their adult children with autism spectrum disorder: A social-ecological approach. *Adapted Physical Activity Quarterly, 34*(4), 401–420.

Burns, S. (2010). Words matter: Journalists, educators, media guidelines and representation of disability. *Asia Pacific Media Educator,* (20), 277–283.

*Caton, S., Chadwick, D., Chapman, M., Turnbull, S., Mitchell, D., & Stansfield, J. (2012). Healthy lifestyles for adults with intellectual disability: Knowledge, barriers, and facilitators. *Journal of Intellectual and Developmental Disability, 37*(3), 248–259.

Centers for Disease Control and Prevention. (2018). *CDC: 1 in 4 US adults live with a disability.* https://www.cdc.gov/media/releases/2018/p0816-disability.html

Chodorow, N. J. (1999). *The power of feelings.* New Haven, CT: Yale University Press.

*Collard, S. S., & Ellis-Hill, C. (2019). 'I'd rather you didn't come': The impact of stigma on exercising with epilepsy. *Journal of Health Psychology, 24*(10), 1345–1355.

*Conchar, L., Bantjes, J., Swartz, L., & Derman, W. (2016). Barriers and facilitators to participation in physical activity: The experiences of a group of South African adolescents with cerebral palsy. *Journal of Health Psychology, 21*(2), 152–163.

Couser, G. T. (2000). The empire of the "normal": A forum on disability and self-representation: Introduction. *American Quarterly, 52*(2), 305–310.

*Cox, B., & Bartle, C. (2020). A qualitative study of the accessibility of a typical UK town cycle network to disabled cyclists. *Journal of Transport & Health, 19,* 1–12.

Davis, L. J. (1999). The rule of normalcy: Politics and disability in the USA [United States of Ability]. In *Disability, divers-ability and legal change* (pp. 35–47). Brill Nijhoff.

Deegan, M. J., & Brooks, N. A. (Eds.). (1985). *Women and disability: The double handicap*. Transaction Books.

DePauw, K. P. (1997). The (in)visibility of disability: Cultural contexts and "sporting bodies." *Quest, 49*(4), 416–430.

Devotta, K., Wilton, R., & Yiannakoulias, N. (2013). Representations of disability in the Canadian news media: A decade of change? *Disability and Rehabilitation, 35*(22), 1859–1868.

Donnelly, P. (1996). The local and the global: Globalization in the sociology of sport. *Journal of Sport and Social Issues, 20*(3), 239–257.

Ellis, K., & Goggin, G. (2015). *Disability and the media*. Macmillan International Higher Education.

Fine, M., & Asch, A. (1988). Disability beyond stigma: Social interaction, discrimination, and activism. *Journal of Social Issues, 44*(1), 3–21.

*Fitzgerald, H. (2005). Still feeling like a spare piece of luggage? Embodied experiences of (dis)ability in physical education and school sport. *Physical Education & Sport Pedagogy, 10*(1), 41–59.

Frank, A. W. (2006). Health stories as connectors and subjectifiers. *Health: An Interdisciplinary Journal for the Social Study of Health, Illness and Medicine, 10*(4), 421–440.

Gaskin, C. J., Andersen, M. B., & Morris, T. (2010). Sport and physical activity in the life of a man with cerebral palsy: Compensation for disability with psychosocial benefits and costs. *Psychology of Sport and Exercise, 11*(3), 197–205.

Goethals, T., Mortelmans, D., Van den Bulck, H., Van den Heurck, W., & Van Hove, G. (2022). I am not your metaphor: Frames and counter-frames in the representation of disability. *Disability & Society, 37*(5), 746–764.

Goodley, D. (2017). *Disability studies: An interdisiplinary introduction* (2nd ed.). London: Sage.

*Hackett, J. (2003). Perceptions of play and leisure in junior school aged children with juvenile idiopathic arthritis: What are the implications for occupational therapy? *British Journal of Occupational Therapy, 66*(7), 303–310.

Haegele, J. A. (2019). Inclusion illusion: Questioning the inclusiveness of integrated physical education: 2019 national association for Kinesiology in higher education Hally Beth Poindexter young scholar address. *Quest, 71*(4), 387–397.

*Haegele, J. A., Hodge, S. R., Filho, P. G., Ribeiro, N., & Martínez-Rivera, C. (2018). A phenomenological inquiry into the meaning ascribed to physical activity by Brazilian men with visual impairments. *Journal of Visual Impairment & Blindness, 112*(5), 519–531.

Hahn, H. (1988). The politics of physical differences: Disability and discrimination. *Journal of Social Issues, 44*(1), 39–47.

Hammond, A., Jeanes, R., Penney, D., & Leahy, D. (2019). "I feel we are inclusive enough": Examining swimming coaches' understandings of inclusion and disability. *Sociology of Sport Journal, 36*(4), 311–321.

Hardin, M. M., & Hardin, B. (2004). The "supercrip" in sport media: Wheelchair athletes discuss hegemony's disabled hero. *Sociology of Sport Online-SOSOL, 7*(1) http://physed.otago.ac.nz/sosol/v7i1/v7il_1.html.

Hargreaves, J. (2000). *Heroines of sport: The politics of difference and identity.* Routledge.

Healy, S., Msetfi, R., & Gallagher, S. (2013). 'Happy and a bit nervous': The experiences of children with autism in physical education. *British Journal of Learning Disabilities, 41*(3), 222–228.

Heumann, J. (1988). Americans with disabilities act of 1988: Joint hearing before the sub-committee on the handicapped of the committee on labor and human resources United States Senate and the subcommittee on select education of the committee on education and labor of the house of representatives. One-Hundredth Congress. Second Session on S.2345: To establish a clear and comprehensive prohibition of discrimination on the basis of handicap. September 27, 1988. Washington, DC: U.S. Government Printing Office.

Howe, P. D. (2011). Cyborg and supercrip: The Paralympics technology and the (dis)empowerment of disabled athletes. *Sociology, 45*(5), 868–882.

Hutzler, Y., Tesler, R., Ng, K., Barak, S., Kazula, H., & Harel-Fisch, Y. (2021). Physical activity, sedentary screen time and bullying behaviors: Exploring differences between adolescents with and without disabilities. *International Journal of Adolescence and Youth, 26*(1), 110–126.

*Jachyra, P., Renwick, R., Gladstone, B., Anagnostou, E., & Gibson, B. E. (2021). Physical activity participation among adolescents with autism spectrum disorder. *Autism, 25*(3), 613–626.

*Jackson, J., Williams, T. L., McEachern, B. M., Latimer-Cheung, A. E., & Tomasone, J. R. (2019). Fostering quality experiences: Qualitative perspectives from program members and providers in a community-based exercise program for adults with physical disabilities. *Disability and Health Journal, 12*(2), 296–301.

*James, L., Shing, J., Mortenson, W. B., Mattie, J., & Borisoff, J. (2018). Experiences with and perceptions of an adaptive hiking program. *Disability and Rehabilitation, 40*(13), 1584–1590.

*Javorina, D., Shirazipour, C. H., Allan, V., & Latimer-Cheung, A. E. (2020). The impact of social relationships on initiation in adapted physical activity for individuals with acquired disabilities. *Psychology of Sport and Exercise, 50*, 101752.

Jensen, L. A., & Allen, M. N. (1996). Meta-synthesis of qualitative findings. *Qualitative Health Research, 6*(4), 553–560.

*Johnston, K. R., Goodwin, D. L., & Leo, J. (2015). Understanding dignity: Experiences of impairment in an exercise facility. *Adapted Physical Activity Quarterly, 32*(2), 106–124.

Kolotouchkina, O., Llorente-Barroso, C., García-Guardia, M. L., & Pavón, J. (2021). Disability, sport, and television: Media visibility and representation of Paralympic games in news programs. *Sustainability, 13*(1), 256.

*Lassenius, O., Arman, M., Söderlund, A., Åkerlind, I., & Wiklund-Gustin, L. (2013). Moving toward reclaiming life: Lived experiences of being physically active among persons with psychiatric disabilities. *Issues in Mental Health Nursing, 34*(10), 739–746.

Lewis, T. A., (2021, January 1). *Working definition of ableism.* Talila A. Lewis. https://www.talilalewis.com/blog/january-2021-working-definition-of-ableism

Lindsay, S., & McPherson, A. C. (2012). Experiences of social exclusion and bullying at school among children and youth with cerebral palsy. *Disability and Rehabilitation, 34*(2), 101–109.

*Mahy, J., Shields, N., Taylor, N. F., & Dodd, K. J. (2010). Identifying facilitators and barriers to physical activity for adults with Down syndrome. *Journal of Intellectual Disability Research, 54*(9), 795–805.

Martin, J. J. (2019). Mastery and belonging or inspiration porn and bullying: Special populations in youth sport. *Kinesiology Review, 8*(3), 195–203.

*McLoughlin, G., Fecske, C. W., Castaneda, Y., Gwin, C., & Graber, K. (2017). Sport participation for elite athletes with physical disabilities: Motivations, barriers, and facilitators. *Adapted Physical Activity Quarterly, 34*(4), 421–441.

Mental Health and Developmental Disabilities National Training Center. (2020). *Self-determination and dignity of risk*. https://www.mhddcenter.org/wp-content/uploads/2020/07/Self-Determination-Dignity-of-Risk-Fact-Sheet.pdf

Mingus, M. (2011, February 12). *Changing the framework: Disability justice*. Leaving Evidence. https://leavingevidence.wordpress.com/2011/02/12/changing-the-framework-disability-justice/

*Moffat, F., & Paul, L. (2019). Barriers and solutions to participation in exercise for moderately disabled people with multiple sclerosis not currently exercising: A consensus development study using nominal group technique. *Disability and Rehabilitation, 41*(23), 2775–2783.

Nichols, C., Block, M. E., Bishop, J. C., & McIntire, B. (2019). Physical activity in young adults with autism spectrum disorder: Parental perceptions of barriers and facilitators. *Autism, 23*(6), 1398–1407.

Oliver, M. (1992). Changing the social relations of research production? *Disability, Handicap & Society, 7*(2), 101–114.

Ouzzani, M., Hammady, H., Fedorowicz, Z., & Elmagarmid, A. (2016). Rayyan—a web and mobile app for systematic reviews. *Systematic Reviews, 5*(1), 1–10.

*Pack, S., Kelly, S., & Arvinen-Barrow, M. (2017). "I think I became a swimmer rather than just someone with a disability swimming up and down:" Paralympic athletes perceptions of self and identity development. *Disability and Rehabilitation, 39*(20), 2063–2070.

Pullen, E., Jackson, D., Silk, M., & Scullion, R. (2019). Re-presenting the Paralympics: (Contested) philosophies, production practices and the hypervisibility of disability. *Media, Culture, and Society, 41*(4), 465–481.

Pullen, E., Jackson, D., & Silk, M. (2020a). (Re-)presenting the Paralympics: Affective nationalism and the "able-disabled". *Communication & Sport, 8*(6), 715–737.

Pullen, E., Jackson, D., Silk, M., Howe, D., & Silva, C. (2020b). Extraordinary normalcy, Ableist rehabilitation, and sporting ablenationalism: The cultural (re)production of Paralympic disability narratives. *Sociology of Sport Journal*. Advanced Online Publication.

Rauscher, L., & McClintock, J. (1997). Ableism curriculum design. In M. Adams, L. A. Bell, & P. Griffen (Eds.), *Teaching for diversity and social justice* (pp. 198–229). New York: Routledge.

*Raymond, É. (2019). The challenge of inclusion for older people with impairments: Insights from a stigma-based analysis. *Journal of Aging Studies*, *49*, 9–15. http://physed.otago.ac.nz/sosol/v7i1/v7il_1.html

Rees, L., Robinson, P., & Shields, N. (2019). Media portrayal of elite athletes with disability–a systematic review. *Disability and Rehabilitation*, *41*(4), 374–381.

*Richardson, E. V., Smith, B., & Papathomas, A. (2017). Disability and the gym: Experiences, barriers and facilitators of gym use for individuals with physical disabilities. *Disability and Rehabilitation*, *39*(19), 1950–1957.

Rimmer, J. H., Riley, B., Wang, E., Rauworth, A., & Jurkowski, J. (2004). Physical activity participation among persons with disabilities: Barriers and facilitators. *American Journal of Preventive Medicine*, *26*(5), 419–425.

*Rolfe, D. E., Yoshida, K., Renwick, R., & Bailey, C. (2009). Negotiating participation: How women living with disabilities address barriers to exercise. *Health Care for Women International*, *30*(8), 743–766.

Schalk, S. (2016). Reevaluating the supercrip. *Journal of Literary & Cultural Disability Studies*, *10*(1), 71–86.

Schell, L. A. B., & Duncan, M. C. (1999). A content analysis of CBS's coverage of the 1996 Paralympic games. *Adapted Physical Activity Quarterly*, *16*(1), 27–47.

Siebers, T. (2001). Disability in theory: From social constructionism to the new realism of the body. *American Literary History*, *13*(4), 737–754.

Silva, C. F., & Howe, P. D. (2012). The (in)validity of supercrip representation of Paralympian athletes. *Journal of Sport and Social Issues*, *36*(2), 174–194.

Smart, B. (2007). Not playing around: Global capitalism, modern sport and consumer culture. *Global Networks*, *7*(2), 113–134.

Stewart, D. L. D. (2018). Using intersectionality to study and understand LGBTIQ people in sport. In V. Krane (Ed.), *Sex, gender, and sexuality in sport: Queer inquiries* (pp. 33–48). Routledge.

Stewart, K., Spurgeon, C., & Edwards, N. (2019). Media participation by people with disability and the relevance of Australian community broadcasting in the digital era. *3CMedia*, *9*, 44–63.

*Taliaferro, A. R., & Hammond, L. (2016). "I don't have time": Barriers and facilitators to physical activity for adults with intellectual disabilities. *Adapted Physical Activity Quarterly*, *33*(2), 113–133.

Taub, D. E., & Greer, K. R. (1998). Sociology of acceptance revisited: Males with physical disabilities participating in sport and physical fitness activity. *Deviant Behavior*, *19*(3), 279–302.

Townsend, R. C., Cushion, C. J., & Smith, B. (2018). A social relational analysis of an impairment-specific mode of disability coach education. *Qualitative Research in Sport, Exercise and Health*, *10*(3), 346–361.

United Nations. (2020). *Pandemic reveals how excluded are society's most marginalized, secretary-general says, launching policy brief on persons with disabilities and COVID-19*. https://www.un.org/press/en/2020/sgsm20074.doc.htm

U.S. Department of Labor, Bureau of Labor Statistics. (2021). *Persons with a disability: Labor force characteristics—2020*. https://www.bls.gov/news.release/pdf/disabl.pdf

*van Schijndel-Speet, M., Evenhuis, H. M., van Wijck, R., van Empelen, P., & Echteld, M. A. (2014). Facilitators and barriers to physical activity as perceived by older adults with intellectual disability. *Mental Retardation, 52*(3), 175–186.

Walsh, D., & Downe, S. (2005). Meta-synthesis method for qualitative research: A literature review. *Journal of Advanced Nursing, 50*(2), 204–211.

Weiller-Abels, K., Everbach, T., & Colombo-Dougovito, A. M. (2021). She's a lady; He's an athlete; they have overcome: Portrayals of gender and disability in the 2018 Paralympic winter games. *Journal of Sports Media, 16*(1), 123–148.

Wendell, S. (1989). Toward a feminist theory of disability. *Hypatia, 4*(2), 104–12.

*Wilhite, B., Devine, M. A., & Goldenberg, L. (1999). Perceptions of youth with and without disabilities: Implications for inclusive leisure programs and services. *Therapeutic Recreation Journal, 33*, 15–28.

Wolpert, J. (1980). The dignity of risk. *Transactions of the Institute of British Geographers, 5*(4), 391–401.

Zhang, L., & Haller, B. (2013). Consuming image: How mass media impact the identity of people with disabilities. *Communication Quarterly, 61*(3), 319–334.

Zuberi, T., & Bonilla-Silva, E. (Eds.). (2008). *White logic, white methods: Racism and methodology.* Rowman & Littlefield Publishers.

Section II

BLACK ATHLETES AS ACTIVISTS

Chapter 6

#SayHerName

The WNBA and Black Women Athletes' Social Activism

Tracy Everbach, Gwendelyn S. Nisbett,
and Karen Weiller-Abels

In summer 2020, after the shooting of unarmed Jacob Blake by police in Kenosha, Wisconsin, WNBA players took the court in a unified effort, wearing T-shirts displaying depictions of seven bullet holes, signifying the number of times officers shot Blake. The WNBA's social justice efforts laid the blueprint for the subsequent NBA walkout to protest police shootings and brutality; the women had staged their own walkout before the men's highly publicized actions. The women's league's commitment to social justice issues has been on display for several years, yet their activism has not received the same amount of media attention as compared to the NBA and professional male athletes like former NFL quarterback Colin Kaepernick (Ayala, 2020; Perry, 2020). This chapter, rooted in Black feminist thought and intersectionality as critical social theory (Collins, 2019; hooks, 1981), as well as queer theory (Butler, 2006; King, 2008), examines the social media activism of WNBA players. Special attention is paid to their marginalized status as women within the arena of sport, the standpoint of queer women of color in the league, and their influence as Black women on other communities (such as their NBA counterparts) who followed and emulated their activism.

BLACK WOMEN ATHLETES AND ACTIVISM

Black women athletes have a long and storied legacy of activism and resistance (Lansbury, 2014). These athletes have been fighting for human rights and social justice for decades. For instance, tennis player Althea Gibson and

Olympic track gold medalist Wilma Rudolph championed civil rights for Black Americans in the 1940s and 1950s. Track athlete Jackie Joyner-Kersee, famous for six medals earned at four Olympic Games from 1984 to 1996, consistently has fought for women's equality in sports. Wendy Hilliard, the first Black woman to participate in rhythmic gymnastics as part of the 1995 US national team, has advocated for equal access and rights for women, particularly Black women (Steidinger, 2020). Toni Smith Thompson, a college basketball player, protested the 2003 invasion of Iraq by turning her back to the American flag. Another college basketball player, Ariyana Smith, in 2014 lay on the court for four and a half minutes to symbolize the four and a half hours Michael Brown's body remained in the street after he was shot by Ferguson, Missouri police (Wulf, 2019). Tennis greats Venus and Serena Williams, who both have been the targets of racist comments and caricatures, have supported both the Black Lives Matter movement and equal pay for women in professional tennis. The women in the WNBA are continuing this history of social justice demonstrations and support as part of their everyday lives. As Seattle Storm player Sue Bird said:

> We've been judged because we're Black, gay, because we're women. Nobody talks about us playing. So you fast-forward 10, 20 years of this and we've developed an identity, and we're being authentic to it. And so far for us, when people say stick to sports it's kind of like, "Yeah 20 years ago we tried, and you wouldn't let us, and now you're saying that?" So it makes no sense to me. (Klar, 2020, para. 9)

The WNBA's current wave of activism first grabbed attention at a July 2016 news conference, when four members of the Minnesota Lynx donned T-shirts reading "Change Starts With Us: Justice and Accountability." Over the next few days, players from the New York Liberty, Indiana Fever, and Phoenix Mercury wore warm-up shirts emblazoned with #BlackLivesMatter and #Dallas5, honoring five police officers who were shot and killed. At that time, the league responded by fining the three teams $5,000 each for wearing unapproved gear on the court (Ayala, 2020, August 29; Bumbaca, 2020, August 6). However, the WNBA players inspired other athletes to speak out on social justice issues and the WNBA later rescinded the fines in support of the players' activism.

Before NFL quarterback Colin Kaepernick gained notoriety for kneeling during the national anthem to protest the killing of Black people by police, the WNBA engaged in its own demonstrations but did not receive anywhere near the amount of attention Kaepernick received. A majority of WNBA players are Black women, and many of its players are out lesbians. Those factors, combined with their platforms as athletes, their status as a marginalized group in sports, and their outspoken advocacy, have made them leaders in social justice movements. The league and the players' union have formed a social justice coalition, called the WNBA Social Justice Council, that addresses issues such as police brutality, gun violence, and criminal justice reform. Players have met in video conferences with such leaders as Michelle Obama and Stacey Abrams to discuss political strategies and causes (Ayala, 2020; Perry, 2020; Streeter, 2020).

In the 2020 season, WNBA players boycotted games to protest police shootings, including the killing of Breonna Taylor in her Louisville apartment. Some players appeared on ESPN's SportsCenter wearing black T-shirts that said, "Arrest the cops who killed Breonna Taylor" (O'Donnell, 2020). One of their rallying cries became the #SayHerName hashtag protesting Taylor's slaying and the deaths of all Black women and girls by police violence. WNBA courts bore the slogan Black Lives Matter. The players also sold #SayHerName T-shirts to support the Breonna Taylor Foundation.

Some players became involved in a Senate political campaign by helping Rev. Rapahel Warnock, a Democratic candidate, get elected to the US Senate in Georgia. Atlanta Dream players protested the political campaign of their own co-owner, Republican Kelly Loeffler, who had held the Georgia Senate seat. The players voiced their support for her opponent, Warnock, and wore "VOTE WARNOCK" T-shirts. The players decided to speak out against Loeffler after she sent a letter to the WNBA denouncing the Black Lives Matter movement (Buckner, 2021a). On January 5, 2021, in a runoff election, Warnock defeated Loeffler for the Georgia Senate seat; Loeffler later sold her interest in the team.

Amira Rose Davis, professor of history and African American studies at Penn State University, argues that players' asserting their personal rights are inherently political.

> The WNBA is a league that is gritty by necessity. It catches so much hate because it's "too Black, too queer." It's full of women. And I think that draws the ire of a lot of people. And so they as a league have always been fairly outspoken, because it's the only way to be. Their very presence on a court, the insistence that they have the right to play and make a living by playing is a political act in itself. (Perry, 2020, para. 11)

BLACK FEMINIST THOUGHT AND INTERSECTIONALITY

Patricia Hill Collins (2019) posits that social actions rooted in Black feminist thought are apt ways to critique the intersection of race, gender, class, and capitalism. The women of the WNBA are uniquely suited to promote social justice issues because of their status as professional athletes, which provides them with social capital and a public voice. Collins points out that Black feminist thought developed as a way of resisting oppression through political expression. Black women have used their own lived experiences through their race, gender, sexuality, and social class, to draw attention to social conditions and raise concerns for members of their communities. Scholar bell hooks notes that while Black women for years participated in the fight against racism, her generation, the women of the mid-twentieth century, were taught to "accept sexual inferiority, and to be silent" (hooks, 1981, p. 2). This spurred the Black feminist movement, which was and is intersectional, to call for an end to both racism and misogyny. Black American women have long been engaged in activism: from Sojourner Truth's mid-nineteenth century rallying cries at anti-slavery and women rights conventions; to Ida B. Wells-Barnett's courageous journalism exposing the lynching of Black people in the American South; to Mary Church Terrell, who fought for women's right to vote and conducted anti-lynching campaigns; to Rosa Parks and many other Black women organizers in the US civil rights movement (hooks, 1981; Roessner & Rightler-McDaniels, 2018). As Collins notes, Black women have long been involved as leaders in community work, which she defines as the effort to help those in their community resist racism and oppression and fight for freedom and justice.

> Whether a moral, ethical tradition that encouraged African American women to relinquish the so-called special interests of issues as women for the greater good of the overarching community, or a survival politics that meant that if Black women didn't do it, it simply didn't get done, Black women's reproductive labor was placed in service to Black communities. (Collins, 2019, p. 169)

As noted by Collins and Bilge (2020), in the 1960s and 1970s, African American women were forced to confront the many injustices that befell them as related to jobs, education, and health care issues. Activism became a strong focus through antiracist movements, feminism, and organizing for workers' rights. These led to a simultaneous approach to social inequality problems on many levels. Collins and Bilge further commented on the use of intersectionality as "black women's specific issues remained subordinated within each movement because no social movement would, or could, address the entirety of discriminations they faced" (p. 3). More recently, Black women have been at the forefront of current social justice movements, founding and influencing others to follow the mobilization of their political activism. In 2006, Tarana Burke founded the MeToo movement, urging other women to speak out about their experiences with sexual harassment and sexual assault. In 2013, three Black women: Alicia Garza, Opal Tometi, and Patrice Cullors, launched the Black Lives Matter movement, which grew worldwide with marches and demonstrations coordinated through social media.

The WNBA is continuing this storied history of political activism through its support for Black Lives Matter and other movements that focus on social justice and inequality, as well as providing an intersectional focus on race, gender, sexuality, class, and social capital. Intersectionality, according to Collins, is a critical social theory still under development that can be used as a "tool for social change" (p. 2). In this chapter, we argue the WNBA's intersectional efforts are creating community and making changes in society.

LESBIAN ATHLETES, ACTIVISM, AND QUEER THEORY

Cooky and Antunovic (2020) addressed activism by women athletes, women of color, and lesbian athletes; noting that changing the larger view of oppressed groups often is difficult. Over the years, activism by women of color—and by sportswomen, in general—has addressed various issues related to social justice. Use of media narratives with respect to activism, particularly within the WNBA, have been marginalized when compared to men's sports and men's activism.

As noted previously in this chapter, the WNBA has been involved in social activism for quite some time in varying capacities and, more recently, the league shifted its focus from feigning heteronormativity to embracing queerness. More than a decade ago, Muller (2007) suggested the WNBA's heteronormativity was "naturalized" (p. 197) by the league. In an article depicting two case studies focusing on marketing strategies promoted by the WNBA, the league maintained a careful presentation that more often promoted a heterosexual, white family (McDonald, 2002). Images of WNBA players after games appeared to reinforce this notion of heteronormativity as players and coaches were shown with their families and children, thus relegating their athletic accomplishments to a secondary status. Even though lesbians are a strong fan base of the league, for years, the WNBA chose to emphasize this heteronormativity.

Two case studies were featured in McDonald's 2002 study: (1) a kiss-in protest by players of the New York Liberty; and (2) the heteronormative view of the Minnesota Lynx management, despite seemingly attempting to provide a welcoming atmosphere. Calling themselves, "Lesbians for Liberty," players of the New York Liberty staged the kiss-in to protest the management of the Liberty's lack of support for Gay Pride Month as well as the league's seeming disregard for the large lesbian fan base. Their protest included kissing during breaks in play and waving banners supporting their lesbian fans, and asking, "Is there really liberty for all?" The Lynx management, on the other hand, seemingly targeted lesbian fans, with fans noting overt marketing strategies of having lesbian local singers post game and advertising in a local gay publication (Muller, 2007). Some respondents indicated fans felt more welcome and safe (safety in numbers) when a larger number of lesbian fans were in the stands. In that time period, it was noted that the Lynx marketing team should try to market more fully to the lesbian community.

In recent years, as political and social views have shifted in the United States with the 2013 passage of the Defense of Marriage Act (DOMA), there is greater acceptance of same-sex marriage, as well as athletes, officials, and sport administrators coming out as gay, lesbian, or bisexual (Becker, 2014; Out Sports, 2014). Marketing to an LGBTQ+ fanbase has also changed. In the 2010s, the WNBA shifted its view and began to openly embrace the LGBTQ+ community, becoming the first pro sport league to specifically provide an outreach to gay fans (Mumcu & Lough, 2017). Since 2014, the league has intentionally marketed to and celebrated the diversity of LGBTQ+ fans. Additionally, as noted by Olson (2020), the WNBA, along with the NBA, has partnered with GLAAD to show their support for Spirit Day, which supports LGBTQ+ youth. The WNBA was an official partner of Spirit Day in 2019, with players Sue Bird, Layshia Clarendon, and Breanna Stewart posting their support on social media. Clearly, the WNBA now notably embraces its LGBTQ+ fan base. In fact, the league is open about the fact that many of its stars identify as queer (Streeter, 2020). Layshia Clarendon, WNBA New York Liberty, who is trans and non-binary, publicly shared her top surgery photos (Kim, 2021). The New York Liberty team has fully supported Clarendon, thus furthering the support and open view of not only fans who identify as LGBTQ+, but players as well.

It is important in this description of lesbian athlete activism to apply queer theory. Within this theoretical approach, the primary tenets reflect identity that is considered fluid, "antinormative (sexual) politics, and a critique of heteronormativity" (Waldron, 2019, p. 26). Women athletes and women athletes of color examine the normative views of heterosexuality and femininity, along with other dominant white discourse. King (2008) noted the use of this antinormative politics suggests gay men and lesbian women may resist a traditional depiction of marriage as it promotes a normalized, dominant view. Furthering this perspective, it is important in sports to support the views of both gender conformers and gender transformers in order to examine gender binary expectations (Travers, 2006). How can athlete activism disrupt what has been gendered, expected athlete norms? As we examine heteronormativity, the activism of Black athletes and queer athletes has and will continue to serve a platform for change. It is important to note this visibility and activism must continue to not be obscured by protests of male athletes (Cooky & Antunovic, 2020).

WOMEN'S SPORTS AS SECONDARY TO MEN'S

Women's sports have never been given the same kind of media attention, promotion, resources, or pay as men's sports on an amateur, school, or professional level (Billings et al., 2014; Cooky et al., 2021; Steidinger, 2020). Only in the Olympic games have women athletes achieved quantitatively similar airtime and coverage as men athletes. Yet, this coverage, and resultant stories, has primarily focused on sports with women wearing bikinis such as beach volleyball or traditionally "feminine" sports such as ice skating or gymnastics emphasizing women's appearance, thus setting them apart for their femininity (Billings et al., 2014).

Tracking women's sports televised coverage for three decades, a 2021 longitudinal study by Cooky et al. found that women continue to receive very limited media coverage. In the most recent iteration of their 30-year study, these authors added social media content and online sports newsletters to their analyses. Even with this additional, non-traditional coverage, Cooky and colleagues still found that men's sports composed an overwhelming majority of the media content. In each of their studies, men's basketball, baseball, and football consumed a majority of the airtime and attention over any other sports. The researchers did note, however, that changes in the manner women's sports were covered had occurred over time. In the 1990s, women athletes often received media coverage based on their beauty and whiteness; hence, much attention was given to a beautiful, white tennis player, Anna Kournikova, who never won a major championship. In the early 2000s, stories that sexualized or derided women athletes began to decline, and the focus of media attention became women athletes' status as wives or girlfriends of men, and/or their roles as mothers. Cooky and her co-authors labeled this type of coverage as "ambivalent" (p. 13). By 2014, the researchers noted that the sexualized coverage and framing of women by their relationship to men and children characteristic of the early 2000s had declined. They dubbed the new nature of coverage "gender-bland sexism" (p. 13) because announcers expressed less excitement and interest about women's sports than men's, often reporting coverage of women with a monotone presentation and less glitzy, less enthusiastic approach. Gender-bland sexism continues today, but with some exceptions. When a women's team represents a nation, such as the US Women's National Team in the 2019 World Cup soccer championship, it is presented as sensational and thrilling rather than dull and bland. Also, when the team is local, a "homer," such as a women's college basketball team in the NCAA March Madness tournament, its local coverage may be elevated. But neither of these instances brings attention to other women's sports, nor enhances overall prominent coverage of women's sports in the same manner as is covered for men's sports, the researchers noted. In addition, while men athletes' community service and social justice activities are often highlighted in sports and news media, women athletes rarely receive such media focus. Cooky and her co-authors point out the US Women's National Team's fight for equal pay (they win more matches and championships than the men) and the WNBA's social justice initiatives and youth education programs are examples of exceptional efforts that have received little sports media coverage (Cooky et al., 2021).

Another element important to note is the pay discrepancy between women's and men's sports. For example, WNBA players receive a fraction of the salaries garnered by NBA players (Steidinger, 2020). Top WNBA player Sue Bird's 2021–2022 salary with the Seattle Storm is $221,450 ("Sue Bird," 2021). In contrast, top NBA player LeBron James's current salary with the Los Angeles Lakers is $39 million ("LeBron James," 2021), meaning Bird's salary is less than 1% of James's salary. Some sports fans argue that men athletes bring in much more revenue and therefore deserve higher pay. However, Bird and other women athletes point out that men and women players work just as hard as each other and therefore should be paid equally for doing the same work (Arail, 2021). Also, Bird notes, investors are willing to put money into men's sports based on potential, while women's sports have never received the same recognition or been given a chance in sports media to prove they can attract large audiences. As Steidinger (2020) asserts, the WNBA has increased its viewership over time, but despite the players' hard work to play well and promote their league, they are often framed negatively in sports media, which holds back their progress. Even though several WNBA players, such as Bird, Brittney Griner, and Diana Taurasi, may have achieved the status of household names, the league remains ignored and marginalized in most sports media.

WNBA ATHLETES AND SOCIAL MEDIA ACTIVISM

In July 2020, Los Angeles Sparks player and president of the Player's Association Nneka Ogwumike and Seattle Storm player Sue Bird announced on social media and in an op-ed that players were dedicating the 2020 WNBA season, which began July 25, to social justice. In a photo, Ogwumike wore a black T-shirt that said "Phenomenally Black" and Bird wore one that read, "Black Lives Matter." In their op-ed they named summer 2020 as, "a moment of national reckoning," and said they were advocating for "a community that reflects incredible diversity, real inclusion, a long tradition of proud activism, and a deep commitment to fighting injustice" (Ogwumike & Bird, 2020). On July 27, 2020, Ogwumike tweeted (see figure 6.1) the op-ed and wrote that "supporting WNBA players means more than just being a fan. It's feminism."

Figure 6.1   Tweet by Nneka Ogwumike (Ogwumike, 2020). *Source*: Screenshot captured from Twitter.

While athlete activism is not a new phenomenon, the popularity and appeal of the modern sports industry creates a powerful platform for activist speech (Kaufman & Wolff, 2010). Increasingly, athletes are also celebrities and social media influencers, with popular athletes appealing to a wide audience (Galily, 2019). Many professional athletes, like LeBron James and Megan Rapinoe, are translating skills in sport to skills in the public arena. Even college-level athletes are not only active in terms of social justice, but they are also savvy about how they weave their beliefs into their personal images (Kluch, 2020).

Celebrities, broadly, can leverage social media to speak out on political issues and persuade fans (Nisbett & Schartel Dunn, 2019). As such, athletes use their celebrity and popularity to channel attention toward social activism and/or political issues (Allen & Miles, 2020). Athletes speaking out on social media can amplify or inspire larger discussions (Frederick et al., 2019) and speak to a wider spectrum of ideological viewpoints (Hayat et al., 2020).

Many WNBA players use their social media influencer status to share personal stories about racism and bias. Layshia Clarendon of the New York Liberty shared on Twitter the daily mental calculus that she and other people of color must do in order to navigate banal situations (like shopping) that can easily escalate into deadly situations (see figure 6.2). These personal narratives are important because feeling connected with an influencer can change people's attitudes and perceptions about political issues (Nisbett & Schartel Dunn, 2019). Moreover, through these individual narratives, the players and coaches quilt together a larger united narrative driving social justice to the forefront of the league's brand and identity.

Celebrity athletes are also employing the power of social media to break the historic confines of sports management and ownership. Athlete activism, be it in person or via social media, continues to be a controversial practice that remains subject to debates over whether athletes should use their platforms for voicing their opinions (Agyemang et al., 2020). A common refrain

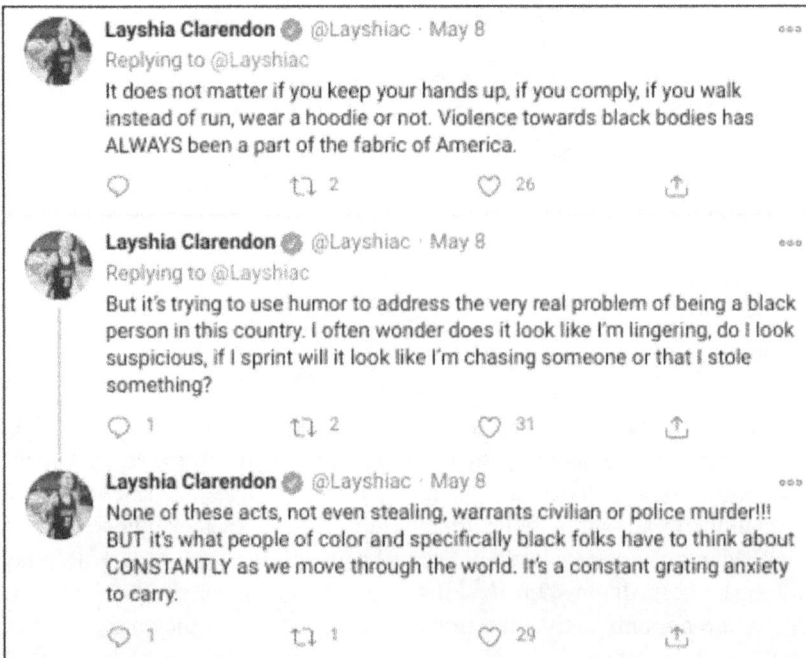

Layshia Clarendon ☑ @Layshiac · May 8
Replying to @Layshiac
It does not matter if you keep your hands up, if you comply, if you walk instead of run, wear a hoodie or not. Violence towards black bodies has ALWAYS been a part of the fabric of America.
♡ 2   ♡ 26

Layshia Clarendon ☑ @Layshiac · May 8
Replying to @Layshiac
But it's trying to use humor to address the very real problem of being a black person in this country. I often wonder does it look like I'm lingering, do I look suspicious, if I sprint will it look like I'm chasing someone or that I stole something?
♡ 1   ♡ 2   ♡ 31

Layshia Clarendon ☑ @Layshiac · May 8
None of these acts, not even stealing, warrants civilian or police murder!!! BUT it's what people of color and specifically black folks have to think about CONSTANTLY as we move through the world. It's a constant grating anxiety to carry.
♡ 1   ♡ 1   ♡ 29

Figure 6.2 Tweets from Layshia Clarendon of the New York Liberty (Clarendon, 2020).
Source: Screenshot captured from Twitter.

among critics and political detractors is that players *should shut up and dribble* (Galily, 2019). The result of this controversy has produced an iterative process whereby athletes who speak out on social and political issues often receive pushback from corporate management and some in the fan community (Galily, 2019; Kaufman, 2008), but, ultimately, break through to a wider audience (Hayat et al., 2020).

The players and coaches of the WNBA, who receive less notoriety and coverage that men's teams or sports do (Cooky et al., 2021), do not rely on the same mechanisms that male athletes use to speak out on social justice. Arguably the mechanism that male athletes use is celebrity, which drives mentions, attention, and coverage. The drawback with this approach is the "shut up and dribble" backlash that male athletes receive for activist speech (Galily, 2019). Based on analysis of the WNBA top athletes, the women athletes seem somewhat able to avoid this backlash. Perhaps, this is due to the lower salaries they receive compared to their male counterparts and the fact that they often present a united front with multiple athletes spreading the same message in a unified, collective way. Unlike prominent men in sports, this gives them strength in numbers and a strong sense of community. Additionally, the WNBA's corporate web site and social media presence, in supporting its players, makes a concerted effort to display community activism, social justice engagement, and the power of women. For instance, tweets from Minnesota Lynx assistant coach Rebekkah Brunson (figure 6.3) exemplify the way the league, players, and the community came together after George Floyd was killed in May 2020.

We argue that athletes are increasingly empowered by social media-based fan communities that go beyond sports fandom. Indeed, social media and social media-based action can circumvent dominant media and corporate narratives, shifting some power to those who traditionally have less agency. This is reflected in the actions of WNBA players and coaches who are less likely to be mega-celebrities like LeBron James, yet who still are doing important activist work via social justice organizations and fan communities established on social media. However, despite the resurgence of athlete activism, individual male athlete actions continue to overshadow the collective work of women athletes (Cooky & Antunovic, 2020).

A perusal of the WNBA's web and social presence suggests that the athletes are at the forefront of integrating calls for social action into their social media sites. Yet, these athletes have had to find a new paradigm in which to enact social change—apparent in their efforts to: (1) build community; (2) engage important stakeholders; (3) protest as a collective action; and (4) enact long-term campaigns and actions. Unlike most other professional sports agencies, the official league content of the WNBA falls in line with the collective tone set by the women athletes. An example of this content—featured on the WNBA

Figure 6.3 Tweets from Rebekkah Brunson, Assistant Coach with Minnesota Lynx (Brunson, 2020). *Source*: Screenshot captured from Twitter.

website (https://www.wnba.com/)—focused on the hashtag #BossWomen, which highlights "all WNBA players" as opposed to highlighting just a few of the more famous players. The content also echoed the calls for social justice (featuring a player wearing a "Say Her Name" shirt) so prevalent in the players' social media from the 2020 season. The WNBA players and the league seem to be more in unison compared to the men's league, which often involves highly publicized differences between players, owner, and league management.

WNBA ATHLETES: MAKING HISTORY, MAKING PROGRESS

Through social media, WNBA athletes leverage their social capital and power as influencers to drive a social justice narrative that circumvents the league's corporate ownership. Indeed, the athletes have been so successful at activist messaging that now, corporate ownership tends to fall in line with the athletes. In this way, we argue the women's collective style is much more productive as compared to the men's individualistic style. In other words, they are finding power in a united voice and a united community. This unity is apparent in the WNBA player's spring 2021 public service announcement featuring Layshia Claredon, A'ja Wilson, Elizabeth Williams, and Nneka Ogwumike, urging Black women to get the COVID-19 vaccine. The ad aims to combat vaccine resistance among Black women as a community and calls upon them to "protect ourselves and our families now" in a campaign called "Our Health is Worth a 'Shot'" (WNBA, 2021, April 15). The players and coaches are emblematic of the power of Black women working to support their community.

With an intersectional approach, the WNBA has responded and continues to respond to the social justice aims that have concerned a community and a nation who have watched the killings of Black men and women at the hands of police, leading to a fight for a more just and inclusive society. Collins (2019) notes that Black women's community work has a long-standing tradition of protecting the lives of young Black people, combating white supremacy, maintaining "families, organizations, and other institutions of Black civil society," and changing institutions (p. 167). WNBA players and coaches are reflecting the work of women dating back to Wells-Barnett's anti-lynching campaigns of the late nineteenth and early twentieth centuries, to the Black women who risked their lives to lead civil rights campaigns of the 1950s and 1960s. This tradition of collective activism for the greater good is a form of "radical resistance," according to Collins (2019, p. 168). Black women's work in this arena has led to Black feminism, which aligns itself with the human rights movement as well as other social justice movements and combines with new technologies like social media to create an intersectional political activist movement that seeks to protect, promote, and advance Black lives. Black women's approaches to "social problems drew upon intersectionality as an analytical tool for analyzing intersectional power relations, and flexible solidarity as a necessary strategy for political action" (Collins, p. 172). By demonstrating publicly for #BlackLivesMatter and other social justice campaigns, as well as walking out on games to promote social justice, WNBA players and coaches are changing the game itself by their collective action of putting themselves on the line on behalf of others. They follow a legacy of American Black women's activism. Their political actions, much like the activism of women such as Rosa Parks in the American civil rights movement, supported and spurred men (such as NBA athletes) to follow and then receive more attention than the women, for the work the women actually did in the first place—an inevitable reflection of masculine hegemony in a patriarchal society. For instance, in May 2021, both the WNBA and NBA used their platforms to urge Congress to pass the George Floyd Justice in Policing Act (Buckner, 2021b); the WNBA has been working toward police reform since at least 2016.

The WNBA also has demonstrated a forward-thinking approach in its current embracing of LGBTQ+ people in all aspects—players, coaches, and fans. While the league for many years tried to hide its gay players behind a cloak of heteronormativity, the WNBA now celebrates it by being open about the fact many of its players identify as queer. As noted by both Kauer (2009) and Travers (2006), queer theory offers the opportunity for inclusion of non-conforming actions and acceptance of the organization of sports beyond traditional gender-conforming behavior. The league now reaches out to gay and lesbian fans, has partnered with GLAAD to assist LGBTQ+ young people, and showed support for players such as Layshia Clarendon of the New York Liberty, who identifies as trans and nonbinary. The WNBA's activism in this area resists the normalization of heterosexuality and of binary gender expectations in society. The players, the coaches and the owners of the WNBA are aware of who the league's players and fans are, and its high-profile, progressive—even radical—actions and activism are changing society and setting the tone and the bar for men's sports to follow.

Response

WNBA Athletes Can Spur Women and Girls
to Speak Out About Injustice

Briana Wallace

As someone who identifies as a Black woman and a female athlete, I know Black female athletes are constantly fighting to be seen, heard, and respected. For instance, as I write this, WNBA star Brittney Griner is in Russian custody and has received very limited media coverage. If she were white and male, everyone would be talking about her case, and it would be all over the news until she was safely home. I also can't help but think that if WNBA athletes were paid equally to NBA athletes, then Griner would not have to play in Russia in the first place. Female athletes are not given the same opportunity and platform to generate revenue like male athletes. For instance, you can most likely go to any sports store and find a jersey of a male athlete, but there will be no jerseys or merchandise of any female athletes.

On a more personal note, I saw the marginalized status of being a woman in sport up-close while I was a college athlete. The male sport teams received more athletic gear, special treatment, recognition, and media attention. In addition to that, the highest paid employee in my college was the men's basketball coach.

As a fan and athlete, watching the WNBA speak out publicly about the injustices going on in the world is truly inspiring. I think the WNBA using their platform and voice is great for young girls to look up to so that they, too, may speak up and stand up for things that are important to them. In college athletics, athletes must attend events with speakers who talk to us about different topics. One time, only the female athletes had to attend. As all the female teams sat down, none of them sat in the first row. When the event began, the three female panelists started by saying that if males were in attendance tonight, then they would have sat in the first row. The panelist then made all the teams get up and sit up closer. She reiterated how important it is for women to use our voices and own any room we walk into.

When I reflect on my own college team's involvement with activism, LGBTQ rights, and women's rights, the discussion was mainly among ourselves in our locker room. We were more comfortable talking to each other about certain issues. For instance, once I walked into the locker room and my teammates were falsely insinuating that Black people do not struggle with mental health problems. One of the players involved was Black and she mentioned that Black people must be strong, and that she does not know of anyone from our race that has suffered from mental health issues or has spoken up about it. My teammates asked my opinion on it since I was majoring in psychology, and I informed them people from all different races and backgrounds can suffer from mental health problems. This instance highlights the importance of people who are in the spotlight (e.g., professional athletes, celebrities) to talk about things they are going through or experiencing, because it shows others if they are struggling, they are not alone.

For me, playing on a predominately white sports team makes it hard to speak up on racial social injustices. At times it just gets swept under the rug and people do not feel comfortable talking about it. However, after I graduated and after the deaths of Breonna Taylor and George Floyd at the hands of police, I had two Black teammates who participated in interviews for our college athletics celebration of Black History Month. It was gratifying to see my teammates talking about issues that relate to race and using their voices to spark discussion. Now that so many professional leagues have stood up against social injustice, more college teams are getting involved and using their voices to speak up. The WNBA league has demonstrated that playing a sport gives people the opportunity to do something they love, but also gives people the platform to use their voices, connect with people, and to shine a light on social issues that are important to them. I have recently been accepted into the Counseling Psychology doctoral program at the University of North Texas. I plan to use my voice in the future as a licensed psychologist and sport psychology consultant. In this role, I will be able to advocate and support female athletes.

REFERENCES

Agyemang, K. J. A., Singer, J. N., & Weems, A. J. (2020). 'Agitate! Agitate! Agitate!': Sport as a site for political activism and social change. *Organization, 27*(6), 952–968. https://doi.org/10.1177/1350508420928519

Allen, S., & Miles, B. (2020). Unapologetic Blackness in action: Embodied resistance and social movement scenes in Black Celebrity activism. *Humanity & Society, 44*(4), 375–402. https://doi.org/10.1177/0160597620932886

Arail, C. (2021, January 26). Sue Bird: "Like, you have to pay the top players." SB Nation Swish Appeal. https://www.swishappeal.com/wnba/2021/1/26/22248717/wnba-sue-bird-podcast-people-mostly-admire-steven-levitt-economics-womens-basketball-pay-salary-cba

Ayala, E. L. (2020, August 29). The NBA's walkout is historic. But the WNBA paved the way. *The Washington Post*. https://www.washingtonpost.com/outlook/2020/08/29/nba-wnba-racial-injustice/

Becker, A. B. (2014). *Examining 25 years of public opinion on gay rights and marriage.* http://blog.oup.com/2014/10/examining-25-years-public-opinion-data-gay-rights-marriage/

Billings, A. C., Angelini, J. R., MacArthur, P. J., Bissell, K., & Smith, L. R. (2014). (Re)Calling London: The gender frame agenda within NBC's primetime broadcast of the 2012 Olympiad. *Journalism & Mass Communication Quarterly, 91*, 38–58. https://doi.org/10.10.1177/1077699013514416.

Brunson, R. [@twin1532]. (2020, May 28). *Tirelessly!!!!!* [Retweet of Minnesota Lynx @minnnestoalynx] [Tweet]. Twitter. https://twitter.com/twin1532/status /1266037047594229760?s=20

Brunson, R. [@twin1532]. (2020, August 26). I'm so very proud to be a part of the WNBA, basketball and the entire sports community. [Tweet]. Twitter. https://twitter.com/twin1532/status/1298768104483364865?s=20

Buckner, C. (2021a, January 7). WNBA players helped oust Kelly Loeffler from the Senate. Will she last in the league? *The Washington Post.* Retrieved from https://www.washingtonpost.com/sports/2021/01/07/wnba-loeffler-warnock-senate-atlanta-dream/

Buckner, C. (2021b, May 25). A year after George Floyd's murder, NBA, WNBA players push to pass police reform. *The Washington Post.* Retrieved from https://www.washingtonpost.com/sports/2021/05/25/nba-wnba-george-floyd-police-reform/

Bumbaca, C. (2020, August 6). Timeline: The WNBA has been on the forefront of racial justice for years. *USA Today.* https://www.usatoday.com/story/sports/wnba/2020/08/06/wnba-players-protest-racial-justice-years-timeline-kelly-loeffler /3304129001/

Butler, J. (2006). *Gender trouble: Feminism and the subversion of identity.* New York: Routledge.

Clarendon, L. [@Layshiac]. (2020, May 8). It does not matter if you keep your hands up, if you comply, if you walk instead of run. [Tweet]. Twitter.

Collins, P. H. (2019). *Intersectionality as critical social theory.* Durham and London: Duke University Press.

Collins, P. H., & Bilge, S. (2020). *Intersectionality.* 2nd ed. Medford, MA: Polity Press.

Cooky, C., & Antunovic, D. (2020). "This isn't just about us": Articulations of feminism in media narratives of athlete activism. *Urban Education, 8*(4–5), 348–364. https://doi.org/10.1177/0042085908318712

Cooky, C., Council, L. D., Mears, M. A., & Messner, M. A. (March 2021). One and done: The long eclipse of women's sports, 1989–2019. *Communication & Sport.* https://doi.org/10.1177/21674795211003524

Frederick, E. L., Pegoraro, A., & Sanderson, J. (2019). Divided and united: Perceptions of athlete activism at the ESPYS. *Sport in Society, 22*(12), 1919–1936. https://doi.org/10.10.1080/17430437.2018.1530220

Galily, Y. (2019). "Shut up and dribble!"? Athletes activism in the age of twittersphere: The case of LeBron James. *Technology in Society, 58.* https://doi.org/10.1016/j.techsoc.2019.01.002

Hayat, T., Galily, Y., & Samuel-Azran, T. (2020). Can celebrity athletes burst the echo chamber bubble? The case of LeBron James and Lady Gaga. *International Review for the Sociology of Sport, 55*(7), 900–914.

hooks, b. (1981). *Ain't I a woman: Black women and feminism.* Boston: South End Press.

Kauer, K. J. (2009). Queering lesbian sexualities in collegiate sporting spaces. *Journal of Lesbian Studies, 13,* 306–318. doi:10.1080/10894160902876804

Kaufman, P. (2008). Boos, bans, and other backlash: The consequence of being an activist athlete. *Humanity & Society, 32,* 215–237 (August). https://doi.org/10.10.1177/016059760803200302

Kaufman, P., & Wolff, E. A. (2010). Playing and protesting: Sport as a vehicle for social change. *Journal of Sport and Social Issues, 34*(2), 154–175. https://doi.org/10.10.1177/0193723509360218

Kim, M. (2021, February 1). Trans WNBA player Layshia Clarendon shares top surgery photos in heartfelt post, gets full support from team. https://www.them.us/story/wnba-layshia-clarendon-top-surgery-photos-team-support?utm_medium=social&utm_brand=them&utm_source=twitter&utm_social-type=owned

King, S. (2008). What's queer about (queer) sport sociology now? A review essay. *Sociology of Sport Journal, 25,* 419–425.

Klar, R. (2020, August 30). WNBA player defends protests against police brutality amid Trump criticism. *The Hill.* https://thehill.com/homenews/news/514326-wnba-player-defends-protests-over-police-brutality-amid-trump-criticism

Kluch, Y. (2020). "My story is my activism!": (Re-)definitions of social justice activism among collegiate athlete activists. *Communication & Sport, 8*(4–5), 566–590. https://doi.org/10.1177/2167479519897288

Lansbury, J. H. (2014). *A spectacular leap: Black women athletes in twentieth century America.* Fayetteville: University of Arkansas Press.

"LeBron James." (2021). Spotrac. https://www.spotrac.com/nba/los-angeles-lakers/lebron-james-2257/

McDonald, M. (2002). Queering whiteness: The peculiar case of Women's National Basketball Association. *Sociological Perspectives, 45,* 379–396.

Muller, T. K. (2007). Liberty for all? Contested spades of women's basketball. *Gender, Place and Culture: A Journal of Feminist Geography, 14*(2), 197–213.

Mumcu, C., & Lough, N. (2017). Are fans proud of the WNBA's 'pride' campaign? *Sport Marketing Quarterly, 26*(1), 42–54.

Nisbett, G., & Schartel Dunn, S. (2019). Reputation matters: Parasocial attachment, narrative engagement, and the 2018 Taylor Swift political endorsement. *Atlantic Journal of Communication.* https://doi.org/10.10.1080/15456870.2019.1704758

O'Donnell, R. (2020, August 27). WNBA players joined together to protest police brutality after postponing more games. SBNation. https://www.sbnation.com/wnba/2020/8/27/21404486/wnba-players-protest-police-brutality-postponing-games

Ogwumike, N. [@nnemkadi30]. (2020, July 27). *We're dedicating our 2020 season to social justice. That's why, more than ever, we need you to show up for us.* [Image attached] [Tweet]. https://twitter.com/Nnemkadi30/status/1287728460291543040?s=20

Ogwumike, N., & Bird, S. (2020, July 27). WNBA players Nneka Ogwumike and Sue Bird: This moment is so much bigger than sports. We need your support. *Phenomenal Media*. https://phenomenalmedia.com/articles/wnba-op-ed

Olson, M. (2020). NBA and WNBA go purple for Spirit Day. *GLAAD*. https://www.glaad.org/blog/nba-and-wnba-community-go-purple-spirit-day

"Our health is worth a shot" campaign (2021). WNBA. Retrieved from https://www.wnba.com/video/our-health-is-worth-a-shot-covid-19-vaccine-psa/

Out Sports. (2014). *109 athletes, coaches, officials, and sport administrators came out publicly this year*. http://www.outsports.com/2104/12/18/7341179/gay-lgbt-athlees coaches-2014

Perry, A. J. (2020, September 4). How Black women athletes paved the way for the NBA strike. *NPR Code Switch*. https://www.npr.org/sections/codeswitch/2020/09/04/909638021/how-black-women-athletes-paved-the-way-for-the-nba-strike

Roessner, L. A., & Rightler-McDaniels, J. L. (2018). *Political pioneer of the press: Ida B. Wells-Barnett and her transnational crusade for social justice*. Lanham, MD: Lexington Books.

Streeter, K. (2020, October 5). The one name the W.N.B.A. won't say. *The New York Times*. https://www.nytimes.com/2020/10/05/sports/basketball/wnba-loeffler-warnock-blm.html

Steidinger, J. (2020). *Stand up and shout out: Women's fight for equal pay, equal rights, and equal opportunities in sport*. Rowman & Littlefield.

"Sue Bird." (2021). Spottrac. https://www.spotrac.com/wnba/seattle-storm/sue-bird-29952/

Travers, A. (2006). Queering sport lesbian softball leagues and the transgender challenge. *International Review for the Sociology of Sport, 4*, 488–207.

Waldron, J. J. (2019). Four perspectives for understanding LGBTIQ people in sport. In V. Krane (Ed.), *Sex, gender and sexuality in sport: Queer inquiries*. New York: Routledge.

WNBA. (2021, April 15). *Our health is worth a 'shot.'* [Video]. https://www.wnba.com/video/our-health-is-worth-a-shot-covid-19-vaccine-psa/

Wulf, S. (2019, January 30). Athletes and activism: The long, defiant history of sports protests. *The Undefeated*. https://theundefeated.com/features/athletes-and-activism-the-long-defiant-history-of-sports-protests/

Chapter 7

How Social Media Gives Black NBA Athletes a Platform to Rally Around Racial Injustice During the #BlackLivesMatter Movement

Teveraishe Mushayamunda and
Mildred F. Perreault

In 2016, just days apart, Alton Sterling was killed at the hands of law enforcement officers in Baton Rouge, Louisiana, and Philando Castile was shot by police in Minneapolis-St. Paul, Minnesota. These events were followed by public protests concerning racial discrimination and mistreatment of Black people and minorities by law enforcement in communities across the United States and the greater world. Protests took place both in-person and offline, and people engaged around "#BlackLivesMatter" with signs, texts, and voices. In the virtual town square of YouTube, Twitter, Reddit, and in the physical town squares, people began to share their experiences and desires for racial justice. As civilians began to speak up for the rights of Black people, among them were professional athletes sharing messages of conviction and hope (Coombs & Cassilo, 2017).

During the 2016 Excellence in Sports Performance Yearly Awards (ESPYs) in Los Angeles, California, National Basketball League All-Stars introduced the show with a speech against police brutality, injustice, and racism in America. During the live event, and after on their social media accounts, athletes spoke out against the systemic injustices toward Black and brown people (Towler et al., 2020). In fall 2016, San Francisco 49ers quarterback Colin Kaepernick became an icon for social change when he knelt before a football game during the national anthem to protest police brutality (Towler et al., 2020). When Nick Wagoner, the San Francisco 49ers reporter for ESPN's NFL (National Football League) Nation, interviewed Kaepernick in 2016, he shared his reasons for action: "Yes. I'll continue to sit. . . . I'm going to continue to stand with the people that are being oppressed" (Wag-oner, August 28, 2016, para. 4).

Black athletes have elevated their voices in the #BlackLivesMatter move-ment. In 2020, the trend of Black athletes' sharing their perspectives on injus-tice continued even given the challenges of social distancing and the health risks of the COVID-19 pandemic. With the sports season on hold, NBA athletes had space and time to engage in social justice on a more personal level. This study investigated statements made about #BlackLivesMatter from 2016 to 2021 by male Black NBA athletes on the social media platforms YouTube and Twitter. It used Colin Kaepernick's demonstration in 2016 as a starting point and limited the study within that three-and-a-half-year period. The paper examined research conducted on media representations of racial inequality. A growing body of research is being done on the social influences and roles of Black athletes and how Black voices have responded to injustices through media and campaigns. The literature review thus is situated in critical race theory (CRT), and the disciplines of political communication, and media studies: specifically public relations and advertising.

One of the researchers was a Black college athlete and because of his experiences during college, he began to observe these issues and events in real time. This study revisited what he observed firsthand, and is based on his experiences and observations as well as the research team's analysis of videos.

PERSPECTIVES ON SPORTS AND RACE

Until the 1960s, scholars of minority races were absent from scholarship on communication and civil rights and therefore minorities were absent from the main story concerning race and civil rights in American history (Zamudio et al., 2011). BIPOC (those who are black, indigenous, and other people of color) scholars began to revolt from the framework of white supremacy in this conversation. The CRT seeks to create a foundation for minority voices while actively dismantling the ideologies of white supremacy. CRT is a collaborative movement between civil rights scholars and activists to use a critical approach concerning issues of *race* and emphasize a focus on *racial justice* (Zamudio et al., 2011). When using CRT as a lens, it is important to situate how it relates to political communication and advertising. CRT asserts that racism exists within a historical context, offers a way to examine how communication is socially constructed, and seeks to understand how humans exist within and interact with these constructions (Simpson, 2010). Therefore, social fields of study like journalism, strategic and political communication have clear connections to how race and racism are perceived within CRT.

Additionally, politics have become connected to history and social movements, and politics creates a more just society (Heywood, 2001). People identify with sports as part of their social lives. Politics has become more intertwined into every aspect of society, including sports (Kobach & Potter, 2013). Research has shown that Black men are often portrayed in the media as detrimental to society (Deeb & Love, 2017). Often, Black athletes must endure stereotypes in a space that is considered "apolitical"; however, sports as a system often augments the focus on stereotypes around racial traits (Deeb & Love, 2017). What happens when the standards of excellence in communication only come from a white lens? In non-critical approaches which have focused on specific racial stereotypes, whiteness is deemed the standard of judgment. When society regards the frame of whiteness as the standard, people of color are rendered inferior in terms of mental, physical, and emotional potential (Deeb & Love, 2017). While political communication is a vast field, this chapter focuses specifically on research concerning injustices and politics in the Black community, and how Black athletes continue to bring awareness to issues in their community. Studies about sports, race, and politics often use CRT to examine the speeches and actions of Black athletes. CRT provides an alternative framework from previous less inclusive, white-dominant theories, and seeks to challenge these perceptions of racism (Hylton, 2010). CRT has been used to research sports media and communication, as well as the portrayals of minorities. When CRT is applied to sports it presents anti-racists with a framework to challenge theorists viewed as fundamentally racist (Hylton, 2010). This literature explores CRT within the context of race and racism, color blindness and anti-racism, speech acts, sports, and other subcategories within CRT. The voices of Black athletes have been influential in elevating Black voices in their fight to challenge and fight society's perspective of inequality in the United States. In this literature, we include the precepts and principles of CRT to guide the conversation, by examining the storytelling and counter-storytelling elements used by these athletes. These factors have been found to provide different versions of the truth, which counter the dominant perspective of white social scientific theories (Hylton, 2005).

When considering CRT, it is important to take into account the social and economic context of the United States, and how that affects Black Athletes. Throughout the course of American history, Black people have been deprived of the opportunity to create wealth. Most of the time they have had to make up ground from past generations being deprived of these opportunities. For example, rather than accruing wealth over time like their white counterparts, people who are from predominantly Black populations deal with pre-existing inequities stemming from capitalism and classism, patriarchy and sexism and other oppressive perspectives (Cooper et al., 2017, p. 14).

Sports and Activism

Sports is often considered an apolitical space, one in which issues of race and power imbalances are absent; however, Carrington (2011) argues that there is indeed a political and racial aspect to sport that dictates behavior and power relations. Building on Feagin's (2020) concept of the white racial frame, Carrington (2011) suggested a white colonial frame exists, there are systematic constraints that highlight white supremacy as a feature of colonialism and produce anti-black racism within white-dominated cultures (Carrington, 2010). CRT provides a perspective that gives a more Black-centered insight into how Black athletes navigate being a part of the industry of professional sports. This presents a challenge because in many ways Black athletes must juggle the pressures of their race and celebrity without being exploited, and perhaps even harness that position as a platform for activism. Being a Black person in America and being a professional athlete both bring their own sets of difficulties. Historically Black athletes must juggle those two aspects of their life while having the responsibility of being an activist (Wulf, 2019). In this task, the main objective of the CRT is to attempt to give BIPOC people a voice, thus providing a more robust account of history, culture, and experiences.

Within the context of sport, the range of Black activist actions has sought social justice through acquiring legitimacy, gaining political access and positional diversity, demanding dignity and respect, and securing and transferring power via economic and technological capital versus the dominant narrative of the Black male as an egotistical misguided agitator (Cooper et al., 2017). In CRT's attempt to debunk myths, it brings a set of themes and goals that it tries to address. For example, social justice and transformation are seen as core goals. CRT also presents a challenge to dominant ideas of "objectivity, metricity, color-blindness, race neutrality, and equal opportunity" (Hylton, 2010, p. 339).

CRT provides a framework to begin the discussion around racial injustice as it continues to develop into racial inequality. Within the framework that is CRT, society is constantly being challenged when it comes to race, and this discussion is increasingly taking place in the public sphere—in online communication, politics, entertainment and sports. CRT has also allowed spaces for sports activists to discuss and advocate for social justice in an "inherently an exploitative space" and "serve as a powerful tool for emancipation, liberation, and empowerment against hegemonic forces" (Cooper et al., 2017, p. 166).

Athletes and Social Media Engagement

Social media engagement is a relational approach to social media strategy which uses images and text to engage audiences (Quesenberry, 2015). Past studies have examined the social media engagement of athletes. Specifically studies have examined cases concerning social justice and (football) soccer, NASCAR, and NCAA, NBA, and NFL athletes (Quesenberry, 2015; Vale & Fernandes, 2018). An understanding of social media engagement around online brand relationships can be found by examining several factors. Social media engagement includes the value of information, entertainment, personal identity, integration and social interactions, personal empowerment, and brand love (Vale & Fernandes, 2018). Audiences grow their loyalty to athletes, teams, and particular sports (Vale & Fernandes, 2018). The connection to audiences through social media allows athletes to establish a consistent brand identity (or the collection of elements that a company creates to portray its image to consumers) without the team, sport, or even traditional media outlets as gatekeepers (Hipke & Hachtmann, 2014). In studying the connections made by marketers with target audiences around sports, Hipke and Hatchmann (2014) found that successful campaigns involved: (1) varied approaches in coordination of postings (i.e., considering timing, linking to events, cross-posting to multiple platforms, visual and graphically appealing posts, video posts), (2) athletic communications as content gatekeepers (i.e., either being held back allowed to post content by team communications and public relations professionals), (3) desire to incorporate sponsors and generate revenue, (4) focus on building fan loyalty through engagement, and (5) challenges of negativity and metrics (or the way negative reception affected engagement with a post). Similarly, another study found that fans who are highly engaged on and offline are more likely to share what they see and hear via word of mouth and with their social media audiences and fan communities (Vale & Fernandes, 2018).

Situating social media engagement requires relating it to *engagement* as defined in public relations, marketing, and strategic communication scholarship. According to public relations research engagement is:

> An affective, cognitive, and behavioral state wherein publics and organizations who share mutual interests in salient topics interact along continua that range from passive to active and from control to collaboration, and is aimed at goal attainment, adjustment, and adaptation for both publics and organizations. (Dhanesh, 2017, p. 925)

Engagement exists within a challenging dichotomy between engagement as *collaboration* or *engagement as control* (Sloan, 2009) which scholars have only recently begun to unpack (Dhanesh, 2017). The concept of engagement has become a foundational yet central concept in public relations and communication scholarship (Dhanesh, 2017). However, the adoption of a postmodern and activist approach to engagement—one which involves two-way dialogue and is more equality based—have become more normalized in strategic communication practice and also in scholarship (Holtzhausen, 2013). Public Relations scholars like Grunig (2001) also encountered these challenges, situating his two-way symmetrical model as one that blended stakeholder engagement as "collaborative advocacy and cooperative antagonism" (Dhanesh, 2017, p. 927). The two-way symmetrical model which focuses on dialogue and attempts to sustain mutually beneficial relationships between an organization and its key stakeholders (Grunig, 2001). This dialogue creates an opportunity for those making a message to advocate for specific causes, and rally those with common beliefs together for action, or collaborative advocacy. However it also allows opportunities for negative thoughts and statements to spread among that same group resulting in cooperative antagonism, or rallying around a common hostility or opposition.

Recently, researchers have also discussed the need for more rich analysis of the development of online content with meaningful stakeholder engagement (Dhanesh, 2017; Greenwood, 2007). Established athletes with several years of experience have the benefit of an established team brand and farther-reaching social media audience than younger athletes or other celebrities, by nature of growth over time. They do not have to rely on social media to create an audience, but rather can use the space to reach beyond those fans who already engage with them online. Typically, social media influencers will seek to engage fans in ways that provide long-term benefits to their brand or affiliated causes in order to support their work through advertising (Woodcock & Johnson, 2019). These could be to encourage engagement in their personal work, causes or interests, but could also be centered around a particular ideology (Delbaere et al., 2021). On social media platforms, consumers can connect with a brand, the media, and each other by resharing the content or commenting below it. This is giving them a more active role in brand storytelling (Gensler et al., 2013; Harrigan et al. 2018).

Intersections of Race and Celebrity

Black athletes may be seen as role models for their heroics in their respective sports. This infatuation with these athletes leads to a variety of challenges when sharing views about social justice. For example, the bodies of athletes are sought after because their physique allows them to perform at a prominent level. In addition, their performance allows them to make a profit from their bodies:

> Although race is a social construct in sport, race is sometimes used to classify athletes into distinct categories, which are then assigned meaning according to the belief in "natural" or "biological" traits. (Deeb & Love, 2017, p. 98)

Because society has created a social construct of devaluing the Black body and people, this concept creates a psychological struggle that Black athletes have had to endure past and present. Black athletes are often assumed to have natural talents for physical strength and agility whereas white athletes are seen as less physically capable, therefore white athletes have been portrayed as harder working than Black athletes with similar accomplishments.

The study recognizes the role intersectionality plays for Black athletes in their fight for equality, including the interactions of race, economic status, and other social challenges like gender (Crenshaw, 1991). Intersectionality addresses the ways in which race, class, gender, and other factors overlap and interdependent systems of discrimination or disadvantage.

Despite the racial integration of sports that began in 1947 with Jackie Robinson (Kelly, 2005), Black athletes were commodity that brought profit to their respective sports (Wulf, 2019). The NBA is made up of 74.2% of Black players (Spears, 2016). Compared to the NFL, the NBA has a longer season, has fewer players to pay, resulting in the players receiving higher wages compared to their football peers. Another factor that separates the leagues is the power that NBA players have. As is the case with other professional sports, NBA players can be vocal about social justice issues, but unlike the NFL, teams are smaller and therefore players might be more noticeable. Social media gives Black athletes the freedom to be open about their personal and political views but also puts more responsibility on the players to speak up (Darroch, 2010). Even though Black athletes are not responsible for creating this social construct of devaluation, many have expressed the pressure to address social injustices both on and off the court and to be a voice of change. The majority of the labor to address these societal issues often falls on Black people while those in the majority, the white population, have the privilege to reject the disparity of inequality in America (Lowery, 2020). In this case, Black athletes use their platforms to bring awareness and are often labeled as social activists. With this perspective from the literature in mind the researchers sought to evaluate two specific foci for the research. First, we sought to understand how Black NBA players were sharing videos about social justice and what that social media engagement with their online audience looked like in response to #BlackLivesMatter. Second, we sought to understand how engagement was taking place around these videos.

DISCOURSE ANALYSIS OF VIDEOS

To provide more context to the research, we used a variety of videos from Black athletes who have been vocal on social justice efforts posted to Twitter, YouTube, and Facebook. In response to the injustices, inequalities, systematic racism, and other factors facing BIPOC communities, various Black athletes have decided to use their platforms to implement and encourage change. For the study, videos were selected based on a variety of keywords in a search engine to identify the discourse around #BlackLivesMatter. The keywords included: #BlackLivesMatter and athletes, LeBron James and social justice, Malcolm Brogden and social justice, Black athletes and activism, Russell Wilson and activism, Jaylen Brown and activism, Malcolm Jenkins and Social Justice, NBA players and racial equality, Milwaukee Bucks statement, Chanse Sylvie and social justice, Deion Sanders Voice, and Fox Sports Voices, Golden State Warriors Skip White House Visit.

Using discourse analysis (which studies written and/or spoken language in relation to its social context) the researchers evaluated these themes by considering narratives, language in context, and how that language is used within a particular institution (Candlin, 2014; Fairclough, 2001). We chose this approach because the research entailed evaluating the videos from the lens of a former Black collegiate athlete, who has done prior research and has previous knowledge of Black athlete activism.

Most of the videos that were studied primarily featured Black NBA athletes who had name recognition (many ranked as ESPN's most influential NBA players of all time) using their personal or team social media platforms (Espn.com, 2018, March 28). When searching, we chose videos based on an initial search of #BlackLivesMatter on YouTube that yielded approximately 264 videos. In order to gain a more in-depth perspective on the videos, we took a smaller sample. To narrow our sample, we chose videos longer than three minutes for more in-depth analysis. The 20 videos were selected based on factors of social media engagement as determined by Hipke and Hachtmann (2014). Officially branded videos from news sources and athletes were selected, and user-generated content from non-NBA athletes was omitted from the sample. We chose 20 videos from the keywords provided. We also aimed for a variety of videos with references to different incidents (Breonna Taylor, George Floyd, etc.). We analyzed the amount of reshares or retweets, comments, logos, number and types of uniforms worn (since that identifies the player's team), views, likes, and the time period they were shared.

In line with qualitative approaches discussed by Lindlof and Taylor (2017), we thematically labeled categories both individually and together. We then compared our tallies to identify consistencies and differences. We came up with a number of themes concerning #BlackLivesMatter and specifically those involving political statements (i.e., encouragement to vote or run for political office), and those concerning social justice (i.e., voicing the idea that all people should have equal access to wealth, health, well-being, justice, privileges, and opportunity regardless of their legal, political, economic, racial, or other circumstances) were identified and tallied. We each discussed the themes and points they recognized from the first five videos and used these to code the remaining 15 videos. We identified a timeline based on events relevant to Black Lives Matter in 2020 and evaluated the responses of teams, players, and the NBA in relation to these events.

The first category coded for in each video was the video type or source. The codes identified were public relations, news source, or blog. Most were from news sources, although some were from private or public relations outlets. Of those videos, most of the videos coded were from a news source while the minority were from a public relations type source. Twitter was the main social media platform used for the distribution of these videos. At the time of data collection (early 2021) all together the videos had 9,637 retweets and shares, with an average of 963.72 per video. The retweets and shares garnered conversion that led to 2,668 comments in total averaging 333.5 comments per video. We also spotted logo recognition throughout the videos, with 93 logos in all 20 videos, and an average of a logo sighting 5.5 times. In addition to the presence of logos, in all the videos there was also the presence of players wearing uniforms. Players wore uniforms a total of 46 times, an average of 3 times per video. From all the videos that were coded they all had a total of 5,564,374 views, while there was an average of 428,028 views per video. Lastly, in all the videos there were a total of 101,673 likes and an average of 7,262.4 likes per video.

SOCIAL MEDIA ANALYSIS

For this study we sought to understand more clearly how Black athletes used videos on social media to engage their followers in social justice discourse. We observed that there were a number of observations concerning the context, topics, and themes of the videos. The videos included specific statements regarding racially charged murders, social justice and political engagement, personal experiences, and interactions with other public comments made by athletes concerning racial injustice. The videos also included groups of athletes as well as individual athletes. In addition, there were some athletes that played a key role in the conversation more than others.

Specific Statements Regarding Racially Related Murders

For example, more than half the videos that were coded were made in 2020. In 2020, the deaths of Ahmaud Arbery, Breonna Taylor, and George Floyd, and other Black people at the hands of police or white vigilantes sparked international protests that involved millions of people. This meant that the majority of the videos from this time period were posted in close proximity to these events. Older content (pre-2018) shared in these videos included images and references to specific events that involved Colin Kaepernik and even older instances of protest including Muhammad Ali's protest of joining the army in 1967 and the "Fists of Fury" protest at the 1968 Olympics by runners Tommie Smith and John Carlos. Lastly, from the videos that were assessed, most of the videos came from Twitter, but were sometimes posted to YouTube and other social media outlets. The videos that came from Twitter received the most engagement—meaning they had more retweets and comments associated with them.

Political Statements

A few of the videos made specific political statements. For example, LeBron James's *More than a Vote* series video gave the history behind voter suppression against Black people in America. This video amplified the problems of the past and used them to empower and persuade others to use their voices to vote in the next election. James partnered with former First Lady Michelle Obama, as well as other athletes and political figures, to create and run the *More than a Vote* campaign to increase voter participation and to fight against voter suppression. Through this video, James narrated as historical and current-day images and videos were used to tell the story of the organization.

Personal Experiences

In a Bleacher Report video, Bradley Beal, CJ McCollum, Andre Iguodala, and other NBA stars spoke up about racism for Black history month. Players highlighted the injustices that Black athletes endure, and the challenges that they face when they decide to speak up. For example, one athlete, Sterling Brown, discussed how he was a victim of harassment from the police, and he opened up to the audience about his experience. The video shared by Brown compiled other images and video clips to tell his personal story, although some of them were not specifically of Brown. Other athletes made statements of solidarity and referenced statements made by civil rights leaders like Martin Luther King, Jr.

Interactions with Public Comments or Events

In the first video with James, he was joined by former president Barack Obama in his series, *The Shop: Uninterrupted*, where they talked about voting. This conversation took place in late October 2020, during the presidential election. The title of that video clip was, *Barack Obama Explains Why It's Our Duty to Fight for Equality* (Uninterrupted, 2020). In this clip

LeBron James, Maverick Carter, and Barack Obama discussed the lasting impact that racism has had within the context of voting. Obama proceeds to elaborate on the importance of staying vigilant and persistent in the fight for equality.

The NBA also posted a video titled *The Truth is #BlackLivesMatter* in summer 2020. This was a short video but featured numerous people, images, and clips of people amid social justice efforts. During this time, the country was experiencing a racial awakening in response to the continual death of unarmed Black people by law enforcement (Worland, 2020). The video showed a compilation of NBA players leading peaceful protests in their cities through marching and speeches. These videos encompassed one of the main messages of this study. Athletes often drew attention to the progress they have made despite the racial and social divide, and in addition they used videos to reference historical and contemporary events where Black athlete's voices have been elevated. Many of these videos included statements concerning social justice similar to those made in the past by Black athletes during national events as acts of peaceful protest. NBA players are influential voices and are seen as community leaders. They recognize that they are expected to speak up and provide a glimpse of hope in these times of tragedy. They speak to this purpose throughout the videos and provide words of encouragement centered around this cause.

Group versus Individual Dynamic

In the videos we analyzed, LeBron James is involved with 5 of the 20. James was highlighted in this study because he is arguably the greatest NBA player of his generation, and with that title comes a tremendous amount of responsibility on and off the court (Coombs & Cassilo, 2017; Jacobson, 2018). He has been able to leverage the title of being the face of the NBA by using his platform to empower and bring awareness to inequality and racism on multiple occasions.

In 15 of the 20 videos, a collection of athletes is involved. Featuring multiple athletes has the potential to garner the attention of multiple audiences (Stever & Lawson, 2013). Therefore, the act of increasing the number of athletes can increase the reach of the audience and increase engagement—as many of these athletes are from many different teams and have different fan bases. One of the videos with the highest viewership had the greatest number of athletes in the frame throughout the video. In the video, the Milwaukee Bucks created a spoken statement on the death of Jacob Blake that took place in Kenosha, Wisconsin. The Bucks protested before their contest against the Orlando Magic, which was a playoff game. Their protest was the first of many protests around the league, as other leagues in sports followed suit.

SOCIAL MEDIA ENGAGEMENT

In considering what social media engagement practices are Black NBA athletes using on their platforms, we found that Black athletes used a variety of
content types and engagement to share their personal views and engage their
publics in the discourse around #BlackLivesMatter. These included using
traditional media (broadcast appearances and events) as well as personal
platforms for multiplatform storytelling approaches.

Traditional Media Platforms

When Black athletes partner with sports channels instead of private channels, their reach grows tremendously. For example, videos on ESPN and
Fox Sports had fewer shares and views as compared to videos posted by
the sports aggregation website Uninterrupted. There were a total of 850,820
views from Fox Sports and ESPN compared to 627,200 views of Uninterrupted. Uninterrupted (uninterrupted.com) is an athlete-empowerment brand
webpage founded by LeBron James and Maverick Carter that cross-posts to
social media platforms and curates news coverage of sports and specifically
Black athletes. When Black athletes had an opportunity to speak out against
inequality on verified sports channels, their words were viewed and shared
widely. Another observation was found that many of the videos were structured as a peaceful form of protest, and actions demanding reparations for
specific racial injustice incidents.

Another video that garnered a lot of engagement was the 2020 ESPYS
video (ESPN, 2020, June 21). It was during the summer of 2020, during
a socially and racially tense season during a pandemic. Therefore, ESPN
recruited Russell Carrington Wilson, a quarterback for the Seattle Seahawks,
FIFA USA, Megan Rapinoe, USA Olympic team women's soccer player,
and Sue Bird, WNBA Seattle Storm and USA Women's Olympic team basketball player. This video used different visuals and mentioned the deaths of
unarmed Black people including George Floyd, Breonna Taylor, and others,
while depicting civil rights violations, death at the hands of law enforcement,
and unequal access to public services. This video's strategic purpose was to
continue the conversation and to bring awareness to the need for dismantling
racism in America.

Personal Platforms

LeBron James has used his platform to help create different platforms like
Uninterrupted, a platform that seeks to empower athletes through effective
storytelling. James has produced several films that have elaborated on the

conversation of inequality and racism from Black athletes' perspectives. James was also an integral part of the *More than a Vote* (https://www.morethanavote.org/, 2021) platform that focused on educating people about their voting rights, dismantling voter suppression, and helping people through the voting process. James has focused beyond the game of basketball and has become the standard of Black athlete activism (Coombs & Cassilo, 2017; Galily, 2019).

Another video that had political statements was one released during the NBA finals in 2018. The video is composed of different statements made during the press conference for The Golden State Warriors and the Cleveland Cavaliers. James also had an interaction with President Trump on Twitter when he "uninvited" the Philadelphia Eagles for a White House visit. During President Trump's presidency, many championship teams opted out of this congratulatory visit to the White House. Throughout President Trump's presidency, he was known for saying offensive remarks seen as divisive. James and various Warriors players spoke up and posted to social media after they decided they were not going to the White House after winning the NBA Finals. James mentioned that neither team would go to the White House because of Trump's derogatory comments concerning acts of protests by Black athletes, and his comments concerning racial injustice and police brutality. Trump's mantra "Make America Great Again" has been seen as a rally cry for many conservatives, but also seen as a divisive tool among Americans. Trump has also been involved in various scandals, including derogatory comments about women. NBA players Kevin Durant, Steph Curry, Draymond Green, and Steve Kerr all made comments regarding the potential White House visit and their disapproval because of Trump.

NBA PLAYERS KEY TO SOCIAL JUSTICE DISCUSSIONS

Through this research we found that NBA players continue to remain key figures in the conversation concerning social justice. Their videos are often shared across platforms, and reshared by celebrities, politicians, fans, and other professionals. Even a year after the murder of George Floyd in May 2020, when this study concluded, NBA athletes were continuing to discuss their concerns openly on their social media platforms as individuals and as a group. The use of social media engagement allows access to broader audiences while also harnessing audiences who identify with different beliefs and opinions. This allows NBA athletes to illuminate social injustices to audiences who might not otherwise experience them.

Examining these different aspects of online videos concerning Black NBA athletes and the Black Lives Matter Movement can give insight into how engaged approaches and storytelling may illuminate the conversation around #BlackLivesMatter. This study recognized the value and potential impact of the narratives shared by Black NBA athletes. Examining social media engagement practices as well as CRT literature provided an opportunity to discuss the implications of this study, and how it alludes to the importance of narratives. Narratives matter, and when people can relate to a narrative purpose is cultivated. When purpose is cultivated, social movements follow—ultimately why it matters. Through the lens of the methodology, a consensus has developed regarding the influence of specific Black athletes. Black athletes are elevated into leaders in times of racial strife concerning the Black community.

Of the 20 videos assessed, LeBron James appeared in several. Some of these were on his own branded social media platform and others involved public statements made at events broadcast on entities like ESPN and Fox Sports. From these videos, the viewership garnered over 1 million viewers in the process, showing a link to a broad audience. James has been able to expand his audience viewership through his platforms such as *Uninterrupted* as well as *More than a Vote* and address several non-sports issues such as voting and civil rights.

Through this analysis, the research affirmed that when James specifically makes a statement, engagement increases. Also, his messages are more likely to be shared than other athletes, but at the same time, if he is part of a panel of voices, there is even more engagement around the topics discussed. In addition to James's success through multiple channels, in this case Twitter and YouTube, James's branded social media content and engagement from his followers and viewers has grown since 2016, and this could be because of his social media engagement around current events and reciprocal relationships with his audience (Hipke & Hachtmann, 2014). Social media engagement can be more impactful if it recognizes the investment of the audience. It can increase viewership but also challenge negative conversations and controversial issues. For example, of the videos assessed, the ones that had the most views were generally the ones that received the most engagement (comments, likes, and shares). Engagement—meaning comments, retweets, reshares, and likes—signify some sort of relationship between the person posting the video and the audience (Quesenberry, 2015). As indicated in the strategies discussed, the key to the increased conversation is engagement. Therefore, social media engagement that affirms previously established relationships between players to their followers and uses various platforms to engage them and supersedes media and team communication gatekeepers, can provide new avenues for engagement. Not only does creating social justice-related content allow athletes to connect with their followers around new topics, but also by sharing videos concerning topics specifically outside of sports and basketball athletes can also build their following and brand recognition. Sharing personalized video content can bring light to issues regarding race, equality, and more, but it serves as an opportunity for Black athletes to network and collaborate. Advocacy in the form of social media engagement also allows audiences to feel connected, and through that connection potentially gain new perspectives on current and volatile social issues.

This research also gives light to how Black athletes today can harness these audiences and perhaps gain more influence than ever before through social media engagement. The National Basketball Association Players Association president executive committee is led by all Black players with Chris Paul as the president. Having an all-Black committee ensures that Black voices are present and heard. Having this platform has allowed the NBA to become more progressive in its actions when approaching racial issues. In addition, the NBPA (players association) is in direct communication with executive figures in the NBA such as Commissioner Adam Silver about ways to implement different programs in NBA cities to help minorities.

In the past, when athletes spoke up about injustice, they faced sometimes permanent consequences, as Olympic medal winners Tommie Smith and John Carlos were stripped of their medals after they raised their fists at the 1968 Olympic Games (Surya, 2019; Wulf, 2019). Black NBA athletes are encouraged by their social media followers to speak about the injustices in America, but also may face negative comments and political objectors. Social media allows athletes to present their experiences and perspectives in a space where they have more control, but can also choose to address negative comments. This takes place both on official NBA platforms and outside of their workplace on personal channels.

In the future athletes will only have more access to online content which they can share with diverse audiences, but may also face more risks of engagement from groups that object to their statements. In addition this study demonstrated the juxtaposition between individual and group videos and the contextualization of both political statements (i.e., encouragement to vote or run for political office), and those concerning social justice (i.e., voicing the idea that all people should have equal access to wealth, health, well-being, justice, privileges, and opportunity regardless of their legal, political, economic, or other circumstances). This chapter seeks to understand not only the volatility and accessibility of social media platforms in relation to #BlackLivesMatter but also the empowerment of Black athletes in the NBA to create authentic statements and endorsements to help these athletes to situate themselves as influencers in the #BLM movement.

Response

Blackness in 2022: A Personal Perspective

Daryl A. Carter

I am a Black man in Tennessee. I am in my mid-40s. I am a highly educated academic and administrator. I am married. I have children. I own my home. My student loans are paid off. I take vacations every year. I own my cars. I am a writer and public intellectual. Yet I am also struggling, as is the country, with the meaning of race in the twenty-first century. It is not easy navigating the waters of race and ethnicity in an era of severe polarization, division, and civil strife.

During the first two decades of the twenty-first century, the United States has been struggling with race, ethnicity, immigration, and culture. Former president George W. Bush, attempting to position the Republican Party as a big-tent party attractive to Americans of all backgrounds, failed to control the growing extremist fringe. This fringe grew into a frighteningly large group of Americans angry over racial progress, immigration, economic dislocation, globalization, and demographic change. As a Black American, I have experienced the past 20 years with both a personal sense of alarm and a high degree of professional curiosity.

It is a bitter piece of avocado toast for one to eat. As a child of the 1980s and early 1990s, I believed that despite the defensive couch in which the Reagan Administration, conservative radio hosts, and Republican elected officials placed Black Americans, we were making progress. Integration of schools and universities, the workplace, and (at least legally) housing had come to be. Furthermore, many mainstream politicians in both political parties took the major victories of the Civil Rights Movement—*Brown v. Board of Education*, Civil Rights Act of 1964, Voting Rights Act of 1965, Fair Housing Act of 1968—as settled issues. The rise of Black professional athletes, such as Earvin "Magic" Johnson, Michael Jordan, and Bo Jackson made me believe the country was changing in profound and long-lasting ways.

Yet those changes today seem singular and momentary. I watched with horror as the right-wing extremism of the 1970s, 1980s, and 1990s became the norm during the twenty-first century. Since the mid-1970s, America had witnessed the growth of separatist groups, neo-Nazi organizations, various militia groups, and others, angered over the ascendancy of Black Americans, Asians, Latinos, LGBTQ individuals, and immigrants. Iraq, Afghanistan, 9/11, and the fraying social fabric conspired to allow for ever greater political, racial, and cultural strife. Equally important, middle-class Americans were badly shaken by the Great Recession, leading many to respond angrily toward others as the economic pie got smaller and smaller. Technology, once thought to be a democratizing tool, generated new divisions and exacerbated old ones.

I watched my personal fortunes grow at a time when Americans, especially Black Americans, saw their futures decline. When Americans were becoming disillusioned with war, I was going into my PhD program. As the recessionary bear came out of its long hibernation in 2007–2008, I was starting a new job as a tenure-track assistant professor of history. Tens of millions of Americans lost their jobs and homes while I was developing a career and increasing my financial and professional security. As many of my fellow Black Americans caught hell after the election of the nation's first Black president (as one astute observer noted), I successfully worked my way through tenure and promotion. Over the next seven years, I became a full professor and went into administration. Simply put, it has been weird and, quite frankly, unsettling to enjoy personal success while so many others have experienced financial insecurity, professional upheaval, and declining opportunity. Yes, I have been blessed, but I also have watched with great anxiety as the cleavages in America have grown larger, deeper, and more profound.

Arguably, nothing has been as frustrating and scary as the extrajudicial violence meted out by law enforcement and vigilantes. The deaths of Black men, women, boys, and girls, as well as Black trans people, in Florida, Georgia, California, Missouri, Texas, Illinois, Wisconsin, Minnesota, New York, Ohio, Pennsylvania, and other places, has greatly troubled me. I am a father. I worry about my kids. My daughter is 21 and my son is 14. How will they be safe? Will they be targeted because of the color of their skin? I cringe at the thought of them being stopped by law enforcement or some vigilante who thinks he/she/they has the right accost my kids. Also, I worry about interactions I might have in the future with law enforcement. Moreover, I fear that evil is being allowed to persist and succeed because of the unwillingness of good people to respond with moral indignation at the suffering of others.

One bright spot, as there are a few, is the increasingly political stance some professional athletes have taken against political brutality and racial injustice. It can be argued the players of the National Basketball Association (NBA) have taken the strongest stand against inequality and injustice. Collegiate athletes have also taken a stand. At my home institution, East Tennessee State University, the men's basketball team took a knee to protest injustice. Despite the fact that many in the region, including self-righteous businessmen and opportunistic politicians, used these events to criticize the players, many supported these students use of their First Amendment rights to draw attention to a national issue. Professional athletes such as LeBron James have used their clout and money to support efforts toward racial equality.

The authors' work forces us to think more deeply and critically about the ways in which Americans view protest and are shaped by it. Americans have been influenced by the Black Lives Matter movement. Tens of millions of people of all races and ethnicities have protested the abuses directed at Black Americans. Millions have advocated for systemic reform of the criminal justice system, banking practices, the American political system, housing policies, education policies (including student loan cancellation and reform), and more. The importance of social movements and the connections between these movements and professional athletes are important to understanding our nation.

It is always difficult for athletes to engage in political activism. For many Americans, sporting events are a way to escape their everyday lives. For me and others, they are an opportunity to see issues that impact me and my community discussed, heard, and seen. Teve Mushayamunda and Mildred F. Perreault have given us a wonderful lens through which we can understand Blackness in 2022.

REFERENCES

Candlin, C. N. (2014). General editor's preface. In Gunnarsson, B. L., Linell, P., & Nordberg, B. (Eds.), *The construction of professional discourse* (pp. viii–xiv). Routledge.

Carrington, B. (2010). *Race, sport and politics: The sporting black diaspora.* Sage.

Carrington, B. (2011). 'What I said was racist—but I'm not a racist': Anti-racism and the White sports/media complex. In *Sport and challenges to racism* (pp. 83–99). London: Palgrave Macmillan.

Coombs, D. S., & Cassilo, D. (2017). Athletes and/or activists: LeBron James and Black lives matter. *Journal of Sport and Social Issues, 41*(5), 425–444. https://doi.org/10.1177/0193723517719665

Cooper, J. N., Davis, T. J., & Dougherty, S. (2017). Not so black and white: A multi-divisional exploratory analysis of male student-athletes' experiences at national collegiate athletic association (NCAA) institutions. *Sociology of Sport Journal, 34*(1), 59–78. https://doi.org/10.1123/ssj.2016-0015

Crenshaw, K. (1991). Race, gender, and sexual harassment. *S. Cal. L. Rev., 65*, 1467.

Darroch, J. (2010). Social media: Giving a voice back to the people. In *Marketing through turbulent times* (pp. 30–38). London: Palgrave Macmillan. https://doi.org/10.1057/9780230251182_4

Deeb, A., & Love, A. (2017). Media representations of multiracial athletes. *Journal of Sport and Social Issues, 42*(2), 95–114. https://doi.org/10.1177/0193723517749598

Delbaere, M., Michael, B., & Phillips, B. J. (2021). Social media influencers: A route to brand engagement for their followers. *Psychology & Marketing, 38*(1), 101–112. https://doi.org/10.1002/mar.21419

Dhanesh, G. S. (2017). Putting engagement in its proper place: State of the field, definition and model of engagement in public relations. *Public Relations Review, 43*(5), 925–933. https://doi.org/10.1016/j.pubrev.2017.04.001

ESPN. (2018, February 18). LeBron James: Athletes have power beyond their sports. YouTube. https://www.youtube.com/watch?v=GpD_IMKlm9A

ESPN. (2018, June 5). What LeBron James, Stephen Curry, Kevin Durant and others said about White House controversy. YouTube. https://www.youtube.com/watch?v=rVlrTb6gt3U

ESPN. (2020, June 21). This is our moment to prove that we know a better world is one where Black lives are valued. YouTube. https://www.youtube.com/watch?v=ZvkIWzi6IbA

ESPN.com. (2018, March 28). #NBArank game changers: The 25 most influential players ever. www.espn.com/nba/story/_/page/nbarank22932314/nbarank-game-changers-25-most-influential-basketball-players-ever

Fairclough, N. (2001). Critical discourse analysis. In McHoul, A., & Rapley, M. (Eds.), *How to analyze talk in institutional settings: A casebook of methods* (pp. 25–38). Continuum Press.

Feagin, J. R. (2020). *The white racial frame: Centuries of racial framing and counter-framing*. Routledge.

Galily, Y. (2019). "Shut up and dribble!"? Athletes activism in the age of twitter-sphere: The case of LeBron James. *Technology in Society, 58*, 101109. https://doi.org/10.1016/j.techsoc.2019.01.002

Gensler, S., Volckner, F., LiuThompkins, Y., & Wiertz, C. (2013). Managing brands in the social media environment. *Journal of Interactive Marketing, 27*, 242–256. https://doi.org/10.1016/j.intmar.2013.09.004

Greenwood, M. (2007). Stakeholder engagement: Beyond the myth of corporate responsibility. *Journal of Business Ethics, 74*(4), 315–327. https://doi.org/10.1007/s10551-007-9509-y

Grunig, J. E. (2001). Two-way symmetrical public relations: Past, present, and future. *Handbook of Public Relations, 11*, 30.

Hayat, T., Galily, Y., & Samuel-Azran, T. (2019). Can celebrity athletes burst the echo chamber bubble? The case of LeBron James and Lady Gaga. *International Review for the Sociology of Sport, 55*(7), 900–914. https://doi.org/10.1177/1012690219855913

Heywood, A. (2001). What is politics? *Politics Review, 11*(2), 2–4. https://www.klshistory.co.uk/uploads/1/1/0/4/110471535/what_is_politics.pdf

Hipke, M., & Hachtmann, F. (2014). Game changer: A case study of social-media strategy in Big Ten athletic departments. *International Journal of Sport Communication, 7*(4), 516–532. https://doi.org/10.1123/IJSC.2014-0022

History.com. (2009, November 16). Muhammad Ali refuses Army induction. Retrieved October 19, 2020, from https://www.history.com/this-day-in-history/muhammad-ali-refuses-army-induction

Holtzhausen, D. R. (2013). *Public relations as activism: Postmodern approaches to theory & practice*. Routledge.

Howard University Law Library. (2021, May 19). A brief history of civil rights in the United States: The Black Lives Matter movement. HUSL Library (n.d.). https://library.law.howard.edu/civilrightshistory/BLM

Hylton, K. (2005). 'Race', sport and leisure: Lessons from critical race theory. *Leisure Studies*, *24*(1), 81–98. https://doi.org/10.1080/02614360412331313494

Hylton, K. (2010). How a turn to critical race theory can contribute to our understanding of 'race', racism and anti-racism in sport. *International Review for the Sociology of Sport*, *45*(3), 335–354. https://doi.org/10.1177/1012690210371045

Jacobson, A. (2018). The greatest basketball player of all time: LeBron vs. Jordan. https://scholar.google.com/scholar_url?url=http://digitalcommons.liberty.edu/cgi/viewcontent.cgi%3Farticle%3D1806%26context%3Dhonors&hl=en&sa=T&oi=gsb-ggp&ct=res&cd=0&d=15706123968666128330&ei=MPCwYO2 7BMPtmQGL8aWAAw&scisig=AAGBfm139WzuS9SdWwaZEhatHT3a3Z -XIg

Kelly, J. (2005). Integrating America: Jackie Robinson, critical events and baseball black and white. *The International Journal of the History of Sport*, *22*(6), 1011–1035.

Kobach, M. J., & Potter, R. F. (2013). The role of mediated sports programming on implicit racial stereotypes. *Sport in Society*, *16*(10), 1414–1428. https://doi.org/10 .1080/17430437.2013.821254

Lindlof, T. R., & Taylor, B. C. (2017). *Qualitative communication research methods*. Sage Publications.

Lowery, B. (2020, July). "Episode 110—The invisibility of white privilege." Speaking of Psychology: The invisibility of white privilege with Brian Lowery, PhD. https://www.apa.org/research/action/speaking-of-psychology/white-privilege

NBA. (2020, June 26). The truth is #BlackLivesMatter. YouTube. https://www.you-tube.com/watch?v=1hJIuVvVQKk

NBA.com. (2021, March 17). LeBron James becomes part owner of Boston Red Sox. https://www.nba.com/news/report-lebron-james-becomes-partner-in-group -that-owns-red-sox.

Quesenberry, K. A. (2015). *Social media strategy: Marketing and advertising in the consumer revolution*. Rowman & Littlefield.

Simpson, J. S. (2010). Critical race theory and critical. *The Sage Handbook of Communication and Instruction*, p. 361.

Sloan, P. (2009). Redefining stakeholder engagement: From control to collaboration. *Journal of Corporate Citizenship*, (36), 25–40. https://www.jstor.org/stable /jcorpciti.36.25

Spears, M. (2016, October 25). *Where are all the White American Players?* https:// theundefeated.com/features/white-american-nba-players/

Stever, G. S., & Lawson, K. (2013). Twitter as a way for celebrities to communicate with fans: Implications for the study of parasocial interaction. *North American Journal of Psychology*, *15*(2), 339–354.

Surya, A. (2019). *The kneel for social justice: Colin Kaepernick, Megan Rapinoe, and The Black lives matter movement* (Doctoral dissertation).

Towler, C. C., Crawford, N. N., & Bennett, R. A. (2020). Shut up and play: Black athletes, protest politics, and black political action. *Perspectives on Politics*, *18*(1), 111–127. https://doi.org/10.10.1017/s1537592719002597

Trolan, E. J. (2013). The impact of the media on gender inequality within sport. *Procedia-Social and Behavioral Sciences, 91*, 215–227. https://doi.org/10.1016/j.sbspro.2013.08.420

Vale, L., & Fernandes, T. (2018). Social media and sports: driving fan engagement with football clubs on Facebook. *Journal of Strategic Marketing, 26*(1), 37–55. https://doi.org/10.1080/0965254X.2017.1359655

Wagoner, N. (2016, August 29). Transcript of Colin Kaepernick's comments about sitting during national anthem. Retrieved November 7, 2020, from https://www.espn.com/blog/san-francisco-49ers/post/_/id/18957/transcript-of-colin-kaeper-nicks-comments-about-sitting-during-national-anthem

Woodcock, J., & Johnson, M. R. (2019). Live streamers on Twitch.tv as social media influencers: Chances and challenges for strategic communication. *International Journal of Strategic Communication, 13*(4), 321–335. https://doi.org/10.1080/1553118X.2019.1630412

Wulf, S. (2019, January 20). Athletes and activism: The long defiant history of sports protests. The Undefeated. https://theundefeated.com/features/athletes-and-activism-the-long-defiant-history-of-sports-protests/

Zamudio, M., Russell, C., Rios, F., & Bridgeman, J. L. (2011). *Critical race theory matters: Education and ideology*. Routledge.

Chapter 8

Athletes as Activists

Exploring Audience Evaluations of Black Celebrity Athlete Activism

Gwendelyn S. Nisbett, Newly Paul,
and Stephanie Schartel Dunn

American sports are influenced by larger societal issues such as sexism, racism, classism, and homophobia (Henricks, 2006; Wolff et al., 2005). Though there is a long history of American athletes protesting on the field against racism and other social and civil rights issues (Kaufman & Wolff, 2010), audiences remain ambivalent about players mixing social activism with sports (Galily, 2019; Peterson, 2009). Sports are often seen by fans as apolitical and neutral, and activist athletes tend to face ostracism, receiving more flak than other activist public figures such as musicians and artists (Coombs et al., 2020; Kaufman, 2008).

Despite the risk, Black players are among the most vocal supporters of civil rights and racial equality (Galily, 2019). Research indicates that high-profile athletes such as LeBron James who have well-defined political affiliations have the ability to appeal to people across the political aisle (Galily, 2019). Moreover, Hayat et al. (2020) argued that athlete celebrities have the ability to appeal across ideological lines and influence those who may not traditionally agree with their viewpoints. Though celebrities are in a unique position to make persuasive appeals, race influences perceptions of source credibility and heuristic evaluation—two indicators of attitude change—which can lessen the persuasive ability of Black celebrities (Schartel Dunn & Nisbett, 2020). This chapter explores the impact of athletes as celebrity spokespersons in the context of social justice issues. Given negative characterizations of Black individuals, including victims of police brutality, are still common in news coverage (Smiley & Fakunle, 2016), this chapter examines the potential for celebrities to appeal to diverse audiences. We conduct a survey to analyze how audiences respond to Black celebrities who talk about racism in society through videos on social media, paying special attention to audience reactions to celebrity messenger and message tone.

This chapter utilizes research on racial stereotypes in sports and social identity theory (SIT) as a framework for understanding the impact of athlete activism. Celebrity influencer research is also incorporated. Celebrity influencer research suggests that well-known people such as LeBron James are good at gaining attention and driving interest. Endorsements in advertisements tend to work best with celebrities that have good source credibility and an association with the cause they are marketing.

CELEBRITY ATHLETE INFLUENCE

Celebrities in marketing and endorsement campaigns are common in product and corporate promotion (Spry et al., 2011). Promotions utilizing celebrity endorsements are considered an effective marketing tool (Brockington & Henson, 2015; Thrall et al., 2008) and celebrity endorsers appear in nearly 20% of advertisements for products and services (Elberse & Verleun, 2012). All types of celebrities are utilized in various campaigns; however, athletic celebrity endorsers are frequently used to target male audiences (Branchik & Gosh Chowdhury, 2013, 2017). Celebrities are popular as spokespersons for social causes, especially on social media (Click et al., 2017). Social media creates the impression of authenticity and closeness between celebrities and fans, because the one-on-one interaction afforded by social media platforms appears unmediated by publicists or the media. This creates strong social bonds between celebrities and fans (Marwick & Boyd, 2011). As a result, celebrities' political messages on social media appear authentic and can affect fans' attitudes and inspire them to identify with the celebrity's politics (Click et al., 2017).

Most celebrity endorsement research has been focused on brand and product marketing (Fleck et al., 2012; Schartel Dunn & Nisbett, 2017). Popularity, celebrity credibility (Fleck et al., 2012), attractiveness (Kahle & Homer, 1985), perceived similarity (Schartel Dunn & Nisbett, 2017), and fan attachment (Choi & Rifom, 2012; Hung, 2014) of the celebrity can determine how effective the endorsement will be. Recent research has also delved into the impact of fandom attachment, narrative engagement, and social media activism (Nisbett & Schartel Dunn, 2019).

In recent years, celebrities have become more prevalent in social and activist roles (Nisbett & Schartel Dunn, 2019; Van den Bulck et al., 2010). Celebrities are in a unique position to bring awareness to social issues (Jackson, 2007) and such celebrity advocacy is especially influential among young audiences (Austin et al., 2008) and in audiences who are less informed and engaged (Baum & Jamison, 2006; Nownes, 2012; Veer et al., 2010). Individuals who encounter celebrities through mediated sources or those who have developed a degree of attachment to a celebrity who then make a political or social statement, are then exposed to messages they may not otherwise encounter. Because of this, celebrity advocacy influences audiences' opinion formation and corresponding behaviors (Becker, 2013; Jackson, 2007; Nisbett & Schartel Dunn, 2019). Furthermore, these messages from celebrities, especially those an audience has a significant fan relationship with, can inspire information-seeking of endorsed views (Nisbett & DeWalt, 2016). Famous examples of celebrity advocacy include Oprah Winfrey endorsing Barack Obama as a political candidate in 2007 (Pease & Brewer, 2008) and videos of sports celebrities Kevin Durant and LeBron James promoting the merits of the Affordable Care Act (Easley, 2014).

Black Athlete Celebrities and Activism

Black activism in sports has a long history going back to the Civil Rights Era, where overt acts of discrimination and racism prompted Black athletes to participate in acts of protest on the playing field (Moore, 2017). In the 1968 Summer Olympics, two Black track stars, Tommie Smith and John Carlos, who won gold and bronze medals respectively, raised a black-gloved fist in the air while they were on the podium as the US national anthem played. The act was regarded as one of the most high-profile shows of protest against racism in the country (Brown, 2018). Though governmental actions outlawed overt racism and discrimination in American institutions, racist ideologies continue to persist in American society, necessitating the need for Black activism even today (Agyemang et al., 2010). Recent examples of Black activism have included Black players from the St. Louis Rams team coming out into the field in 2014 with their hands raised to protest the death of Michael Brown in Ferguson, Missouri; the Milwaukee Bucks basketball team refusing to play in August 2020 to protest the death of Jacob Blake in Kenosha, Wisconsin, causing the NBA to cancel the next three games; and tennis champion Naomi Osaka wearing face masks at her US Open matches in 2020 that displayed the names of Black people killed in violent confrontations with the police.

A prominent example of activism in American sports occurred in 2016, when Colin Kaepernick, an NFL quarterback, took a knee in protest of racial injustice and police brutality. His protest demonstrated the power athletes have to shape the dialogue surrounding major issues, including systemic racism (Cramer, 2019). Following him, many other Black athletes have engaged in public acts of protest (Cooper et al., 2017; Cramer, 2019; Frederick et al., 2017; Sappington et al., 2019). Kneeling, boycotting games, or wearing T-shirts and sports gear with slogans such as "I can't breathe," which is associated with the Black Lives Matter Movement, are active forms of protest (Duval, 2020). Such protests are likely to draw attention and strong reactions, especially given the wide fan following that sports commands and the media attention these events get. However, activism in sports also exists off the field in the form of anti-racist messages that are posted online by fans, by advertisements from sporting brands, or by players on their social media pages. We know comparatively less about how audiences react to such anti-racist messages delivered by Black athletes off the field. We rely on existing literature on audience response to Black athletes' activism on-the-field, social identity, and white racial frames theory (Feagin, 2013) to understand audience reactions for off-the-field activism by Black athletes.

RESPONDING TO ATHLETE ACTIVISM

Black Athlete Stereotypes

Prior research on sports and race has documented that media coverage of athletes varies depending on their race. Broadly speaking, this research found that Black athletes are described in terms of their physical strength rather than their mental abilities; their successes are attributed more to skill and experience than hard work, which is associated with white athletes; and white athletes are more likely to be portrayed as modest and averse to fame compared to Black athletes (Billings, 2003; Billings & Eastman, 2002; Eastman & Billings, 2001). Though later works have found that explicit stereotypes used by sports announcers and journalists to describe Black and white athletes have declined (Angelini & Billings, 2010), a culture of white supremacy still exists in American sports (King et al., 2007).

White supremacy in sports exists in three major ways: persistent, resurgent, and veiled (King et al., 2007). Persistent white supremacy draws from ideologies of the Jim Crow era and scientific racism which relied on physical characteristics to determine supremacy. Examples of this type of white supremacy include fans' racist and sexist comments on tennis star Serena Williams' physical appearance and strength (Desmond-Harris, 2016), and discourses about the unnaturalness of interracial sexual relationships in regard to the Duke lacrosse case (Leonard, 2007). Resurgent white supremacy includes ideas that the racial progress of non-white groups is threatening to white culture, and that there is a need to protect and reestablish the dominance of white culture. This idea includes the "tendency to express such positions in coded, sanitized language" (King et al., 2007, p. 6). Finally, veiled white supremacy manifests itself in comments and attitudes that deny the presence of racism in society and promotes the idea of a colorblind world.

White supremacist ideas in sports influence audiences' attitudes toward Black athletes (Rada & Wulfemeyer, 2005). In a 2013 study, Ferrucci et al. (2013) found that white respondents were likely to perceive Black athletes as having superior strength and innate athletic ability compared to white athletes, but also were unlikely to perceive white athletes as having more intelligence or leadership qualities. The authors concluded that the audience's perceptions were triggered by out-group stereotyping. When presented with photos of Black athletes, the respondents, who were mostly white, found their stereotypes to be activated, which prompted them to perceive Blacks as physically strong. The absence of such stereotypes toward the in-group of white athletes prompted the white respondents to not perceive white athletes as naturally intelligent. Thus, existing research documents examples of covert stereotyping in audience perceptions of athletes, depending on their race. But how do audiences' attitudes of white supremacy and social identity affect their perception of athletes' off-the-field political activism? Are Black celebrity athletes immune to racial stereotyping? We explore these questions in the next section.

Responses to Black Athletes' Activism

Audiences' responses to Black athletes' activism have ranged from expressions of support, to indifference and dismissal, to outright hostility. Negative responses to athlete activists have come from team owners and public officials (Sappington et al., 2019) as well as from individuals posting on social media (Frederick et al., 2017). Given the prevalence of white supremacist attitudes in American sports, athletes who engage in acts or speeches of protest are perceived as disrupting the dominant status quo, interrupting the idea of escapism and entertainment associated with sports, and causing fans to confront facts about structural racism (Finley et al., 2020). There is also evidence that fans react in contrary ways to the same event, as they did in 2015 when University of Missouri football players staged a walkout to protest racial inequality. In this case, some fans encouraged advocacy, while others trivialized and dismissed racism and criticized the players' activism on the field (Frederick et al., 2017). Similar contrasting behavior among fans was discovered in a study of comments posted on social media in 2016 when prominent Black basketball players used an ESPN awards show to discuss racial profiling and the racial divide in the country (Frederick et al., 2018). The authors found that while some fans dismissed the existence of racism, supported the police, attacked the Black Lives Matter Movement, and framed "Blacks" as criminals, there were others who criticized the racist dialogues, and discussed the need to address systemic racism and accountability of the police.

Some of this behavior can be explained by SIT and white racial frames. According to SIT (Tajfel & Turner, 1979), individuals tend to sort themselves into various groups depending on similarities related to their beliefs, behaviors, and attitudes. People who are members of a given group tend to consider themselves as part of an in-group; they rely on one another to uphold group ideals and build self-esteem. As part of this process, they celebrate the ideals that are common to the in-group and denigrate those who do not share the group's characteristics. Such outsiders are deemed members of the out-group and in-group members often assign derogatory stereotypes to these out-group members, especially when their in-group identity is threatened or delegitimized (Brewer, 1999). Threats can be in the form of value threats or distinctiveness threats (Branscombe et al., 1999). While value threats are those that attack the in-group's shared beliefs and customs and devalue group membership, distinctiveness threats are those that undermine the group's uniqueness from out-groups and portray in-group members as similar to out-groups.

The idea of the white racial frame (Feagin, 2013) posits that mass media and society promote the idea of whiteness as a normative ideal. According to Feagin (2013), "the White racial frame is an 'ideal type' . . . drawn on selectively by White individuals acting to impose or maintain racial identity, privilege, and dominance vis-à-vis people of color in recurring interactions" (p. 15). Our institutions favor white identity and ways of life while othering non-white culture and treating non-whites as members of out-groups. Taken together, SIT and the white racial frame lay the foundation for studying audience responses to Black athletes' messages of activism. American sports tend to favor the dominant white identity and treat black athletes as others (Schmittel & Sanderson, 2015). Audiences tend to identify more and develop emotional bonds with sportspersons who share their racial identity (Pan & Zeng, 2017), and when these in-group bonds are threatened, fans tend to lash out by criticizing and vilifying the sportspersons who do not fit the norm.

Individual characteristics of sports fans also color their responses to athlete activism. Rasinski and Czopp (2010) found that racially prejudiced individuals are more likely to report perceptions of rudeness from speakers challenging racism. On one hand, individuals who believe the world is fair and equal are likely to view protests and protest messages negatively (Sappington et al., 2019), but on the other hand, if individuals are not aware of injustice or do not perceive race-related issues to exist in society, they are likely to have a strong negative reaction to athletes' protest behaviors. People who hold strong nationalistic ideals are more likely to respond negatively to athletes' activist messages than others (Smith, 2019).

Yet, the benefits of anti-racist messages as a whole are undeniable. When people confront interpersonal biases through anti-racist messages, they tend to exhibit reduced instances of prejudice in future (Czopp et al., 2006; Rasinski & Czopp, 2010). When white people learn about their unearned privilege, they are motivated to mitigate their feelings of discomfort (Chow et al., 2010; Littleford & Jones, 2017). Duval (2020) analyzed social media messages of people in far-right groups denigrating Colin Kaepernick for his peaceful protest in response to systemic racism. Findings in their study suggest members of far-right groups experience a type of bonding when participating in denigration of a perceived other. Therefore, when messages counter to those of the protestor are shared in response to protest messages, they can serve to reinforce negative schemas and reinforce existing ideas. Ultimately, protest messages can either help correct incorrect schema, or they can reinforce negative perceptions of race.

EXPLORING AUDIENCE RESPONSES DURING 2020 BLACK LIVES MATTER PROTESTS

To explore the topic further, two social media activism examples from the summer of 2020 were examined via audience response data. Responses ($n = 270$) were collected via an online survey among college students fielded during the late summer/fall 2020, capturing attitudes from both the summer social protests and fall election season. Respondents were shown one of two videos. In one video clip, LeBron James discusses Black Lives Matter with reporters at a media press conference in July 2020. He explains, "When you're black it's not a movement, it's a lifestyle." In the second video clip, former NFL player Michael Bennett discusses what Black Lives Matter means to him in an interview conducted as part of ESPN's sports and pop culture website "The Undefeated." Both clips were relatively short, 1:32 and 1:42 respectively. The clips were selected because of their similarities in subject matter and length; however, we were primarily interested in looking at how respondents reacted to the two different levels of celebrity and different styles utilized by James and Bennett. James is one of the biggest celebrities in the world and used a very matter-of-fact style, while Bennett is a recognizable athlete (but much less well known) using an heartfelt style.

A thematic analysis of the audiences' comments was conducted to gauge the major narratives that were generated. For reference, survey respondents were 63.7% women, 35.1% men, and 1.1% non-binary. In terms of race, participants were 5% Asian, 1.9% Indigenous American, 14.9% Black, 17.2% Hispanic/Latinx, 56.1% White, and 5% other. Moreover, 24.8% reported being Hispanic/Latinx regardless of race. The average age was 24. In terms of ideology identification, 19% were Republican, 39.9% were Democrat, 16.3% were Independent, 5.4% were Libertarian, and 19.4% reported no affiliation.

Thematic Analysis

Identification with the Athletes

This theme arose from James's statement in the video that he sees Black Lives Matter as a lifestyle, not simply as isolated acts of protest. This theme appeared as three subparts in the comments: (1) identification with Black people, (2) understanding racism in society, and (3) celebrity and racism. Participants who identified with Black people and the discrimination they face stated that they understood that Black Lives Matter was not just a movement or a trendy meme; Black respondents, in particular, mentioned that they too lived the Black experience and the message held special relevance for them. One respondent stated about the James video: "It's true. I've never seen Black Lives Matter as a movement. It was always a statement and/or acknowledgment to me. We're simply saying Black lives matter. Not more, not less, just simply matter."

Others explained that while they were not Black, the statement was illuminating and helped them better understand both Black Lives Matter and the lived experience of others. Previous research noted the potential for confronting people about their own privilege may inspire changes in attitude. A common theme centered on thoughts of empathy and attempting to understand. One respondent noted, "I believe black lives matter, but I'm white. For me it will never be a lifestyle, I can never understand what it's like to be black in America." Other respondents noted how the athletes inspired them to ponder their own privilege. One respondent offered, "As a white woman, I recognize my privilege in society and I am saddened at our static criminal justice system. It really hit me—kids are growing up not knowing if they will survive the day because of their race." Though these may be musings in the immediate response to seeing an emotional plea for equality, it is interesting that some respondents were moved to question their own white privilege.

Celebrity does not shield a person from racism, and this idea constituted a sub-theme of responses. In reaction to Bennett's video, a respondent said:

> It makes me sad that not only are African [American] people affected by this but so are African [American] athletes who are more in the spotlight and may have more wealth. It shows that this problem is mainly because of their skin color and not because of their wealth or profession.

Respondents discussed macro issues about racism in society in response to both messages. The messages seemed to make them ponder about the past, present, and future of race relations in the country. Respondents brought up larger issues such as denial of civil rights, discrimination, structural inequality, political inaction, and police brutality in response to the videos. The athletes struck a personal chord and prompted respondents to examine race and BLM in the context of their own lives.

Messenger Matters

A major theme was audience reaction to who was speaking, their message tone, and ultimately, their level of celebrity. Respondents reacted to the heartfelt manner in which Bennett delivered the message, saying it sounded like he was speaking from his heart. Respondents also reacted emotionally to his mention of his daughter and his struggle with explaining racism to her. One respondent noted, "It was especially devastating when he explained the part about his daughter and how he does not know how to explain to her that she does matter even though the world says otherwise." Reacting to James's video, a respondent offered,

> My honest reaction was that this man is correct. Being black isn't just a move-ment, it's something that people live through everyday. Racism shouldn't just be an issue when it's popular and there should be a constant push for equity. Although I understand what he's trying to say, but it didn't come off as well thought out.

More people mentioned being moved by Bennett's tone and none brought up his celebrity status, while people were more likely to refer to James's celebrity status and describe his message as a "motivational speech" meant to explain his thoughts on Black Lives Matter and as "informative, and powerful and helpful." Bennett's message, on the other hand, was described as "honest opinion" as him "speaking the truth" and as "raw, vulnerable, and real." This shows that respondents seem to have found Bennett's message more heartfelt; though many agreed with James's message, they were unable to separate the celebrity from his message. This was probably a result of James's popularity. While most respondents identified him by name, a majority of respondents referred to Bennett simply as a Black athlete. Overall, James's message made people deliberate whether or not they agreed with him that Black Lives Matter is a lifestyle not a movement, while the reaction to Bennett's message was more emotional.

Using Their Platform

This theme represented an ambivalent response to the videos. At once respondents agreed with the BLM movement, but some wanted to see more action from the speakers. Some respondents who were non-Black mentioned that hearing from the players—both Bennett and James—reminded them about their own lack of action and the need for society to do more. One respondent noted,

> I completely agree with the statements made by LeBron. Black athletes are not exempt for the treatment that is passed out to black people in the rest of the world. Black athletes should use their platform to fight injustices in society.

Another offered: "As a professional athlete he has the choice to speak out and people will listen because he is a place of power."

Of Bennett, one participant remarked, "I believe he has every right to wear that hat and people owe it to him to listen, he has a platform and I appreciate that he is using it for the right purposes regardless of others opinions." Another said, "There is so much racial injustice in this country and I find it inspiring that athletes are willing to risk their careers to stand up against the inequality in this country."

Another frequent sub-theme centered on the common dismissive refrain that athletes should stick to sports and not venture into activism. This is a trope present in both media coverage and political discourse (Galily, 2019). Some comments focused on celebrities not being authentic and being shills for corporations, as one respondent said, "He's just another athlete that gets bought by different corporations and individuals to say or promote what they'd like."

A sub-theme focused on money and wealth from being an athlete. As one respondent noted of Bennett, "It makes me angry that someone successful who made millions of dollars playing a game is telling me this country doesn't give people like him a chance. This feels like a virtue signal." No matter how earnest the message, people find it difficult to evaluate a celebrity's message in isolation. There may be an assumption that celebrities are unlikely to know or be genuinely interested in issues that affect average people because they are uniquely gifted or wealthy. One respondent said,

> I think that we all have to live our lives, and can't blame someone else because we had to work harder or didn't get the fancy house or pay. The man speaking probably makes a million dollars+ a year, and he is saying how hard he has it. Poor little rich guy, I wonder how much of his own money he actually spends to help out those who are less fortunate than him.

Some respondents also expressed skepticism that the athletes had experienced serious racism. They doubted the lived experience of the athletes based on their wealth and celebrity status. One respondent commented about LeBron James's video,

> I understand what the speaker was talking about, even though I am not African American. It would be frustrating to suddenly have people of other races speaking out about something that they may not have actually experienced firsthand. However, this gentleman is obviously wealthy and well-known, so one has to wonder how much discrimination that he actually experiences.

ATHLETE CELEBRITIES AND ANTI-RACISM ACTIVISM

We often call upon celebrities to use their platforms to call attention to social issues and push for civil rights. With increased public attention to social and civil rights issues, this trend has become more common. In this context, our chapter explored the reactions audiences have to celebrity activist messages. We found that fans' responses, as in society, were mixed in terms of those supporting the celebrities and those questioning why celebrities were using their platforms to push political messages. The responses exhibited evidence of SIT, with many respondents zoning in on racial identification in their responses to the messages, as opposed to identifying as a fan of the athlete or the team. While a majority of the negative responses about the videos came from white respondents, we did find several comments from white respondents that reflected ambivalence about racism or solidarity with BLM and an understanding of the players' arguments. The negative respondents indicate the presence of white supremacy in sports, especially veiled white supremacy that questions the presence of racism in society and uses Black athletes' success as evidence of an equitable world.

Celebrities make us ponder about social issues, but we find that entrenched racism persists in American sports culture. This is not surprising, but study findings suggest it is important that people understand that money and fame do not absolve our society from dealing with systemic racism. While we saw some evidence of audience members who were able to use the athletes' messages to imagine how life is for a member of the out-group, this depended on the emotional content of the message and the audience's own beliefs, not the celebrity status of the athlete. Overall, we found a limited influence of the celebrity appeal of Black athletes in influencing people's attitudes about social issues. In some cases, audiences were unable to connect with the athletes' messages *because* of the athletes' celebrity appeal, which made respondents question the sincerity of the messages. Athletes such as LeBron James who have a nuanced record of mixing brand management and activism have become more outspoken about racial issues (Coombs & Cassilo, 2017), but we find that while they may be effective in bringing awareness about issues, they may be less effective in changing minds.

Clearly, Black athletes alone cannot bring about a change in the racist sporting culture of our country. Some organizations are taking heed of this, and trying to question racist structures. For example, the WNBA is leading the way on integrating activism and marketing by supporting their athletes and paving the way for leagues such as the NBA to take on more responsibility to speak out (Ayala, 2020). But activism through sports needs to go beyond just Black athletes stepping up and sports organizations using performative virtue signaling, even if this comes at the risk of backlash from fans.

Response

Being Black Is Life

Rebekah Sears

While I have never had the celebrity of a LeBron James or Colin Kaepernick, I have occupied the identities of being a Black person and athlete simultaneously in a predominantly white space. As such, there are a number of emotions that I feel when thinking about this topic. It is saddening that tragedies such as the police killings of George Floyd and Breonna Taylor are serving as the catalysts for Black athlete activism. Despite everything that has been said about working hard and achieving the "American dream," Black athletes who have done just that are still subject to the effects of white supremacy. I am hopeful, though, that activism continues and the effects of this activism throughout society and sport continue to inspire and motivate the general population to seek change. As LeBron James said, being Black is "not a movement; it's a lifestyle. . . . This is a walk of life. When you wake up and you're Black, that is what it is." (James, 2020). I was unaware of many of the theories that have been used as explanations for systemic racism and white supremacy, such as those that are currently in the spotlight of politics. However, now that I have been exposed to them, they simply describe the experience of being a Black person in the United States.

Social media has a variety of uses. For example, I use it (primarily Twitter) to keep up with sports news. However, because of the vastness of the Internet, I have been exposed to social justice issues and the discourse that surrounds them. Often over the past five or six years, I have seen athletes engaging in this discourse. Sports and politics have always been tied together, and now with the influence of social media, they will likely be tied together forever. Because of my experience on social media, I think it is unfair and almost impossible to demand that sports and politics be separate. Additionally, social media has made fan and opponent access to athletes easier than it has ever been. Another side of this is that some athletes have been more open about giving glimpses of their lives to fans, as well. To me, this gives athletes a certain level of relatability; there are some identities that everyone shares, regardless of what our stations are in life. We are all brothers and sisters, mothers and fathers, and friends and family. From what I have seen, though, the reaction to Black athletes' lives can be wildly different from their white peers. The common thought that I have seen is that people think Black athletes do not experience racism once a specific threshold of wealth is reached. It is unfortunate that people discount the effects that systemic racism and white supremacy have on Black peoples' lives, especially Black athletes. Wealth does not prevent one from experiencing discrimination. On the contrary, I would argue that it makes that individual—in this case, a wealthy Black athlete—an even bigger target for discrimination, as they have gained an advantage in a system that was specifically designed to keep them from being successful and wealthy. The term "Black athlete" contains two identities: Black and athlete. While the "athlete" identity will eventually be shed to some degree, the same cannot be said about Blackness. At the end of the day, Black athletes will always be Black, and they operate in a society that has been taught to see race first and ask questions later (or never).

REFERENCES

Agyemang, K., Singer, J. N., & DeLorme, J. (2010). An exploratory study of black male college athletes' perceptions on race and athlete activism. *International Review for the Sociology of Sport, 45*(4), 419–435.

Angelini, J. R., & Billings, A. C. (2010). An agenda that sets the frames: Gender, language, and NBC's Americanized Olympic telecast. *Journal of Language and Social Psychology, 29*(3), 363–385.

Austin, E. W., Vord, R. V., Pinkleton, B. E., & Epstein, E. (2008). Celebrity endorsements and their potential to motivate young voters. *Mass Communication & Society, 11*, 420–436. https://doi.org/10.1080/15205430701866600

Ayala, E. L. (2020, August 29). The NBA's walkout is historic. But the WNBA paved the way. *The Washington Post.* https://www.washingtonpost.com/outlook/2020/08/29/nba-wnba-racial-injustice/

Baum, M. A., & Jamison, A. S. (2006). The Oprah effect: How soft news helps inattentive citizens vote consistently. *The Journal of Politics, 68*, 946–959. https://doi.org/10.1111/j.1468-2508.2006.00482.x

Becker, A. B. (2013). Star power? Advocacy, receptivity, and viewpoints on celebrity involvement in issue politics. *Atlantic Journal of Communication, 21*, 1–16.

Billings, A. C. (2003). Portraying tiger woods: Characterizations of a "Black" athlete in a "White" sport. *Howard Journal of Communication, 14*(1), 29–37.

Billings, A. C., & Eastman, S. T. (2002). Gender, ethnicity, and nationality: Formation of identity in NBC's 2000 Olympic coverage. *International Review for the Sociology of Sport, 37*(3), 3497368.

Branchik, B. J., & Gosh Chowdhury, T. (2013). Self-oriented masculinity: Advertisements and the changing culture of the male market. *Journal of Macromarketing, 33*(2), 160–171.

Branchik, B. J., & Gosh Chowdhury, T. (2017). Men seeing stars: Celebrity endorsers, race, and the male consumer. *Journal of Marketing Theory and Practice, 25*(3), 305–322. https://doi:10.1080/10696679.2017.1311216

Branscombe, N. R., Ellemers, N., Spears, R., & Doosje, B. (1999). The context and content of social identity threat. In N. Ellemers, R. Spears, & B. Doosje (Eds.), *Social identity* (pp. 35–59). Oxford: Blackwell.

Brewer, M. B. (1999). The psychology of prejudice: Ingroup love or outgroup hate? *Journal of Social Issues, 55*(3), 429–444.

Brockington, D., & Henson, S. (2015). Signifying the public: Celebrity advocacy and post-democratic politics. *International Journal of Cultural Studies, 18*(4), 431–448.

Brown, D. (2018, October 16). 'A cry for freedom': The Black Power salute that rocked the world 50 years ago. *The Washington Post.* Retrieved from https://www .washingtonpost.com/history/2018/10/16/a-cry-freedom-black-power-salute-that -rocked-world-years-ago/

Choi, S. M., & Rifom, N. J. (2012). It is a match: The impact of congruence between celebrity image and consumer ideal self on endorsement effectiveness. *Psychology and Marketing, 29,* 639–650.

Chow, R. M., Lowery, B. S., & Knowles, E. D. (2010). To be fair or to be dominant: The effect of inequality frames on dominant group members' responses to inequity. In M. Neale (Ed.), *Fairness and groups* (Research on Managing Groups and Teams, Vol. 13, pp. 183–204). Emerald Group Publishing Limited.

Click, M. A., Lee, H., & Holladay, H. W. (2017). 'You're born to be brave': Lady Gaga's use of social media to inspire fans' political awareness. *International Journal of Cultural Studies, 20*(6), 603–619.

Coombs, D. S., & Cassilo, D. (2017). Athletes and/or activists: LeBron James and Black Lives Matter. *Journal of Sport and Social Issues, 41*(5), 425–444. https://doi .org/10.1177/0193723517719665

Coombs, D. S., Lambert, C. A., Cassilo, D., & Humphries, Z. (2020). Flag on the play: Colin Kaepernick and the protest paradigm. *Howard Journal of Communications, 31*(4), 317–336. https://doi.org/10.1080/10646175.2019.1567408

Cooper, J. N., Macaulay, C., & Rodriguez, S. H. (2017). Race and resistance: A typology of African American sport activism. *International Review for the Sociology of Sport,* 1–31. https://doi.org/10.1177/1012690217718170

Cramer, L. (2019). Cam Newton and Russell Westbrook's symbolic resistance to whiteness in the NFL and NBA. *Howard Journal of Communication, 30*(1), 57–75. https://doi.org/10.1080/10646175.2018.1439421

Czopp, A. M., Monteith, M. J., & Mark, A. M. (2006). Standing up for a change: Reducing bias through interpersonal confrontation. *Journal of Personality and Social Psychology, 90*(5), 784–803. https://doi.org/10.1037/0022-3514.90.5.784

Desmond-Harris, J. (2016, September 7). Serena Williams is constantly the target of disgusting racist and sexist attacks. *Vox.* Retrieved from https://www.vox.com /2015/3/11/8189679/serena-williams-indian-wells-racism

Duval, S. S. (2020). Too famous to protest: Far-right online community bonding over collective desecration of Colin Kaepernick, fame, and celebrity activism. *Journal of Communication Inquiry, 44*(3), 256–278. https://doi.org/10.1177/0196859920911650

Easley, J. (2014, March 19). Pro athletes come out in force for ObamaCare. *The Hill.* Retrieved from http://thehill.com/policy/healthcare/201248-pro-athletes-come -out-in-force-for-obamacare

Eastman, T., & Billings, A. (2001). Biased voices of sports: Racial and gender stereotyping in college basketball announcing. *Howard Journal of Communications, 12*(4), 183–201.

Elberse, A., & Verleun, J. (2012). The economic value of celebrity endorsements. *Journal of Advertising Research, 52*(2), 149–165.

Feagin, J. R. (2013). *The White racial frame: Centuries of racial framing and counter-framing* (2nd ed.). New York, NY: Routledge.

Ferrucci, P., Tandoc, E. C. Jr., Painter, C. E., & Leshner, G. (2013). A black and white game: Racial stereotypes in baseball. *Howard Journal of Communications, 24*(3), 309–325.

Finley, S., Gray, B., & Martin, L. (2020). T*he religion of white rage white workers, religious fervor, and the myth of Black racial progress*. Edinburgh: Edinburgh University Press.

Fleck, N., Korchia, M., & Le Roy, I. (2012). Celebrities in advertising: Looking for congruence or likability? *Psychology & Marketing, 29*, 651–662.

Frederick, E., Sanderson, J., & Schlereth, N. (2017). Kick these kids off the team and take away their scholarships: Facebook and perceptions of athlete activism at the University of Missouri. *Journal of Issues in Intercollegiate Athletics, 10*, 17–34.

Frederick, E. L., Pegoraro, A., & Sanderson, J. (2018). Divided and united: Perceptions of athlete activism at the ESPYS. *Sport in Society*.

Galily, Y. (2019). "Shut up and dribble!"? Athletes activism in the age of twittersphere: The case of LeBron James. *Technology in Society, 58*. https://doi.org/10.1016/j.techsoc.2019.01.002

Hayat, T., Galily, Y., & Samuel-Azran, T. (2020). Can celebrity athletes burst the echo chamber bubble? The case of LeBron James and Lady Gaga. *International Review for the Sociology of Sport, 55*(7), 900–914. https://doi.org/10.1177/1012690219855913

Henricks, T. S. (2006). *Play reconsidered: Sociological perspectives on human expression*. University of Illinois Press.

Hung, K. (2014). Why celebrity sells: A dual entertainment model of brand endorsement. *Journal of Advertising, 43*, 155–166.

Jackson, D. J. (2007). The influence of celebrity endorsements on young adults' political opinions. *The International Journal of Press/Politics, 6*, 67–83.

James, L. (2020, July 23). *LeBron James speaks on BLM: 'When you're Black, it's not a movement; it's a lifestyle.'* [Video]. YouTube. https://www.youtube.com/watch?v=T6CkKIObfws

Kahle, L. E., & Homer, P. M. (1985). Physical attractiveness of the celebrity endorser: A social adaptation perspective. *Journal of Consumer Research, 11*, 954–961. https://doi.org/10.1086/209029

Kaufman, P. (2008). Boos, bans, and other backlash: The consequence of being an activist athlete. *Humanity & Society, 32*, 215–237. https://doi.org/10.1177/016059760803200302

Kaufman, P., & Wolff, E. A. (2010). Playing and protesting: Sport as a vehicle for social change. *Journal of Sport and Social Issues, 34*(2), 154–175. https://doi.org/10.1177/0193723509360218

King, C. R., Leonard, D. J., & Kusz, K. W. (2007). White power and sport: An introduction. *Journal of Sport & Social Issues, 31*(1), 3–10. https://doi.org/10.1177/0193723506296821

Leonard, D. J. (2007). Innocent until proven innocent: In defense of Duke lacrosse and White power (and against menacing Black student-athletes, a Black stripper, activists, and the Jewish media). *Journal of Sport and Social Issues, 31*(1), 25–44.

Littleford, L. N., & Jones, J. A. (2017). Framing and source effects on White college students' reactions to racial inequity information. *Cultural Diversity and Ethnic Minority Psychology, 23*(1), 143.

Marwick, A., & Boyd, D. (2011). To see and be seen: Celebrity practice on Twitter. *Convergence: The International Journal of Research into New Media Technologies, 17*(2), 139–158.

Moore, L. (2017). *We will win the day: The Civil Rights Movement, the Black athlete, and the quest for equality.* Santa Barbara, CA: Praeger.

Nisbett, G. S., & DeWalt, C. C. (2016). Exploring the influence of celebrities in politics: A focus group study of young voters. *Atlantic Journal of Communication, 24*(3), 144–156. https://doi.org/10.1080/15456870.2016.1184664

Nisbett, G., & Schartel Dunn, S. (2019). Reputation matters: Parasocial attachment, narrative engagement, and the 2018 Taylor Swift political endorsement. *Atlantic Journal of Communication.* https://doi.org/10.1080/15456870.2019.1704758

Nownes, A. J. (2012). An experimental investigation of the effects of celebrity support for political parties in the United States. *American Politics Research, 40*, 476–500. https://doi.org/10.1177/1532673X11429371

Pan, P.-L., & Zeng, L. (2017). Parasocial interactions with basketball athletes of color in online mediated sports. *Howard Journal of Communications, 29*(2), 196–215. https://doi.org/10.1080/10646175.2017.1354790

Pease, A., & Brewer, P. R. (2008). The Oprah factor: The effects of a celebrity endorsement in a presidential primary campaign. *The International Journal of Press/Politics, 13*, 386–400. https://doi.org/10.1177/1940161208321948

Peterson, J. (2009). A 'race' for equality: Print media coverage of the 1968 Olympic protest by Tommie Smith and John Carlos. *American Journalism, 26*(2), 99–121. https://doi.org/10.1080/ 08821127.2009.10677714

Rada, J. A., & Wulfemeyer, K. T. (2005). Color coded: Racial descriptors in television coverage of intercollegiate sports. *Journal of Broadcasting & Electronic Media, 49*(1), 65–85. https://doi.org/10.1207/s15506878jobem4901_5

Rasinski, H. M., & Czopp, A. M. (2010). The effect of target status on witnesses' reactions to confrontations of bias. *Basic and Applied Social Psychology, 32*(1), 8–16.

Sappington, R., Keum, B. T., & Hoffman, M. A. (2019). "Arrogant, ungrateful, anti-American degenerates": Development and initial validation of the Attitudes Toward Athlete Activism Questionnaire (ATAAAQ). *Psychology of Sport and Exercise, 45*, 1–11. https://doi.org/10.1016/j.psychsport.2019.101552

Schartel Dunn, S. G., & Nisbett, G. S. (2017). Does sport celebrity advocacy work? Testing the potential for endorsements to backfire. *Atlantic Journal of Communication, 25*(3), 197–206. https://doi.org/10.1080/15456870.2017.1324193

Schartel Dunn, S. G., & Nisbett, G. S. (2020). If Childish Gambino cares, I care: Celebrity endorsements and psychological reactance to social marketing messages. S*ocial Marketing Quarterly, 26*(2), 80–92. https://doi.org/10.1177 /1524500420917180

Schmittel, A., & Sanderson, J. (2015). Talking about Trayvon in 140 charac-ters: Exploring NFL players' tweets about the George Zimmerman verdict. *Journal of Sport and Social Issues, 39*(4), 332–345. https://doi.org/10.1177 /0193723514557821

Smiley, C. J., & Fakunle, D. (2016). From "brute" to "thug:" The demonization and criminalization of unarmed Black male victims in America. *Journal of Human Behavior in the Social Environment, 26*(3–4), 350–366. https://doi.org/10.1080 /10911359.2015.1129256

Smith, L. (2019). Stand up, show respect: Athlete activism, nationalistic attitudes, and emotional response. *International Journal of Communication, 13*, 22.

Spry, A., Pappu, R., & Cronwell, B. (2011). Celebrity endorsement, brand credibility and brand equity. *European Journal of Marketing, 45*(6), 882–909. https://doi.org /10.1108/03090561111119958

Tajfel, H., & Turner, J. C. (1979). An integrative theory of intergroup conflict. In S. Worchel & W. G. Austin (Eds.), *The social psychology of intergroup relations* (pp. 33–48). Monterey, CA: Brooks-Cole.

Van den Bulck, H., Panis, K., Van Aelst, P., & Hardy, A. (2010, June). Celebrity activists in social profit campaigning: A survey with the Flemish public on views and effectiveness. Annual Conference of the International Communication Asso-ciation, Singapore.

Veer, E., Becirovic, I., & Martin, B. A. S. (2010). If Kate voted conservative, would you? The role of celebrity endorsements in political party advertising. *European Journal of Marketing, 44*, 436–450. https://doi.org/10.1108/ 03090561011020516

Wolff, E. A., Hums, M. A., & Fay, T. (2005). Fear factor: Fear of disability and the unspoken reality – Implications in sport. Presented at the annual conference of the North American Society for Sport Sociology, Winston-Salem, NC.

Section III

AFTER THE LIGHTS GO OUT

Chapter 9

Fairness, Without the Inclusion

A Critical Discourse Analysis of Trans-Exclusionary Sports Bans

Vincent Peña

While historically many have argued that transgender people have been made invisible or ignored by the media, there has been a slow but steady improvement in trans representation over the last decade or so. Trans folks have experienced an undeniable increase in visibility, with prominent trans women such as Laverne Cox starring in major Netflix programs, or athletes like Chris Mosier being included in ESPN's *The Body Issue*, or the election of Sarah McBride as the first transgender woman to serve in the US Senate. Most recently, actor Elliot Page came out as transgender and weightlifter Laurel Hubbard is poised to become the first transgender woman to qualify for the Olympics in Tokyo in 2021. All of these examples point to the increase in transgender representation and visibility for a group that has long been marginalized and stereotyped by the media as well as excluded from various realms of public life.

However, this increased visibility hasn't always meant greater acceptance, as many trans people still experience discrimination, bias, and vitriolic rhetoric. More importantly, this increase in visibility hasn't led to an accompanying increase in transgender inclusion in many spaces, such as in politics, the media, and especially sports (Fischer & McClearen, 2020). Sports at nearly every level are organized based on a division of the sexes, and transgender people who want to compete have more often than not been disallowed from participating according to their gender identity. Not being able to play according to one's identity amounts to exclusion. The visibility of transgender athletes has prompted political backlash and a wave of bills banning transgender women from high-school and college sports as well as led to an extended and ongoing debate about the inclusion of transgender athletes in sports. This debate has taken center stage in high-school sports across the country, and two recent cases in Idaho and Connecticut have been at the center of it all. These two examples are among the first of many efforts to codify transgender exclusion, and exploring them will allow for a greater understanding of the debate and its implications for transgender high-school athletes.

In 2019, several cisgender female track athletes filed a lawsuit against Connecticut's policy that allows high-school athletes to compete according to their gender identity and argued that two black transgender athletes in particular had unfair advantages against the cisgender female runners. Though the lawsuit initially had the support of Donald Trump's US Department of Education, who ruled in 2020 that the Connecticut policy was in violation of Title IX, that ruling has since been rescinded and the case dismissed (Kelley, 2020; Riley, 2021).

In 2020, Idaho passed a law called the "Fairness in Women's Sports Act," which banned transgender athletes from competing in women's sports, becoming the first state to pass such a law (Minsberg, 2020). A federal judge temporarily blocked the law in August 2020, but the legal battle is far from over—and the athletic status of trans women and girls in Idaho is far from settled (Brassil & Longman, 2020). This chapter features a critical discourse analysis around these two important legal decisions. Transgender media representations can shape public perceptions and attitudes about whether they should be included in sports. Therefore, I was primarily concerned with analyzing the news coverage of these trans-exclusionary efforts across the country. The goal here is not just to highlight the way trans athlete inclusion is being framed, but also to interrogate the relationship between the media discourse and the efforts to exclude transgender individuals from sports.

In this chapter, I conduct a critical discourse analysis surrounding the attempts to exclude transgender girls from high-school sports in states like Idaho and Connecticut, focusing on both traditional and sports media organizations and their ability to frame how others rationalize the logic of trans exclusion. In particular, this chapter analyzes the news media coverage of the Connecticut lawsuit and the Idaho bill and outlines the various ways trans athletes and their inclusion is discussed within the media. The analysis will attempt to highlight not only the framing of these cases and the athletes involved, but also the way hegemonic notions of gender, sexuality, and race are perpetuated in the media. It will also attempt to explore the ways in which media outlets portray trans athletes amid a discussion about their inclusion in sports.

What follows is an examination of the way sports are a site where gender is constructed and policed, followed by previous scholarly work outlining the way transgender people, and athletes in particular, are portrayed in the media. The analysis at the heart of this chapter elucidates several aspects of the discourse that echo previous research findings in addition to implications for journalists covering—or not covering—transgender athletes. The discussion section highlights these implications and considers ways to improve media representations of trans athletes. Therefore, this work not only addresses a gap in the literature but examines how discourse of trans high-school athletes compares to that about professional trans athletes while also critically analyzing coverage about the bills themselves.

POSITIONALITY, REFLEXIVITY, AND THEORETICAL FRAMEWORK

As a straight, cisgender man, I acknowledge my own positionality in relation to the group I am studying. My interest in studying transgender athlete discourse comes from my research focus of gender and race representation in sports media. As such, understanding the ways transgender people are covered in the media is an important aspect of that research. Transgender has been used as an umbrella term to include "everyone who challenges the boundaries of sex and gender" and also to distinguish between "those who reassign the sex they were labeled at birth, and those of us whose gender expression is considered inappropriate for our sex" (Feinberg, 1996, p. x). I use "transgender" or "trans" to include any number of gender identities that do not align with the sex one was assigned at birth. This includes queer, gender nonconforming, non-binary, transgender, transsexual, two-spirit, genderfluid, and others whose gender identity challenges the gender binary. My goal in using transgender so universally is not to essentialize a variety of different gender identities, but to use a common language in order to more coherently complete my analysis. It's important to note that individuals may define themselves using different terminology, but the focus of this chapter is on the discourse about them rather than the various ways they might self-identify. There is a lot of scholarship about the proper terms, but for the purposes of this chapter, transgender will be inclusive of all non-normative gender identities. Although as this chapter highlights, anti-trans efforts in youth sports are focused only on trans girls and trans women, and the examples of state-level bills and lawsuits that aim to exclude trans folks are only targeted at trans girls.

Importantly, this work functions within a critical perspective informed by queer theory and feminist media studies, especially the work of Crenshaw (1989), Collins (1990), Butler (1994) and others. This critical discourse analysis is concerned with examining the power of the media to disseminate dominant narratives about trans athletes that have been found to stereotype, pathologize, and demonize them (Namaste, 2000; Birrell & Cole, 1990; Barker-Plummer, 2013). Additionally, though the focus here is on transgender athlete rules and discourse, it is impossible to separate issues of gender from race, class, ability, or other social identities. Therefore, the perspective of intersectionality is of utmost importance in this study. Intersectionality explains how people can experience oppression in a multifaceted way based on their overlapping identities and positionalities. Coined by Crenshaw (1989) but rooted in black feminist thought of the Combahee River Collective, the term is focused on the way race, gender, ability, religious and other identities can compound to subject people to a multilayered oppression.

Queer theory application includes a variety of academic disciplines and perspectives, but is focused primarily on questioning and critiquing heteronormativity, the gender binary, biological determinism and other social apparatuses that shape our constructions of gender and sex (Waldron, 2018). In addition to challenging the gender binary, a queer theory perspective "allows us to recognize that the issues that arise when trans athletes seek to play sports are not a result of trans athletes' participation, but rather a social problem rooted in limited understandings of the fluidity and performance of gender" (Semerjian, 2018, p. 159). Gender, according to Butler (1990), "is an identity tenuously constituted in time, instituted in an exterior space through a stylized repetition of acts. The effect of gender is produced through the stylization of the body" (p. 140). In other words, Butler has argued that gender is performative, in that people enact the socially agreed upon traits of a specific gender so as to be that gender. Nothing is natural about our gender and sexual binary, she argues, through our gender performativity we perpetuate the heterosexual matrix, where sex, gender, and sexuality are normatively linked (Butler, 1993). Therefore, gender should be understood not as something concrete and fixed, but rather contextual and fluid. This social problem mentioned above is in part rooted in the way sports function on a societal level, which has long been to cultivate distinct gender categories that are indeed concrete and fixed. A transgender identity poses a direct challenge to any gender binary, as it represents the possibility that gender exists outside the limited notions that currently shape our social world. And because trans identity upends this binary assumed to be "natural," their very presence in sports spaces works against the traditional function of sports, which has been to facilitate the construction of ideal masculinities and femininities. Cromwell (1999) wrote that trans people, especially those who have undergone surgery, are "dangerous actors" because "they demonstrate that the relationships between the body, sex, and gender are arbitrary" (Semerjian & Cohen, p. 38).

SPORTS AND THE CONSTRUCTION OF GENDER

Countless scholars have noted that sports function as a means to reinforce strict gender hierarchies and many have argued that sports are one of the primary (if not *the* primary) places that masculinity is performed, perpetuated, and defined (Messner, 2007; Lorber, 1993). Sports have been a historically masculine space and have therefore long reflected the values and dominant ideologies of the men who have participated. As researchers have noted, sports, especially at the youth level, have long served to create ideal gendered subjects and have been used in educational settings to uphold strict gender binaries (Messner, 1996).

Therefore, the feigned alarm toward transgender athletes competing isn't just about keeping them out but maintaining a sex-segregated system not just in sports but in society more broadly. Because sport has historically been a male domain and is one of the most sex-segregated realms in our society, it serves to perpetuate heteronormative gender norms and ideals (Semerjian & Cohen, 2006, p. 3). In fact, it's one of the few places in society so strictly adherent to sex segregation (Anderson, 2008). The inclusion of women in sport already posed problems to hegemonic masculinity, and as Semerjian notes, "Transgender athletes' presence in sport serves to further conflagrate an environment that remains one of the strongest bastions of sex segregation and biological determinism in society" (2006, p. 30). Women were long barred from sporting competitions, and though women largely have access to sports today, the media coverage they get continues to pale in comparison to men's sports (Cooky et al., 2021). Thus, the hurdles for trans inclusion are seemingly even greater. Perhaps unsurprisingly, the presence of trans women in sports is much more problematic than trans men in sports, largely because of heteronormative and sexist assumptions about athletic ability. Much of this is based on pseudo-science. There are rarely any public debates or legislation drafted to block transgender men competing in sport. Most of the concern about trans athletes is about trans women, coupled with discussions about fairness. Many professional and amateur trans women athletes have been accused of unfair advantages by virtue of being assigned male at birth, a discourse that is readily apparent in coverage of prominent trans athletes (Semerjian, 2018; McClearen, 2015).

Sports are a very heteronormative, hegemonically masculine space that is not incredibly welcoming of women, let alone transgender people (Anderson & Travers, 2017). Understanding the way media, and sports media especially, cover trans people is vitally important to creating inclusive sporting spaces. It allows us to examine the way discourse shapes reality, and in particular the way discourse about trans-athlete bans further perpetuates problematic assumptions about the way gender operates in sports. As feminist scholars have noted, the media discourse of trans folks usually involves the mapping of heteronormative assumptions in a way that reifies the typical sex and gender hierarchy upon which society is structured, especially within sports (McClearen, 2015). But, as McClearen and others have said, transgender media representation is nuanced and complex.

MEDIA REPRESENTATION AND DISCOURSE
OF TRANSGENDER PEOPLE

Scholars have long claimed that trans individuals have been erased and made invisible in society (Namaste, 2000). When they were included, research has shown that media representations of trans people have tended to marginalize, exoticize, and delegitimize them and their experiences, and has typically resorted to sexist and (cis)sexist rhetoric (Love, 2018; Billard, 2016; Sloop, 2004). Additionally, discourse related to trans athletes is often portrayed in ways that uphold rather than disrupt the gender binary, thereby ignoring and overlooking the experiences of many trans individuals (Birrell & Cole, 1990). However, more recent scholarship and current events have indicated that trans representation has increased and improved over the last couple decades. Semerjian (2018) argues that trans individuals, and trans athletes in particular, have made significant gains in the realm of representation, especially with the coming out of athletes such as Caitlyn Jenner in 2015. But there are, of course, downsides to that, and researchers have noted that trans individuals are usually framed in unflattering and often problematic ways (Arune, 2006; Willox, 2003; Anderson & Travers, 2017). Scholars studying representation of trans people in the media have identified several frames the media have typically used to discuss trans people: the pathologizing, marginalizing, and disciplining of transgender identity and gender non-conformity (Sloop, 2004; Willox, 2003); the "wrong body" discourse that focuses on "fixing" of gender non-conformity (Barker-Plummer, 2013); the focus on legitimacy and fairness, which is of course the primary focus of the coverage being analyzed. This last aspect of transgender media coverage is one that tends to focus on the "science," on the notion of legitimate (trans)gender identity, and biological difference (Fausto-Sterling, 2000).

Previous research on trans athletes and trans athlete representation has highlighted how trans athletes are framed by the media (when they are included), and the sexist and heteronormative rhetoric used to talk about trans folks from both advocates and opponents of trans sports inclusion. Most studies have focused on examples of professional trans athletes, especially those focused on media coverage of athletes—but few if any have focused on the coverage of high-school trans athletes, especially amid a wave of anti-trans legislation across the country aimed specifically at regulating and "protecting" girls high-school sports (Sewell, 2020a). As mentioned previously, many scholars have examined the media representation of trans athletes, but because of the lack of visibility of trans athletes, as well as the dearth of examples of prominent trans athletes to focus on, many of these studies have focused on a small group of prominent trans athletes, such as Fallon Fox or

Caitlyn Jenner (Lovelock, 2017; Brady, 2016), or on adult amateur trans athletes (Semerjian & Cohen, 2006; MacKinnon, 2016; Travers, 2006).

The improvement in coverage that occurred had seemingly turned a tide in the struggle for transgender inclusion. Love (2017) argued that the period from 2014 to 2016 was a period of relative trans-inclusion improvement and offered hope that new guidelines were a sign of changes to come. But he cautioned that the simultaneous advances in trans visibility are being met with the increasing anti-trans backlash in the form of legislation at the state and national level, arguing that "the potential for greater acceptance and inclusion of transgender athletes is tenuous at best" (p. 201). As Mia Fischer (2019) argued in her book, *Terrorizing Gender*, increased visibility for trans people leads to increased surveillance and scrutiny, which can manifest in myriad ways. That all these bills are being introduced now can be viewed as a direct consequence of that increase in visibility. Additionally, the current wave of legislation seemingly originates with the efforts to ban trans girls in Connecticut, adding a racialized aspect to this backlash because the two trans girls who were the target of a lawsuit, Yearwood and Miller, are both Black. It is exactly at this juncture that we find ourselves. Though there is ever greater trans visibility, anti-trans backlash from all levels of government is stunting progress for LGBTQ+ rights in general, and transgender people in particular. States across the country are attempting to place restrictions on trans athletes or banning them from playing sports altogether. The wave of backlash is reflective of society's general view of people who challenge categories like gender or sex, which is one dictated by prejudice, ignorance, and discrimination. Transgender folks have been deemed threatening to the status quo, and therefore state and local legislators are desperately trying to control what spaces transgender folks can even exist.

Several studies on trans athlete media representation have focused on Fallon Fox, the first openly transgender fighter in professional mixed martial arts (MMA) (McClearen, 2015; Love 2018; Fischer & McClearen, 2020). McClearen (2015), in her examination of popular media discourse about Fallon Fox, the first openly transgender professional MMA fighter, found that both supporters and detractors of Fox relied on sexist and cissexist language in discussing her participation in the sport. For those advocating for Fox's inclusion and right to compete, McClearen argued they often relied on sexist assumptions about the athletic inferiority of females in arguing that Fox was sufficiently female because she wasn't that athletic or strong. As McClearen noted, Fox's supporters

> rely on a sexist characterisation of female athletes as substandard to speak against the cissexism that challenges Fox's right to fight as a woman. In fact,

their primary arguments hinge on the science of weakness and unexceptionality of female athletes to prove their case for Fox. (2015, p. 87)

For example, Liz Carmouche, a fellow UFC fighter, came out in support of Fox because the latter was medically cleared and had "sufficiently proven that she was no stronger than the average female MMA fighter" due to decreased levels of testosterone and unexceptional athletic ability (McClearen, 2015, p. 85).

Meanwhile, those who were critical of Fox, especially the professional MMA fighters who often used transphobic, sexist, and racist language, were unquestionably guilty of sexism and cissexism, wherein the sexism is based on the heteronormative assumptions of gender roles and abilities. These people often talked about protecting the female MMA fighters from Fox because of the apparent natural advantage Fox would have over another woman. For instance, UFC commentator Joe Rogan engaged in cissexist language by affirming Fox's right to be transgender but arguing:

> If you want to be a woman in the bedroom and you know you want to play house and all of that other shit and you feel like you have, your body is really a woman's body trapped inside a man's frame and so you got a operation, that's all good in the hood. But you can't fight chicks. Get the fuck out of here. You're out of your mind. You need to fight men, you know? Period. You need to fight men your size because you're a man. You're a man without a dick. (Quoted in McClearen, 2015, p. 81)

McClearen points out that both sides are ultimately concerned with maintaining a sex and gender binary that reaffirms patriarchal systems of power. Despite these concurrent discourses of sexism and cissexism from both supporters and opponents, many of them supported some version of trans-inclusivity (McClearen, 2015). Underscoring the paradoxical and contradictory nature of transgender athlete coverage, Love (2018) noted that articles about Fox simultaneously pathologized or marginalized her by their inclusion of oppositional or medical perspectives alongside statements from trans advocates challenging the gender binary. Drawing from the "queer art of failure" as theorized by Halberstam (2011) and Muñoz (2009), Fischer and McClearen (2020) argue that Fox occupies a precarious position; in order to prove that she is a woman—that is, prove that she is inferior athletically to men—she must lose fights. Therefore, she can only win by losing. To be seen as a woman, she must fail as an athlete, which perpetuates the sexist and pseudoscientific assumptions about male athletic superiority. Underlying all the findings of the research presented above is that the rhetoric of inclusion regarding trans athletes usually centers on discussions of fairness. The concern about fairness is limited to whether it's fair for cisgender girls and women because of these aforementioned assumptions about sexual difference. And in both of the cases this chapter analyzes, the issue of fairness occupies a large portion of the discussion, albeit the fairness rhetoric is mostly used to obfuscate more directly transphobic motivations for seeking to exclude transgender athletes.

Different States, Same Story

In 2019, three cisgender high-school girls in Connecticut—Selena Soule, Chelsea Mitchell, and Alanna Smith—filed a Title IX complaint against the state over its law allowing people to participate in high-school sports based on their gender identity (Putterman & Riley, 2019). The three girls argued that because of the presence of two transgender girls, Andraya Yearwood and Terry Miller, they were deprived of podium spots, recognition, and even college scholarships as a result. The lawsuit sought to reverse the Connecticut Interscholastic Athletic Conference (CIAC) rule that permits high-school athletes to compete according to their gender identity. The lawsuit, if successful, would have changed the rule to mandate high-school athletes compete based on their assigned sex at birth. Another desired outcome of the lawsuit was to prevent Yearwood and Miller from competing in their last track season in 2020, which never happened due to the emergence of the COVID-19 pandemic. Yearwood and Miller had earned several state championships in track and field for their respective schools, and the plaintiffs contended that they themselves were denied those spots, despite the lead plaintiff in the case, Soule, placing eighth in a race that Miller and Yearwood finished first and second. Additionally, another plaintiff in the case, Chelsea Mitchell, defeated Miller and Yearwood on multiple occasions and won 11 state championships (Webb, 2020). The complaint to the US Department of Education's Office of Civil Rights found support within the Trump administration's Department of Justice, with former attorney general William Barr signing a statement of interest in March 2020. The Office of Civil Rights also threatened to withhold federal funding from the state if the CIAC did not change its rule. Both of those official stances by both departments were rescinded after Joe Biden was elected president, and Biden went so far as to sign an executive order in February on "Preventing and Combating Discrimination on the Basis of Gender Identity or Sexual Orientation" (Riley, 2021). In April 2021, a federal judge officially dismissed the lawsuit against the CIAC, claiming that because Yearwood and Miller had already graduated, there was no example of any transgender athlete still competing (Riley, 2021).

The situation in Idaho is slightly different, although seemingly inspired by the efforts in Connecticut and elsewhere to exclude trans girls from high-school sports. Aside from the involvement of the Alliance Defending Freedom

(ADF), which has a hand in nearly all legislative attempts to ban trans athletes, the instances are quite different. Barbara Ehardt, a state representative and former NCAA athlete and coach, introduced a bill before the Idaho legislature, HB500, that aimed at outlawing transgender participation in sports at the high-school and college levels in the state of Idaho. The bill would require high-school and college athletes to compete based on their assigned sex at birth, which would need to be verified if called into question via sex-verification testing. Despite widespread criticism from local businesses, trans advocates, and other Idaho lawmakers, the bill was signed into law by Governor Brad Little in August 2020. It has since been halted by a federal judge because of its likelihood to lose in court on the grounds it's likely to be deemed unconstitutional (Keyser, 2020). While Idaho was the first state to officially pass such a law banning trans girls and women from playing according to their gender identity, more than 30 states have since joined in on these efforts and have proposed or passed similar legislation, including Mississippi, Tennessee, and Georgia (Block, 2021). However, this chapter focuses on the two instances in Connecticut and Idaho because they have set the stage for all the subsequent efforts to limit transgender girls and women from accessing women's sports.

Considering these specific examples, several questions guide this study, including the following: How does the media cover trans exclusionary bans across the United States? Are there any differences in coverage based on the outlet, the geographic location, the gender/race of the athletes involved? Are the typical representations of trans athletes present in the media coverage? To what extent has coverage improved in the last several years? What does the discourse about trans athletes and trans-exclusionary legislation reveal about the power of sports media? To what extent does the media coverage challenge anti-trans rhetoric and transphobia? What does the discourse about trans athletes from news and sports outlets say about power dynamics between athletes, sporting organizations, and sports journalists?

METHODOLOGY

Critical discourse analysis is concerned with identifying and analyzing the manifestations of power that are embedded within discourse, such as news media coverage (Fairclough, 2013; van Dijk, 1998). As Gill notes, discourse analysis perspectives "share a rejection of the realist notion that language is simply a neutral means of reflecting or describing the world, and a conviction in the central importance of discourse in constructing social life" (2000, p. 172). The discourse surrounding trans athlete inclusion certainly reflects cultural ideologies and attitudes, and this chapter is concerned with highlighting the implications of that discourse.

Utilizing an intersectional feminist framework, this chapter reports on a critical analyzes of these cases on both a local and national scale. As such, the corpus for this analysis includes local—that is, in Idaho and Connecticut—in addition to national news coverage. In particular, it will feature the largest newspapers in both states, such as the *Idaho Statesmen* and the *Hartford Courant*, as well as national media outlets such as the *New York Times*, the *Washington Post*, *USA Today*, and sports media outlets such as ESPN, *Sports Illustrated*, and others. Only print or digital publications were used. I utilized the search function on the respective sites using the search terms of the names of the people directly involved in each case, such as "Lindsay Hecox" in Idaho and "Andraya Yearwood" in Connecticut, the terms "transgender" and "transgender athlete," as well as terms like "HB500," for the trans-exclusionary bill in Idaho. For the other outlets, I utilized Dow Jones' news database, Factiva, as well as Google searches for the same terms used above for each of the outlets included. Both news articles and opinion or commentary pieces longer than 300 words were included in the analysis, leaving me with a sample of 90 articles.

NEWS COVERAGE OF TRANSGENDER BANS

Examining the journalistic discourse about trans athletes yielded several trends that were evident across the sample, such as the paradoxical nature of the coverage that was both critical and benevolent toward trans athletes; the privileging of cisgender perspectives over transgender perspectives; and the juxtaposition of the cisgender desire to win versus the transgender desire to participate. Aspects of the coverage at times represented an improvement, however small, from the problematic coverage outlined in previous research on trans athletes. For instance, there were many more articles in favor of trans inclusion than expected, and many journalists avoided using transphobic language themselves. However, that being said, several of the characteristics of media coverage of trans athletes found in previous research were present, such as the focus on fairness and inclusion (Love, 2018), the use of gender and sex stereotypes, the aforementioned misgendering of trans people (Willox, 2003), and reliance on medical experts to invalidate trans identity (Henne, 2014).

Because of the different context and people involved, as well as the social, cultural, and political climate of the areas in which each took place, the findings and implications for each have both similarities and differences. The discourse analysis for Idaho involved the passing of a bill aiming to ban trans girls from high-school and college sports in the state, while the discourse analysis of the Connecticut lawsuit focused on the challenge to an existing law that permits the participation of athletes according to their gender identity. Thus, the latter is a response to a perceived threat while the former is a pre-emptive attempt by lawmakers to exclude trans athletes. These two examples also represent the two most common ways local governments have attempted to exclude trans athletes across the country. The parties involved in the Connecticut lawsuit and the state representatives in Idaho who are trying to push this legislation are both trying to achieve the same goal, which is the exclusion of trans girls and women from high-school sports. They don't just have the same goal, but also employ the same tactics and anti-trans rhetoric. That's not an accident. Both efforts are supported and funded by the ADF, an evangelical Christian organization responsible for many of the anti-trans bills being introduced across the country. Southern Poverty Law Center has classified ADF as an anti-LGBT hate group because they support the criminalization of same-sex marriage, state-sanctioned sterilization of trans folks in Europe, and claims that homosexuality will ruin society (Putterman, 2020).

This analysis was not concerned with quantifying the number of frames used or the frequency of any characteristics, but rather was intended to identify new themes of coverage in addition to applying findings from previous research on trans athletes. The entire focus of the coverage—the debate on transgender inclusion—centers on one of the most common frames of transgender athletes, according to Love (2017), which is that trans athletes are granted legitimacy in their identity but in a way that reinforces a gender binary and perpetuates a gender hierarchy that assumes men are biologically (i.e., athletically) superior to women. This assumption is at the core of the push to "protect" women's and girl's high-school sports. While some have argued for an end to a sex-segregated system of sports, many advocates for trans inclusion argue simply to let people play in the sport according to their gender identity.

Privileging of Anti-Trans and Cisgender Perspectives

In coverage of these two legal battles, news and sports outlets alike tended to prioritize the anti-trans perspective, especially when it came from a cisgender or lesbian woman or doctor/medical professional who validated the scientific logic behind sex-segregated sports. Cisgender women and girls in particular were generally quoted first, indicating at least some level of significance in the overall framing of the issue. In one Yahoo Sports article explaining tennis legend Martina Navratilova's opposition to trans athlete inclusion, the author examines the various perspectives of the debate, but centers Navratilova's transphobic response. When listing the different arguments, the first one reads, "Transgender women have an unfair advantage over other female competitors" (Mah, 2019, para. 10) and includes three excerpts from various people highlighting that point, including a transgender runner and medical physicist. The other aspects of the debate included in the article, all of which are in favor of trans inclusion, only feature one perspective per argument. According to Mah (2019), the other prominent augments of the debate are "Biology doesn't matter, there are already factors that create differences among competitors" (para. 16); "This debate is bigger than transgender athletes on the field, it's about inclusion in sports and is a broader part of a broader social and political movement" (para. 18); "Fairness claims about trans athletes are rooted in prejudice and phobia" (para. 21); and "Pushing transgender youth away from sports is harmful" (para. 23). Though the arguments in favor of transgender inclusion clearly outnumber those against, the positioning of the arguments in this order, with the transphobic perspective at the top, implies some degree of importance, especially because it is accompanied in the article by several aggregated perspectives supporting the claim in an attempt to provide "both sides," as journalism often does. The organization of the arguments gives the impression that though there are more arguments in favor of trans inclusion and exclusion, the one argument against weighs more and is deemed more credible.

Both local papers featured a number of cis girls and women as op-ed writers, as if being cis gender makes them an expert or authority and grants them credibility over their trans counterparts, who don't get space in the op-ed section. Indeed, even those who supported the rights of high-school athletes to compete according to their gender identity were often cisgender. The implication of the use of cis women to argue against trans women as authorities is the assumption that they are "real" women and therefore their experiences are more valid and authentic. And most of those arguing in favor of the anti-trans bill were women, at least in terms of the sponsors of the bill and those who wrote columns. This discursive move to situate cis women against trans women might be unintentional, but it has the effect of perpetuating a biological gender binary and authenticating the experiences and perspectives of cis women while ignoring or dismissing trans experiences. In the *Idaho Statesman*, several cisgender women wrote columns advocating in favor of the bill, relying on arguments that the bill isn't anti-transgender, but "pro-female" (Burt, 2020) or urging people to "please protect women's sports from transgender athletes," (Kenyon, 2020). Cisgender female athletes commonly argue in favor of the anti-trans efforts in articles and columns throughout the sample, and it's often implied their cisgender identity and former or current athlete status justifies their inclusion as experts on the topic. In a *Hartford Courant* article, a cisgender woman who opposes transgender inclusion is introduced in a way that signals her credibility in a way that doesn't happen for trans sources:

But Betty Remigino-Knapp says cis females are at a biological disadvantage. Remigino-Knapp, a former UConn track and cross country coach, is now an assistant track coach at Hall High School who spent 20 years as the West Hartford school athletic director.

"I have great empathy for all transgender kids," Remigino-Knapp said. "I don't object to it morally at all. I think the issue at hand is the inequity—if you are a biological male you have an advantage because of testosterone. It's a proven medical fact. I think our female student-athletes and our coaches feel there's no longer a level playing field" (Riley, 2018, para. 19–20).

Paradoxical Nature of Trans Athlete Coverage

The second primary theme of the coverage was the contradictory aspects of the news and sports media discourse, which pertains mostly to the way even defenses of trans athletes can be counterproductive. The paradoxical coverage featured simultaneously problematic and supportive rhetoric or reframed the issue of trans exclusion as an economic issue, which distracts from the core issue at hand. Despite this, there were examples of coverage overall that indicated an improvement in coverage, echoing previous work on the legitimizing nature of recent transgender news coverage (Billard, 2016).

Benevolent Anti-Trans Rhetoric

As feminist scholars have argued (Gill, 2007), gender representations in the media have become increasingly complex and difficult to interpret and thus require a "postfeminist sensibility" that finds meaning in that nuance and doesn't view things via a good-bad binary. This paradox of coverage, as several have called it (McClearen, 2015; Love, 2018), was also evident in the coverage of the Connecticut lawsuit and the Idaho bill, as both supporters and opponents of transgender inclusion can deploy similar hegemonic rhetoric that reinforces gender binaries. But as McClearen (2015) noted previously, even the advocates for trans inclusion inevitably employ sexist rationale when their arguments in favor of trans inclusion focus on the biological or scientific evidence of their gender identity:

> Fox's supporters in more progressive media institutions rely on a sexist characterization of female athletes as substandard to speak against the cissexism that challenges Fox's right to fight as a woman. In fact, their primary arguments hinge on the science of weakness and unexceptionally of female athletes to prove their case for Fox. The result is that Fox endures cissexism from those who oppose her participation in women's MMA and sexism from those who support her inclusion. (p. 87)

The most problematic aspects of this type of coverage included the uncritical inclusion of quotes by sources that intentionally misgender or deadname transgender athletes. Sports journalists would repeatedly include quotes that referred to trans women as "biologically male" or some other phrase that is intended to delegitimize their gender identity. In many instances, both sports and news media provided a mouthpiece for the anti-trans rhetoric and allowed it to continue circulating unchallenged. This occurred in discussions about the lawsuits and in the language of the bill in Idaho, which is obviously rooted in an anti-transgender perspective, as evidenced by the bill's language and timing. In the *Idaho Statesman*, Ehardt is quoted first in most stories, and it's often a similar refrain about the biological advantages between men and women, such as

> Boys and men already have too many advantages over young girls participating in sports. . . . There is absolutely an inherent advantage that boys and men have, and we simply cannot compete. I just want us to keep the playing field fair. (As quoted in McIntosh, 2020, para. 6)

Others like Madison Kenyon, who joined in a lawsuit in defense of the new Idaho bill, consistently referred to transwomen and girls as "males" and "biological male." She writes:

> During the fall 2019 cross-country season, I was told we'd be competing against a male who identifies as female. This biological male had competed on the male cross-country team for three years before identifying under a female name. In the men's division, the athlete had recorded times in several events faster than the college women's national record. . . . I already knew how it feels to compete against—and lose to—a male athlete in women's sports. Other girls and women, I learned, were facing the same problem. (2020, para. 3)

However, there were also a few instances of journalists challenging and even correcting these statements in their articles, to the extent that they would clarify the offensiveness of the phrase or declare their opposition to it. One example was in Kliegman's *Sports Illustrated* feature, in which she supplements a quote by the author of the bill, Barbara Ehardt, by saying that Ehardt incorrectly referred "to transgender women as 'biological males'" (2020, para. 33). Another example of more progressive coverage can be found in an ESPN.com feature about the national debate that centers the experiences of the trans girls at the heart of these two legal cases, in particular Miller, Yearwood and Hecox (Barnes, 2020). Like the example in *Sports Illustrated*, Barnes also called out and/or contextualized the quotes used in the story, especially when the source misgendered trans athletes. They wrote statements like, "Throughout its 29-page complaint to the Department of Education, the ADF referred to Miller and Yearwood as males" (Barnes, 2020, para. 12). However, much of ESPN's coverage of the transgender debate and these cases comes from wire services, and many of the articles from ESPN are written by the same author, who themselves is non-binary.

Focus on Economics

With the Idaho ban in particular, many opponents to the bill argued against the transgender ban in sports not because of the discrimination of trans students or the unconstitutionality of the bill, but rather the economic impact the bill could have on the state and the city, especially involving NCAA events that bring in a large amount of revenue and boost the local economy. One of the primary differences between the two legal cases in Idaho and Connecticut is that Idaho's bill is focused on both high-school and college sports, which has much different economic and political implications because of the money involved in major college sports. *The Idaho Statesman* featured several articles focusing on the economic impact as well as op-eds written by people who argued against the ban but on the grounds that it's bad for Idaho businesses. Indeed, many of Idaho's largest businesses signed a letter against it, and the NCAA itself threatened to pull events out of the state should it move the bill forward and sign it into law (Sewell, 2020b). The NCAA has previously used this tactic in response to other instances of anti-trans legislation, such as in 2016, when it pulled events from North Carolina because of its so-called bathroom bill (Forde, 2020).

This economic focus diverts attention away from the issue and indeed ignores the transphobia inherent in the bill, legislature, and society more broadly. Instead of arguing against the bill on moral or ethical grounds, many opponents to the bill simply urged people to think about the money that could be lost (Rubel, 2020). Another op-ed in the Statesman explicitly stated the authors weren't interested in the transgender ban, but only on the economic impact:

> The unintended economic consequences of these two bills will materially harm our industry and detrimentally impact businesses throughout Idaho. Our intent is not to debate the merits of the legislation. But it is vital that Idahoans understand the economic repercussions that will further devastate our already hard-hit tourism industry. (Muchow, Westergard, & Pidgeon, 2020, para. 2)

They continued,

> Unfortunately, these transgender bills have the unintended potential to inflict significant damage on the already ailing tourism industry and our reputation as an attractive tourist destination. We are hopeful that a solution—either

legislatively or in the courts—will allow travelers from all 50 states to enjoy the benefits that Boise and all of Idaho have to offer (2020, para. 8)

This last quote underscores how the economic focus erases the core of the issue, rendering the rights of trans women and girls to compete in sports secondary to tourism and the economy.

"I Want to Win" versus "I Want to Participate"

Throughout the coverage, one of the major threads is the juxtaposition of the cisgender desire to win and the transgender desire to simply compete. In many of the stories featuring trans athletes, those athletes were often quoted saying something along the lines of not wanting to dominate their sport, but just be included and have an opportunity to compete. For example, an article in the *Hartford Courant* quotes a 14-year-old trans student, Sarah Huckman, who says she and other trans athletes play sports "for the love of it" (2021). Lindsey Hecox, who wants to run for the women's track-and-field team at Boise State and the plaintiff in a lawsuit against the state, is often quoted through the coverage about just wanting to run, to have an opportunity to "compete." "I just want to run at whatever level I'm at. But I always have the fear that if I run too fast, it's going to be a problem," Hecox said to *Sports Illustrated* (Kliegman, 2020, para. 22). Others, like Yearwood and Miller, echoed similar sentiments and reiterated their gender identity and their desire to run in statements following the initial Title IX complaint. Yearwood stated, "I have known two things for most of my life: I am a girl and I love to run" (Riley, 2019, para. 17), while Miller said, "I am a girl and I am a runner. I participate in athletics just like my peers to excel, find community and meaning in my life" (Riley, 2019, para. 16).

Conversely, almost all cisgender girls and women featured in the articles focused on winning, the impact of trans girls on their chances of winning, and the risk they pose to their future athletic careers. As Idaho State University cross-country runner, Madison Kenyon, wrote in the *Idaho Statesman*,

Sports was the air I breathed growing up; it's the air I breathe now. I want my future daughters and other young girls to be able to have the same experiences and opportunities I've enjoyed. I want my teammates' and my own hard work to pay off. I'm not competing for a participation trophy. I'm competing to be the best . . . to medal . . . to win. (Kenyon, 2020, para. 12)

As one of the plaintiffs in the Connecticut lawsuit, Chelsea Mitchell, said, "No girl should have to settle into her starting blocks knowing that you don't have a fair shot at winning" (Brechlin & McFarland, 2020, para. 5), although she herself was named the *Hartford Courant*'s female athlete of the year. This juxtaposition of trans athlete desire to compete with cisgender desire to win underscores the discursive attempts to situate trans athletes as standing in the way of cisgender success on the field. Stating one's motivation for participation is winning is often framed as more important than just wanting to be there. Because such an emphasis is placed on winning in sports in general, and in the discourse about the transgender exclusion bills in particular, the pleas from cisgender girls and women arguing for trans athlete bans seemingly carry more weight because their goals are aligned with the goal of sports more broadly (i.e., winning). The cisgender focus on winning implies that the presence of trans girls threatens that enterprise. In fact, many of them make that specific claim, as the three cisgender girls did in their lawsuit challenging the CIAC policy. This also supports the rationale behind the sex-segregated nature of sports, which "purported to protect the integrity of women's competition under the logic that female athletes would not otherwise have a fair shot at winning" (Henne, 2014, p. 792). To be clear, this dichotomy of winning versus participating doesn't mean transgender girls aren't interested in being successful, but that the coverage has discursively positioned these two motivations in opposition to each other.

NEW WAVE OF (UN)FAIRNESS AND EXCLUSION

Similar to previous research on trans athletes, particularly trans women, this analysis underscored the paradoxical nature of coverage of transgender people, which is at once both exclusionary toward and at times accepting of them; highlighted the way news and sports media tended to privilege cisgender and anti-trans perspectives; and outlined how the rationales from athletes involved are split between wanting to win and wanting to compete. In the case of the trans-athlete bans examined here, the coverage reflected this seemingly contradictory disposition that arises in these discussions. Many who argued either in favor or against the inclusion of trans girls in girls' sports were clear in their acceptance of transgender identity, yet still framed the debate in a problematic fashion (Sloop, 2004), engaged in discussions of "biology" and "science" to designate authentic gender identity (Fausto-Sterling, 2000; Henne, 2014), and provided a mouthpiece for opponents of trans inclusion to say more overtly transphobic or sexist comments. These findings about the coverage of the trans-exclusionary efforts across the country might not be new or novel necessarily, but they are significant for their implications for journalists. Sports journalists need to talk about and cover trans issues; not covering them is just as bad as demonizing or delegitimizing them. It almost goes without saying, but the lack of discussion mandates it be repeated. However, increased representation isn't a cure-all for problems that arise within news coverage. Visibility can only be so beneficial to gaining gender equity in sports (McClearen, 2021). It requires not just including trans identities in the coverage and seeking trans perspectives, but also employing transgender journalists.

This discourse analysis highlighted the media's ability to define the debate and frame it in a way that gives credibility to "both sides" whereby one calls for inclusion based on self-identification and the other mandates exclusion based on state-defined, biologically deterministic identities. So, while the coverage at times seems progressive, sometimes even benevolent, it still has the effect of demonizing trans people by the inclusion of perspectives that are unchallenged by the journalist. Transgender journalists and writers covering this were a notable exception, especially because they often pushed back on anti-trans rhetoric and centered trans voices, both in terms of athletes and other sources. As scholars have noted previously, coverage of women's sports in particular no longer features overt examples of sexism, but that doesn't mean the coverage is harmless, especially when considering the intersectional identities of the athletes in these examples (Cooky et al., 2015; Love, 2018). Rather, sexism, misogyny, racism, and other hateful and problematic ideologies come through in more subtle, seemingly innocuous ways. To combat this, journalists should be mindful and reflexive about their rationale for using certain quotes and sources in their reporting, especially if it only serves to further demonize and marginalize trans folks. For journalists covering issues of racial discrimination, it is not necessary to solicit quotes from racists. Likewise, when covering transgender issues, one need not quote transphobic sources just because they have an opinion. Doing so creates a false sense of neutrality and delegitimizes the experiences—and the existence—of transgender athletes. And for the journalists covering these issues, they also need to understand the ways in which transgender people of color, especially black girls like Yearwood and Miller, are impacted by the intersectionality of their identity.

Journalism is often called the first draft of history. But being the first draft of history, while not always the more accurate account of current events, is immensely powerful, and comes with the ability to define, to set boundaries, to establish standards, and so on, especially about groups of people deemed to be outsiders or who might pose a threat to the status quo. As this chapter seeks to present, a problem with legacy and sports media organizations is that even if they cover a topic like transgender inclusion in sports, they often resort to tropes about transgender people, rely on biology to determine the legitimacy of trans folks, center the debate around potential economic consequences, and focus on "fairness."

Trans representation in the newsroom is important. The outlets with some of the most balanced, sensitive coverage of the debate about trans inclusion came from places employing trans journalists, who center and include trans voices throughout their coverage, such as Outsports. Although, good coverage shouldn't have to come only from trans folks, just like women shouldn't have to write about "women's issues" and black journalists shouldn't be limited to covering race-related topics. Having the perspectives of the communities being covered undoubtedly improves the coverage of minority groups, but it can't just be their responsibility. Cisgender journalists need to improve the way they cover trans issues, especially by adding context to problematic quotes, fact-checking unverified information provided by sources, and centering the experiences of those most at risk of discrimination, prejudice, and vitriol so as to not further symbolically annihilate them from the media.

Representation in journalism has always been an industry issue, especially regarding newsroom demographics. Some have argued that if representation of minority groups were representative of the actual population, coverage might be better (Robinson & Culver, 2019). Others have argued the same in favor of gender equity in sports journalism (Hardin, 2013). To some degree this is true. I believe greater representation leads to better coverage to an extent. But what is needed is the critical eye of journalists to challenge racist, transphobic, heteronormative assumptions, and to not include quotes from people expressing those types of beliefs without calling it out or at least providing some context. In the debate on transgender inclusion, many arguments against inclusion are framed as "scientific" or "biological" or "about competition" or "fairness" in order to obscure the fact that they are arguing for trans erasure, not exclusion. If you can keep transgender people out of sports, a realm in society often dubbed "a microcosm" or "a reflection" of society, then surely you can exclude them from many other areas of public life.

Given this all-too-common argument that the inclusion of trans athletes is not fair for cisgender athletes, most of the legislation intended to restrict or ban trans athletes is not framed as anti-trans but rather about fairness or about maintaining the "integrity" of women's sports. The sponsor of the Idaho bill, Barbara Ehardt, has said as much:

> Some have labeled these as transgender bills, falsely so. I don't see that at all. This legislation, it doesn't care how you identify. That's the beauty of it. You can identify however you want. This is all about sex, because in the arena of sport, one's biological sex matters. It just simply does. You can't get around that. (Block, 2021, para. 37)

However, scholars have argued the contradiction inherent in such rhetoric:

> The obsession to determine what is fair, and where people have a right to compete misses the point. While competitive athletes will strive to gain every advantage through training, there must be a respect for the training that trans athletes do. There must be an understanding they are not trying to gain an unfair

advantage, but simply need places to express their physical abilities, to strive and struggle and achieve. Until we make space for all to play sports, it is quite simply, not fair. (Semerjian, 2018, p. 159)

This discussion of fairness and the intentional attempts to claim the bills are not anti-trans obfuscates the very real anti-trans attitudes that provide the impetus for proposing them in the first place.

While writing this book chapter in the first half of 2021, more than 30 states across the country introduced new legislation aimed at restricting transgender access to sports. Six states have actually passed bills while others are working their way through statehouses all over the United States. The problematic, transphobic language seen in the coverage of the cases in Idaho and Connecticut is even more pronounced in some instances, such as Tennessee, where the governor said that transgender girls will "destroy women's sports" (Mattise & Kruesi, 2021). States such as Mississippi, Georgia, and Tennessee have passed bills actually banning trans girls and subjecting any girl to sex verification testing should someone challenge her, while states such as Texas are trying to pass similar laws. Though this chapter points to examples of more nuanced and less overtly problematic coverage of trans athletes, the sudden increase in these bills speaks to the culturally rooted anti-LGBTQ— and particularly anti-trans—attitude that permeates much of American social, and especially legal, life. And as these efforts pick up steam, it's imperative for journalists to be reflexive about how they cover them and critically consider how to avoid perpetuating troublesome transgender stereotypes and assumptions and work toward creating an inclusive sporting environment.

For starters, journalists can begin by educating themselves about transgender identity and start to take stock of their own biases and predilections about gender identity and its role in structuring sports. Journalists have a responsibility not only to provide more equitable coverage of transgender people in sports, but to push back against efforts within and outside of sports to exclude transgender people from participating. This includes prioritizing trans perspectives, using correct pronouns, and not giving space to transphobic voices and perspectives. Indeed, if adhering to a queer theory perspective, people must do more than challenge anti-trans rhetoric and legal efforts, but must also question the sex-segregated nature of sports and the gender binary itself (Semerjian, 2018). Research has pointed to slight improvements in coverage of transgender athletes over time, but there is still work to do, especially as these exclusionary efforts gain steam across the country. Sports journalists play an outsized role in the discourse around trans inclusion in sports, thus the way they write about trans athletes is undeniably key to achieving that. Sports journalists, writers, bloggers and other media members need to understand their part in this problem, which starts with having some critical self-reflexivity about whose voices are being included, who is being left out, and how they can improve.

Response

I Am Trans. I Am Human.

Karleigh Webb

What frustrates me the most as a journalist when discussing transgender rights is that too often the fourth estate seeks the easy story at the expense of the humanity of transgender people.

I find much of coverage dehumanizing. For example, "Transgender Athletes vs Women." You might as well pitch it as Godzilla versus Mothra.

There is the numbing complicity of the mainstream press in parroting the press releases of groups like the ADF. Groups like the ADF thrive on painting issues without context, deal in gross falsehoods about trans people, and play on the general ignorance and fear of the cisgender public.

When you merely recap their points without greater analysis, this harms trans people. There is no excuse whatsoever for terms such as "biological males" and "transgendered" to be a news story in a professional media environment. When you allow gaslighting tactics to pass without due challenge, or examination, you cede you the title of a journalist and become a mouthpiece of legalized discrimination!

We also must reexamine how we approach and tell stories of my people. Too often, a trans person as a subject finds their humanity in the background and the "debate" at the center. My people are cast as a "contention," a "case study," or a "talking point." It's a "disaster movie" mentality and it needs to stop.

We are human beings with lives, hopes, fears, and ambitions of our own.

Our lives are placed in the constant context of the continuing struggle for legal recognition, but rarely does that context include letting the reader or viewer see life beyond the relationship to the "debate." So much of our story is placed in terms of cisgender perceptions of transgender lives and experiences. If the core of the discussion isn't on the "hows" and "whys" of our transition, it is on trying to present the narrative of "they were this person and now they are this person."

Our lives and stories are much richer than this. To place the mechanics of what we go through ahead of the organic, human pulse of who we are is the most dehumanizing thing that happens to us and its tiring!

The constant "before" and "after" approach to how we are covered is demeaning and often insulting. It sends a subliminal message underneath that we as trans people are "not quite real" and have "something to hide."

We spend so much of an interview filling in some arbitrary "resume" because that is the cisgender frame of reference. Rote listing of date and years to fit simple formulas to tell "simple stories" instead of delving into the complex realities and the bright joys of our existence.

That word is the most ignored in the discourse—joy!

Contrary to common cis perception, there is a lot of color, beauty, and joy in being who we are. We push for our rights and step into the struggle because of this beauty and joy. It would make for better understanding if the press centered "trans is beautiful" as much as they center "trans under siege."

I challenge my fellow journalists to get out of the "monster movie/disaster movie" mentality of covering my trans community.

REFERENCES

Anderson, E. (2008, June). "I used to think women were weak": Orthodox masculinity, gender segregation, and sport. *Sociological Forum, 23*, 257–280. https://doi.org/10.1111/j.1573-7861.2008.00058.x

Anderson, E., & Travers, A. (2017). *Transgender athletes in competitive sport. Transgender athletes in competitive sport.* https://doi.org/10.4324/9781315304274

Arune, W. (2006). Transgender images in the media. In L. Castañeda & S. B. Campbell (Eds.), *News and sexuality: Media portraits of diversity* (pp. 111–134). London: Sage.

Barker-Plummer, B. (2013). Fixing Gwen: News and the mediation of (trans) gender challenges. *Feminist Media Studies, 13*, 710–724. https://doi.org/10.1080/14680777.2012.679289

Barnes, K. (2020, June 23). The battle over Title IX and who gets to be a woman in sports: Inside the raging national debate. ESPN. Retrieved from https://www.espn.com/espnw/story/_/id/29347507/the-battle-title-ix-gets-woman-sports-raging-national-debate

Birrell, S., & Cole, C. (1990). Double fault: Renee Richards and the construction and naturalization of difference. *Sociology of Sport Journal, 7*, 1–21.

Block, M. (2021, May 3). Idaho's transgender sports ban faces a major legal hurdle. NPR. Retrieved from https://www.npr.org/2021/05/03/991987280/idahos-trans-gender-sports-ban-faces-a-major-legal-hurdle

Brassil, G. R., & Longman, J. (2020, August 19). Who should compete in women's sports? There are 'Two almost irreconcilable positions.' *The New York Times.* Retrieved from https://www.nytimes.com/2020/08/18/sports/transgender-athletes-womens-sports-idaho.html

Brechlin, D., & McFarland, S. (2020, February 14). Families of three Connecticut high-school students file lawsuit seeking to prevent transgender athletes from participating in girls sports. *Hartford Courant.* Retrieved from https://www.courant.com/sports/high-schools/hc-sp-ciac-transgender-federal-lawsuit-20200212-20200212-wjk3p4i3evh25ayp7kksefmf4i-story.html

Burt, C. (2020, April 21). Idaho's transgender athlete bill is pro-female, not anti-transgender. *Idaho Statesman.* Retrieved from https://www.idahostatesman.com/opinion/readers-opinion/article242055826.html

Butler, J. (1990). *Gender trouble: Feminism and the subversion of identity*. New York: Routledge.

Butler, J. (1993). *Bodies that matter: On the discursive limits of "sex"*. New York: Routledge.

Collins, P. H. (1990). Black feminist epistemology. In P. H. Collins, *Black feminist thought: Knowledge, consciousness and the politics of empowerment* (pp. 251–271). New York: Routledge.

Cooky, C., Messner, M. A., & Musto, M. (2015). "It's Dude Time!" *Communication & Sport, 3*(3), 261–287. https://doi.org/10.1177/2167479515588761

Cooky, C., Council, L. T. D., Mears, M. A., & Messner, M. A. (2021). One and done: The long eclipse of women's televised sports, 1989–2019. *Communication and Sport, 9*(3), 347–371. https://doi.org/10.1177/21674795211003524

Crenshaw, K. (1989). Demarginalizing the intersection of race and sex: A black feminist critique of antidiscrimination doctrine, feminist theory and antiracist politics. *University of Chicago Legal Forum, 78*(2), 139–167. https://doi.org/10.1016/0011-9164(90)80039-E

Cromwell, J. (1993). *Transmen and FTMs*. Chicago: University of Illinois Press.

Fairclough, N. (2013). Critical discourse analysis. In J. P. Gee & M. Handford (Eds.), *The Routledge handbook of discourse analysis* (1st ed., pp. 9–20). London: Routledge.

Fausto-Sterling, A. (2000). *Sexing the body: Gender politics and the construction of sexuality*. New York: Basic Books.

Feinberg, L. (1996). *Transgender warriors: Making history from Joan of Arc to Dennis Rodman*. Boston: Beacon Press.

Fischer, M. (2019). *Terrorizing gender: Transgender visibility and the surveillance practices of the U.S. security state*. Lincoln, Nebraska: University of Nebraska Press.

Fischer, M., & McClearen, J. (2020). Transgender athletes and the queer art of athletic failure. *Communication and Sport, 8*(2), 147–167. https://doi.org/10.1177/2167479518823207

Forde, P. (2020, June 10). Athletes ask NCAA not to host events in Idaho due to state's transgender girls and women's sports ban. *Sports Illustrated*. Retrieved from https://www.si.com/college/2020/06/10/ncaa-idaho-transgender-law-sports

Gill, R. (2007). Postfeminist media culture: Elements of a sensibility. *European Journal of Cultural Studies, 10*, 147–166. https://doi.org/10.1177/ 1367549407075898

Halberstam, J. (2011). *The queer art of failure*. Durham: Duke University Press.

Hall, S. (1997). *Representation: Cultural representations and signifying practices*. London: SAGE Publications.

Hardin, M. (2013). Want changes in content? Change the decision makers. *Communication and Sport, 1*, 241–245. https://doi.org/10.1177/2167479513486985.

Henne, K. (2014). The "science" of fair play in sport: Gender and the politics of testing. *Signs, 39*(3), 787–812. https://doi.org/10.1086/674208

Kelley, A. (2020, May 28). U.S. rules against state allowing transgender athletes to compete in women's sports. *The Hill*. Retrieved from https://thehill.com/changing

-america/respect/equality/499960-us-rules-against-state-allowing-transgender-ath-letes-to

Kenyon, M. (2020, June 7). I'm a female student athlete in Idaho. Please protect women's sports from transgender athletes. *Idaho Statesman*. Retrieved from https://www.idahostatesman.com/opinion/readers-opinion/article243283701.html

Keyser, J. (2020, August 17). Federal judge in Idaho stops state from implementing ban on transgender athletes. *Idaho Statesman*. Retrieved from https://www.idahostatesman.com/news/politics-government/article245032205.html

Kliegman, J. (2020, June 30). Idaho banned trans athletes from women's sports. She's fighting back. *Sports Illustrated*. Retrieved from https://www.si.com/sports-illustrated/2020/06/30/idaho-transgender-ban-fighting-back

Lorber, J. (1993). Believing is seeing: Biology as ideology. *Gender and Society, 7*(4), 568–581.

Love, A. (2017). The tenuous inclusion of transgender athletes in sport. In E. Anderson & A. Travers (Eds.), *Transgender athletes in competitive sport* (pp. 194–205). New York: Routledge.

Love, A. (2018). Media framing of transgender athletes: Contradictions and paradoxes in coverage of MMA fighter Fallon Fox. In *LGBT athletes in the sports media* (pp. 207–225). https://doi.org/10.1007/978-3-030-00804-8

Lovelock, M. (2017). Call me Caitlyn: Making and making over the "authentic" transgender body in Anglo-American popular culture. *Journal of Gender Studies, 26*, 675–687. https://doi.org/10.1080/09589236.2016.1155978

MacKinnon, K. (2017). An introduction to five exceptional trans athletes from around the world. In E. Anderson & A. Travers (Eds.), *Transgender athletes in competitive sport* (pp. 43–53). New York: Routledge.

Mah, P. (2019). The debate over transgender athletes. *Yahoo*. Retrieved from https://www.yahoo.com/news/debate-transgender-athletes-021911396.html

Mattise, J., & Kruesi, K. (2021). Governor: Transgender athletes will 'destroy women's sports.' *Yahoo Sports*. Retrieved from https://sports.yahoo.com/governor-transgender-athletes-destroy-womens-190552748.html

McClearen, J. (2015). The paradox of Fallon's Fight: Interlocking discourses of sexism and cissexism in mixed martial arts fighting. *New Formations, 86*, 74–88. https://doi.org/10.3898/NEWF.86.04.2015

McIntosh, S. (2020, January 12). Idaho is about to join national debate over transgender student-athletes. *The Idaho Statesman*. Retrieved from https://www.idahostatesman.com/opinion/from-the-opinion-editor/article239121313.html

Messner, M. A. (1996). Studying up on sex. *Sociology of Sport Journal, 13*, 221–237.

Messner, M. (2007). *Out of play: Critical essays on gender and sport*. Albany, NY: State University of New York Press.

Minsberg, T. (2020, May 2020). 'Boys are boys and girls are girls': Idaho is first state to bar some transgender athletes. *The New York Times*. Retrieved from https://www.nytimes.com/2020/04/01/sports/transgender-idaho-ban-sports.html

Muchow, K., Westergard, C., & Pidgeon, K. (2020, June 29). Idaho's anti-transgender bills will have a deep economic impact on tourism and business. *Idaho*

Statesman. Retrieved from https://www.idahostatesman.com/opinion/readers -opinion/article243819502.html

Muñoz, J. E. (2009). *Cruising Utopia: The then and there of queer futurity*. New York: New York University Press.

Namaste, V. (2000). *Invisible lives: The erasure of transsexual and transgendered people*. Chicago: The University of Chicago Press.

Putterman, A. (2020, February 14). Who is alliance defending freedom? The religious-conservative legal group has targeted transgender high school athletes in Connecticut. *Hartford Courant*. Retrieved from https://www.courant.com /sports/hc-sp-alliance-defending-freedom-transgender-athletes-lawsuit-20200214 -20200214-3rb6tjsiwfaijhqalhlvw7ys2i-story.html

Putterman, A., & Riley, L. (2019, June 18). Connecticut high school athletes file complaint over transgender policy. *Hartford Courant*. Retrieved from https:// www.courant.com/sports/high-schools/hc-sp-transgender-high-school-track-law- suit-20190618-20190618-4mjx7gllrjarlpidhnjeecfosq-story.html

Riley, L. (2018, June 5). Coaches, parents question policy for high school transgender athletes. *Hartford Courant*. Retrieved from https://www.courant.com/sports/high -schools/hc-sp-hs-transgender-high-school-athletes-0520-story.html

Riley, L. (2019, June 21). Complaint over Connecticut high school athletics transgen- der policy has merit, former federal prosecutor says. *Hartford Courant*. Retrieved from https://www.courant.com/sports/high-schools/hc-sp-hs-transgender-0620 -20190620-su5xszoz5fgqtpof77g3ea6hu4-story.html

Riley, L. (2021, April 26). Federal judge dismisses lawsuit that sought to block trans- gender female athletes from competing in girls high school sports in Connecticut. *Hartford Courant*. Retrieved from https://www.courant.com/sports/high-schools /hc-sp-hs-transgender-case-dismissed-20210425-twgpmkmsrvhnhl64u2tr32tg3y -story.html

Robinson, S., & Culver, K. B. (2019). When White reporters cover race: News media, objectivity and community (dis)trust. *Journalism, 20*(3), 375–391. https://doi.org /10.1177/1464884916663599

Rubel, I. (2020, June 22). Guest opinion: GOP transgender laws are affecting Idaho businesses. *Idaho Statesman*. Retrieved from https://www.idahostatesman.com/ opinion/readers-opinion/article243720302.html

Semerjian, T. Z. (2018). Making space: Transgender athletes. In V. Krane (Ed.), *Sex, gender, and sexuality in sport: Queer inquiries* (pp. 145–162). London: Routledge.

Semerjian, T. Z., & Cohen, J. H. (2006). "FTM means female to me": Transgender athletes performing gender. *Women in Sport and Physical Activity Journal, 15*(2), 28–43. https://doi.org/10.1123/wspaj.15.2.28

Sewell, C. (2020a, March 31). The ACLU will see the governor in court. Groups react to passage of anti-transgender bills. *Idaho Statesman*. Retrieved from https://www .idahostatesman.com/news/politics-government/state-politics/article241645901 .html

Sewell, C. (2020b, March 5). 5 of Idaho's largest companies just called out the Leg- islature for not supporting diversity. *Idaho Statesman*. Retrieved from https://www

.idahostatesman.com/news/politics-government/state-politics/article240919661
.html

Sloop, J. (2004). *Disciplining gender: Rhetorics of sex identity in contemporary U.S. culture*. Amherst: University of Massachusetts Press.

Travers, A. (2006). Queering sport: Lesbian softball leagues and the transgender challenge. *International Review for the Sociology of Sport, 41*, 431–446. https://doi.org/10.1177/1012690207078070

van Dijk, T. A. (1988). *News as discourse*. Hillsdale, NJ: Lawrence Erlbaum.

Waldron, J. J. (2018). Four perspectives for understanding LGBTIQ people in sport. In *Sex, Gender, and Sexuality in Sport: Queer Inquiries* (pp. 15–32). https://doi.org/10.4324/9781315114996-3

Webb, K. (2020, February 18). Cisgender athlete behind anti-trans lawsuit defeats top trans rivals. *Outsports*. Retrieved from https://www.outsports.com/2020/2/18/21140680/high-school-connecticut-terry-miller-chelsea-mitchell-track-andraya-yearwood-ciac-adf-transphobia

Willox, A. (2003). Branding Teena: (Mis)representations in the media. *Sexualities, 6*, 407–425. https://doi.org/10.1177/136346070363009

Chapter 10

In High Demand

Friday Night Prime Time and High School Athletes with Disabilities

Alison R. Tsuchida and Nathan M. Murata

Imagine a Friday night in your hometown high-school gym or on the football field. The stands are full of enthusiastic family members, classmates, and community advocates matching the energy on the court or field. The cheerleaders are out, and the band is playing. The excitement in the air is almost tangible. It is an experience that some take for granted and one that some high-school students may never experience. This is often the unfortunate reality of interscholastic athletics and the high-school experience for students with disabilities.

In the United States, approximately 71.8% of all children ages 6–12 participated in sport in 2018 (Aspen Institute, 2019). However, in the 2018–2019 school year, less than half of the enrolled 16.9 million high-school students participated in high-school athletics (National Federation of State High School Associations [NFHS], 2019; U.S. Census Bureau, 2019). The value of sport has been touted for so many reasons. The benefits for extracurricular sport participation include but are not limited to fitness, improved academics, teamwork, cooperation, social relationships, and positive mentors/role models (US Department of Health and Human Services, 2019). Consequently, extracurricular sport opportunities are being reduced for the sake of academic and financial priorities despite recommendations to expand such activities (Shaffer, 2019). This author also noted that some of the positive motivational outcomes of sport include school grades, coursework selection, educational and occupational aspirations, self-esteem, and educational attainment (Shaffer, 2019). While the benefits are well known for students without disabilities, those with disabilities may not necessarily have equal opportunities to participate in authentic interscholastic, recreational, and leisure activities (Solish et al., 2010).

Inequality and authentic sport participation are seen throughout history despite the clear and obvious benefits of sport to all participants. Traditionally, interscholastic sports target, and are geared toward, not only the able-bodied students but the top athletes and performers in and out of the classroom. Inclusion on a high-school sport team typically means that you are physically superior to your peers and can perform the given sport-skill at an above-average ability. Additionally, you are in good academic standing and can cognitively understand and apply tactical concepts with some ease. This current design of interscholastic athletic participation limits inclusion and opportunities for all students to gain health and social-related benefits of physical activity and sport participation.

In fact, the opportunities to participate in interscholastic sports are even fewer for students with disabilities if they are unable to make it onto their high-school team. Throughout the 50 states, only 14 states report having adapted sport programs for boys, and 15 states report having adapted sport programs for girls (NFHS, 2019). This means that of the nearly 8 million students who participated in high-school sports, only 15,541 of them were students who participated in adapted sport programs, which comes out to a staggering 0.02% of high-school student athletes (NFHS, 2019).

More recently, Kozub and Samalot-Rivera (2020) posited that states have consistently varied interscholastic programming for students with disabilities in high school. This is despite a previous report that indicates interscholastic sports for students with disabilities as a benefit to school programs as a whole (Kozub & Porretta, 1996). Bailey (2005) argues that participation in sport has the potential to fend off social exclusion which he defines as a "lack of access to power, knowledge, services, facilities, choice and opportunity" (p. 76) by bringing people together around a shared interest, increasing a sense of belonging, and providing opportunities to develop skills, social networks, and community pride. His argument is in line with the notion that sport can play a role in achieving social justice and equality for all, particularly in schools (Darnell & Millington, 2019).

If so many benefits of sport exist to participants and programs, why aren't there more opportunities? Well, for one, there have been "loopholes" in laws aimed at expanding opportunities. For instance, while different definitions of disabilities do exist, Section 504 of the Rehabilitation Act of 1973 has perhaps the broadest coverage for students. Section 504, governed by the Office of Civil Rights, covers any individual of any age who has a physical or mental impairment that results in a major impairment or limitation to the individual's activities of daily living (29 U.S.C. § 794). Section 504 has important implications for students with disabilities as it first and foremost grants greater and equal access to participation in educational and non-educational activities. These activities may be separate or different from those offered to students without disabilities, but they must be comparable, and the difference must be necessary to ensure safety and or health of those individuals participating in the activity (Galanter, 2013). The 504 mandate applies to all recreational and competitive sport and sport training; however, it does not mandate that all individuals with disabilities can participate in all activities. Schools and other agencies can use the "otherwise qualified" criterion to grant access or deny participation in extracurricular activities (Smith, 2001). The result, given the nature of interscholastic athletics, is fewer opportunities for students with disabilities.

Furthermore, not all states have progressive legislation that promotes inclusion and expanding opportunities as seen in the 2008 Maryland Fitness and Athletic Equity Act for Students with Disabilities that

> requires local boards of education to develop policies to include students with disabilities in all curricular and extracurricular physical education and athletic programs. Specifically, the schools must provide students with reasonable accommodations to participate, the opportunity to try out for school teams, and access to alternative sport programs. (U.S. Department of Education, Office of Special Education and Rehabilitative Services, & Office of Special Education Programs, 2011, p.17)

This type of legislation has been one of the first to specifically address equality in athletic participation and has helped to open doors previously closed to students with disabilities while also serving as a catalyst for program development and inclusion. However, not all states have been this progressive, and hence the responsibility to create opportunities often falls upon the individual schools or districts.

This chapter describes an inclusive interscholastic basketball program implemented in the state of Hawaii and how its three guiding constructs helped to facilitate and promote social and physical activity opportunity equality through an authentic sport experience which can be essential toward one's long-term community assimilation and health.

FRIDAY NIGHT PRIME TIME

Friday Night Lights, a film by Berg (2004), was a movie based on a town in Texas that lived for football games on Friday nights. The movie eclipsed how team spirit, team pride, and being a part of a team were beneficial in so many ways, not only winning. The attention to sports played on Friday nights can also be felt throughout our community here in Hawaii. Families, students, community members, businesses, and media all flock to school fields and gymnasiums to relish the limelight and to be part of something special. The Friday Night Prime Time (FNPT) program offered that same type of impact: *Interscholastic athletic participation opportunities for students with disabilities.* The impact of this program also created the following ancillary benefits for students with disabilities: (1) created equal opportunity and access to after-school athletics; (2) provided a venue for after-school programming for those with and without disabilities; (3) expanded opportunities for all students (those who did not make it on to a varsity team can elect to serve as a peer coach); (4) impacted quality of life for students with disabilities through continued physical activity development and participation; and (5) promoted school spirit and pride.

FNPT assisted schools in preparing students with disabilities and their peers for interscholastic competition by training coaches, providing ample and adequate practice time by securing gym time, supporting interscholastic games between schools (i.e., minimum two games—one at each school's gymnasium), by securing transportation, and supplying officiating for the games. Two Honolulu area schools participated in this program (Straus, 2017). The sport of basketball was used to foster and promote interaction within and between schools. There is research to support the notion that schools are able to provide equal opportunities for students with disabilities and their peers with extracurricular athletic activities (Team Prime Time, n.d.).

Geographical Context

The state of Hawaii is known for its diverse cultures. For individuals with a disability, however, we are similar to anywhere else in the world; inclusive extracurricular activities and sport opportunities are limited. To address this issue, the University of Hawaii at Mānoa's College of Education, Department of Kinesiology and Rehabilitation Science teamed up with local public high schools to create a program to give students with disabilities, students who are at-risk, and students without disabilities the opportunity to experience interscholastic athletics. The program, Friday Night Prime Time is modeled after Team Prime Time Games High School League where peers are paired with students with disabilities to form "Varsity" teams that play against other high schools (Team Prime Time, n.d.). Often impacted by physical level, cognitive level, and in some cases behavior, students with disabilities may not have the opportunity to participate on their high-school interscholastic teams for a variety of reasons, with the most prominent being that individuals with a variety of disabilities wouldn't even be able to participate in a typical team tryout. Other reasons include but not limited to the capping of a typical team roster, coaching philosophies are different and more aligned with a win at all cost mentality which is more exclusive than inclusive especially for students with disabilities, and cost may be several reasons why only those who are capable of making a varsity or junior varsity team, actually do so. Consequently, as previously noted, federal law has stated that opportunities should be provided and even created to foster and encourage participation in these important opportunities for students with disabilities. In this regard, Friday Night Prime Time provides these changes for students with disabilities. With high-school bands playing, cheerleaders, and the bleachers full of fans, you wouldn't know that the teams playing weren't competing for a State Championship.

Three Guiding Constructs

In creating FNPT, we sought to develop the fundamental need for sport as the catalyst to physical, emotional, and psychological well-being for students with and without disabilities. FNPT is rooted in equity, motivation, sense of purpose, and relationship building between students with disabilities and students without disabilities. We believe a portion of human motivation, social justice, and acknowledging federal and state laws has been captured in our FNPT games.

We found the following constructs to be relevant to the project which were illuminated through sports. These constructs are *Sense of Belonging*, *Self-Esteem and Self-Efficacy*, and *Social Justice*. While the purpose of this chapter is not to provide a detailed examination of these constructs; rather, we want to stress it is the essence of these constructs and how they were captured in our FNPT program that afforded students with disabilities the opportunity to participate on an interscholastic athletic team and represent their school in an authentic sporting event.

Sense of Belonging

Developing a sense of meaning and purpose propels an individual to be passionate about the task at hand. The need for interpersonal relationships with peers, classmates, teachers, and coaches defines a sense of belonging (McLeod, 2018). This author surmised that a sense of belongingness with meaning and purpose include friendship, intimacy, trust, and acceptance. Being part of a group or team helps fulfill this sense of belonging. Within the FNPT program, students with disabilities were provided an opportunity to fulfill this "belonging" need by being part of a team, representing their school in a sanctioned basketball game. Each member had a responsibility to do well in school, engage with peers and teachers in a positive way, attend practices, and demonstrate proper gamesmanship. By being a good teammate, team members showed each other trust, honesty, and being trustworthy. Consequently, "school belongingness, or the psychological sense of school membership, is the feeling of being personally accepted, respected, included, and supported by others in the school social environment and is an antecedent to a successful learning experience" (Vaz et al., 2015, pp. 1–2). The need to belong in school is critically important for adolescents and perhaps even more important for students with disabilities who for years have been marginalized. Coupled with sports, the sense of belonging became magnified twofold for adolescents. Zhao et al. (2021) argue that "the intersecting area of sport participation and belonging for young adults with intellectual and developmental disabilities is important to understand as it has significant implications for the development of sport programs for this population" (p. 403).

In the 1970s, past research in sport participation motivation included enjoyment, learning and improving sport-skills, fitness, and socially being with friends (Alderman & Wood, 1976). During the 1980s sport participation motivational theorists developed a knowledge base to develop theory. With the onset of the studies generated in the 1980s, themes emerged as to why athletes participate in sport: physical competence, social acceptance, and enjoyment (Gould & Petlichkoff, 1988; Weiss & Petlichkoff, 1989; Weiss & Williams, 2004). The emergent themes led to more theories being developed to increase our understanding of motivation. One of the most prevalent theories that is often still being refined today is the Self-Determination Theory (SDT) (Deci & Ryan, 1985, 2000, 2008). The aforementioned themes support involvement in sport for social reasons and wanting to be a part of a team. Given that much of an athlete's time is spent with teammates in both sporting and non-sporting contexts, friendships are perceived as being easy to form (Weiss & Petlichkoff, 1989).

Self-Esteem and Self-Efficacy

Self-esteem can be classified into two distinct categories: (1) esteem for self, and (2) respect from others (McLeod, 2018). Self-esteem is having a sense of value, confidence, and self-worth. Respect from others is another important construct within the context of the program. The latent value placed on respect allows the individual to feel safe, confident in his/her ability, and self-respect. Moreover, sport is evidenced as being a mediator in the development of positive global self-concept and self-esteem in adolescent athletes with and without disabilities which can contribute to better socialization and mental health (Scarpa, 2011; Shapiro & Martin, 2010).

During the FNPT event, students with disabilities demonstrated their physical ability, understanding of how the game is played, and camaraderie associated with playing on a team. The students were playing on a team that represents their school, as full-fledged members of the high-school team; they were not simply playing for a feel-good moment from the crowd or to get token minutes for a viral video. They participated alongside their peers for the entirety of the game. Self-esteem for these student athletes really began to emerge as they were counted on by teammates, family, teachers, peers, and the community.

Self-efficacy is a by-product of knowledge and is one's belief that they have the ability to be successful in a particular act or activity (Block et al., 2010). These beliefs in one's self, coupled with positive support from parents and teachers, can lead to autonomous motivation and positive attitudes toward physical activity (Vierling et al., 2007). For youth, participation in physical activity is often motivated by these feelings of self-efficacy, especially youth with disabilities, who are often less motivated to participate in physical activity. Consequently, youth are more likely to be active if they have social support from peers, and when they believe that they will be successful (Kodish et al., 2006). These feelings of self-efficacy translate into adulthood as there is a linear relationship between behavioral and cognitive processes change and self-efficacy (Kosma et al., 2006). Furthermore, Dixon-Ibarra and Driver (2013) highlight the importance of performance attainment, verbal persuasion, and social influence in increasing self-efficacy and physical activity participation among individuals with disabilities. Positive support and encouragement from peers is equally, if not more, important than the skill attainment and performance success for some individuals in maintaining physical activities.

FNPT affords the student athletes the opportunity to practice not only the sport skills but also to experience socialization skills with their peers. Positive encouragement and verbal persuasion were provided by the coaches, parents, and peer mentors who participated alongside the students with disabilities on the same team and worked toward the same goals. The more one is able to utilize their skill sets, the more likely they are to become proficient and develop a sense of confidence in their abilities.

Social Justice

Because most children are educated in schools, interscholastic sports and extracurricular activities provide valuable physical activity opportunities. Interscholastic sports have the ability to promote and enhance sport skills, physical fitness, confidence, and many more positive effects as well as life skills, lessons, and morals (Shaffer, 2019). In fact, coaches themselves can be terrific role models and help the individuals they work with learn to lead positive lives. In this connection, participation in interscholastic sport programs has multiple benefits and should be encouraged for individuals of all abilities (Lumpkin & Stokowski, 2011).

Despite federal and state laws that govern and support sports participation for students with disabilities, some state athletic associations have been slow to acknowledge the positive impact students with disabilities offer with regard to extracurricular activities and sport. The historical aspect of disallowing students with disabilities to engage in authentic interscholastic activities has been witnessed for decades. While federal and state laws have made a positive impact on the education and quality of life for students with disabilities, equal opportunities in sports and extracurricular activities continue to lag behind. In his Dear Colleague Letter, Seth M. Galanter, Acting Assistant Secretary for Civil Rights offered the following:

> Students with disabilities who cannot participate in the school district's existing extracurricular athletics program—even with reasonable modifications or aids and services—should still have an equal opportunity to receive the benefits of extracurricular athletics. When the interests and abilities of some students with disabilities cannot be as fully and effectively met by the school district's existing extracurricular athletic program, the school district should create additional opportunities for those students with disabilities. . . . OCR urges school districts, in coordination with students, families, community and advocacy organizations, athletic associations, and other interested parties, to support these and other creative ways to expand such opportunities for students with disabilities. (Galanter, 2013)

Our ability to promote and provide equal opportunities and access in extracurricular activities and sports for individuals with disabilities can serve as the nexus to Social Justice in education. Social justice issues continue to be debated in schools especially in addressing students with disabilities (Connor, 2014). For example, within the Special Education domain, traditional scholars have argued against the trajectory of special education since it does not address social justice and suggested changes (Connor, 2014). For example, Within this corpus of special education differences in implementing social justice, sports and extracurricular activities can be a catalyst for promoting social justice in schools and particularly for students with disabilities. Social justice and participation in sports exists in a society where there is justice for all, individuals have a voice in the formation of social norms, policies and practices all the while demonstrating dignity and autonomy for each individual and valuing diversity (Bredemeier & Shields, 2019). The impact of equal opportunity provides students with disabilities an opportunity to fully engage with non-disabled peers in representing the high schools in a sanctioned interscholastic event, which can be one mechanism to address social justice in our schools.

Amid inequality in extracurricular sports in schools, advocates have argued for rekindling attention to sports with its social benefits, charitable fundraising potential, and positive impact on after-school programs. Sports have contributed and will continue to contribute to the pursuit of social justice (Darnell & Millington, 2019). The authors surmised, "Sport, when used in a manner that is attuned to the context and complexities of social structures and cultural differences does indeed hold potential to contribute to positive social change" (p. 185). Sport can have a positive interplay with equal opportunity and social justice. When considering how equality, human motivation, sense of purpose, and building relationships can all be interrelated into one tangible episode, team sports is that conduit.

AUTHENTIC EXPERIENCE

Students who participated in this program were a part of an authentic interscholastic experience. The students had to make it through "tryouts" (although, more like a regular practice because everyone made the team), meet behavioral expectations, and attend scheduled practices not unlike any other competitive interscholastic program. Once game day arrived, the students made sure to wear their team gear and let their peers and teachers know about the big game. The team bus would arrive as the gym filled up with fans, the band playing, the cheerleaders cheering, and the concession stands whipping up their finest foods. High fives and cheers during warm-ups indicated that the teams were ready. Each member on the team was introduced with great fanfare rather than just the starters only. And, with the referees in place, the first whistle signaled the game was on.

The rules of the FNPT game were no different than a regular interscholastic game, yet there was a lot of room for flexibility by the referees as their main job was to keep the game moving rather than to end up as a focal point as they sometimes do in competitive athletic events. After all, the competition itself is only part of the full sport experience for these athletes. The peers who participated alongside their teammates with disabilities were responsible for helping to facilitate the play by bringing the ball up the court, rebounding, and essentially being the "quarterback" of the team. With the final buzzer, there was a winner and a loser but you wouldn't have been able to tell who won by looking at the faces of the players. Appreciation and pride exuded from players, families, coaches, and teachers alike. Each game was one to remember.

Another salient outcome was the ability for both schools to be able to *sustain* these extracurricular sport programs for students with disabilities. This proactive approach demonstrated that schools were able and willing to provide equal opportunities for *all students* and were not reactive to formal complaints or even the possibility of litigation toward participation.

Outcomes

In order to determine the efficacy of FNPT, data were collected in the form of questionnaires and interviews with teachers, parents, and student athletes. Following the completion of the FNPT program teachers/coaches, parents, and participants were asked to provide post-participation feedback which described the social implications of interscholastic athletic programs for adolescents through their firsthand examples and experiences from FNPT. All identifiers have been removed and any name utilized in this chapter are pseudo names to protect the anonymity of the participants.

Teachers/Coaches Feedback

As if teachers didn't have enough on their plate already, they are also frequently found coaching interscholastic sports at their schools; they have built a rapport with the students and can be terrific role models. Similarly, this program relied heavily on not only teacher involvement for coaching but also support and encouragement. Administrators, teachers, and educational assistants recruited students to participate and they assisted with coaching the team, logistics and administration, or the ever-important cheer and support squads. Their relationship and rapport with the students and families allowed the teams to run smoothly, engage parents, and maximize student participation while also getting to see their students in a new light.

Post-program evaluation was solicited via feedback forms. Two teachers/coaches agreed that the basketball program had the same physical and affective benefits that come with physical activity and interscholastic participation for all students. Specifically, they cited "increased socialization, leadership skills, and sportsmanship" as positive affective outcomes. One of the teachers further explained that participation in this program meant that "the students who required less assistance were able to take on leadership roles while other students were able to benefit from greater and positive socialization. They got lots of high fives and would root for one another." The other teacher noted that it was "interesting to see the students outside of their typical classroom environment and to see them shining on the court" adding that the program gave the students something to look forward to:

"They got to look forward to game day. And, now they are already looking forward to the next season."

Overall, there was an agreement that there is a need for this type of program for students with disabilities in schools because it provides positive outcomes such as, "increased physical activity" and "increased social interactions and relationships." As one of the teachers stated, "The program gave the students a chance to build life skills like the other athletes on campus. They had to turn in forms on time, act responsibly and respectfully, show up to practice, and earn their playing time." This comment highlighted the fact that coaches can develop character and help student athletes learn to be productive members of society through interscholastic programming (Lumpkin & Stokowski, 2011). The teachers also agreed that the participants enjoyed the program, but there were a few students who may have preferred a different activity.

Parent Perspectives

Family and parent support can either be a barrier or facilitator to participation in physical activity. Positive parent and family support is an important factor in building positive associations with physical activity (King et al., 2003). And, as one can imagine, negative or lack of family support may deter or deny participation. Following the completion of the FNPT program, parents were encouraged to complete a short survey to assist the organizers in evaluating the program.

Ten parents completed the voluntary post-program survey out of forty that were distributed. There was a consensus that extracurricular opportunities that allow for physical activity are valuable. Parents noted they saw a positive difference in their child's leisure time physical activity behavior at home (9 out of 10) and in their child's confidence and/or attitude toward participating in physical activities (8 out of 10). While these are important takeaways, follow-up questioning indicated not only positive observations surrounding their child's experience but also brought to light the sense of happiness and pride that they felt as parents watching their child participate in the sport. One parent further explained that this was their child's first time participating in an extracurricular activity or sport. "I didn't know what to expect," she said, "But, the teachers and coaches were supportive and knowledgeable, the program was organized, all the kids got to play, and everyone was so encouraging!" She was so ecstatic for her child and said that they are both looking forward to the next season.

As evidenced from the parent feedback, parents overwhelmingly described the sense of achievement, pride, and excitement that this activity gave to their child. The enjoyment and opportunity to be a part of a team with their peers made the season feel too short. And, the opportunity for their child to be a part of their school team and to have the chance to represent their school was something they won't soon forget. It is positive feelings and experiences like these that are likely to encourage support for future participation in sport and physical activity.

Student Athlete Response

Student athletes with disabilities from the program were asked to voluntarily complete a post-participation survey. Fifteen participants (11 males, 4 females) completed the survey out of the 40 that were distributed to the teams. The participants were asked to respond to two different scales. The first scale was a happiness scale with response options of: Really Happy (4), Happy (3), Not So Happy (2), and Didn't Like It At All (1). Participants were then asked to rank a second set of questions from: Absolutely Yes (4), Yes (3), A Little (2), and Not At All (1). The results of the survey can be found below. Results indicated that the students with disabilities had a very positive experience.

All students with disabilities who completed the survey were either really happy or happy with the way the sport made them feel, with playing against other schools, and with their self-confidence at school. One of the students with a disability who participated in the program for the first time said that, "I felt like a star. I felt like a Warrior (University of Hawaii mascot)." Further explaining that it was the first time he ever played in a game in front of "the whole school and he even got a lei like the Warriors." He said that it was the "best day ever." Based on a 4-point Likert scale: 4—Really Happy, 3—Happy, 2—Not So Happy, 1—Didn't Like It at All, student athletes reported on how they felt about the sport they were playing, how they felt competing against other schools and their self-confidence during school. (See table 10.1.)

Student athletes with disabilities were also probed on the social aspect of playing in FNPT. Questions in the survey asked about friendships, school pride, being on a team, having more fun, and other related social aspects of

Table 10.1   Questions Posed to Student Athletes with Disabilities

QUESTIONS	Average Score	Really Happy	Happy	Not So Happy	Didn't Like It At All
How did the sport make you feel? (n%)	3.8	12 (.80)	3 (.20)		
How did you feel about playing in the games against other schools? (n%)	3.6	9 (.60)	6 (.40)		
How do you feel about your self-confidence at school? (n%)	3.73	11 (.73)	4 (.27)		

this event. Employing a categorical scale from "Absolutely Yes, Absolutely Yes, Yes, A Little and Not At All," student athletes with disabilities rated the following in table 10.2.

The student athletes with disabilities also mentioned that they were happiest about being able to play on the team. They really liked making new friends on the team and hearing the crowd cheer. In fact, the program was so well received that every student who left comments said that they wanted more games and a longer season. This was a common theme throughout the student athletes, teachers, and parents. They wanted more.

Furthermore, outside of the survey, a peer mentor who participated in the program shared this anecdotal in school observation. "Before, most people just walked by the special ed class. But since they got to play on Friday Night other students are giving them high fives in the hall and saying 'hi' all the time. It's like everyone is happier." She explained that people knew "their" names and everyone just seemed excited to root for the team now that they felt more comfortable saying hi and giving high fives, adding to the evidence that inclusive interscholastic programs have benefits for all students, not just the students with disabilities.

BEYOND SCHOOL TRANSLATION

Social interaction through physical activities and integrated team sports help to limit social exclusion and have numerous benefits that include physical health, cognitive and academic development, mental health, crime reduction, and reduction of truancy and disaffection (Bailey, 2005). The aforementioned benefits provide further evidence that the lack of sport opportunities for students with disabilities is detrimental to both the physical and social health of these individuals (Kozub & Samalot-Rivera, 2020). Although access and equal opportunities in extracurricular activities are mandated by law, the lack of interscholastic opportunities for students with disabilities persists (Kozub & Samalot-Rivera, 2020).

Findings from the FNPT program indicated that it is the type of program that can and should continue to be supported by parents, students, and teachers alike. Shields et al. (2012) reported that the family has a major role in facilitating positive physical activity experiences and social interactions with peers through such physical activities, which can be especially beneficial to physical activity engagement. Encouraging extracurricular participation, particularly in sport, can enhance one's likelihood of social and peer-group integration. Similarly, coaches and teachers can be equally important in ensuring quality programming and interactions. Albeit, simply having the opportunity to be a part of an interscholastic team, compete, and represent your school may be the most motivating factors.

Table 10.2 Social Aspects of Participating in Friday Night Prime Time

Question	Average Score	Absolutely Yes	Yes	A Little	Not At All
Did you make new friends because you played on these teams? (n%)	3.4	9 (.60)	3 (.20)	3 (.20)	
Do you have more school pride because you played on these teams? (n%)	3.53	9 (.60)	5 (.33)	1 (.07)	
Do you feel like a more important person at school because you played on a team? (n%)	3.6	9 (.60)	6 (.40)		
Do more students at school know who you are because you played on a team? (n%)	3.53	8 (.53)	7 (.47)		
Do you think people at your school are friendlier since joining the team? (n%)	3.6	9 (.60)	6 (.40)		
Do you want to do more activities at school since you played on a team? (n%)	3.67	11 (.73)	3 (.20)	1 (.07)	
Do you want to go to school more because you were on the team? (n%)	3.2	7 (.47)	4 (.27)	4 (.27)	
Do you feel like you want to play sports after high school more than you did before joining the team? (n%)	3.6	10 (.67)	4 (.27)	1 (.07)	
Is high school more fun because you joined a team? (n%)	3.53	9 (.60)	5 (.33)	1 (.07)	
Do you feel more accepted on campus because you were on the team? (n%)	3.33	5 (.33)	10 (.67)		
Do you have more friends because you played on these teams? (n%)	3.27	9 (.60)	3 (.20)	1 (.07)	2 (.13)
Do you want to play these sports again at your school? (n%)	3.73	11 (.73)	4 (.27)		

The overwhelming positive support for this program adds to the body of evidence that more organized inclusive sport opportunities are needed in our communities and school settings. Enjoyment and positive health and social outcomes were cited by teachers as benefits of the program. These positive health and social outcomes along with the positive perceptions of physical activity, self-efficacy, self-esteem, and belongingness that it creates, could be the biggest benefits of this inclusive program. Programs that are accessible and have the capability to adapt activities for inclusion of all participation levels are needed to create positive physical activity experiences to enhance overall health in both our schools and communities (Lorenzi, 2014).

When individuals feel competent and capable of performing a sport or skill, they are more likely to participate in the said activity. Self-efficacy and self-esteem are linked and can lead to participation in sport or social activities for that matter, beyond the school years. As such, Individual Transition Plans (ITP) which are required for special education students who are 14 years and older, under the IDEA, must have recreation/leisure addressed as part of their ITP in their Individualized Education Plan (IEP) (Murata & Jansma, 1999). The ITP considers the student's strengths and interests to determine expected outcomes for life beyond school. Participation in extracurricular sport, recreation, or health-related physical activities, that if practiced during the adolescent years and in school, can lead to positive lifelong behaviors and a greater sense of overall well-being.

Inclusive physical activities have a multitude of benefits for all participants beyond the activity itself, including, but not limited to, increased comfort levels with social interactions and increased positive attitudes toward athletes with disabilities (McConkey et al., 2013; Sullivan & Glidden, 2014; Wilski et al., 2012). While social interactions are important for persons with disabilities, other constructs such as enhanced relations with peers, expanded social networks, and initiation of other social activities have value beyond measure (Smith et al., 2015). Consequently, there is a perpetual need for more programs that are accessible and have the capability to adapt activities for inclusion of all individuals that will also help to promote social and physical health benefits within our communities (Shields et al., 2012).

Schools and interscholastic sports can serve as a stepping stone toward social justice for all (Darnell & Millington, 2019). After all, being part of a team is achieving a slice of equality. As Lorenzi (2014) explains, we need to move beyond the "awe" and "feel-good" sports moments and create more authentic and meaningful interscholastic sport experiences and opportunities for students with disabilities. Programs such as Special Olympics, Unified Sports by Special Olympics, and Team Prime Time's Prime Time Games, have stepped up to create more opportunities for sport participation; however, there is still room to improve and grow.

In High Demand

Despite withstanding laws, such as Section 504 of the Rehabilitation Act, IDEA, and the ADA, that protect individuals with disabilities from discrimination and increased access to public facilities and programs, research has shown that physical activity levels among children and adolescents with disabilities are considerably lower than children and adolescents without disabilities (Jung et al., 2018; McCoy & Morgan, 2020). Because adolescents with disabilities will have to transition from school life to community living, increasing physical activity levels, social and recreational inclusion and involvement, as well as learning skills needed to initiate and maintain active and healthy lifestyles is of utmost importance.

While there are different factors that determine lifelong physical activity participation, our findings suggest that intrinsic motivation to participate in the sport of basketball may have improved alongside their feelings of competence and relatedness. The happiness the participants felt about the program, the desire to participate in more extracurricular activities, the feelings of belongingness and school spirit, and the support from their peers, coaches, teachers, and parents can all be motivating factors that are in line with the SDT and the building of self-esteem and self-efficacy (Deci & Ryan, 1985, 2000, 2008; Shapiro & Martin, 2010). All of which leads to a greater and more positive sense of one's abilities and social relationships that can improve mental and physical health.

Unfortunately, there remains a lack of organized, inclusive, interscholastic athletic programs and as such there is insufficient evidence that these programs promote and provide fitness, health, and social-related outcomes. Although mandated by law, there remain much fewer extracurricular opportunities for individuals with disabilities than there are for individuals without disabilities (Kozub & Samalot-Rivera, 2020). Thus, there remains a high demand for the creation of interscholastic sport opportunities from which all students can benefit.

Perhaps a program like this, modeled after or partnering with Team Prime Time Sports, would be a good starting point for high schools across the country. Adapted physical activity advocates or coaches, special education teachers, proactive administrators, and supportive parents can collaborate to create a program that meets the needs of their students. Additionally, partnering with a local University might help to mobilize experts in the field and generate manpower and other resources.

Schools can and should be progressive by instating more interscholastic options and programming so that all students can have the opportunity to benefit from authentic participation in sport. Skill attainment, socialization, and positive persuasion and encouragement from peers are only the tip of the iceberg when it comes to the benefits of interscholastic sport participation. As a society, we can do better by maximizing opportunities to be physically active and prioritizing the health of all students.

Response

Atypical Students Benefit from Friday Night Prime Time

Greg Taguchi

"Eh Mister, are you coming to our game tonight?" is a question often asked by the student-athletes at our school on game day. However, this time the question was being asked by an atypical student-athlete on a Friday.

This was a student with a disability who was participating in a FNPT adaptive basketball program. As the only adaptive interscholastic program in the state of Hawaii, FNPT provided some of our non-typical students with special needs (NTSNS) an opportunity to participate in interscholastic athletics, specifically the sport of basketball. It allowed them to have the same experiences and benefits of participation in athletics as their typical peers. Participants of FNPT gained a sense of belonging and team spirit as they competed alongside some of their typically developing peers. Members of this team learned valuable life lessons that mirrored those of a typical athlete experience, such as teamwork, commitment, pride, sportsmanship, and competition.

The FNPT participants were proud to represent their school in athletic competition. After all, in order to participate, they needed to try out for the school team. During the tryouts, they expressed feelings of anxiety and hope that they would make the team. I observed them give their best effort during tryouts and subsequent practices as they were excited to have made the team.

In the days to follow, the students were so proud that they had made the team. They would share this information with their peers and adults on campus. Team members were held to team rules and expectations that were similar to expectations of their typical peers who participated on interscholastic school teams to further develop a sense of accountability.

Exuberant expressions from our students were on full display during the pre-game introductions. One student was ready to erupt off the bench as soon as the introductions started and did just that as his name was called; he jumped around and waved to the spectators, full of joy. Team members and coaching staff stood proudly together during the playing of the National Anthem, Hawaii Pono'i, and school alma maters. Then it was game time! The teams were participating in an authentic interscholastic athletic event.

The student athletes had the experience of competing in the limelight and being cheered on by all those who attended the games. The participants were embraced by the entire school community. The bleachers were full of peers, faculty, family, friends, and the school band.

The only big difference: the unusual cheering. There was no negative or antagonistic cheering occurring from anyone in the gym. Often at typical athletic events it is common to hear people cheering negatively and making demeaning statements about the opposing team. Not at these games. People in attendance were cheering for both schools, excited when either team scored.

The peer mentors who participated alongside the atypical student athletes were equally as proud to be on the team and pumped up for game time. The program helped to break down invisible barriers between the peers and students with special needs as both sides were more comfortable talking to one another at school.

Following the completion of the game, several participants and coaches had the opportunity to be interviewed by the media in attendance. What an experience for them to be interviewed. Scores and game statistics were printed in the local newspapers and several television news broadcasts covered the events. In the days to follow, the student athletes were enthusiastic to share about their game experience. Similar to any other team chatter, they discussed who played, and who did what during the game. They understood that in competition there is a winner and a loser. We were fortunate at our school that we were able to go undefeated through the season, making the unofficial claim of reigning league champs.

REFERENCES

Alderman, R. B., & Wood, N. L. (1976). An analysis of incentive motivation in young Canadian athletes. *Canadian Journal of Applied Sport Sciences*, *1*(2), 169–175.

Aspen Institute. (2019). *State of play: Trends and developments in youth sports.* https://www.aspeninstitute.org/wp-content/uploads/2019/10/2019_SOP_National _Final.pdf

Bailey, R. (2005). Evaluating the relationship between physical education, sport and social inclusion. *Educational Review*, *57*(1), 71–90. https://doi.org/10.1080 /0013191042000274196

Berg, P. (2004). Friday night lights. Universal pictures; imagine entertainment. https://www.uphe.com/movies/friday-night-lights

Block, M., Taliaferro, A., Harris, N., & Krause, J. (2010). Using self-efficacy theory to facilitate inclusion in general physical education. *Journal of Physical Education, Recreation & Dance, 81*(3), 43–46. https://doi.org/10.1080/07303084.2010 .10598448

Bredemeier, B. L., & Shields, D. L. (2019). Social justice, character education, and sport: A position statement. *QUEST, 71*(2), 202–214. https://doi.org/10.1080 /00336297.2019.1608270

Connor, D. J. (2014). Social justice in education for students with disabilities. In L. Florian (Ed.), *The SAGE handbook of special education: Two volume set* (Vol. 1, pp. 111–128). SAGE Publications, Ltd. http://dx.doi.org/10.4135/9781446282236.n9

Darnell, S. C., & Millington, R. (2019). Social justice, sport, and sociology: A position statement. *QUEST, 71*(2), 175–187. https://doi.org/10.1080/00336297.2018.1545681

Deci, E. L., & Ryan, R. M. (1985). *Intrinsic motivation and self-determination in human behavior*. New York: Plenum.

Deci, E. L., & Ryan, R. M. (2000). The "what" and "why" of goal pursuits: Human needs and the self-determination of behavior. *Psychological Inquiry, 11*(4), 227–268. https://doi.org/10.1207/S15327965PLI1104_01

Deci, E. L., & Ryan, R. M. (2008). Facilitating optimal motivation and psychological well-being across life's domains. *Canadian Psychology, 49*(1), 14–23. https://doi.org/10.1037/0708-5591.49.1.14

Dixon-Ibarra, A., & Driver, S. (2013). The role of self-efficacy in physical activity participation for persons with disabilities. *Palaestra, 27*(4), 31–36.

Galanter, S. M. (2013). *Dear colleague letter*. Office for Civil Rights. https://www2.ed.gov/about/offices/list/ocr/letters/colleague-201301-504.html

Gould, D., & Petlichkoff, L. (1988). *Participation motivation and attrition in young athletes*. Champaign, IL: Human Kinetics, 1988.

Jung, J., Leung, W., Schram, B. M., & Yun, J. (2018). Meta-analysis of physical activity levels in youth with and without disabilities. *Adapted Physical Activity Quarterly, 35*(4), 381–402. https://doi.org/10.1123/apaq.2017-0123

King, G., Law, M., King, S., Rosenbaum, P., Kertoy, M., & Young, N. (2003). A conceptual model of the factors affecting the recreation and leisure participation of children with disabilities. *Physical & Occupational Therapy in Pediatrics, 23*(1), 63–90. https://doi.org/10.1080/J006v23n01_05

Kodish, S., Kulinna, P. H., Martin, J., Pangrazi, R., & Darst, P. (2006). Determinants of physical activity in an inclusive setting. *Adapted Physical Activity Quarterly, 23*(4), 390–409. https://doi.org/10.1123/apaq.23.4.390

Kosma, M., Gardner, R., Cardinal, B., Bauer, J., & McCubbin, J. (2006). Psychosocial determinants of stages of change and physical activity among adults with physical disabilities. *Adapted Physical Activity Quarterly, 23*(1), 49–64. https://doi.org/10.1123/apaq.23.1.49

Kozub, F. M., & Porretta, D. L. (1996). Including athletes with disabilities: Interscholastic athletic benefits for all. *Journal of Physical Education, Recreation and Dance, 67*(3), 19–24. https://doi.org/10.1080/07303084.1996.10607216

Kozub, F. M., & Samalot-Rivera, A. (2020). Interscholastic participation for athletes with disabilities revisited: Are today's programs doing enough? *Journal of Physical Education, Recreation and Dance, 91*(2), 42–51. https://doi.org/10.1080/07303084.2019.1693453

Lorenzi, D. G. (2014). Creating authentic sport experiences for individuals with disabilities. *Journal of Physical Education, Recreation & Dance, 85*(9), 3–5. https://doi.org/10.1080/07303084.2014.958025

Lumpkin, A., & Stokowski, S. (2011). Interscholastic sports: A character-building privilege. *The Education Digest, 77*(4), 50–54.

McConkey, R., Dowling, S., Hassan, D., & Menke, S. (2013). Promoting social inclusion through Unified Sports for youth with intellectual disabilities: A five-nation study. *Journal of Intellectual Disability Research, 57*(10), 923–935. https://doi.org /10.1111/j.1365-2788.2012.01587.x

McCoy, S. M., & Morgan, K. (2020). Obesity, physical activity, and sedentary behaviors in adolescents with autism spectrum disorder compared with typically developing peers. *Autism, 24*(2), 387–399. https://doi.org/10.1177/13623 61319861579

McLeod, S. A. (2018, May 21). *Maslow's hierarchy of needs*. Retrieved from https:// www.simplypsychology.org/maslow.html

Murata, N. M., & Jansma, P. (1999). *Individualized transition plans*. In P. Jansma (Ed.), *Psychomotor domain training and serious disabilities* (5th ed., pp. 361–370). University Press of America.

National Federation of State High School Associations. (2019). *2018-19 high school athletics participation survey: Conducted by the national federation of state high school associations based on competition at the high school level in the 2018-19 school year* [Data Set]. National Federation of State High School Associations. https://www.nfhs.org/media/1020412/2018-19_participation_survey.pdf

Scarpa, S. (2011). Physical self-concept and self-esteem in adolescents and young adults with and without physical disability: The role of sports participation. *European Journal of Adapted Physical Activity, 4*(1), 38–53. https://doi.org/10.5507/ euj.2011.003

Section 504 of the Rehabilitation Act of 1973, 29 U.S.C. § 794 (1973). https:// www.govinfo.gov/content/pkg/USCODE-2010-title29/pdf/USCODE-2010-title29 -chap16-subchapV-sec794.pdf.

Shaffer, M. L. (2019). Impacting student motivation: Reasons for not eliminating extracurricular activities. *Journal of Physical Education, Recreation and Dance, 90*(7), 8–14. https://doi.org/10.1080/07303084.2019.1637308

Shapiro, D., & Martin, J. J. (2010). Multidimensional physical self-concept of youth athletes with disabilities. *Adapted Physical Activity Quarterly, 27*(4), 294–307. https://doi.org/10.1123/apaq.27.4.294

Shields, N., Synnot, A. J., & Barr, M. (2012). Perceived barriers and facilitators to physical activity for children with disability: A systematic review. *British Journal of Sports Medicine, 46*(14), 989–997. https://doi.org/10.1136/bjsports-2011-090236

Smith, L., Wedgwood, N., Llewellyn, G., & Shuttleworth, R. (2015). Sport in the lives of young people with intellectual disabilities: Negotiating disability, identity, and belonging. *Journal of Sport for Development, 3*(5), 61–70.

Smith, T. (2001). Section 504, the ADA, and public schools: What educators need to know. *Remedial and Special Education, 22*(6), 335–343. https://doi.org/10.1177 /074193250102200603

Solish, A., Perry, A., & Minnes, P. (2010). Participation of children with and without disabilities in social, recreational and leisure activities. *Journal of Applied*

Research in Intellectual Disabilities, 23(3), 226–236. https://doi.org/10.1111/j
.1468-3148.2009.00525.x

Straus, P. (2017). The prime time games: It's inclusion, but who's including who?
Palaestra, 31(4), 32–37.

Sullivan, E., & Glidden, L. M. (2014). Changing attitudes toward disabilities through
unified sports. *Intellectual and Developmental Disabilities, 52*(5), 367–378. https://
doi.org/10.1352/1934-9556-52.5.367

Team Prime Time. (n.d.). *Prime time games.* https://teamprimetime.org/programs/
game-changing-stats/

U.S. Census Bureau. (2019). *School enrollment: American community survey 1-year
estimates subject tables* (Table S1401) [Data set]. U.S. Department of Commerce.
https://data.census.gov/cedsci/table?q=S1401&tid=ACSST1Y2019.S1401

U.S. Department of Education, Office of Special Education and Rehabilitative Services,
& Office of Special Education Programs. (2011). *Creating equal opportunities for
children and youth with disabilities to participate in physical education and extracurricular athletics.* https://www2.ed.gov/policy/speced/guid/idea/equal-pe.pdf

U.S. Department of Health and Human Services. (2019). *National youth sports strategy.* https://health.gov/sites/default/files/2019-10/National_Youth_Sports_Strategy
.pdf

Vaz, S., Falkmer, M., Ciccarelli, M., Passmore, A., Parsons, R., Black, M., Cuomo,
B., Tan, T., & Falkmer, T. (2015). Belongingness in early secondary school: Key
factors that primary and secondary schools need to consider. *PLOS ONE, 10*(9).
https://doi.org/10.1371/journal.pone.0136053

Vierling, K. K., Standage, M., & Treasure, D. C. (2007). Predicting attitudes and
physical activity in an "at-risk" minority youth sample: A test of self-determination
theory. *Psychology of Sport & Exercise, 8*(5), 795–817. https://doi.org/10.1016/j
.psychsport.2006.12.006

Weiss, M. R. (1993). Psychological effects of intense sport participation on children
and youth: Self-esteem and motivation. In B. R. Cahill & A. J. Pearl (Eds.), *Intensive participation in children's sport* (pp. 39–69). Human Kinetics.

Weiss, M. R., & Petlichkoff, L. M. (1989). Children's motivation for participation in
and withdrawal from sport: Identifying the missing links. *Pediatric Exercise Science, 1*(3), 195–211. https://doi.org/10.1123/pes.1.3.195

Weiss, M. R., & Williams, L. (2004). The why of youth sport involvement: A developmental perspective on motivation processes. In M. R. Weiss (Ed.), *Developmental sport and exercise psychology: A lifespan perspective* (pp. 223–268). Fitness
Information Technology.

Wilski, M., Nadolska, A., Dowling, S., McConkey, R., & Hassan, D. (2012). Personal
development of participants in special Olympics unified sports teams. *Human
Movement, 13*(3), 271–279. https://doi.org/10.2478/v10038-012-0032-3

Zhao, W. M., Thirumal, K., Renwick, R., & DuBois, D. (2021). Belonging through
sport participation for young adults with intellectual and developmental disabilities: A scoping review. *Journal of Applied Research in Intellectual Disabilities,
34*(2), 402–420. https://doi.org/10.1111/jar.12817

Chapter 11

Migrant Children with Disabilities in Italian Schools

Educational and Sport-Related Experiences

Paolo Lucattini

The rising number of children with disabilities and with a migratory background attending nursery school, kindergarten, primary, and secondary school describes one of the most evident features of the constant evolution of the Italian intercultural society.[1] With the expression "migratory background," I refer to the following three scenarios: (1) young second-generation foreigners, born in Italy to parents both born abroad (from here onward, abbreviated as G2); (2) young Italian children of mixed couples, born in Italy but with one parent born abroad; and (3) young first-generation foreigners, born abroad to parents born abroad.

A recent report[2] of the Italian Ministry of Education, University and Research (in Italian language, MIUR)—published in November 2020 and concerning the 2018/2019 academic year—highlights that those students with disabilities and migratory background make up 13.4% of the total number of students with disabilities. The presence of students with disabilities in Italian schools increased from about 174,000 young people in 2009 to just under 284,000 in the 2018–2019 academic year (out of a total of 8.6 million young people in Italy). This significant increase in migrants is attributable to different factors such as policies aimed at inclusive processes, the improvement of diagnostic criteria, the increase in the use of certifications, and growing attention of family members and teachers in intercepting the difficulties of children and young people. The increase in the last 10 years has affected all school levels, with a more pronounced growth in secondary school, where the participation of students with disabilities has increased by 64%.

Both at a national (Armani, 2018; Caldin, 2012; Goussot, 2011; Mei, 2011) and international level (Albrecht et al., 2009; El-Lahib, 2016; El-Lahib

255

& Wehbi, 2011; Oliver & Singal, 2017; Pisani & Grech, 2015; Spagnuolo et al., 2019), there are only a few scientific studies that focus their research on the interconnection of these two conditions—disability and migration—of the human experience. Moreover, as well as exacerbating the risk of promoting field-specific action that lacks the fundamental dialogue between special education and intercultural education (Friso & Pileri, 2020), the neglect of this dual belonging does not align with the much-advocated right to integration and inclusion highlighted by the Salamanca Statement (United Nations Educational, Scientific and Cultural Organization [UNESCO], 1994) and by the Convention on the Rights of Persons with Disabilities (CRPD) (United Nations [UN], 2006).

MIGRATORY PHENOMENA AND
THE SCHOOL SYSTEM

On a global level, the serious humanitarian crises present in the African continent and in the Middle East, as well as in the countries of Venezuela and Myanmar, force millions of people to leave their habitual residence due to persecution, conflicts, violations of human rights, and events that seriously compromise public order (Fondazione ISMU, 2021). During 2019, more than 79.5 million people had to flee their homes. Among them, 45.7 million were internally displaced people (civilians forced to flee from wars and persecutions, who remain within their country of origin), 26 million were refugees, and 4.2 million were those who have requested international protection (United Nations High Commissioner for Refugees [UNHCR], 2020). The Mediterranean region and in particular Turkey have been at the center of these enormous, forced movements of human beings in the last decade. However, together with the forced movements of people, we must remember that 40% of permanent migratory phenomena toward countries considered "developed," including the countries of the European Union, are linked to family reunification (Organisation for Economic Co-operation and Development [OECD], 2021).

Given the enormous complexity of the decision to flee one's home, there may be differences in the way that double belonging (i.e., disability and migratory phenomena) influences an individual's choice (Caldin et al., 2010). The health and education systems of the countries where people begin their new phase of life are called upon to do everything possible to create relationships of trust, paying particular attention to the cultural dimension of dialogue. The presence of the linguistic-cultural mediator, in school as well as in other institutional contexts of the territory, becomes decisive in these circumstances (Bini, 2018; Pescamarona, 2019). Through dialogue, educators, teachers, and specialists can assume the perspective of the family and know the motives (or causes) of the migration, alongside present needs, and future expectations. School, particularly for migrant children, and even more so for migrant children with disabilities, represents a constant challenge in their daily life; for instance, these children often face difficulties overcoming language-related problems (Bonifacci, 2010; Branchi, 2015; Folgheraiter & Tressoldi, 2003; Murineddu et al., 2006).

When considering the dual dimension from the perspective of the family, belonging to a culture can influence whether one believes in different care practices (Moro, 2012) and, similarly, it represents one of the contributing elements to making families predisposed (or not) to collaborating with the local school (Goussot, 2010, 2011), and recognizing the role of the teacher as a person with whom to think and plan the educational path of the child.

Meanwhile, Italian schools have attempted to become a recognized place of social and relational reference to welcome the individual person and the individual family, regardless of their stories, experiences, and affiliations. Examples of how schools are trying to move in this direction include: (1) adapting and personalizing the teaching as much as possible and devising and implementing projects that involve the territory and the realities present in it; (2) involving students in official bodies for comparison and evaluation of the school system together with school managers, teachers, family members; planning formal (and non-formal) moments of dialogue with family members; and also, (3) by establishing within the school some institutional positions dedicated to intercultural issues, inclusive policies, technological innovations, and sports practices (de Anna, 2014; Ianes & Cramerotti, 2015; Lombardi, 2020; MIUR, 2014, 2015; Zollo, 2019).

Taking into consideration the dispositions of Italian Law No. 92/2019,[3] and the principles of a European Commission White Paper (European Commission, 2007), in this chapter, we analyze two recent studies (Autorità Garante per l'Infanzia e l'Adolescenza, 2018; Accorinti et al., 2018) that look at school-related and extracurricular experiences and projects of children and young people with disabilities (the first study) and children and young people with a migratory background (the second study), with particular attention on the themes of play and sport activities. By identifying relevant educational and sports opportunities and experiences present in Italian school and extra-curricular contexts, and with the awareness of being faced with a recent and not commonly analyzed phenomenon, I believe these studies could, indirectly, offer significant operational ideas. Based on the results, I suggest that intercultural dialogue, teaching strategies, teacher training, involvement of peers and/or family members, and networking are crucial for recognizing and enhancing the differences present in the classroom, for decreasing conflicts, and for triggering new friendships and meaningful sharing within the activities, experiences, and projects.

A Swift Characterization of Italian Schools

Before proceeding with the analysis of the research, I will further highlight some helpful characteristics of the Italian school context in relation to the dual dimension as well as sport. Primarily, in Italian schools, regardless of ability, cultural, economic, religious, or social affiliations, children have a right to education. The goal was to ensure that everybody is *equally* present in the class environment as well as in extracurricular projects related to leisure and motor activities and sport (such as after-hours volleyball training).

Second, in kindergarten and primary school,[4] physical education—considered an expression of a personal right, an instrument of cognitive learning, and support for harmonious growth, health, well-being, and full development of the individual (MIUR, 2012, 2018a)—as of writing this chapter, appears as having less value compared to other subjects. While in first- and second-level secondary school, teaching physical education is overseen by the national curriculum and done by qualified PE teachers, in kindergarten and primary school, physical education is similarly part of the curriculum, but is taught by teachers with general qualifications not specialized in motor sciences; though, the teachers at the kindergarten and primary level do receive short-term support throughout the school year from local and national projects more directly specialized in sports. The introduction of external specialists offers added richness in terms of experience and education; contrarily, this situation introduces a potential risk of differing quality and quantity of the educational offer (theoretical and practical activities) due to territorial funding dependent on the differing economic resources specific to each Italian region. In other words, these practices may not be delivered *equally*. This can, in turn, lead to different recreational, physical, and sports-related experiences for children who reside in one region over another.

To illustrate the significance of educational projects, I will highlight the project, "Classroom Sports" ("Sport in Classe"), initiated in 2014 to promote the enhancement of Physical Education in Italian primary schools. The project included a new sport governance system for schools whereby the organization of activities was delegated to national entities such as The Italian Ministry of Education, University and Research, the Italian National Olympic Committee, and the Italian Paralympic Committee. These organizations worked collaboratively with regional/provincial coordinating entities and in synergy with the sports centers within schools. The project led to significant changes, such as: (1) the inclusion of two hours per week of mandatory physical education in the curriculum; (2) the introduction of a "sport tutor" that helped the classroom teacher during the planning and creation of activities; (3) more focus on students with disabilities (thanks to the collaboration of Italian Paralympic Committee representatives in the management bodies);

and (4) an initial training of involved teachers as well as ongoing professional development in the classroom.[5]

The architecture of Italian schools required two fundamental elements: (1) the presence of a support teacher (a specialized teacher who supports the curricular teacher) from kindergarten until second-grade secondary school: and (2) the systematic involvement of children, teenagers, and young adults with Special Educational Needs[6] (in Italian language, Bisogni Educativi Speciali [BES]) from kindergarten until university. As pointed out by Lombardi (2020, p. 32), a school model toward which to strive should include the presence and mediation of specialized teachers applied as resources at the service of the class group. The skills of the specialized teacher are used in the collective planning of future activities for all students. Yet, those same skills are crucial when planning diversified activities while respecting individuality. In the Italian school system, the term, "special education needs," stands for particularly different personal characteristics and life situations. Notably, this expression included all conditions of disability, specific learning disorders (SLD), and socioeconomic, linguistic, and cultural disadvantages. Unlike in the United States, "special education needs" is not solely a euphonism for students with disabilities.

These two elements (i.e., a specialized support teacher and active engagement with students with special educational needs) characterize the inclusive model of Italian schools which keeps trying to put the focus of its everyday actions on the people, their peculiarities, and their importance in belonging to as well as enriching the community. This model also presents various critical aspects. For instance, the school administrators, as well as those in the broader community, perceive support teachers as the only professional figures who must devote themselves to inclusive practices and policies. Within the school and the single class, the student with disabilities often becomes entrusted to the support teacher, while the search for inclusiveness should be a collective undertaking (Booth et al., 2006). Furthermore, the number of specialized support teachers does not appear sufficient in relation to requests by schools; in fact, specialized teachers represent only 64% of the total number of support teachers (Istituto Nazionale di Statistica [ISTAT], 2019).

A Brief Historical Path of Italian Schools

Most broadly, the last 100 years of the historical path of Italian schools include phases of exclusion (until 1960), medicalization (1960–1970), insertion (1970–1977), integration (1977–2009) and inclusion (from 2009 to present), which can be witnessed being linked to, and overcoming, one another (Bocci, 2017). To provide further context for our analysis, I will provide a snapshot of the recent and current historical perspective.

In the 2000s, the International Classification of Functioning, Disability and Health (ICF) compiled by the World Health Organization (World Health Organization [WHO], 2001; 2007), together with the UN CRPD, drawn up on December 13, 2006, and ratified by Italy with the Law No. 18/2009, generated changes on a global level with considerable effects at the local level. This in turn has led to a revisiting and consequent new representation of the concept of disability, highlighting on one hand the totality of the person (and not their impairment or illness) and, on the other, the complexity of the interactions between health conditions and the nature of the contexts (environmental, family, work, school, social). This new representation invites individuals as well as governments to no longer: (1) perceive incapacity as an individual problem but as discrimination produced by society; (2) consider people with disabilities as invisible citizens and objects of decisions made by others, but as persons with human rights and as conscious individuals who want to make decisions on their own life; and (3) design policies based on assistance, but instead on inclusion and mainstreaming (Griffo, 2009, p. 13).

SCHOOL AND DOUBLE BELONGING

The presence of children and young people with a migratory background in Italian schools can, from its origins to today, be described through three distinct scenarios. In the initial period, the increase in students with non-Italian citizenship was slow and progressive. In the academic year 1985/86, there were 7,050 such students enrolled in Italian schools while in 1997/98 the number had grown to 70,657. Subsequently, between the academic years 1997/98 and 2011/12, Italy experienced a second phase of acceleration, with significant increases from one year to the next. During this phase, attendance of Italian schools by students with non-Italian citizenship increased tenfold over a period of 14 years, reaching a total of 755,939 students. The most recent and shortest phase, between academic years 2012/13 and 2016/17, signified a stagnation, with a slowdown in the growth trend (Santagati & Colussi, 2019). In 2016/17, there were 826,091 children and young people with non-Italian citizenship in Italian schools, or 9.4% of the total school population (MIUR, 2018b). But if we go beyond the quantitative aspect of the phenomenon and reflect on the fact that people come to Italy from more than 190 countries, we can join those who tend to consider the Italian society a sort of *migratory archipelago* (Fiorucci et al., 2017). The most-represented countries are Romania, Morocco, Albania, China, and Ukraine (Lombardi & Lucattini, 2020).

The empirical studies that refer to the mixture of the dimension of disabilities on the one hand and that of interculturality on the other, are relatively recent (Goussot, 2010). For example, within official documents (Colombo & Ongini, 2014; MIUR, 2013), the expression "foreign students with disabilities" was introduced only from the 2012/13 school year. The adoption of this expression means focusing teachers' attention on dimensions that can (and should) be observed, studied, and addressed as a single characteristic of the human condition (Lombardi & Lucattini, 2020). As argued by national and international scholars, double belonging appears to be a poorly investigated phenomenon because adding difficulties to a situation that is complex requires a particularly in-depth level of analysis (Pennazio & Bochicchi, 2020).

The Right to Play and Sport of Children and Young People with Disabilities

In May 2019, the Guarantor Authority for Childhood and Adolescence (in Italian language, Autorità Garante per l'Infanzia e l'Adolescenza)[7] together with the Institute of the Innocents (in Italian language, Istituto degli Innocenti),[8] published their research "The Right to Play and Sport of Children and Young People with Disabilities." It builds upon a set of actions (e.g., meetings, interviews, focus groups and specific hearings) that started in May 2018 with the aim of showing recent developments of the right to play and sport for children and young people with disabilities, and with the prospect of identifying potential political and cultural strategies. Quantitative data was collected through the administration of questionnaires to local authorities (173 municipalities with a total of 4 million people, or 7% of the Italian population). Qualitative data was collected through document analysis (standards, studies, and international, European, and national reports), focus groups (involving 238 people, of whom 207 were minors across north, center and south of Italy), and expert interviews (Ministry of Education, University and Research, the Italian Society of Pediatrics, the Italian Society of Child and Adolescent Neuropsychiatry, and the Italian Union for the Fight Against Muscular Dystrophy).

Common themes stressed across all the different respondent groups were: (1) the lack of reference regulations and dedicated political and social planning when it came to nurturing the importance of play and sport in people's lives (including people with disabilities); and (2) the need to develop adequate spaces for inclusive practices and prioritize specific training courses on the subject. While in terms of adopting principles and translating them into laws, Italy can be considered a *pilot country* on an international level; the research has highlighted how much still needs to be achieved in terms of concrete implementation. As evidence of this, and in reference to the right to health, the quality of services, social inclusion, opportunities for play and sport, the social inequalities involving children and young people are particularly evident. When considering only the presence of physical-structural barriers, only 32% of Italian schools are accessible. If sensory-perceptive barriers and the related sensory facilitators (acoustic signals, relief maps, tactile paths, visual signals, etc.) are included, the accessibility of Italian schools drops to 18% (ISTAT, 2019). Moreover, Italy has little research, periodic studies and, consequently, updated data, on children and young people with disabilities (United Nations Children's Fund [UNICEF], 2013) and their families. Even scarcer is information, both national and local, on how children with disabilities manage their free time. Regarding sport, the research indicates baskin as an inclusive sporting activity of particular interest. Baskin is a sport that was born in Italy (Cremona) in the early 2000s thanks to family members and physical education teachers. Compared to Olympic or Paralympic basketball, baskin expresses values of full accessibility and total participation through the introduction of new rules that allow athletes, people with and without disabilities, to play together within the same team, same sports facility, and for the same championship (Bodini et al., 2007; Magnanini, 2009; Moliterni & Mastrangelo, 2016; Tatulli, 2014).

The available research highlights numerous differences between the north and south of the country in terms of families' consideration and institutional attention given to the importance of play and sport, and in terms of effective accessibility of spaces and services. In the north of Italy, families have a greater awareness of the benefits of play and sport, and the services and institutions pay more attention to the needs of the community. Also, the accessibility of available opportunities is better. Generally, parents in the south tend to see play and sport as rehabilitative elements and not as actions of pleasure or fun that are fundamental for the development of children and young people with disabilities (Bianquin, 2017). Further differences exist in accessing certain recreational or sports practices due to the characteristics of the disabilities (e.g., physical, intellectual, sensory disabilities, etc.). Specifically, people with physical disabilities have greater opportunities to access sports than people with intellectual disabilities or those on the autism spectrum (de Anna et al., 2018). Unfortunately, the culture of play as a constitutive element of educational and social processes for the health and well-being of children and young people with disabilities is not widespread, particularly in the south (Bulgarelli & Stancheva-Popkstadinova, 2017).

At the same time, there is a lack of training courses, research, studies, and, more generally, pedagogical attention on how to support the possibility of play in connection to different situations of disability (for example, intellectual developmental disorder, communication disorders, autism spectrum disorder). At a structural level, inclusive playgrounds are still not widespread, especially in the south, and the existing playgrounds are mainly centered on accessibility for people with physical or sensory disabilities. Ultimately, though "inclusion" is a hallmark of how Italian school is viewed, there is a lack of adequate policies or dedicated resources to trigger the necessary inclusive projects that involve schools, private sector organizations, and sports associations in these territories. In terms of communication and awareness, there is a lack of mapping of spaces, experiences, play activities and sports dedicated to people with disabilities, just as correct information on accessible and usable resources is limited.

Finally, with the aim of stimulating the adoption of measures and provisions at a regulatory and cultural level, the available research promotes a series of recommendations addressed to the government, the parliament, the regions, local authorities, social, health and educational services, sports agencies, and certain categories of professionals. The recommendations can be divided into three areas of intervention:

1. Promote actions raising awareness of the culture of play and sport for children and young people with disabilities, regardless of the characteristics of the disability, reference contexts, and age. Examples include using (a) World Sports Day (April 6) and Play Day (May 28) to organize initiatives highlighting the importance of sport and play for the well-being of children and young people with disabilities; (b) bringing families, teachers, and specialists closer to these issues through the production and distribution of informational materials; and (c) welcoming these themes within training courses for teachers, specialists working at playrooms and libraries, entertainers, and specialists in the sports sector. More generally, this involves the promotion of training and other activities raising awareness of the right to play for those who, directly or indirectly, work with and for people in the developmental age (UN, 2013).

2. Establish stable methods for collecting information and data on children and young people with disabilities, with particular attention to the issues of play and sport, aiming to have a dynamic, useful, and usable mapping for specialists and family members. This could include establishing a database of disabilities at national level, focusing on the infant–17 age group. Such database could function via monitoring systems spanning between different administrative levels (national, regional, and municipal) and services present in the territories, to obtain a detailed and constant description of the national and local situation over time. Additionally, this promotes the development of systems and methods for ludic contexts, accessible sports associations, and the simultaneous development of apps dedicated to spreading such information among the population.

3. Promote the creation and development of ludic and sportive contexts that are fully accessible and inclusive, also through collaborative projects supported by economic incentives and regulatory requirements. Monitor the quality of inclusiveness (UNESCO, 2015) with direct involvement of children and young people, together with their families. For example, regulations could be introduced that make the right to play and sport during the developmental age a tangible reality. These regulations, in addition to guaranteeing the usability of ludic and sportive contexts, should take into consideration the criteria of inclusiveness, accessibility, equality, territoriality, and characteristics of different disabilities. Further examples include: (a) the introduction of communications and signs facilitating the accessibility and usability of ludic and sportive contexts; (b) the allocation of specific structural funds for the creation of innovative projects and inclusive services at the local level, favoring the re-appropriation and use of urban public spaces; (c) the inclusion of programs in the political agenda that encourage the promotion and national diffusion of amateur sports associations committed to the full involvement of children with disabilities; (d) the activation of working groups dedicated to promoting sports opportunities for people with intellectual disabilities (Special Olympics model) within schools, sports associations, and third sector organizations; and (e) encouraging the adoption of sports practices, such as baskin, to involve children and young people with and without disabilities in a context of shared rules.

It Does Not Matter if We Are Foreigners; We Must All Play Together

The second research paper that focused on in this contribution is related to the *Brothers of Sport* survey, carried out by the Institute for Research on Population and Social Policies (in Italian language, IRPPS) together with the National Research Council (in Italian language, CNR), as part of the program agreement between the Italian Ministry of Labor and Social Policies and Italian National Olympic Committee for the promotion of integration policies through sport.[9] Representing a valuable contribution to the understanding of the role of sport in the integration paths of young generations, the research was carried out at the beginning of the 2016/17[10] school year through over 1,287 interviews with female (48%) and male (52%) students of Italian first-level secondary schools (ages 11–14), and with some of their teachers (34). As I will show from the data collected, this research does not fulfill the central desire of this contribution as it does not analyze the double belonging of young people. Despite this, I believe it is strategic to focus on this research because it allows us to collect the perspectives of those directly involved, young people, on issues strictly related to at least two of the main themes of our contribution: sport and migratory background.

Overall, the schools involved in the survey had at least 15% of young people with a migratory background; those included in interviews were evenly dispersed about the referenced northeast, northwest, and center and south of the country (29%, 36%, 35%, respectively). As for the sample within the interviews, 41% were young people with a migratory background; more specifically, 23% of the total sample were considered young G2, 5% were young Italian children of mixed couples; and 13% were young first-generation foreigners. Of those teachers that were included, at the time of the survey, 41% were engaged in teaching physical education and predominantly identified as female (65%). The questions used covered interpersonal relationships, opinions and attitudes, phenomena of exclusion, stereotypes, sports practices, and the perception of sport. Through these questions, the dimensions considered within the research highlight: (1) the characteristics of the friendship network; (2) the recognition of the values of sport; (3) opinions on ethnic and gender diversity in sport; and (4) cheering.

Regarding the participation of young people in sports, 79% practiced at least one sport outside school hours at the time of the survey. More specifically, that is 86% of young Italians, 79% of children of mixed couples, 70% of G2s, and 63% of young first-generation foreigners. The most popular activities are football (soccer), volleyball, and basketball, followed by swimming. The least popular are martial arts, dance, and artistic gymnastics. The geographical origin and the socioeconomic condition of families are particularly decisive for the choices of young people. Given that 50% of the sample of young people belong to families of medium status,[11] 32% to a low status, and 18% to a high status, sports activities are practiced by almost all (92%) young people belonging to a high status while over a half (65%) of young people belonging to a low-status practice sport. Among young people with migratory backgrounds, the highest percentages of those participating in sport are of Asian origin (69%), followed by those who come from Central Africa (67%) and finally, those from Central and South America (62%). The lowest percentages are found among young people from Eastern Europe (56%) and North Africa (58%). Football (soccer) appears to be the activity favored by young people with a low financial status, while martial arts and tennis by young people with a high status. Swimming appears to be more common among those who belong to families with a medium status.

Among the reasons that guide young people to practice sports, pleasure and entertainment prevail in 83% of cases, followed by the possibility of socializing (51%), being in good health (44%), and paying attention to physical well-being (38%). Contrarily, the reasons for not practicing sports include the desire to devote oneself to something else (in 35% of cases), lack of time on the part of family members to accompany the children (15%), and the economic burden of doing sport (12%).

The migratory background and the socioeconomic condition of families furthermore influence the lack of any sporting activity among young people. For example, 38% of young first-generation foreigners, 34% of G2s, and 13% of Italians have never practiced sports. The study shows 28% of young people belonging to families with low status have never practiced sports, while this percentage drops to 10% in high status situations. More importantly, however, these data provide evidence to suggest that playing sports increases the chances of meeting friends (regardless of gender) compared to those who do not. This relationship is particularly evident among young people with a migrant background engaged in some sport outside school hours, who declare that they have a circle of friends that is less segregated and more open to their Italian peers, compared to those who do not practice sports. However, participating in sports activities is also characterized by episodes and moments of exclusion. From the responses of young people, it emerges that this is a frequent phenomenon; in fact, more than half (54%) of them have suffered a refusal or in some way been made fun of at least once compared to only 1 in 10 young people from non-migratory backgrounds. Thankfully, following the occurrence of an episode of exclusion, in most cases (60%), the situation is resolved directly by the young people involved. In one-third of the cases (30%), those directly affected decide to give up. Only rarely (7% of cases) do adults intervene. This happens particularly if younger children are also present. When creating teams for a match, for example, with victory in mind we tend to choose the best, the strongest, the biggest, the males and, consequently, individuals are often excluded based on presumed abilities that may be related to age or gender. In the cases captured in these data, the reasons attributable to differences in nationality were not particularly relevant; thus suggesting that the context of sport may be a dimension in which the differences of origin are less incisive, and the languages less marked by cultural belonging.

The survey further focuses on the values and representations of sport, discrimination in sports, the spreading of prejudices, and stereotypes relating to migratory phenomena. In answering the questions, "But what purpose does sport serve? What opportunities arise by doing sport?," as partially observed above, young people underlined that sport is synonymous with having fun with friends, sharing, and team play ranging from successes to defeats. For some of them, without distinction between young Italians and youth with migratory background, sport is a place where everyone can feel equal and at ease. Young people with foreign origins emphasize the importance of the same rules for everyone and the incentive to resolve disputes without the use of violence. Thanks to sport, one learns: (1) how to lose (as 66% of the interviewees expressed); (2) how to overcome envy toward those who are stronger (44%); (3) how to value sacrifice (43%); (4) how to give one's all to win (41%); and (5) how to achieve desired goals.

Yet, sport can also become a scenario of intolerance and racism, despite possessing an extraordinary potential for inclusion and for overcoming inequalities. The young people interviewed expressed a consistent disagreement (77%) with the introduction of rules that limit the presence of non-Italian players in football, basketball, women's volleyball, and rugby teams involved in national championships. Similarly, young people strongly disagreed (75%) with the racist stereotype that recognizes the physical superiority of Black athletes over white athletes (though, a quarter of young people agreed with this statement). Finally, the young people were also interviewed about certain widespread forms of racism that manifest themselves above all in football, through banners and chants against non-Italian players of the opposing team. Most young people (80%) clearly reject the possibility of tolerating these forms of chants or considering them a way of cheering. At the same time, the remaining amount of young people who do define themselves as very (7%) or quite tolerant (13%) toward such modalities (those who practice at least one sport are less tolerant than those who do not practice any) is sobering.

As previously mentioned, the research also involved a group of teachers (34 in total, of whom 22 were women), mostly graduates in motor sciences and with a long professional experience (on average 25 years). The majority (80%) of teachers expressed that family members of young people with migratory background are scarcely present in school activities and that they often encounter socioeconomic problems. Difficulties in the linguistic competencies of young people with migratory background negatively affect communication with teachers and peers (Beneduce, 2013; Goussot, 2015; Miconi & Moscardino, 2017). The teachers highlighted that participation in sports projects at local and regional level tends to be a particularly positive and useful experience.[12] These experiences also facilitate the inclusion of students with relational and social difficulties and enhance motor skills acquired during ordinary school activities. The strong presence of adolescents with a migratory background in lower secondary schools is a positive factor because it allows young people to grow up with fewer prejudices and to know, understand, and approach different cultures. Despite this, the teachers confirmed the occurrence of episodes of discrimination mainly due to physical appearance, gender, situations of disability, and also due to language and religious affiliation (Mauro, 2016; Refrigeri, 2011).

For what concerns the operational proposals aimed at promoting integration through sport, the teachers pointed out the possibility, on the part of the school, to provide free sports services in the afternoon and evening for young people with greater economic problems and difficulty with socialization. Another particularly useful action is the financing of sports equipment needed at an individual level (e.g., overalls, shoes, etc.). Finally, the most-practiced sports in the countries of origin of young people with migratory background should become objects of greater attention. From a structural and organizational point of view, the teachers' responses underline the importance of diversified sports opportunities, the use of sports testimonials to convey the educational aspects of sport to young people, and the organization of tournaments that promote the participation of mixed teams, made up of young Italians and young people with a migratory background (Damiani et al., 2018; Gramegna, 2020; Madonna & Merolla, 2017; Mangone, 2016).

With the conviction that physical education must take on greater weight within the school system and across the different classes/teachings, when asked what should be done (at a social and, above all, political and institutional level) to strengthen the role of sport in the process of social integration, the teachers called for: (1) decreasing the emphasis on competitive practices; (2) improving the structures and equipment available for sports in schools; (3) taking care of young people, especially of those with migratory background and with poor economic capacity, promoting access to extracurricular sport; (4) introducing the role of the physical education teacher starting from kindergartens and primary schools; and (5) increasing the number of hours for sports activity per week in all school levels (Carraro, 2008; Ceciliani, 2018; de Anna, 2007; Gori & Tanga, 1996; Pesce et al., 2015).

CONCLUSION

Despite the lack of specific research on educational and sport-related experiences involving children and young people with disabilities and migratory backgrounds, the recommendations and data emerging from the documents analyzed allow for the development of considerations and hypotheses. Both at school level and the extracurricular level, the term *disability* is mainly associated with the inclusive dimension of practices and policies while *migratory background* is more closely connected to integration. On one hand, the importance of play and sport in the life of each student represents a transversally recognized element of value. On the other hand, the shortcomings in terms of regulations, political and social planning, contexts, and training courses are evident. Italian schools have only recently begun to reflect in an intercultural perspective, while the training opportunities for children and young people with disabilities are widely established.

The growing presence of children and young people with disabilities and migratory background documented at the school level, currently represents a common phenomenon also in extracurricular activities directed at promoting recreational and sporting activities. In addition to the activities widely promoted on the national level by baskin and the (international) Special Olympics movement (example activities encountered in one of the two studies),[13] we also want to mention the emerging experiences of social football, visionary football, and inclusive rugby.[14] In different Italian regions, these initiatives are fueling innovative practical, educational, and cultural activities, adapting regulations, taking care of contexts, enhancing the dialogue, and putting the person at the center with the conviction that there is no "lowercase and uppercase life" (Gardou, 2016).

Response

The Story of "A"

Maria Elena Mastrangelo

In 2019, the "Baskin team" lined up among its basketball players an athlete of Moroccan nationality with a mild intellectual disability, significant socio-cultural disadvantage, and previous experiences of discrimination and racism. Thanks to this inclusive sport he was finally able to feel welcomed, to experience the sense of belonging to a group, and to have successful experiences that have contributed considerably to fortifying his self-esteem and his sense of self-efficacy.

"A," a teenager of Moroccan origin, tall and slender, agile and elegant in his movements, had been involved in Baskin training by the coach of the "Baskin team," at the request of a close friend of his, a director of an association promoting the social inclusion of immigrants and political refugees.

"A" did not speak Italian very well, but he could understand exactly what he was being told.

The boy was far from his family, he was not even sure if his parents were still alive, and he had been entrusted by the social services to a shelter for minors. His background was marked by experiences of exclusion and moments in which he felt marginalized, mocked, teased, and not considered by anyone.

"A" had no friends and had difficulty actively seeking contact with peers, either because of language-related difficulties or because he felt inadequate.

The Baskin group was heterogeneous—in addition to me, the coach, and an educator, there were two boys with Down syndrome, three boys with mild intellectual disabilities, a boy with quadriparesis, one non-disabled boy older than him, and three non-disabled girls of his age.

At first, "A" avoided the glances of his teammates and was not interested in having a conversation with them, he displayed behaviors of avoidance. The coach, using group strategies and games, created conditions that allowed the boy to gradually interact with his teammates, although "A" seemed to be doing it half-heartedly, performing the group exercises out of a sense of duty and respect for the coach.

When the coach gave the basketball players the opportunity to shoot freely for the basket, "A's" attitude began to change, he enjoyed himself, tried to shoot for the basket from different angles and managed to hit the basket.

In subsequent training "A" was able to make the basket even from a distance; his eyes no longer had that veil of melancholy that usually characterized his gaze, they were full of life.

The coach never missed an opportunity to highlight "A's" talent; the boy became increasingly aware of his abilities and began to relate to his teammates; above all he was flattered by the compliments he received from his teammates.

For the first time, he felt looked upon with admiration, someone was appreciating his abilities. He was not used to it, but he liked it; he trained with ever greater commitment and with each day became better and more capable than the day before.

During the training matches he had become a point of reference for his team, he heard his name being called, his teammates were looking for him, his presence on the pitch was important for the team. "A" smiled, he was proud of himself, he felt himself capable and important to someone. Every day, "A" seemed more confident and more satisfied.

His posture had also changed, he walked with his shoulders straight and his head held high, he looked his teammates in the eyes. It was nice to see him smile. Unfortunately, after a few months "A" was transferred to another city, he was far away and could no longer participate in trainings.

I don't have any news from him, but I like to imagine that wherever he is, he is jumping, dribbling, and shooting with the enthusiasm, determination, and *joie de vivre* he learned on the Baskin pitch.

NOTES

1. Nursery school is a non-mandatory educational environment for children until the age of 3. Kindergartens represent the first level of the Italian educational system; they take care of children aged 3–5. Primary schools take care of the educational and training paths of children aged 6–10; secondary schools, of children aged 11–19. More specifically, first-level secondary school lasts three years, starting at the age of 11 and ending at the age of 14, whereas second-level secondary school includes two mandatory years (until the age of 16) and in most cases, the next three years (until the age of 19) are not mandatory.

2. The report can be found in the following link:

https://miur.gov.it/documents/20182/0/I+principali+dati+disabilit%C3%A0_a.s.2018_2019.pdf/038e3480-952d-7d15-4879-dcf9b86e3fce?version=1.0&t=1609762580854

3. The law establishes the transversal teaching of civic education in the whole school community. This specific teaching is fundamental not only to promote the knowledge regarding the Italian Constitution and the institutions of the European Union, but it is also fundamental to shape responsible and active citizens, to promote a full and conscious contribution to the "civic life," a social and cultural contribution in respect of the rules, the rights and duties. This teaching also facilitates the sharing

of principles of legality, an active as well as a digital citizenship, environmental sustainability, and the right to health and well-being. The law can be found in the following link: https://www.gazzettaufficiale.it/eli/id/2019/08/21/19G00105/sg

4. This section refers to the Parliamentary Bill 992 "Delega al Governo in materia di insegnamento curricolare dell'educazione motoria nella scuola," currently under examination in respective commissions. Further explanations are available at http://www.senato.it/leg/18/BGT/Schede/FascicoloSchedeDDL/ebook/51085.pdf

5. Further explanations can be found at https://www.camera.it/temiap/documentazione/temi/pdf/1105624.pdf?_1629205421201

6. Further explanations are contained in the following link https://www.miur.gov.it/bisogni-educativi-speciali

7. The authority that promotes the implementation of the *New York Convention* and other international instruments concerning the promotion and protection of the rights of children and adolescents, the full application of the European and national legislation in force on the promotion of the protection of childhood and adolescence, as well as the right of minors to be welcomed and educated primarily in their own family and, if necessary, in another supportive familiar environment. To learn more, consult the link https://www.garanteinfanzia.org/

8. The institute promotes the active rights of childhood and adolescence as enshrined in the Convention on the Rights of the Child, adopted in New York on November 20, 1989, and enforced in Italy with the law of May 27, 1991, no. 176. To learn more, consult the link https://www.istitutodeglinnocenti.it/

9. As documented within the respective institutional portal https://www.lavoro.gov.it/temi-e-priorita/immigrazione/focus-on/politiche-di-integrazione-sociale/Documents/8C-Accordo-di-programma-sport-integrazione-Coni.pdf in 2014, the Ministry of Labor and Social Policies signed a program agreement with the Italian National Olympic Committee for the implementation of activities aimed at promoting the integration of people with migratory background through sport, and countering forms of discrimination and intolerance. The activities carried out (until the 2018/2019 academic year) involved educational institutions, universities, sports clubs, and sports federations.

Educational institutions were involved through an educational-information campaign called "Champions of Fair Play." As part of the campaign, primary school classes participated in a project called "Classroom Sports," which involved reflection on the topic of integration and created drawings and texts on the subject with the aim of promoting the principles of fair play. Older primary school students (grades 4–5) additionally elaborated on fair play and its values, such as respect for the rules, for others and for oneself, and the appreciation of diversity, uniqueness, equality, loyalty, and integration.

Universities were involved through the creation of a pilot didactic module "Sport and Integration," launched experimentally within the motor sciences undergraduate degree. After the first experience gained in 2018 with the Tor Vergata University of Rome, the module was adopted by four other universities across the country (University of Naples "Parthenope," University of Verona, University of Turin, and University of Parma) in an attempt to offer an unprecedented training opportunity to future graduates in motor sciences, with the aim of stimulating reflection on educational processes related to the world of sports and enhancing professionalism in this specific area.

Sports clubs and federations were involved through the "Brothers of Sport" campaign and an open call for the enhancement of specialists involved in the social sector. The campaign was aimed at sports associations of the national territory to spread to technicians, managers, operators, athletes and family members a greater awareness of the role played by sport as a tool for the inclusion of multicultural groups. The call was aimed at the enhancement of technicians strongly committed to social issues and attentive to the role of sport as a tool for inclusion and integration.

Sports clubs and federations were also involved through free participation in the courses for "Operators in Sport" aimed at young people with a migratory background, and through the creation of a program to promote sportive practices aimed at 1,000 children and young people, aged 5–17, with a migratory background and with economically disadvantaged family situations.

10. We must point out that the research was carried out in a period of growing interest in the topic of "Sport and Integration," testified both by the presence of publications (Conti & Porro, 2016; Croci, 2016; Mangone, 2016) and by the implementation of initiatives and projects (for example, the project *Fondo Asilo Migrazione e Integrazione 2014–2020*, available at https://fami.dlci.interno.it/fami/ and the initiative *Dinamiche sociolinguistiche e interculturali nei contesti sportivi 2018*, available at https://dipartimento.unistrasi.it/163/435/Dinamiche_sociolinguistiche_e_interculturali_nei_contesti_sportivi,_15_-_16_novembre_2018.htm).

11. Based on the rates of income tax for physical persons (IRPEF), an annual income can be considered low until 15,000 euros, medium–low between 15,000 and 28,000 euros, average between 28,000 and 50,000 euros, and high over 50,000 euros (ISTAT, 2021).

12. A story particularly present not only in the Italian media but also on a global level (SpecialOlympics.org, International and Cultural Association, Peace and Sport, ESPN.com, sportanddev.org) is that of Gerald Mballe, a young man who in 2015, after a long and complex journey, managed to arrive from Cameroon to Italy, where he now lives and works.

He is a partner athlete (athlete without intellectual disability) within the Special Olympics Pro Settimo Eureka Team (Piedmont Region). Gerard is a positive example of the global efforts of the Special Olympics movement to involve young refugees or young people with a migrant background in sport, regardless of skill levels.

The example of Gerard testifies how sport can contribute to giving a sense of purpose to young people.

In becoming athletes within the Unified Sports program, young people can also experience new sense of belonging in their communities.

13. Regarding baskin, an example particularly engaged with children with disabilities and migratory background is the AS.SO.RI Onlus https://www.assori.it/ while with regard to Special Olympics, one example is the All Stars Arezzo Onlus https://allstarsarezzo.it/

14. More information about Social Football, Visionary Football, and Inclusive Rugby is available at the following links http://www.centroaccoglienzaempoli.it/, https://quartotempofirenze.it/, https://chivassorugby.it/

REFERENCES

Accorinti, M., Caruso, M. G., Cerbara, L., Menniti, A., Misiti, M., & Tintori, A. (2018). *Non conta se siamo stranieri, dobbiamo giocare tutti insieme.* Roma: Consiglio Nazionale delle Ricerche—Istituto di Ricerche sulla Popolazione e le Politiche Sociali. (IRPPS Working papers n. 106/2018).

Albrecht, G. L., Devlieger, P. J., & Van Hove, G. (2009). Living on the margin: Disabled Iranians in Belgian society. *Disability & Society, 24*(3), 259–271.

Armani, S. (2018). *Benessere e intercultura. Nuove prospettive per favorire l'inclusione dei malati disabili e migranti.* FrancoAngeli.

Autorità Garante per l'Infanzia e l'Adolescenza. (2018). *Il diritto al gioco e allo sport dei bambini e dei ragazzi con disabilità. Documento di studio e di proposta.* Tipografia Eurosia. Available at https://www.garanteinfanzia.org/sites/default/files/diritto-al-gioco-sport-bambini-ragazzi-disabilita.pdf

Beneduce, R. (2013). Illusioni e violenza della diagnosi psichiatrica. *Aut Aut, 357,* 181–205.

Bianquin, N. (2017). LUDI—Play for Children with Disabilities: l'interdisciplinarietà a supporto di un nuovo modello di intervento per il gioco del bambino con disabilità. *Italian Journal of Special Education for Inclusion, 5*(1), 15–31.

Bini, E. (2018). Accogliere famiglie con bambini disabili in contesti migratori. Scenari inclusivi a Bologna. *REMHU Revista Interdisciplinar da Mobilidade Humana, 26*(52), 209–222.

Bocci, F. (2017). Dall'integrazione all'inclusione: lo sguardo si sposta sul contesto. In A. Morganti & F. Bocci (A cura di), *Didattica inclusiva nella scuola primaria. Educazione socioemotiva e Apprendimento cooperativo per costruire competenze inclusive attraverso i "compiti di realtà"* (pp. 12–23). Giunti Edu.

Bodini, A., Capellini, F., & Maggio, G. (2007). Il Baskin: fondamenti sportivi, sociali e culturali. *L'Integrazione Scolastica e Sociale, 6*(1), 76–81.

Bonifacci, P. (2010). Lo sviluppo cognitivo bilingue. In S. Contento (A cura di), *Crescere nel bilinguismo. Aspetti cognitivi, linguistici ed emotivi* (pp. 29–40). Carocci.

Booth, T., Ainscow, M., & Kingston, D. (2006). *Index for inclusion: Developing play, learning and participation in early years and childcare.* Centre for Studies on Inclusive Education. Available at https://www.eenet.org.uk/resources/docs/Index%20EY%20English.pdf

Branchi, C. (2015). Proiezioni. Appunti sui test psicodiagnostici e il loro uso in sede di valutazione del minore straniero e della sua famiglia. *AM. Rivista della Società italiana di antropologia medica, 39–40,* 201–216.

Bulgarelli, D., & Stancheva-Popkstadinova, V. (2017). Play in children with intellectual disabilities. In S. Besio, D. Bulgarelli, & V. Stancheva-Popkostadinova (Eds.), *Play development in children with disabilities.* Berlin: De Gruyter.

Caldin, R. (A cura di). (2012). *Alunni con disabilità, figli di migranti. Approcci culturali, questioni educative, prospettive inclusive.* Liguori Editore.

Caldin, R., Argiropoulos, D., & Dainese, R. (2010). Genitori migranti e figli con disabilità. Le rappresentazioni dei professionisti e le percezioni delle famiglie. *Ricerche di Pedagogia e Didattica, 5*(1), 1–38.

Carraro, A. (2008). *Educare al movimento.* Lecce: Pensa Multimedia.

Ceciliani, A. (2018). Didattica integrata quali-quantitativa, in educazione motoria-sportiva, e benessere in età evolutiva. *Formazione & Insegnamento, 16*(1), 183–193.

Colombo, M., & Ongini, V. (A cura di). (2014). *Alunni con cittadinanza non italiana. L'eterogeneità dei percorsi scolastici. Rapporto nazionale A.s. 2012/2013.* Fondazione ISMU. Available at https://www.istruzione.it/allegati/2014/Miur_2012_2013.pdf

Conti, F., & Porro, N. (A cura di). (2016). Sport and migrations in the global (dis)order. *International Journal of Migration Studies, 203,* Centro Studi Emigrazione Roma.

Croci, P. (2016, 22–24 settembre). *Sport, immigrazione ed integrazione delle seconde generazioni.* IX Càonferenza ESPAnet Italia, modelli di welfare e modelli di capitalismo, le sfide per lo sviluppo scoio-economico in Italia e in Europa, Macerata, Italy.

Damiani, P., Colzani, E., & Gomez Paloma, F. (2018). Rugby Mixed Ability e Inclusione. Un'analisi di caso tra Sport, Pedagogia e Neuroscienze. *Formazione & Insegnamento, 16*(1), 195–203.

de Anna, L. (2007). Le attività motorie e sportive nella scuola dell'infanzia e primaria in una prospettiva inclusiva. *L'integrazione scolastica e sociale, 6*(4), 307–314.

de Anna, L. (2014). *Pedagogia speciale. Integrazione e inclusione.* Carocci.

de Anna, L., Rossi, C., & Mazzer, M. (2018). *Inclusione, narrazione e disturbi dello spettro autistico. Ricerche e prospettive della pedagogia speciale.* Cafagna.

El-Lahib, Y. (2016). Theoretical dimensions for interrogating the intersection of disability, immigration and social work. *International Social Work, 60*(3), 640–653.

El-Lahib, Y., & Wehbi, S. (2011). Immigration and disability: Ableismin the policies of the Canadian state. *International Social Work, 55*(1), 95–108.

European Commission. (2007). White Paper. White Paper on Sport. Available at https://eur-lex.europa.eu/legal-content/EN/TXT/?uri=CELEX%3A52007DC0391

Fiorucci, M., Pinto Minerva, F., & Portera, A. (A cura di). (2017). *Gli alfabeti dell'intercultura.* Edizioni ETS.

Folgheraiter, K., & Tressoldi, P. E. (2003). Apprendimento scolastico degli alunni stranieri: Quali fattori lo favoriscono? *Psicologia dell'Educazione e della Formazione, 3,* 365–387.

Fondazione ISMU. (2021). *Ventiseiesimo Rapporto sulle migrazioni 2020.* FrancoAngeli.

Friso, V., & Pileri, A. (2020). Migrant Children with disabilities in primary school. Research perspectives. *Educazione Interculturale. Teorie, ricerche, pratiche, 18*(2), 70–86.

Gardou, C. (2016). *Nessuna vita è minuscola. Per una società inclusiva.* Mondadori Università.

Gori, M., & Tanga, M. (1996). *Il corpo e l'azione motoria. Note per la costruzione di una nuova prassiologia.* Torgiano (PG): Calzetti & Mariucci.

Goussot, A. (2010). Bambini stranieri con bisogni speciali: rappresentazione della disabilità dei figli da parte delle famiglie migranti e degli insegnanti. Una ricerca sperimentale a Cesena: bambini figli di migranti con bisogni speciali. *Ricerche di Pedagogia e Didattica - Infanzie e Famiglie, 5*(1), 1–26.

Goussot, A. (2011). Disabilità, rappresentazioni e mondi culturali. *Educazione Interculturale. Culture, esperienze, progetti, 9*(1), 11–26.

Goussot, A. (2015). I rischi di medicalizzazione nella scuola. Paradigma clinico-terapeutico o pedagogico? *Educazione democratica, 9,* 15–47.

Gramegna, B. (2020). Con i piedi, con la testa, con il cuore - il gioco del calcio per imparare. *Bollettino Itals, 18*(82), 78–88.

Griffo, G. E. A. (2009). La Convenzione delle Nazioni Unite sui diritti delle persone con disabilità e l'ICF. In G. Borgnolo, R. de Camillis, C. Francescutti, L. Frattura, R. Troiano, G. Bassi, & E. Tubaro (A cura di), *ICF e Convenzione ONU sui diritti delle persone con disabilità. Nuove prospettive per l'inclusione* (p. 13). Erickson.

Ianes, D., & Cramerotti, S. (A cura di). (2015). *Compresenza didattica inclusiva. Indicazioni metodologiche e modelli operativi di co-teaching.* Erickson.

ISTAT. (2019). *L'inclusione scolastica: accessibilità, qualità dell'offerta e caratteristiche degli alunni con sostegno.* Available at https://www.istat.it/it/files/2019/01/Alunni-con-sostegno-as-2017_18.pdf

ISTAT. (2021). *Annuario statistico italiano 2021.* Available at https://www.istat.it/it/archivio/264305

Lombardi, G. (2020). *Il Team nei processi d'inclusione Come costruire interdipendenze positive nel contesto educativo. Conversando con gli "addetti ai lavori".* Pensa Multimedia Editore.

Lombardi, G., & Lucattini, P. (2020). Gli allievi con disabilità di cittadinanza non italiana: oltre i confini e le barriere. In L. Chiappetta Cajola (A cura di), *Come fare Sostegno a scuola. Teoria e pratica nella didattica inclusiva* (pp. 373–380). Anicia.

Madonna, G., & Merolla, M. (2017). I progetti del Settore Giovanile e Scolastico della F.I.G.C. per l'Integrazione Sociale. *Giornale Italiano di Educazione alla Salute, Sport e Didattica Inclusiva, 1*(4), 81–85.

Magnanini, A. (2009). Lo Sport . . . per tutti. Una risorsa per l'integrazione. In L. de Anna (A cura di), *Processi formativi e percorsi di integrazione nelle scienze motorie. Ricerca, teorie e prassi.* FrancoAngeli.

Mangone, E. (A cura di). (2016). *Adolescenti e sport. Trasformazioni sociali e pratiche motorie.* FrancoAngeli.

Mauro, M. (2016). *The Balotelli generation. Issues of inclusion and belonging in italian football and society.* Bern: Peter Lang AG.

Mei, S. (A cura di). (2011). *Disabili stranieri: un doppio sguardo per l'inclusione sociale. Rileggere criticamente saperi, modelli e strumenti.* Bologna: Centro Ri.E.Sco.

Miconi, D., & Moscardino, U. (2017). La valutazione psicologica di bambini e famiglie migranti. In S. Bonichini (A cura di), *La valutazione psicologica dello sviluppo. Metodi e strumenti* (pp. 395–414). Carocci.

MIUR. (2012). Annali della Pubblica Istruzione. Indicazioni nazionali per il curricolo della scuola dell'infanzia e del primo ciclo d'istruzione. Available at http://www.ind icazioninazionali.it/wp-content/uploads/2018/08/Indicazioni_Annali_Definitivo.pdf

MIUR. (2013). *L'integrazione scolastica degli alunni con disabilità dati statistici A.S. 2012/2013.* Available at https://www.istruzione.it/allegati/integrazione_sco-lastica_degli_alunni_con_disabilita.pdf

MIUR. (2014). *Linee guida per l'accoglienza e l'integrazione degli alunni stranieri.* Available at https://www.miur.gov.it/documents/20182/2223566/linee_guida _integrazione_alunni_stranieri.pdf/5e41fc48-3c68-2a17-ae75-1b5da6a55667?t =1564667201890

MIUR. (2015). *Diversi da chi?* Available at https://www.miur.gov.it/documents/20182 /2223566/DIVERSI+DA+CHI.pdf/90d8a40f-76d2-3408-da43-4a2932131d9b?t =1564667199410

MIUR. (2018a). Indicazioni Nazionali e Nuovi Scenari. Available at https://www .miur.gov.it/documents/20182/0/Indicazioni+nazionali+e+nuovi+scenari/

MIUR. (2018b). *Gli alunni con cittadinanza non Italiana A.S. 2016/2017.* Available at https://www.miur.gov.it/documents/20182/0/FOCUS+16-17_Studenti+non +italiani/be4e2dc4-d81d-4621-9e5a-848f1f8609b3?version=1.0

Moliterni, P., & Mastrangelo, M. E. (2016). Verso il canestro e oltre! Baskin per promuovere inclusione e prosocialità: uno studio pilota. *Italian Journal of Special Education for Inclusion, 4*(2), 171–188. Pensa Multimedia Editore.

Moro, M. R. (2002). *Genitori in esilio. Psicopatologia e migrazioni.* Raffaello Cortina Editore.

Murineddu, M., Duca, V., & Cornoldi, C. (2006). Difficoltà di apprendimento scolastico degli studenti stranieri. *Difficoltà di apprendimento, 12*(1), 49–70.

OECD. (2021). *International migration outlook 2021.* Available at https://doi.org/10 .1787/29f23e9d-en

Oliver, C., & Singal, N. (2017). Migration, disability and education: reflections from a special school in the east of england. *British Journal of Sociology of Education, 38*(8), 1217–1229.

Pennazio, V., & Bochicchio, F. (2020). Promote the intercultural inclusion of migrant families of children with disabilities in early childhood education services. *Educazione interculturale. Teorie, ricerche, pratiche, 18*(2), 14–25.

Pescarmona, I. (2019). I piccolissimi dell'immigrazione. Sfide e dilemmi pedagogici sulla prima infanzia nelle società multiculturali. *Rivista Formazione, Lavoro, Persona, 9*(29), 65–74.

Pesce, C., Marchetti, R., Motta, A., & Bellucci, M. (2015). *Joy of moving. Movimenti e Immaginazione. Giocare con la variabilità per promuovere lo sviluppo motorio, cognitivo e del cittadino.* Torgiano (PG): Calzetti & Mariucci.

Pisani, M., & Grech, S. (2015). Disability and forced migration: Critical intersectionalities. *Disability and the Global South, 2*(1), 421–441.

Refrigeri, L. (A cura di). (2011). *Sport e razzismo. Il ruolo dell'educazione*. Lecce-Brescia: Pensa MultiMedia.

Santagati, M., & Colussi, E. (A cura di). (2019). *Alunni con background migratorio in Italia. Emergenze e traguardi. Rapporto nazionale*. Fondazione ISMU.

Spagnuolo, N., El-Lahib, Y., & Kusari, K. (2019). Participatory training in disability and migration: Mobilizing community capacities for disability advocacy. *Qualitative Research, 20*(2), 213–228.

Tatulli, I. (2014). Attività motoria sportiva integrata. Decostruzione di modelli, nuove sfide inclusive nella formazione. *L'integrazione Scolastica e Sociale, 13*(1), 59–66.

UN. (2006). *Convention on the rights of persons with disabilities*. Available at https://www.un.org/development/desa/disabilities/convention-on-the-rights-of-persons-with-disabilities.html

UN. (2013). *Convention on the rights of the child. General comment No. 17 (2013) on the right of the child to rest, leisure, play, recreational activities, cultural life and the arts (art. 31)*. Available at https://www.refworld.org/docid/51ef9bcc4.html

UNESCO. (1994). *The Salamanca statement and framework for action on special needs education*. Available at https://www.european-agency.org/sites/default/files/salamanca-statement-and-framework.pdf

UNESCO. (2015). *Quality physical education: Guidelines for policy makers*. Available at https://en.unesco.org/inclusivepolicylab/sites/default/files/learning/document/2017/1/231101E.pdf

UNHCR. (2020). *Global trends. Forced displacement in 2019*. Available at https://www.unhcr.org/statistics/unhcrstats/5ee200e37/unhcr-global-trends-2019

UNICEF. (2013). *La condizione dell'infanzia nel mondo 2013. Bambini e disabilità*. Available at https://www.datocms-assets.com/30196/1607934752-rapporto-20unicef-202013.pdf

WHO. (2001). *International classification of functioning, disability and health: ICF: short version*. Available at https://apps.who.int/iris/handle/10665/42417

WHO. (2007). *International classification of functioning, disability and health: Children & youth version: ICF-CY*. Available at http://apps.who.int/iris/bitstream/handle/10665/43737/9789241547321_eng.pdf;sequence=1

Zollo, I. (2019). "Affermare valori inclusivi": la prospettiva del Nuovo Index per l'inclusione. *Italian Journal of Special Education for Inclusion, 7*(2), 322–339. Pensa MultiMedia Editore.

Chapter 12

Criticism of Stereotypes in Paralympism and Expectations of Media Portrayals of Latin American Athletes

Sandra Meléndez-Labrador

The Paralympic Games are, according to International Paralympic Commit-tee (IPC), the parallel games to the Olympic Games and illustrate how the two movements exist side by side. Even though the Greek preposition "para" means "next to," in the Dictionary of Spain Academy, "paralelo" means two or more lines or planes equidistant from each other and no matter how long they are, *they cannot be found*. This is one of many paradoxes in the Paralym-pian world, as will be addressed in this chapter.

These games were born in 1948, as a competition called Stoke Mandeville Games for World War II veterans with spinal injures. In 1952, they became became an international competition, with the first Paralympic Summer Games on American soil held in Toronto, Canada, in 1976. In 2016, Rio de Janeiro (Brazil) became the first South American country to host the Games. The Rio Games became the main media platform for people with disabili-ties in the region and an opportunity to transform the negative stereotypes about disability in the media. Given historic injustices faced by those with disabilities among South American countries, it is vital to understand how people with disabilities want society to think of them and what they want to project through the media, which is why this chapter will focus on the opin-ion of Latin American Paralympic athletes as the main promoters of positive images of disability. Thus, taking into account that media representations of disability in Latin America can range from an iconic analysis "passively as they do nothing more than pose or are represented by their condition, by that which must be cured or replaced" (Vergara-Heidke & Torres-Calderón, 2019,

p. 159), to "content that focuses on the sporting activity and not on the disability" (Meléndez-Labrador, 2021a, p. 157).

The Paralympic Games are not the only sporting events for people with disabilities. Other less-known events are the Deaflympics and Special Olympics; yet the Paralympic Games is the third most-publicized sporting event in the world behind the FIFA world cup and the Olympic Games. As Castillo and Sáenz said, "After more than 40 years of presence in society, disability in elite sport has accepted the mercantilist forms of the Olympic Games, and its members have adopted the well-known roles of fame and unprecedented television visibility" (2011, p. 91). In this order, although, the Paralympic Games is not traditionally viewed as a top television sports event (Boyle, 2012), the Paralympics has allowed for a wide concentration of studies on disability and the media concerning sport at a global level because it is a popular sporting mega-event and one of the most hyper-visible displays of disability in the media (Pullen et al., 2020). Indeed, this chapter is the first exploration into the expectations of Paralympic athletes from several Latin American countries about media portrayal of the Rio Paralympic Games 2016.

MEDIA AND PARALYMPIC GAMES RESEARCH

Studies on disability and communication have roots reaching back to the 1960s. For example, Taylor (1957) and Gerbner (1961) found that mental illness was the most commonly portrayed disability on television and magazines. In the 1980s, this work was extended (Ferrante, 2021) as a result of the claims of organizations of people with disabilities: "alternative modes of living full lives, free of stigma, prejudice, or any sense of inferiority" (Silva & Howe, 2012, p. 179). These claims translated into guaranteeing the human rights of persons with disabilities (Shapiro, 1994), as Article 8 of the Convention on the Rights of Persons with Disabilities (CRPD) said:

a) To raise awareness throughout society, including at the family level, regarding persons with disabilities, and to foster respect for the rights and dignity of persons with disabilities; b) To combat stereotypes, prejudices and harmful practices relating to persons with disabilities, including those based on sex and age, in all areas of life;

The States Parties signatories of the Convention must ensure the promotion of images respectful of the rights of persons with disabilities. Currently this struggle continues about media representation of people with disabilities and how to convey and perpetuate stereotypes that portray people with disabilities as charitable objects rather than as subjects of rights (Meléndez-Labrador, 2018). This type of representation can and does continue to be harmful to athletes with disabilities in how they are perceived, from the "supercrip" portrayal, because "presumed deserving of pity—instead of respect—until he or she proves capable of overcoming a physical or mental limitation through superhuman feats" (Englandkennedy, 2008, p. 98).

In relation to sport, Boyle states that the study of communication "should continue to tell us truths about the values that we have as a society" (2012, p. 97); and, additionally, in relation with a disability, Hodges et al. (2014), state that the journalistic coverage of the Paralympics "provides significant opportunity to influence public attitudes regarding disability and disability sport; challenging dominant stereotypes and encouraging a continued move away from disability sport as therapeutic value, towards prestigious elite-level competition" (p. 6). Additionally, Claydon, Gunter and Reilly (2015) argue that the Paralympics are "heralded as a source of inspiration to disability communities to engage with sport" at the same time "provided a platform for the representation of disability, which shifted the focus from 'disabilities' per se to the sporting abilities and achievements of high-performance athletes who happen to be disabled" (p. 70). But there is a thin line between showing an inspirational athlete and a sport hero and a superhuman athlete with a disability that overcomes limitations until they have succeeded in sport.

Throughout history, the social perception of people with disabilities and their physical performance changed from social segregation (sport for people with disabilities vs. sport for people without disabilities) and contempt to progressive social integration and appreciation of their athletic abilities (Paralympic and elite athletes). In that process, the media have been central: "continues to play a significant role in leading progressive social change" (Alexander, 2015, p. 21), taking into account Clogston's (1990) two models of media representation of disability: (1) the traditional disability model that presents a disabled person as defective in a medical or economic way, assuming that problems arise because an individual is disabled, not from society; (2) the progressive model (opposite) that views people as disabled by society, not a physical attribute.

Maika and Danylchuk argue that "much of the information the general public receives about disability is disseminated by media rather than directly from people with lived experiences" (2016, p. 1). Generally, media do it through stereotypes or categories: the key expressions, speeches, or narrative fragments used to talk about an issue have certain characteristics that shape a stereotype that ultimately frames the media approach or approach (Shoemaker & Reese, 1991). As noted by Tejkalová and Strielkowski (2015),

Representation plays a dominant role in the construction of identity, the reflection of "us" and "them." It is natural and it starts when human beings are born, on the other hand it can be a germ of prejudices and stereotyping of other people,

and from the media because "mass media convey a certain representation of reality using the process of stereotyping" (p. 579).

Stereotypes of disability are the cultural narratives of the body constructed from ideological categories manifested in brands or labels. In the case of people with disabilities, the most recognized "brand" refers to those wiith physical disabilities. More precisely, the body and its potentialities are the central axis of sport, in addition to being the main resource applied in visual sports journalism. As Bertling (2012) points out, "Pictures attract attention, perception, emotion, and involvement. In sport coverage press pictures primarily have an emotional, entertaining and/or illustrative function and often use eroticism, general aesthetics (especially athletic body composition) or even humor (sarcasm)" (p. 57).

Within sport for people with disabilites, media coverage shows the athletes as monuments of tragedy, deviance or freakery, or as fetishes; "some iterations of these representations risk encoding the disabled body as a science fiction superhero 'other' and as 'inspiration porn'" (Alexander, 2015, p. 143). A tentative definition is given by Grue (2016):

> Inspiration porn is the representation of disability as a desirable but undesired characteristic, usually by showing impairment as a visually or symbolically distinct biophysical deficit in one person, a deficit that can and must be overcome through the display of physical prowess. (p. 838)

Precisely, the little knowledge about the Paralympic Games by a majority of journalists leads to stereotypical coverage despite events that "represent a unique opportunity to educate the public on different types of impairment and how to combat stereotypes related to the question of impairment" (Pappous & Souza, 2016, p. 4).

The superhero and inspirational person are common stereotypes in media representation of Paralympic athletes. That media model is part of the "supercrip" frame, which suggests that Paralympic athletes have approximated able-bodied athletic performance despite their disability "problem." As Kolotouchkina, Llorente-Barroso, and Pavón (2021) argued:

> The complexity of the understanding of disability and its public acceptance is reflected in its media representation, ranging from simplistic, cruel, and discriminating frames anchored in stigma and stereotypes to inspirational positive discourses that enhance abilities, normality, and equality.

Many scholars have demonstrated that "supercrip" is the predominant journalistic narrative in Paralympics. This approach is also true for Latin American researchers: (Marques et al., 2014; Meléndez-Labrador, 2021b; Ferrante, 2021). For example, McGillivray et al. (2019) noted athletes with disabilities presented during the Rio 2016 Paralympic Games were featured in a stereotypical way, suggesting a sense of perplexity and lack of training of media professionals on how to cover disability sport. The "supercrip" narratives are criticized for problematic effects of pity, that might lead to negative perceptions of persons with disabilities in general (Berger, 2008; Bartsch et al., 2018; Silva & Howe, 2012; Mason, 2013; Suggs & Guthrie, 2017). Recently, Pullen et al. (2020) provided a supercrip frame through three types of disability narratives in contemporary Paralympic media coverage: (1) *Extraordinary normalcy*: depicts overcoming disability in discourses of disability inclusion that include the ability to successfully navigate ableist institutions; (2) *Ableist rehabilitation:* portrays para sports to restore the "normal" life and body that led to an impairment from an accident, occupational hazard, or military service; and (3) *Sporting ablenationalism*: visual images centered on bodies of successful athletes where impairment has been "exceeded" through technological or is not visible or severe enough to disrupt neoliberal ableist bodily norms impairment. The third is the most dominant narrative on Paralympic coverage according to Pullen et al. and are most recognized in Latin America as "Personal tragedy-focused narratives" (Figueiredo, 2017), "Narratives of overcoming adversity" (Santos et al., 2020b), and "Identity narrative of supercrip Ave Fenix" (Ferrante, 2021).

Research on Paralympic sport and media has increased substantially in the last decade. In Latin America and it has been of particular interest to academics in Brazil (Meléndez-Labrador, 2022). This is likely due to the work of Brazilian disability rights activists and their involvement in raising the visibility and changing perceptions of people with disabilities in Brazil (de Souza & Brittain, 2020). But it is necessary to measure the status of claims in Latin America in regard to the rights of persons with disabilities perspective and their relationship with the role played by the media in this guarantee. This could be the first step to get there.

METHOD

This chapter seeks to address the relationship between media and disability, specifically focusing on the area of sports journalism in Latin America during the 2016 Paralympic Games in Rio de Janeiro, Brazil. Specifically analyzed were the expectations expressed by Latin American athletes about the way they wished to be portrayed by the media during the 2016 games in a meeting video. One month before the Paralympic Games in Rio 2016, on July 29, 2016, an alternative media company, *Inspire Latin America*—which specializes in Paralympic sport coverage—held a virtual meeting on Latin American Journalism and Paralympism with the support of Americas Paralympic Committee (APC), called "Hangout con atletas paralímpicos latinoamericanos." This media company sought, according to cofounders Hernando Ayala and Juan Pablo Prieto, to establish a regional alliance to build a proposal for a Latin American narrative around the most popular and advanced Paralympic Games in history. In pursuit of this goal, Ayala and Prieto invited 10 Latin American Paralympic athletes to tell them what they expected from the journalistic coverage of Rio 2016 in that hangout.

The research was developed from a critical-interpretative approach, through discourse analysis applied to the hangout video, published on Inspire's YouTube channel with the interviews conducted by the Latin American Alliance of Journalism and Paralympic Sport[1] to 10 Paralympic athletes from Argentina (1), Brazil (1), Colombia (3), Chile (1), Ecuador (1), Peru (1), and Venezuela (2). (See table 12.1.) This is a qualitative descriptive study that seeks to understand responses onto an existing framework about the coverage of Rio Paralympic Games supported by previous research.

Ethical Statement

Although the researcher took part in the hangout as a commentator, the responses analyzed in this chapter were taken from a secondary analysis of the public interview on Inspire LatinoamericaYouTube Channel. The purpose of

Table 12.1 Para Athletes Interviewees

Athlete	Sport	Classification*	Country
Daniela Gimenez	Swimming	S9, SB9, SM9	Argentina
Renato Nunes Da Cruz	Athletics	T64	Brazil
Érica María Castaño Salazar	Athletics	F55/56	Colombia
Maritza Arango Buitrago	Athletics	T11, F11	Colombia
Nelson Crispín Corzo	Swimming	S6, SB6, SM6	Colombia
Cristian Exequiel Valenzuela Guzmán	Athletics	T11, F11	Chile
Darwin Gustavo Castro Reyes	Athletics	T11, F11	Ecuador
Efraín Sotacuro	Athletics	T46	Peru
Víctor Hugo Garrido Márquez	Cycling	C2	Venezuela
Zuray Marcano	Para powerlifting		Venezuela

Source: Own elaboration.
* According to the International Paralympic Committee website, "classification is the cornerstone of the Paralympic Movement, it determines which athletes are eligible to compete in a sport and how athletes are grouped together for competition. In Para sports, athletes are grouped by the degree of activity limitation resulting from the impairment. This, to a certain extent, is similar to grouping athletes by age, gender or weight" (IPC, 2021).

the interview was to know how people with disabilities who are media figures (in this case Latin American Paralympic athletes) expected to be portrayed by the media in their participation in Rio. After a professional exercise as a photographer on-site in Rio Paralympic Games and finding that a guide for covering these Paralympic Games was provided there by Brazilian Paralympic Committee (based on previous research), the researcher decided to review again the responses of the interviewees given a month before the event.

PARALYMPIC NARRATIVES

The questions asked by Hernando Ayala (Inspire Latinoamerica) were: (1) *What is the story, the narrative, the journalism type that you want to portray your performance in the Paralympic Games in Rio 2016?*; and (2) *How has Paralympic journalism evolved in your country?* (Inspire, 2016). The responses of the athletes interviewed agreed with the "Media Guide: How to Cover the Rio 2016 Paralympic Games" designed by Athanasios Pappous (University of Kent, UK) and Doralice Lange de Souza (Universidade Federal do Paraná, Brazil) and supported by Brazilian Paralympic Committee. With the support of the Brazilian Paralympic Committee, this guide was provided to the Brazilian media during the Paralympic Games (shortly after this interview) to enable Brazilian media professionals to promote a more inclusive image of people with disabilities based on positive and accurate coverage. This guide is the only publication based on the research work on media and disability and was the only recommended for the IPC on the Rio and Tokyo Paralympic Games. Additionally, Pappous demonstrated with other colleagues that the media have failed to harvest the opportunity of the Paralympic Games to alter stereotypes about what it means to be disabled (Pappous et al., 2011).

Based on his own research work as an worldwide expert on the interdisciplinary between sport sociology, disability studies, and communication sciences, Pappous along with Souza proposed five guidelines for writing texts on Paralympic sport: (1) put the athlete first, not their disability; (2) disability does not equal suffering; (3) avoid grouping people by disability; (4) prioritize the athletes' sporting events, not their disability; (5) use of appropriate terms (Pappous & Souza, 2016).

The comments below from the interviewees suggest how they support these statements and what their hope is for media depiction.

Focus First on the Athlete and Not the Impairment

It is important to understand that we are high-performance athletes, that we sweat as much or perhaps with a little more difficulty than conventional athletes, while we try to represent our country in the best way. (Cristian Valenzuela)

In Peru there is not much diffusion of the Paralympic athletes; they (sports journalists) put us aside unlike the Olympic athletes. (Efraín Sotacuro)

By moving the athlete first and not their disability, normalization is sought, since athletes with disabilities must be portrayed with the same respect as athletes without disabilities. Pappous and Souza (2016) argued that the basic rule is to address the athlete first, instead the impairment. Paralympic athletes want to be treated first and foremost as athletes, preferably using the name without qualifiers.

Impairment Does Not Equate to Suffering

The Paralympic sport is the same as the Olympic Games. It is a high-performance sport and journalists help society see that reality. In Argentina frequently the disabled [*sic*] is showed like a victim or poor thing that is not right truly. I believe that sport gives the disabled [*sic*] a lot of physical freedom and leads them to do things unthinkable. (Daniela Giménez)

Paralympic sport is also an investment issue and if there is no support we will continue to be seen as the poor people in a discriminatory society. (Víctor Hugo Garrido)

Addressing disability should not be equated with suffering. Expressions such as "victim of," "afflicted by," or "suffer" are commonly used by journalists, reinforcing the stereotype that disability equals suffering, using terms that portray athletes with disabilities as fragile or in situations of tragedy. They must be presented in a context of possibilities and high performance, as people who can have a happy life and who reach a high level of sports performance. Pappous and Souza (2016) argue, "The Paralympic athletes don't see themselves as victims of suffering in some way. Their impairment is part of who they are" (p. 5). Nevertheless, is not only a matter of highlighting the athlete's sporting value, overcoming, performance, normality, and the very conception of disability are presented in ways that challenge dominant stereotypes and disengage the association between disability and sport only as therapeutic value (Hodges et al., 2014).

First and Foremost Athletes

It is time to show not only our disability but also our technical capacity and our competencies to make significant marks in the world of para-sports. In the world we have to understand that Paralympic athletes cannot be valued as a quality-of-life program, we are high-performance athletes. We need the help of journalists who show what is happening in the parasport's world. There is a very big difference in the way European and North American athletes are pictured. The Paralympic Games are the opportunity for transformation. (Renato Nunes Da Cruz)

Pappous and Souza (2016) suggest showing the qualities of the athlete, rather than focusing on the disability. It is also important to refer to the sporting situation first, and the disability second. Examples might include, framing athletes with disabilities, such as wheelchair athletes, runners, or swimmers, rather than in terms such as blind, amputees, disabled; "If it is necessary to refer to an impairment, this should come after identifying the athlete and achievement" (p. 6). But, at this point, the most important priority for the journalist should be to ask the athlete who he or she is and what he or she considers to be his or her essence, to allow them to talk about themselves in the first place.

Prioritize the Sporting Achievements of the Athletes and Not Their Impairment

I invite to journalists to be more aware of the paralympic system, to cover us on equal terms with conventional athletes, that make our performances more visible. Journalists must be understood that Paralympic sport can be covered as the conventional sport because we give all on the track, we have a strong training plan, we can obtain the same results and represent the countries in the same way. (Maritza Arango)

To consider the Paralympic athletes as high performance, who have a disability but also the dream of obtaining a gold medal for their country. (Darwin Castro)

Our message is of high performance, high level—we are athletes who first won disability, then we train as hard as possible and then we face the best athletes in the world. (Cristian Valenzuela)

The reality of the journalists is to cover the news in a very short time and space; therefore, they must focus more on the results. When they need to talk about the disability, the approach should not be to bring it up first, because "paralympic athletes are competitive athletes who have worked hard to get to where they are. Although the narrative of victory over adversity and physical challenges may be a legitimate part of the story, we should prioritize the sporting achievements" (Pappous & Souza, 2016, p. 6). This point is clearly problematic, because that adversity can include narratives with the negative effect of inspirational and elevated emotions generated by representations of overcoming or "supercrip." That image sets unrealistic standards of comparison that can foster unfavorable judgments about people with disabilities, especially those who are not athletes (Bartsch et al., 2018), that hide the adversities beyond sports performance that people with disabilities face in terms of discrimination on a daily basis, especially in "undeveloped" countries.

Terminology

> The media in Colombia and South America need to know more about the categories of competence and the types of disability to ensure they do not use the wrong terms that make me feel bad because they are not giving me the importance that given to a conventional athlete. (Nelson Crispín Corzo)
>
> Make changes in the language that eliminate unpleasant labels, because we do not feel identified with them. There are technical terms and an inclusive language with which we do identify. I would propose as a narrative the "paralympic lyric," which highlights the feelings and emotions of the Paralympic athletes before competing, for example in training and those emotions that we make feel to the public with our performances. (Zuray Marcano ✝)

In relation to the coverage of disability sport, the use of language and terminology by newspaper journalists often reaffirms traditional, medicalized views of the people with disabilities, without acknowledging the sociogenetic dimensions of disability (Marcellini, 2012). In this regard, Pappous and Souza (2016) proposed to use "athlete," and "athlete with an impairment," or "athlete with an amputation/cerebral palsy/spinal cord injury," where further explanation is required, and never use "deficient," "crippled," "paralyzed," "handicapped," or "invalid," as these expressions reinforce negative stereotypes of physical disability and defects. The Pappous and Souza recommend use of "an athlete had a car accident which damaged his spine," or "which led to an amputation," instead of "suffers from," "victim of," or "afflicted by." These latter terms stigmatize and suggest tragedy, whereas athletes see themselves as high achievers who shouldn't be seen as victims. Finally, they suggest writing or saying "an athlete who uses a wheelchair" or "wheelchair athlete" instead of "confined to a wheelchair," because to the athlete concerned, the chair is an instrument of freedom and movement, not confinement.

This proposal that the journalists use feelings and emotions within all of their coverage, not just those about disability sport, would increase the normalized treatment of athletes. In general, as Alexander (2015) argued, "The work must be to foster societies in which disabled people can be, simply, human" (p. 145), that is to say, the human dignity approaches rather than simple "inclusivity."

Photo Coverage

If the journalist wants to portray qualities such as power, energy, attitude in the field, I suppose it will be necessary to photograph me in full-body, throwing, in official competitions, that depends on the purpose of the journalist, the type of information and the audience. (Érica Castaño)

The authors agree with the Paralympic brand's physical/visual character-istics and style from IPC: athletes should be portrayed as "dynamic, trium-phant, international individuals" like the motto of the Paralympics: "Spirit in Motion." They argue "photographs transmit emotions and help us express how we would like to be perceived. They also tell a story and can have a big-ger impact than words in themselves. In addition, their impact is immediate" (Pappous & Souza, 2016, p. 8).

In that regard, the photos must avoid: (a) Passive poses that accentuate the impairment; (b) Photos that portray failure; (c) Photos which portray the athletes in conditions of isolation and dependency, or which hide their faces; (d) Photos that hide deficiency; (e) Photos that accentuate impairment. Pap-pous and Souza propose images that promote a positive image and empower Paralympic athletes with the following characteristics: (a) The athletes are portrayed in action in the field of competition; (b) They are wearing sports clothes; (c) They are photographed in action; (d) Their facial expression por-trays competition and effort; (e) Any impairment is not hidden.

The Pappous and Souza guide and other similar ones such as EFDS (2016) and IPC (2014) take into account aspects of written and verbal language, forms and means of expression, and interaction with Paralympic athletes during interviews. Even so, it is possible to take into account the Universal Communicative Accessibility Model (Meléndez-Labrador, 2022) that sug-gests including an intersectional contextualization perspective. This perspec-tive explains the social reality of people with disabilities from the interaction of social, economic, political, cultural, and symbolic factors. At the same time, aspects of participation can help co-construct the image of Paralympic athletes (Meléndez-Labrador, 2021a). These guidelines need to be tested with the same Paralympic athletes to know other aspects that these Paralym-pic athletes consider important in the way they are presented by the media (Meléndez-Labrador, 2021b). There is also a need for this information to be tested with the worldwide activists for the rights of people with disabilities. These claims are intended to transcend the postulates in which the legacy of Ludwig Guttmann and his Stoke Mandeville games was built, currently questioned for maintaining "the ideology of normality, medical paternalism, and segregation" (Ferrante, 2021, p. 26). As Maika (2014) said, "clearly the development of sport for people with disabilities is rooted in a rehabilitation and medical setting. This sets the stage for a history of medicalized framing of Paralympic athletes" (p. 15).

In general terms, the expectations of Latin American Paralympic athletes from the media align with those of other Paralympic athletes, although they have been analyzed in only a few Brazilian and Colombian studies (Figueiredo, 2017; Meléndez-Labrador, 2021b) where Paralympic athletes with disabilities were defined by their achievements and competence rather than their disabilities even though "Paralympic" is a medical label. This perspective is part of the cultural pluralism model (progressive media model) by Haller (2000), which recognizes a person with disability in media representation and auto-representation as multifaceted and not defined by the disability. In Brazilian research, Santos et al. (2018) called this "esportividade paraolímpica," a new framing category in the photographic coverage of Rio 2016 Paralympic Games which discourse that values the sportsmanship (esportividade) of the athlete with disability as of the characteristics of photo coverage of institutional media guides (e.g., Pappous & Souza, 2016). Likewise, Hilgemberg (2019) categorized as "esportivo" terms associated with the practice of sports such as the modality practiced and expressions like "champion," "record holder," medalist, winner, and so on.

Additionally, athletes highlighted the lack of knowledge that sports journalists have of the Paralympic system. In this regard Solves et al. (2018) found the editors of media coverage of the 2008 and 2012 Paralympic Games in Spain did not recognize the sporting nature of this event. Kolotouchkina and colleagues (2021) pointed out, "the difficulty in understanding the rules and regulations of specific Paralympic disciplines" (p. 21), as one of the main barriers to normalizing the visibility of the parasports competitions. This is not a new problem, unfortunately, as Golden, in 2003, suggested: "Media professionals need to become more knowledgeable about Paralympic sport and its peculiarities so that they can recognize the sportsmanship involved" (as cited in Santos et al., 2020a, p. 4).

EVOLUTION OF PARALYMPIC SPORTS JOURNALISM IN LATIN AMERICA

In regard to the second question of the hangout analyzed: *How has Paralympic journalism evolved in your country?* Paralympic-focused journalism has been poorly developed over the nearly 70-year existence of the event, even with the extensive research conducted on the topic. In Latin America—outside of predominately Brazilian and some Colombian research on the subject—the journalistic production, media representations, and perceptions about Paralympic sport are poorly explored (Meléndez-Labrador, 2022). So, these interviews with the Latin American Paralympic athletes from Rio 2016 (*Inspire*, 2016) give the first major regional contribution to the analysis of the subject. Indeed, the Latin American athletes spoke about the evolution of Paralympic journalism in each country; their voices led to the following conclusions.

Low Diffusion

The low diffusion of Paralympic sport on the Latin American media persists, although Paralympic sport is experiencing an intense process of mediatization on a global scale (Santos et al., 2020a). Brazil had the advantage of being the Olympic hosts and confirmed, as in London 2012, the number of news stories has grown significantly in the Paralympic Games (Pappous et al., 2011; de Souza and Brittain, 2020; dos Santos et al., 2019; Hilgemberg, 2019). But, in other places of Latin America, this aspect is unknown. For example, one private and two public mainstream media of Colombia attended the Paralympic Games in Rio 2016 (Meléndez-Labrador, 2021a). In addition, the athletes believed there was no media interest in the subject for many years. In fact, in Latin America, this aspect has not been demonstrated in the region, except for Brazilian media coverage of Rio. Historical Paralympic sports journalism wasn't attractive for researchers despite Paralympic Games Rio 2016's impact in the continent (Meléndez-Labrador, 2022). The participants also demanded that media portrays Paralympic sport with the same interest, recognition, and technical accuracy as conventional sport.

Journalism as Promoter

The journalism and sports institutions were recognized as promoters of adapted and Paralympic sports. Rojas and Torrijos (2021) argued that both maintain the social relevance of the social acceptance and integration of people with disabilities "by pushing public opinion toward more comprehensive consideration and respect for their physical efforts and feats" (p. 229). However, it is necessary to check details based on the "supercrip" style of parasport portrayal (Silva & Howe, 2012; Busch et al., 2013; Crow, 2014; Walsh, 2015; Hodges et al., 2015; Ferrante, 2021).

> I highlight the work that Coldeportes has done in Colombia together with the Olympic and Paralympic Committee to go to forgotten regions [. . .] and teach people with disabilities that there are adapted sports. It is very important to continue showing all these projects and the benefits for the disabled population. (Érica Castaño)
> In Venezuela, it is deficient, apathetic, in my career I noticed marketing must influence governments so that they invest in the media and can transmit

our values to society. Society has not yet been able to perceive the importance of having a Paralympic Games taking place on the continent. (Víctor Garrido)

Mainstream Media Prioritizes Medalists

The mainstream media tends to prioritize medalist athletes. Florence (2009) found that the Brazilian Paralympic athletes claim that the media only covers the big Paralympic events and highlights only the gold medals. Novais and Figueiredo (2010) found greater media exposure of Olympic athletes regardless of the number of medals won compared to Paralympic athletes in Brazilian and Portuguese digital media. Santos, Solves, and Souza (2020a) called to this new value "athletic merit" and Novais and Figueiredo analyzed it as "Relacionadas à vitória." As Léseleuc et al. (2010) argued: "that medals, records, and other achievements constitute one of the cornerstones of the sporting press. This is equally applicable to both the Olympic and the Paralympic Games" (p. 288).

> London was my first Paralympic Games and I was very excited about how the media was going to depict us. They showed Moisés Fuentes because he did something very important, but very little was said about the other delegation. A change is being seen here in Colombia for Rio. The Colombian Paralympic Committee has made links with television channels and our work is being shown. (Nelson Crispín Corzo)

From Overcoming to Sport Narratives

The Paralympic news shift from a "supercrip" (overcoming) representation framework to a focus first on the athlete and the sporting achievements, means there are genuine attempts by journalists to cover the Paralympics beyond stereotypes (Ellis & Goggin, 2015; Meléndez-Labrador, 2021a).

> It has gone from an editorial of overcoming to seeing and criticizing us as athletes. Media such as Fuerza Paralímpica and the Chilean Paralympic Committee have contributed to making society understand that our message is one of high performance, of a high level. (Cristian Exequiel Valenzuela)

Further studies are needed on this aspect, particularly about other Latin American countries.

Recognition for Other Media

The work of independent/alternative media were recognized by the Paralympic athletes that felt they identified with their portrayals. The independent and institutional media portray athletes as high level.

In Argentina, it did not exist before Paradeportes. [. . .] I think there is a long way to go but we are on the right path. In Latin America there was very little diffusion so the work you do is great. (Daniela Gimenez)

I feel represented and identified with this alliance of Latin American journalists and independent media. (Zuray Marcano ✝)

CONCLUSION AND DISCUSSION

The purpose of this chapter was to learn about the expectations of Latin American athletes regarding media representations of their performance in the Rio 2016 Paralympic Games. In this regard, this chapter describes how the Latin American Paralympic athletes interviewed have a high level of empowerment that goes hand-in-hand with their sports experience and access to progressive references, among others. Many athletes have also managed to build a self-perception that blurs the stereotypes of disability, since they expressed a critical position on the media's representation of their sports performance and made contributions to complement the guidelines on media coverage of the Paralympic Games and, by extension, any other adapted sport event. However, it must be noted, their notoriety rarely, if ever, reaches the status of non-disabled athletes.

Research is urgently needed about the news production process (historical, critical, and comparative) and perceptions about Paralympic portrayals in other Latin American countries after the Tokyo 2020 Paralympic Games. Especially considering that (1) society influences the way journalists work and routine problems in the production of Paralympic news in mainstream media (Santos, Solves, & Souza, 2020a) and alternative media (Meléndez-Labrador, 2021a) and (2) at the same time journalists influence the social construction of reality. As Hilgemberg (2019) argued, because the journalist is inserted in a certain culture, with his/her thoughts and ideas, and is often one who writes for a newspaper (or other media outlet) that has guidelines to be followed.

In the present chapter, athletes indicated that there is interest and institutional efforts to improve the treatment of Paralympic sport, and by extension, broader adapted sports coverage, in the media, based on the guide by Pappous and Souza (2016). This contains, in general terms, the requirements as expressed by Latin American para-athletes. Aspects such as the inclusion of feelings and emotions, as the "Paralympic lyric" (suggested by the athlete Mirandina Zuray Marcano ✝) that emerge in sports performance before, during, and after competitions could be added as news value, emphasizing that the "drama" of disability or dramatic life stories (Santos et al., 2020a) should be excluded from future coverage.

On the other hand, it is necessary to take into account not only the symbolic issues of the journalists, but also those of the athletes (e.g., self-perception and perception of other athletes), who may be influential (e.g., a media interview) in the news production process. Davis (2013) argued:

> For stigmatized people, the idea of normality takes on an exaggerated importance. Normality becomes the supreme goal for many stigmatized individuals until they realize that there is no precise definition of normality except what they would be without their stigma. (p. 155)

Finally, there is a distance between the real Paralympic coverage and the athletes' media expectations because the "supercrip" narrative continues to be the major frame to portray the Paralympic athletes in the media (Meléndez-Labrador, 2022). Yet, even of those interviewed, athletes don't expect superfluous or hypercongratulatory media coverage; instead, they want their sports achievement to have the same exposition of non-disabled athletes.

Response

Keep Quiet and Let the Results Speak for You

Erica María Castaño Salazar

I have the firm conviction, "Where there's a will, there's a way." I reinforced this phrase when I acquired my disability on December 8, 2008, the Day of Candles in my country, to be more exact. One bullet crossed my path, severed my spinal cord and also bifurcated my life, one before and one after. Now, I want to talk about the "one after," where I am today.

I remember many moments, some sweet and others bitter, how I had to start from scratch, to reinvent myself in everything of my everyday life, simple things like bathing, dressing, feeding myself, cleaning the house, going from one place to another, taking a cab, going to a subway station, and so on. I had to relearn to live with my disability, and I had to learn to love my wheelchair as a part of myself. Keep quiet and let the results speak for you.

It was a process of rapid acceptance. With the doubts circling my head, I remember one day looking up to heaven and praying to God fervently: "Lord, do with me whatever you want!" Undoubtedly, it was the beginning of my sporting journey and the turn of my life and my family.

Suddenly, God sends people who would help me build this path. Without thinking, I start practicing adapted sport—ParaAthletics—and became a discus thrower. This sports discipline has allowed me to enjoy success as God's purpose in my life.

When I was a child, I dreamed to be a prosecutor; I wanted to be that. I studied law at the Universidad Autónoma Latinoamericana in Medellín, Colombia; after that, I studied criminal procedure for a postgraduate degree, but God had other plans for me: to be a world champion.

The last seven years, I have sacrificed family moments and special dates, lived in other cities away from the people who love me. Every morning, when my alarm clock rings at five o'clock, I have had to find the strength to train twice a day. Now, I am a different woman than I used to be: I have bigger muscles, I have my nails short and unpainted, my face has no make-up, my hair is always tied up, my skin and clothes are still wet from sweat. Nevertheless, I am extremely proud of my triumphs and grateful for all the satisfactions harvested in this time. Fill my soul of happiness—my mother's tears of joy—when she knows that in other place in the world, that I am harvesting the fruits that God taught me to sow in silence.

I love my mother and my two brothers. I wish my father was alive so he could see me succeed as an athlete, because he taught me to love sports. Also,

I feel blessings for my husband, the most wonderful man on the planet. God in his infinite mercy put him in my life to give me more happiness than I already had. My "eternal boyfriend," as I call him, came when my health was not the best, but with his love, dedication and care, he supported me throughout my illnesses. Best of all, he is a thrower, a para-athlete like me, a champion. Together we love God above all things; we are made for each other.

In hindsight, these are some of the things that leave me amazed. Despite the adversity there are so many opportunities hidden behind this. The decision was in my hands, choose whether to take advantage of the opportunities or let them go.

Here I am, working to participate in my second Paralympic Games: Tokyo 2021, in silence, focused, dedicated, more motivated. I am certain that God will make the noise with the results that he has in store for me.

NOTE

1. That Alliance was formed by Latin American alternative media and journalists specialized in Paralympics: Inspire Latinoamérica; María Fernanda Jiménez, Nexos TV, Costa Rica; Maximiliano Nobili, Paradeportes, Argentina; Efrén Galván, Deporte Adaptado, México; Carlos Rizki, Adaptado Sport, Venezuela; Manuel Castro, Plan Sinergia, Perú; Marcela Garrido, Fuerza Paralímpica, Chile; Sandra Meléndez, Discomunica, Colombia; Seu Esporte y RS Paradesporto, Brazil. And institutional members: José Luis Campo +, President of the Americas Paralympic Committee (APC) and Eduardo Montenegro, Vice President of the APC and Sports Director of the Colombian Paralympic Committee; Manuel Campo, community manager of the APC; Hernán Goldzycher, editorial coordinator of the International Paralympic Committee (IPC); Gabriela Bedoya, Public Relations and Communications of the Ecuadorian Paralympic Committee; and Miguel Villamil, Communications Director of the Colombian Paralympic Committee. There were five virtual and face-to-face sessions in which topics such as journalism on Paralympic sport from the media and the athletes, as well as the keys of the Paralympic system of the Americas for the development of Latin American Paralympic sport, were addressed. The final session was the International Seminar on Journalism and Paralympics—Paralympic Games Rio 2016, supported by Universidad Sergio Arboleda, Colombia.

REFERENCES

Alexander, J. (2015). 'Superhumanity' and the embodiment of enlightenment the semiotics of disability in the official art and advertising of the 2012 British Paralympics. In D. Jackson, C. E. Hodges, M. Molesworth, & R. Scullion (Eds.),

(2014). *Reframing disability?: Media, (dis)empowerment, and voice in the 2012 Paralympics.* Routledge.

Bartsch, A., Oliver, M. B., Nitsch, C., & Scherr, S. (2018). Inspired by the Paralympics: Effects of empathy on audience interest in para-sports and on the destigmatization of persons with disabilities. *Communication Research, 45*(4), 525–553.

Berger, R. J. (2008). Disability and the dedicated wheelchair athlete: Beyond the "supercrip" critique. *Journal of Contemporary Ethnography,* 37, 647–678.

Bertling, C. (2012). Disability sport in the German media. In O. J. Schantz & K. Gilbert (Eds.), *Heroes or Zeros? The media's perceptions of Paralympic sport* (pp. 55–64). Champagne, IL: Common Ground Publishing LLC.

Boyle, R. (2012). Reflections on communication and sport: On journalism and digital culture. *Communication & Sport, 1*(1–2), 88–99.

Castillo, S. S., & Sáez, M. T. M. (2011). Narrativa audiovisual y discapacidad. Realización televisiva comparada de los Juegos Olímpicos y Paralímpicos de Pekín 2008. *ZER: Revista de Estudios de Comunicación Komunikazio Ikasketen Aldizkaria, 16*(31), 89–107.

Claydon, E., Gunter, B., & Reilly, P. (2015). Dis/Enablement? An analysis of the representation of disability on British terrestrial television pre-and post-paralympics. In Jackson et. al. (Eds.). *Reframing Disability? Media, (Dis)Empowerment, and Voice in the 2012 Paralympics,* pp. 37–65. London: Routledge.

Crow, L. (2014). Scroungers and superhumans: Images of disability from the summer of 2012: A visual inquiry. *Journal of Visual Culture, 13*(2), 168–181. https://doi.org/10.10.1177/1470412914529109

Davis, L. J. (2013). *The disability studies reader.* Fourth edition. Routledge.

de Souza, D. L. & Brittain, I. (2020). The Rio 2016 Paralympic games: The visibility of people with disabilities in Brazil as a possible legacy. *Communication and Sport, 10*(2), 334–353 https://doi.org/10.10.1177/2167479520942739.

dos Santos, S. M., Furtado, S., Poffo, B. N., et al. (2019). Mídia e Jogos Paralímpicos no Brasil: A cobertura da Folha de S. Paulo entre 1992 e 2016. *Revista Brasileira de Ciências do Esporte, 41*(2), 190–197.

EFDS. (2016). *Media guide: Reporting on disabled people in sport.* English Federation of Disability Sport.

Ellis, K., & Goggin, G. (2015). *Disability and the media.* London: Palgrave Macmillan.

Englandkennedy, E. (2008). Media representations of attention deficit disorder: Portrayals of cultural skepticism in popular media. *The Journal of Popular Culture, 41*(1), 91–117.

Ferrante, C. (2021). Rising Phoenix y la filosofía del "deporte para discapacitados" de Ludwig Guttmann ¿Un legado para romper prejuicios? *Lecturas: Educación Física y Deportes, 26*(275), 2–34.

Figueiredo, T. H. (2017). Atleta real x Atleta de Papel: A perspectiva individual dos atletas paralímpicos e sua representação na mídia impressa. Doctoral thesis.

Florence, R. B. P. (2009). *Medalhistas de ouro nas paraolimpíadas de Atenas 2004: reflexões de suas trajetórias no desporto adaptado.* São Paulo (SP): Universidade Estadual de Campinas, Faculdade de Educação Física.

Gerbner, G. (1961). Psychology, psychiatry, and mental illness in the mass media: A study of trends, 1990–1959. *Mental Hygiene, 45*, 89–93.

Grue, J. (2016). The problem with inspiration porn: A tentative definition and a provisional critique. *Disability & Society, 31*(6), 838–849.

Hardin, B., & Hardin, M. (2003). Conformity and conflict: Wheelchair athletes discuss sport media. *Adapted Physical Activity Quarterly, 20*(3), 246–259. https://doi.org/10.10.1123/apaq.20.3.246

Hilgemberg, T. (2019). Jogos Paralímpicos: História, mídia e estudos críticos da deficiência. *Recorde, 12*(1), 1–19.

Hodges, C. E. M., Jackson, D., & Scullion, R. (2014). Voices from the armchair: The meanings accorded to the Paralympics by UK television audiences. In D. Jackson, C. Hodges, M. Molesworth, & R. Scullion (Eds.), *Reframing disability? Media, (dis)empowerment and voice in the London Paralympics* (pp. 172–185). London: Routledge.

Hodges, C. E., Scullion, R., & Jackson, D. (2015). From awww to awe factor: UK audience meaning-making of the 2012 Paralympics as mediated spectacle. *The Journal of Popular Television, 3*(2), 195–212.

Inspire. (2016). Hangout con atletas paralímpicos latinoamericanos—inspire webtv [Video]. Youtube. https://www.youtube.com/watch?v=gAcDkBbkAOI&t=390s.

IPC. (2014). *Guide to reporting on persons with an impairment.* International Paralympic Committee.

IPC. (29 de octubre de 2021). What is classification? https://www.paralympic.org/classification

Kolotouchkina, O., Llorente-Barroso, C., García-Guardia, M. L., & Pavón, J. (2021). Disability, sport, and television: Media visibility and representation of paralympic games in news programs. *Sustainability, 13*(1), 256.

Maika, M. (2014). The "Other" athletes: Representations of disability in Canadian print media during the London 2012 Paralympic Games (Tesis de maestría). University of Western Ontario, Canadá.

Marcellini, A. (2012). French perspectives on the media and Paralympics. In O. Schantz & K. Gilbert (Eds.), *Heroes or zeroes?* Champaign, IL: Commonground.

Marques, R., Gutierrez, G., Almeida, M., Nunomura, M., & Menezes, R. (2014). Media approach to Paralympic sports: The view of Brazilian athletes. *Movimento, Porto Alegre, 20*(3), 989–1012.

Mason, F. (2013). Athletic, but ambivalent, and in brief: Canadian newspaper coverage of sledge hockey prior to Vancouver 2010. *Sport in Society, 16*(3), 310–326.

McGillivray, D., O'Donnell, H., McPherson, G., & Misener, L. (2019). Repurposing the (super)crip: Media representations of disability at the Rio 2016 Paralympic Games. *Communication & Sport, 9*(1), 3–32.

Meléndez-Labrador, S. (2018). Formación de estereotipos sobre discapacidad, movilización ciudadana y medios alternativos. El caso de No Más Teletón en Colombia. Ponencia presentada en el GT8 del XIV Congreso ALAIC realizado en la Universidad de Costa Rica. Publicado en Memorias pp. 206–212. ISSN 2179-7617.

Meléndez-Labrador, S. (2021a). Periodismo alternativo, alfabetización y co-construcción del imaginario social de la discapacidad en los juegos de Río 2016. Chasqui. *Revista Latinoamericana de Comunicación, 1*(146), 141–158.

Meléndez-Labrador, S. (2021b). Límites y oportunidades de la investigación en Comunicación y Discapacidad en Hispanoamérica. En J. Solves y S. Sánchez (Eds.), *Nuevos retos de la discapacidad y la comunicación en la sociedad del conocimiento* (pp. 55–80). Tirant lo Blanch, España.

Meléndez-Labrador, S. (2021c). Autoidentidad y discursos mediáticos de la discapacidad en la prensa deportiva digital. Quaderns de Filologia—Estudis Lingüístics vol. 26, Universitat de València (pre print).

Meléndez-Labrador, S. (2022). El lugar de la lengua de señas como lengua minoritaria en la Accesibilidad Comunicativa Universal. *Anuario Electrónico de Estudios en Comunicación Social "Disertaciones", 15*(1), 1–21. https://doi.org/10.12804/revistas.urosario.edu.co/disertaciones/a.10127

Novais, R., & Figueiredo, T. (2010). A visão bipolar do pódio: olímpicos versus paraolímpicos na mídia on-line de Brasil e de Portugal. *Logos 33 – Rio de Janeiro, 17*(2), 78–89.

Pappous, A. & Souza, D. (2016). *Media guide: How to cover the Rio 2016 Paralympic Games* (pp. 1–16). University of Kent. Recuperado de https://kar.kent.ac.uk/64890/

Pullen, E., Jackson, D., Silk, M., Howe, P. D., & Silva, C. F. (2020). Extraordinary normalcy, ableist rehabilitation, and sporting ablenationalism: The cultural (re)production of Paralympic disability narratives. *Sociology of Sport Journal, 38*(3), 209–217.

Rojas-Torrijos, J. L., & Ramon, X. (2021). Exploring agenda diversity in european public service media sports desks: A comparative study of underrepresented disciplines, sportswomen and disabled athletes' coverage on twitter. *Journalism Studies, 22*(2), 225–242. https://doi.org/10.10.1080/1461670X.2020.1809497

Santos, S. M. D., Solves, J., & Souza, D. L. D. (2020a). The news production process in the Brazilian journalistic coverage of the 2016 Rio Paralympic Games. *Journalism, 23*(6), 1319–1337.

Santos, S., Almela, J., & Souza, D. (2020b). The influence of broadcasting rights on sports journalism: A study with journalists on the coverage of the Rio/2016 paralympics games. *Movimento, 26.* https://doi.org/10.22456/1982-8918.90427

Shapiro, J. (1994). Disability rights as civil rights: The struggle for recognition. In *The disabled, the media and the information age* (pp. 59–72).

Shoemaker, P. J., & Reese, S. D. (1991). *Mediating the message—Theories of influence on mass media content.* New York: Longman.

Silva, C. F., & Howe, P. D. (2012). The (In)validity of supercrip representation of Paralympian athletes. *Journal of Sport & Social Issues, 36*(2), 174–194. https://doi.org/10.10.1177/0193723511433865

Suggs Jr, D. W., & Guthrie, J. L. (2017). Disabling prejudice: A case study of images of Paralympic Athletes and attitudes toward people with disabilities. *International Journal of Sport Communication, 10*(2), 258–276. https://doi.org/10.10.1123/IJSC.2017-0030

Taylor, W. L. (1957). Gauging mental health content in the mass media. *Journalism Quarterly, 34*, 191–201.

Tejkalová, A. N., & Strielkowski, W. (2015). Media coverage of summer Paralympic games (1992–2008): A case study of the Czech Republic. *Mediterranean Journal of Social Sciences, 6*(2), 578–578.

United Nations. (2007). *Convention on the rights of persons with disabilities* (resolution 61/106). New York, NY: United Nations.

Vergara-Heidke, A., & Torres-Calderón, G. (2019). Representación de las personas con discapacidad en los anuncios publicitarios en Costa Rica: revisión desde el análisis multimodal. *Logos (La Serena), 29*(1), 149–164.

Walsh, A. (2015). Out of the shadows, into the light? The broadcasting legacy of the 2012 Paralympics for Channel 4. In Jackson et. al. (Eds.). *Reframing Disability? Media, (Dis)Empowerment, and Voice in the 2012 Paralympics* (pp. 42–52). London: Routledge.

Conclusion

Leveraging Sport for Justice

Karen Weiller-Abels, Andrew M. Colombo-Dougovito, and Tracy Everbach

Sport, in its myriad variations and ever-changing contexts, has existed as a constant of human culture for about as long as the human construct of community. It has played a humble role in the creation of a common unity—often providing a touchstone for seemingly incompatible persons to find agreement and provide a target for their social unity or a place to dream. In fact, during an ongoing pandemic, approximately 57.5 million viewers in the United States watched digital live sports content at least once per month in 2020 (Statista, 2021). It is projected that figure would rise to over 90 million in the United States and around 3.5 billion globally by 2025 (Boston Consulting Group & Signa Sports United, 2021). Viewership of the National Women's Soccer League (NWSL) increased nearly 300%—making it on par with viewership of the English Premier League and Major League Baseball games (Gao, 2020). Indeed, soccer itself is arguably the most popular sport in the world, commanding anywhere between 3 billion and 4 billion fans (WorldAtlas, 2020).

With a global fan base and a sporting culture that has been and continues to be rooted in nationalism (Arnold, 2021), it is hard to ignore the enormous influence sport has on broader society. Indeed, examples of sport competition and games are embedded into the very fabric of society and have existed across documented human history. This is so intensely a part of our world that sport events such as the Olympic Games or "world cup" matches can pause global action or shift geopolitical alliances. For instance, in response to the global repudiation of the ongoing apartheid, South Africa was barred from global competition. Though, in the abolition of apartheid, the narrative of nationalism within sport in South Africa has been used to excuse ongoing injustices (Alegi, 2020), it is difficult to overlook the strength sport has in shifting cultural identity. In 1972, during the Summer Olympic Games in

Munich, Germany, commanding the attention of the world, the Black September Organization (BSO)—an offshoot of the Palestinian Liberation Organization (PLO)—took nine Israeli hostages in the Olympic Village, drawing the attention of nearly 4,000 journalists and 2,000 television commentators (Silke & Filippidou, 2019). Ultimately, the terrorists killed 11 Israeli Olympic athletes, witnessed by nearly 900 million viewers globally, thus, forever changing our sense of safety during sport competition.

More recently, international sport athletes have used their platforms to nonviolently draw attention to ongoing social injustice. In 2021, during the Tokyo Summer Olympic games, several US athletes—including Raven Saunders, Race Imboden, and Gwen Barry—used an "X" with their hands as protest to support oppressed people, primarily during medal ceremonies. According to Saunders, the X was meant to represent "the intersection of where all people who are oppressed meet" (Pells & Graham, 2021, para. 2). Drawing an investigation from the International Olympic Committee (IOC), in violation of Rule 50 of the Olympic Charter, which bars athletes from participating in "[any] kind of demonstration or political, religious or racial propaganda" (IOC, 1983, p. 90), Barry stated, "Protest on a podium . . . it is a human right. It is not for the IOC to decide" (Gregory, 2021, para. 6). Further drawing political ire from mostly Republican politicians in the United States, Barry said:

> If anything, I am being extremely American by stating my rights. By exercising my constitutional right to say, I believe in freedom and justice for us all. And if I don't see it, I have a right to peacefully protest until I see what I know America is capable of. I am protesting for America to be good for everybody. And just not for the elite or the white supreme. (Gregory, 2021, para. 4)

Although the IOC has attempted to maintain its "neutrality" by limiting protest, it must be recognized that the limitations themselves are a political act—one taken by those with privilege to remain "neutral" and that supports the status quo, thus continuing to maintain ongoing oppression.

Using the Olympic Games as a platform, protesting has long coexisted with modern coverage. In one of the earliest examples, Irish track-and-field athlete Peter O'Connor in 1906—a decade before the Irish War of Independence—was angered by having to run under the British flag, so he scaled a 20-foot flagpole and waved the Irish flag (Godin, 2020). As a long-standing symbol of the power of protest, John Carlos and Tommie Smith raised their fists to draw attention to the ongoing racial tensions in the United States and human rights violations of the Vietnam War. Ultimately, this act ruined the athletes' careers—including that of Australian Peter Norman, who shared the podium with Carlos and Smith. In 2016, Carlos said he remained, "proud of what we did." Smith added, "They never let us forget that we were wrong . . . we were not wrong. We were only ahead of our time" (Rhoden, 2016, para. 31).

As we follow the activism of athletes and its interwoven history with the social acceptance within broader global culture, the influence of sport is undeniable. Even if certain acts of protest don't make immediate change, their impact is seen in their wake. As we live through yet another era of increasing protest and civil unrest across the globe, we are treated to real-time examples of the impact of protest and how bad faith actors can use misrepresentations of protest for political gains. Moreover, we gain insight into how media representation of such events can further the reach of certain causes, as well as poorly represent the progress that is being made. Only through critical reflection and constant pressure from activists and scholars can such progress be made permanent.

As we have learned through the scholarly and personal narratives in this collection, sport and associated recreation have provided spaces for certain groups of athletes to build community. Sport also provides a microcosm in which to study how traditionally conflicted identities find mutual coexistence. In examining the media's role in this discourse, we have provided examples of how influential coverage can be and how discursive language persists. In this discourse, we must remain aware of the faults of sport in our pursuit of justice. Being coopted, sport can give excuses for ongoing persistence of social oppression; it can also be used as a tool to break down the discriminatory walls of exclusion.

Within the United States, sport is centered within the broader culture. Indeed, in the wake of our changing media landscape, sport has garnered the bulk of our attention and has been a source of immense wealth generation. It is the centerpiece of the identity of many academic institutions and is a major motivator for students to continue their high school education or is weighed disproportionately in students' choices for college attendance, even if they are not participating in athletics. Yet, sport participation comes with its own problems that have been ill addressed. Across predominantly contact sports, concussions continue to be an issue of grave concern but with little progress in understanding the long-term impacts or preventative measures (Martini & Broglio, 2018). Increased specialization in sport—defined as, focusing on one sport, quitting all other sports to focus on the one sport, and spending greater than eight months of training each year—has led to increased rates of injury and burnout particularly among youth (DiSanti & Erickson, 2019; Jayanthi et al., 2019; Wiersma, 2000). Moreover, within our capitalist system, athletes are often disposable in pursuit of victory. Organizations from amateur through professional are ripe with scandal. For instance, just in the last few years, we have learned of decades-long abuse scandals occurring at Penn State University (Jerry Sandusky), Michigan State University/USA Gymnastics (Larry Nassar), and within girls' and women's gymnastics programs (Bela Karolyi). Overwhelmingly white, older male owners of sport teams and organizations continue to grow their wealth from the labor of predominately Black and brown teams or from the abuse of young women athletes.

As we have shown, sport, and the representation thereof, continues to provide a venue for the growth of individual identity. It provides a space for people to learn about themselves, as well as one another. It also serves to reinforce the already existent inequality that is present across society. For instance, Black athletes continue to fight systemic racist practices within society and are subject to racial attacks despite their wealth and social status. Women athletes lack pay equality despite winning more national and international championships than their male counterparts. Disabled athletes lack the basic access to society that is taken for granted by their able-bodied counterparts and live with ingrained inadequacy due to the lack of acceptance of disability in broader society. Transgender athletes are constantly questioned, tested, and excluded from competitions because they do not conform to our hegemonic constructions of gendered sport.

As we conclude this book, we wanted to end on positivity . . . but that did not prove to be an easy task. Though there exists a wealth of examples of the progress that has been made across all domains of sport, conversely, there exists even more examples of how much further society has to go to reach a place of equity. In pursuit of a more just future, Martínková (2020) suggests organizations use "open" categories for sport competition to reduce the inequality that exists among gendered competitions. In this model, Martínková, suggests that "unisex sports" be added that "are suitable for participants of athletes of all sexes, based on merit (p. 256)" as opposed to egalitarian "mixed sports" that allocate spots on the team to male and female athletes. Though it is hard for many to conceptualize how certain sports could be made unisex, moving from our current paradigm of sport is an absolute necessity if justice is to prevail—meaning our construction of sport may have to move to a space that is unfamiliar to those sports that exist presently.

The modern construction of sport and our media coverage of its events is a twentieth-century construct; built during a time of great expansion and change in the development of society. Our continual tweaking of its design has led to greater inclusion; however, finding just and equitable solutions within a designed oppressive system remains elusive. Power, within these structures, does not yield willingly. As scholars, stakeholders, participants, and advocates, we must take a more active role in the way sport is leveraged in society—holding those in power and those who maintain that power imbalance accountable. We must think broadly about what sport can be and reflect on its inadequacies, to use it to the greatest benefit. We must create together a paradigm shift that is broader in scope and applies to all.

Will you join us?

REFERENCES

Alegi, P. (2020). Beyond master narratives: Local sources and global perspectives on sport, apartheid, and liberation. *The International Journal of the History of Sport, 37*(7), 559–576.

Arnold, R. (2021). Nationalism and sport: A review of the field. *Nationalities Papers, 49*(1), 2–11.

Boston Consulting Group & Signa Sports United (2021, May 11). *New study reports $1.1 trillion global sports market and predicts 3.5 billion in global sports participation by 2025* [Press release]. https://ir.signa-sportsunited.com/new-study-1-1-trillion-global-sports-market-and-predicts-3-5-billion-in-global-sports-participation-by-2025/index.html

DiSanti, J. S., & Erickson, K. (2019). Youth sport specialization: A multidisciplinary scoping systematic review. *Journal of Sports Sciences, 37*(18), 2094–2105.

Gao, M. (2020, December 13). Women's soccer set viewership records in 2020—now it needs to keep them watching. *CNBC.* https://www.cnbc.com/2020/12/13/womens-soccer-viewership-records-paving-expansion.html

Godin, M. (2020, January 14). Athletes will be banned from protesting at the 2020 Tokyo Olympics. But the games have a long history of political demonstrations. *TIME Magazine.* https://time.com/5764614/political-protests-olympics-ioc-ban/

Gregory, S. (2021, July 16). 'I won't shut up.' Team USA hammer thrower Gwen Berry discusses protest and the Olympics. *TIME Magazine.* https://time.com/6080430/gwen-berry-olympics-team-usa/

International Olympic Committee. (1982). *Olympic charter, 1983.* Lausanne: Comite International Olympique.

Jayanthi, N. A., Post, E. G., Laury, T. C., & Fabricant, P. D. (2019). Health consequences of youth sport specialization. *Journal of Athletic Training, 54*(10), 1040–1049.

Martini, D. N., & Broglio, S. P. (2018). Long-term effects of sport concussion on cognitive and motor performance: a review. *International Journal of Psychophysiology, 132*, 25–30.

Martínková, I. (2020). Unisex sports: Challenging the binary. *Journal of the Philosophy of Sport, 47*(2), 248–265.

Pells, E., & Graham, P. (2021, August 1). Incredible Raven: Saunders lend her voice to the Olympics. *Associated Press.* https://apnews.com/article/2020-tokyo-olympics-track-and-field-raven-saunders-769bc8c5816d9a228463c530ff04e1b6

Rhoden, W. C. (2016, July 17). Two Olympians need an apology, even if it comes years too late. *The New York Times.* https://www.nytimes.com/2016/07/18/sports/olympics/john-carlos-tommie-smith-committee-apology.html

Silke, A., & Filippidou, A. (2019). What drives terrorist innovation? Lessons from Black September and Munich 1972. *Security Journal, 33*, 210–222.

Statista. (2021). *Number of digital live sports viewers in the United States from 2021 to 2025.* https://www.statista.com/statistics/1127341/live-sport-viewership/

Wiersma, L. D. (2000). Risks and benefits of youth sport specialization: Perspectives and recommendations. *Pediatric Exercise Science, 12*(1), 13–22.

WorldAtlas. (2020). *The most popular sports in the world.* https://www.worldatlas.com/articles/what-are-the-most-popular-sports-in-the-world.html

Resources for Sport Scholars, Athletes, and Stakeholders

To assist in jumpstarting or assisting your own pursuit of justice within your sport communities, we have provided links to organizations that are working for equity and justice within sport and recreation.

ORGANIZATIONS

Athletes for Impact: https://athletesforimpact.com/
Association for Women in Sports Media: http://awsmonline.org/
Camp Aranu'tiq: https://www.camparanutiq.org/
Chicago Metropolitan Sports Association: https://chicagomsa.org/
Dart Center for Journalism and Trauma: https://dartcenter.org/
Federation of Gay Games: https://gaygames.org/
GLAAD Sports Program: https://www.glaad.org/programs/sports
Gotham Volleyball: https://www.gothamvolleyball.org/
Institute for Sport and Social Justice: https://sportandsocialjustice.org/
International Association of Gay/Lesbian Country Western Dance Clubs: https://www.iaglcwdc.org/main.php
International Paralympic Committee: https://www.paralympic.org/
Latin American Sports Association: https://lasainc.org/
Latin America and Paralympic sport promotion: https://www.obladic.org/latamtokio2020
LGBT Sport Safe: www.lgbtsportsafe.com
Move United: https://www.moveunitedsport.org/
National Alliance for Youth Sports: https://www.nays.org/
National Black Professional Athletes Foundation: https://www.nbpaf.org/
National Center on Disability and Journalism: https://ncdj.org

National Council of Youth Sports: https://www.ncys.org/
National Sports Center for the Disabled: https://nscd.org/
North American Gay Volleyball Association: https://nagva.org/
Outsports: https://www.outsports.com
RISE (Ross Initiative in Sports for Equality): https://risetowin.org/
Team New York Aquatics: https://www.tnya.org/
United States International Council on Disabilities: https://usicd.org
WNBA Social Justice Council: https://www.wnba.com/social-justice-council
    -overview/
Women's Sports Foundation: https://www.womenssportsfoundation.org/
You Can Play Project: https://www.youcanplayproject.org

BOOKS AND OTHER WRITING

How To Be An Antiracist by Dr. Ibram X. Kendi [print, 2019]
Resistance and Hope: Essays by Disabled People by Alice Wong [print, 2017]
Why Are All the Black Kids Sitting Together In the Cafeteria? And Other
    Conversations About Race by Beverly Daniel Tatum [print, 2017]
10 Principles of Disability Justice by Sins Invalid [digital, September 2015:
    https://www.sinsinvalid.org/blog/10-principles-of-disability-justice]
The Icy Elegance of Arthur Ashe . . . And the Passion of Muhammed Ali by
    Stephen Tignor [digital, August 2016: https://longreads.com/2016/08/31/
    the-icy-elegance-of-arthur-ashe-and-the-passion-of-muhammad-ali/]
The Renaissance of Ableism by David Gray-Hammond [digital, Septem-
    ber 2021: https://emergentdivergence.com/2021/09/25/the-renaissance-of
    -ableism/]
SI's 2020 Sportsperson of the Year: The Activist Athlete by the Editors of
    Sports Illustrated [digital, December, 2020: https://www.si.com/sportsper-
    son/2020/12/06/sportsperson-2020-james-stewart-mahomes-osaka-duver-
    nay-tardif]
Making gym classes in schools gender neutral is a brilliant idea by Karen
    Fratti [digital, January 2018: https://apple.news/AYnM2GEbVTAOeyk
    TWG7AByg]
#StacyTaughtUs Syllabus: Work by Stacey Park Milbern by Leah Lakshmi
    Piepsna and Alice Wong [digital, May 2020: https://disabilityvisibilityproject
    .com/2020/05/23/staceytaughtus-syllabus-work-by-stacey-milbern-park/]

MEDIA

Hella Black Podcast: https://www.hellablackpod.com/
Strange Fruit podcast: https://open.spotify.com/show/1kol6yriTdonBDc
b03g9Ei?si=Bey8Ax50SsaZ1qxAIrzEHA
Pod for the Cause: https://civilrights.org/podforthecause/
Scene on Radio podcast: Season 2: Seeing White: https://www.sceneonradio
.org/seeing-white/
The 1619 Project: https://www.nytimes.com/interactive/2019/08/14/maga-
zine/1619-america-slavery.html
The Disability Visibility Project: https://disabilityvisibilityproject.com

GUIDES

Building an Anti-Racist Workplace: https://timesupfoundation.org/work
/equity/guide-equity-inclusion-during-crisis/building-an-anti-racist
-workplace/
Disability Language Style Guide: https://ncdj.org/style-guide/

Index

Page references for figures are italicized

About the Contributors

EDITORS

Dr. Andrew M. Colombo-Dougovito (andrew.colombo-dougovito@unt
.edu) is an assistant professor of sport pedagogy and motor behavior at the
University of North Texas. There, he also serves as the director of the UNT
Physical Activity and Motor Skills Program, and as the head of the Disability and Movement Research Collective. His research focuses on examining
the political and socio-environmental elements that influence the physical
activity engagement of disabled populations, particularly autistic individuals, across their lifespan. He has authored or coauthored over 20 journal
articles and book chapters and has given over 50 presentations to diverse,
international audiences. In recognition for his work, he was awarded the Elly
D. Friedmann Young Professional Award from the International Federation
of Adapted Physical Activity (2019) and the Dr. Doris R. Corbett Johnson
Leaders for Our Future Award from SHAPE America (2021). In April 2021,
he was inducted as a fellow of the Research Council within SHAPE America.
When not at work, he tries to spend as much time as possible outdoors—
climbing, mountain biking, and hiking—and with family.

Dr. Tracy Everbach (tracy.everbach@unt.edu) is a professor of digital/
print journalism at the Mayborn School of Journalism, University of North
Texas. Her research focuses on gender and race in media, gender representations in sports, sexual harassment in media, and women in journalism. She
is co-author of the 2018 book *Mediating Misogyny: Gender, Technology &
Harassment* and the 2020 book *Testing Tolerance: Addressing Controversy*

in the Journalism and Mass Communication Classroom. She has written numerous book chapters and published in journals such as *Journalism & Mass Communication Quarterly, Newspaper Research Journal, Journal of Sports Media,* and *Columbia Journalism Review.* A former newspaper reporter, she teaches classes on race, gender and media, qualitative research methods, and writing, editing, and reporting.

Dr. Karen Weiller-Abels (karen.weiller@unt.edu) is an associate professor in the Department of Kinesiology, Health Promotion and Recreation, University of North Texas. Her research centers on media representation of gender issues in sport. She is the author/co-author of numerous publications in this area in journals such as *Sport and Society, Journal of Sport and Social Issues, Sociology of Sport Journal,* and *Women in Sport and Physical Activity.* She has presented at state, regional, national, and international levels. She teaches courses in Sociology of Sport at the undergraduate and graduate levels, as well as a course in Women, Leisure, and Sport.

CONTRIBUTORS (ALPHABETICALLY)

Dr. Austin R. Anderson (austin.anderson@unt.edu) is an assistant professor in the Kinesiology, Health Promotion and Recreation department at the University of North Texas (UNT). His main research focuses on issues of diversity, inclusion, social justice and public policy in leisure and recreation through examinations of sport-specific recreation and management areas. These issues include stigma and belonging in aquatic, sport and campus recreational spaces, with an emphasis on social justice-based goals for people who often find themselves marginalized due to prejudice, discrimination and/ or lack of access. He also has an active research agenda investigating aquatic safety and management, particularly those involving minority population groups. He has authored or co-authored articles in journals such as *Leisure Sciences, Annals of Leisure Research, Recreational Sport Journal,* and *Health & Place.*

Lisa Carlsen (lcarlsen@niu.edu) is the head women's basketball coach at Northern Illinois University. She was hired in 2015 shortly after being named the Women's Basketball Coaches Association Division II National Coach of the Year. She led Lewis University to four NCAA Division II tournament appearances and two Great Lakes Valley Conference championships. Charged with rebuilding NIU's program, her teams have a combined record of 89–90, highlighted by a 21-win season in 2017. That same year NIU was runner-up in the Mid-American Conference tournament and earned a sport in the Women's National Invitational Tournament, the team's first post-season appearance in 22 years. She is a graduate of Northwest Missouri State University where she earned all-conference honors in both basketball and softball. She holds a master's degree from the University of Nebraska Omaha and played professional basketball for the Nebraska Express of the Women's Basketball Association.

Dr. Daryl A. Carter (carterda@estu.edu) is the director of Black American Studies and a professor of history at East Tennessee State University. He has taught numerous courses and students in the program during his career at ETSU. As a trained historian in American political history and African American history, he brings a deep knowledge and understanding of the complexities of African American history. He is the author of the highly regarded *Brother Bill: President Clinton And The Politics of Race and Class*. Currently, he has been working on a book length examination of American liberalism, Edward M. Kennedy, and the United States since 1980. He holds a B.S. in Political Science and M.A. in History from East Tennessee State University.

Dr. William P. Cassidy (bcassidy@niu.edu) is professor of journalism in the Department of Communication and a faculty associate of the Center for the Study of Women, Gender and Sexuality at Northern Illinois University. His major research area is sports journalism with a focus on the representation of gay and lesbian athletes. He is the author of two books, *Sports Journalism and Coming Out Stories: Jason Collins and Michael Sam* and *Sports Journalism and Women Athletes: Coverage of Coming Out Stories*. His scholarship has appeared in journals such as *Communication & Sport*, *International Journal of Communication*, *Journal of Computer-Mediated Communication*, *Journalism & Mass Communication Quarterly*, and *Journal of Sports Media*. He is vice president of Kappa Tau Alpha, the national honor society in journalism and mass communication and a 2020 recipient of the Dorothy Bowles Public Service Award from the Association of Education in Journalism and Mass Communication.

Erica María Castaño Salazar (ecastao231@hotmail.com) is a two-time Columbian national medalist (Ibagué 2015; Bolívar 2019), a two-time Paranamerican Games medalist (Toronto 2015; Lima 2019), and a two-time World Medalist (London 2017; Dubai 2019). She placed fourth at the 2016 Paralympic Games in Rio and is the current representative of Colombian Para-athletes. She was the first Colombian woman to win a gold medal in a world para-athletics championship. She is a specialist in sports management.

Dr. Suzanna Rocco Dillon (sdillon@twu.edu) is a professor of adapted physical activity in the School of Health Promotion and Kinesiology at Texas Woman's University at Denton (TWU). She has a history of advocacy and service to the field of adapted physical activity including serving as president and the Advocacy and Policy Chair for the National Consortium for Physical Education for Individuals with Disabilities (NCPEID). She is also the Adapted Physical Education National Standards (APENS) executive director and a member of the SHAPE America National Physical Education Standards Task Force. She is a faculty scholar in the Sherrill Teaching and Research Lab and a member of the Pioneers in Teaching and Learning Academy at TWU. Her research interests center on the occupational socialization of physical educators and physical activity specialists providing programming for individuals with disabilities, as well as the use of evidence-based practices for individuals with autism spectrum disorder within integrated and segregated physical activity settings that lead to improved outcomes for individuals on the autism spectrum.

Dr. Stephanie G. Schartel Dunn (scharteldunn-s@mssu.edu) is an assistant professor and the W. Robert Corley Professor of Marketing in the Plaster College of Business at Missouri Southern State University. Her research examines mediated social influence, consumer behavior, and attitude change. She has published in journals such as *Western Journal Communication, Social Marketing Quarterly*, and the *Howard Journal of Communication*.

Louis Jenkins is one of the contemporary masters of the prose poem. He authored multiple books, including *Where Your House Is Now: New and Selected Prose Poems* and *In the Sun Out of the Wind*, and was featured regularly on the radio show, *A Prairie Home Companion*, until his death in late 2019. His brief accessible prose poems use humor, wry observation, and hypothesis to tease out the absurdity of everyday situations. Permission to reprint his poem, *Football*, was gracious granted by his spouse and literary heir, Ann Jenkins.

Dr. Eric Knee (eknee@adelphi.edu) is an assistant professor of health & sport sciences in Adelphi University's Ruth S. Ammon College of Education & Health Sciences in New York. His main research focuses on social justice within leisure, recreation, and sport contexts with particular emphasis in the intersectional experiences of queer individuals and communities, dominant organizational and societal frameworks of "inclusion" within leisure contexts, and critical and counter-hegemonic pedagogy. Examples of these works include the exploration of power and hierarchies of in/exclusion within queer spaces, organizational responses to LGBTQ+ inclusion within campus recreation spaces, examinations of queer youth experiencing homelessness and housing insecurity, the historical and contemporary role of queer spaces in community-formation and activism, and the creation of a class analyzing queer history and lives through a leisure lens. He has authored or co-authored articles in journals such as *Leisure Sciences, Leisure Studies, Journal of Leisure Research, Journal of Homosexuality, Recreational Sports Journal,* and *American Journal of Recreational Therapy.*

Dionne L. Koller (dkoller@ubalt.edu) is a professor of law and director of the Center for Sport and the Law at the University of Baltimore. Prior to entering law teaching, she was an attorney with Akin, Gump, Strauss, Hauer & Feld, L.L.P. in Washington, DC, specializing in complex commercial litigation. Her scholarly focus is Olympic and amateur sports law, and she is a frequent media commentator and consultant to state and federal legislatures on issues related to sports and the law.

Paula Lavigne (pmlavigne@gmail.com) is an investigative reporter at ESPN, where she has worked since 2008. She is also the co-author of *Violated: Exposing Rape at Baylor University Amid College Football's Sexual Assault Crisis,* a book she and ESPN.com senior writer Mark Schlabach wrote about Baylor University and its handling of sexual violence among students. She has been recognized for her investigative journalism with several awards including a George Foster Peabody Award for her work investigating sexual assaults within Michigan State athletics and an Alfred I duPont-Columbia University Award for an investigation on a youth football gambling ring. She has a bachelor's of journalism degree from the University of Nebraska-Lincoln and an MBA from Creighton University.

John Loeppky (john@jloeppky.com) is a disabled theatre artist and arts administrator, freelance journalist, current MFA student and former athlete. He works for Listen to Dis' Community Arts, Saskatchewan's only disability-led disability arts organization. His journalistic work has been published by CBC, FiveThirtyEight, Defector, the Globe and Mail, among many others. He lives in Regina, Saskatchewan, Canada.

Frank D. LoMonte (flomonte@ufl.edu) is a professor of media law and director of the Brechner Center for Freedom of Information at the University of Florida, where his research focuses on the public's right of access to civically essential information. He is executive producer of the investigative podcast, "Why Don't We Know," exploring issues of government secrecy and hosted by Pulitzer Prize winner Sara Ganim. He practiced law with Sutherland Asbill & Brennan LLP in Atlanta, clerked for federal judges on the Northern District of Georgia, and for nearly 10 years served as director of the nonprofit Student Press Law Center in Washington, DC.

Dr. Paolo Lucattini (paololucattini@gmail.com) received his PhD in Inclusion and Training within Physical Activity and Sports Sciences from the University of Rome "Foro Italico" (Italy). Prior to this, he earned two master's degrees specializing in international cooperation in the disability sector, and in education and integration of people with disabilities, social hardships, and elderly people via motor and expressive activities. After two decades of working in one of Tuscany's largest private healthcare centers and 10 years of serving as the regional director of Special Olympics Italy, as well as being the organizer of numerous inclusive events and projects, he is currently a lecturer at the University of Pisa and at the University of Rome "Foro Italico" and collaborates with various other Italian universities conducting national qualification training for support teachers. His primary research interests are migratory phenomena and intersectionality; inclusive play, sports, animated movies and related technologies.

Dr. Maria Elena Mastrangelo (mariaelenamastrangelo@assori.it) earned a PhD in Human Movement and Sport Sciences at the Foro Italico University of Rome. Her professional activity takes place mainly in three areas: training and research, psychotherapy and planning for the social inclusion of people with disabilities through work, sports, artistic and recreational activities at the ASSORI ONLUS Foundation of Foggia and L'Arte nel cuore onlus in Rome. She holds the position of National Eligibility Officer (NEO) VIRTUS and carry out training activities with the Italian Federation of Relational Intellectual Disability Sports (FISDIR) and the Italian Ente Sport Inclusivi (EISI) within the Italian Paralympic Committee (CIP).

Dr. Sandra Meléndez-Labrador (smelendezcom@gmail.com) is a social communicator, Master in Strategic Communication, PhD in Communication by Universidad del Norte, scholarship Ministry of Science of Colombia. She was an independent adapted sports journalist at Rio Paralympic Games with Discomunica. She is an activist and is a member of the Colombian Coalition for the Implementation of the Convention on the Rights of Persons with Disabilities. She is director and cofounder of the Latin American Observatory on Disability and Communication—OBLADIC. She is a researcher in disability and communication since 11 years and focuses her work on intersectional and participatory research in critical studies. She is an external member of the

Research Group on Disability and Communication—GIDYC of the Universidad CEU Cardenal Herrera in Spain. She is vice-coordinator of the Working Group 8 of the Latin American Association of Communication Researchers—ALAIC from where promote disability and communication research in the region. She has published studies about disability and communication in academic journals and books.

Dr. Nathan M. Murata (nmurata@hawaii.edu) is a professor and dean in the College of Education at the University of Hawaii at Mānoa. He is a certified adapted physical educator (C.A.P.E.) and his research focuses on adapted physical education and traumatic brain injury. He was the recipient of numerous US DOE Personnel Preparation grants and has authored or co-authored numerous articles in an array of journals from the *Journal of Physical Education, Recreation, and Dance* to the *Journal of Applied Neuropsychology*. Additionally, he is author of a chapter in *Physical Activity and Health Promotion in the Early Years—Evidence Based Practices for Early Childhood Educators* and co-author of *Essentials of Teaching Adapted and General Physical Education: Culture, Diversity and Inclusion* and *Case studies in Adapted Physical Education (2nd ed.): Empowering Critical Thinking*.

Teveraishe Mushayamunda (tmushayamunda@gmail.com) is a master's student at East Tennessee State University in the Brand and Media Strategy program. He is a former college athlete who was born in Zimbabwe. He moved to the United States when he was three years old and has grown up in an African culture in an American environment. He graduated from Milligan University with a Bachelor of Science in Communications with a focus in public relations and advertising.

Dr. Gwendelyn S. Nisbett (gwen.nisbett@unt.edu) is an associate professor of public relations at the Mayborn School of Journalism, University of North Texas. Her research examines the intersection of mediated social influence, campaign communication, and popular culture. Her research incorporates a multi-methods approach to understanding the influence of fandom and celebrity in social and civic engagement. She has published in journals such as *Political Communication, Health Communication*, and the *Atlantic Journal of Communication*. She teaches courses in social influence, social media, and ethics in strategic communication.

Dr. Newly Paul (newly.paul@unt.edu) is an assistant professor of journalism at the Mayborn School of Journalism University at the University of North Texas in Denton. Her research areas include political communication, race and gender in politics, and media coverage of elections. She has taught principles of news, news reporting and writing, copyediting, political reporting, and minorities in media. Her research has won grants and awards and has been published in top journals such as *Political Research Quarterly* and *Journalism and Mass Communication Quarterly.*

Vincent Peña (vincent.pena@utexas.edu) is a fourth-year doctoral candidate in journalism and media at the University of Texas at Austin and incoming professor of sports communication at DePaul University. His research focuses on the intersection of sports, media, identity, and politics. His work has been published in the *Journal of Sports Media, The International Journal of Sport and Society,* and the *U.S. Latina/o Oral History Journal.*

Dr. Mildred F. Perreault (perreault@etsu.edu) is an assistant professor in media and communication at East Tennessee State University. She has researched local journalists, public relations practitioners, and citizen scientists as both stakeholders and disaster communicators. After working as a journalist and public relations professional in Washington, DC and South Florida, she sees the role of the local journalist as one that can engage community response and build community resilience. She has been published in *American Behavioral Scientist, Games and Culture, Disasters, Communication Studies,* and *Journalism Education.*

Warren Perry (warrenperry3@gmail.com) has over 20 years of experience coaching swimming on the club, scholastic, and collegiate levels. Having grown up in coastal North Carolina, he has been around water his whole life. He began competitive swimming at the age of seven, quickly worked up the state and national rankings, and was recruited to swim at the University of North Carolina. After college, Warren worked in the Sports Science labs at Duke University and coached the varsity team at East Carolina University. Currently, he is the aquatics director and head coach at Convent of the Sacred Heart in New York City and an adjunct instructor in East Carolina's Department of Kinesiology.

Dr. Joshua D. Rubin (jrubin2@bates.edu) is a visiting assistant professor in anthropology at Bates College, where he also serves on the Program Committee for Africana. He is a theorist and ethnographer of the political significance of "everyday aesthetics." His work devotes particular attention to the cultural and historical modes of perception and aesthetic assessment that people deploy in the course of their everyday lives. He has published about South African rugby (in *Cultural Anthropology* and *Safundi*) as well as about art and natural gas distribution in Zimbabwe (in the journal *Africa*). His monograph on the aesthetic politics of rugby in South Africa was published in 2021, and a second book project about the political significance of user research to videogame development is presently under contract.

Rebekah Sears (rebekahsears22@gmail.com) is a second-year master's student in the Kinesiology program with emphasis in the psychosocial aspects of sport at the University of North Texas, Denton, Texas. She has 14 years of competitive sport experience including 4 years of varsity high-school basketball. Upon graduation, she plans to pursue a doctoral degree in the field of sport psychology.

Greg Taguchi (GregTaguchi@gmail.com) is a physical educator and the chairperson of the Health and Physical Education Department at Kalani High School. He has been an educator for over 25 years and is well respected in the community and beyond for his work with youth in the classroom and in athletics as he was named the Oahu Interscholastic Association Coach of the Year in both baseball and football over the span of his coaching career. He received his Master of Science in Physical Education from the University of Hawaii at Manoa and has been a key community partner with the College of Education and Department of Kinesiology and Rehabilitation Science, filling many roles including but not limited to serving as a cooperating teacher to mentor student teachers, the health education coordinator for a TBI-related project, and a lecturer for a variety of graduate level Adapted Physical Education courses. He was also instrumental in the creation and coordination efforts of the "Friday Night Prime Time" program in Hawaii, in which he is still actively involved.

Dr. Allison R. Tsuchida (artsuchi@hawaii.edu) is an assistant professor in adapted Physical Education, Physical Activity, and Health & Exercise Science within the Kinesiology and Rehabilitation Science Department at the University of Hawaii at Mānoa. She has her PhD in Adapted Physical Education and is a C.A.P.E. certified. She helped to create, coordinate, and direct the "Friday Night Prime Time" program that is supported by Prime Time Sports. The program has expanded from two high schools to 12 across the state of Hawaii and has been a novel approach to providing all students the opportunity to participate in interscholastic athletic competition. She has also worked extensively on an externally funded project from the State Department of Health, dealing specifically with TBI, curriculum development, online delivery, and sports/fitness for students with disabilities.

Briana Wallace (BrianaWallace@my.unt.edu) is a master's student in kinesiology with an emphasis in the psychosocial aspects of sport at the

University of North Texas. She is a former Division 1 softball athlete from Seton Hall University. She identifies as a Black and Hispanic female.

Karleigh Webb (karleighsportsvideo@gmail.com) has been in sports journalism and sports broadcasting for 26 years. She is currently a writer-contributor to *Outsports*, and the host of the Trans Sporter Room podcast centering on the intersection between transness and sports. She is also a videographer/editor/producer for her firm, *Karleigh Webb Video*, in Connecticut. When not chasing a story, she is a crisis operator for *Trans Lifeline*, North America's only 24-hour-a-day, 7-days-a-week hotline dedicated to the need of transgender people. She considers her service as an honor as great as the awards and commendations she has earned as a journalist. It is this work that also fuels her work as an activist centering around human rights, anti-war issues, and the fight against economic violence placed upon working people. Sports is not just a piece of her craft and passion, it is also her hobby. A lifelong athlete, she is an active, budding duathlete-triathlete, and loves to get behind the plate in softball and be the signal-caller behind center in flag-football.

www.ingramcontent.com/pod-product-compliance
Lightning Source LLC
Chambersburg PA
CBHW022301280326
41932CB00010B/932